Food Security and Development

The global food system is characterized by large numbers of people experiencing food insecurity and hunger on the one hand, and vast amounts of food waste and overconsumption on the other. This book brings together experiences from different countries addressing the challenges associated with food security. Seen through various disciplinary lenses the different cases included are countries at various stages of food security, with diverse stories of success as well as failures in their efforts: China, Brazil and India, as well as less developed countries in Africa and Asia, such as Malawi, Ethiopia, Tanzania, Myanmar, Bangladesh and the Philippines. The authors pay special attention to the environmental and socioeconomic challenges in the respective chapters and how they contribute to food insecurity. Each of the case studies identifies and analyses which factors or drivers (environmental, economic, policy, technology, markets) have been the most powerful shapers of the food system and their future impact.

The case studies identify interventions at regional, national and local levels that contribute positively to food security, highlighting solutions that are effective to implement for all levels of decision makers. Overall, the book provides insights in order to foster a greater understanding of the issues surrounding food security and support progress towards the goal of a sustainable food system for all.

Udaya Sekhar Nagothu is Professor and Director of International Projects at The Norwegian Institute for Agricultural and Environmental Research (Bioforsk), Ås, Norway.

'This timely and comprehensive volume ably highlights the complexity and multifaceted nature of the food security issue. Whilst recognizing that food security goes far beyond simply increasing production, the importance of access to water and irrigation as a major determinant of land productivity, particularly in an era of climate change, is explored. The book clearly articulates the critical role that agricultural research will play in enabling food production to keep pace with population growth without compromising vital natural systems.'

Jeremy Bird, Director General of the International
Water Management Institute, Sri Lanka

'This book combines political, economic and agro-ecological analyses to examine the causes of food insecurity and through in-depth country case studies provides important insights to the need for diverse approaches to solving the problem of food insecurity, making it clear that political economy as well as technical approaches are necessary.'

Leslie Lipper, EPIC Programme Director and Senior Environmental
Economist, Food and AgricultureOrganization of the United Nations, Rome, Italy

'The issue of food insecurity is still high on the agenda of many developing countries. This well-researched and clearly-written book presents country specific studies and sets out recommendations to deal with the structural problems of food insecurity. It is my firm belief that the book will be an excellent source of timely, useable, and relevant information to policy makers, the academic community and development practitioners.'

Belay Kassa, Professor of Agricultural Economics and Interim Deputy Rector,
Pan African University and African Union Commission, Addis Ababa, Ethiopia

'Dr Udaya Sekhar Nagothu and his colleagues deserve our gratitude for preparing this timely book which shows the way for sustainable food and nutrition security. The experiences of nine different countries are analyzed and their strengths and weaknesses have been pointed out. The book is timely because of the launching of the Zero Hunger Challenge next year for the United Nations. The book compiled by Dr Nagothu gives very interesting information on the policies and strategies adopted by countries like China and India as well as seven other countries for removing the scourge of hunger. The book is comprehensive and deals with the multiple dimensions of food and nutrition security. I hope it will be widely read and used by all concerned with the achievement of zero hunger. I congratulate and thank Dr Udaya Sekhar Nagothu and his colleagues for this labour of love for a hunger free world.'

M.S. Swaminathan, UNESCO Chair in Ecotechnology, Founder Chairman of
the M.S. Swaminathan Research Foundation, former Director General of
the International Rice Research Institute and former President of the International
Union for the Conservation of Nature and Natural Resources

Food Security and Development

Country case studies

Edited by Udaya Sekhar Nagothu

Routledge
Taylor & Francis Group

LONDON AND NEW YORK

earthscan
from Routledge

First published 2015 by Routledge

2 Park Square, Milton Park, Abingdon, Oxon OX14 4RN

711 Third Avenue, New York, NY 10017, USA

Routledge is an imprint of the Taylor & Francis Group, an informa business

First issued in paperback 2017

British Library Cataloguing in Publication Data
A catalogue record for this book is available from the British Library

Library of Congress Cataloguing in Publication data
   Food security and development : country case studies / edited by Udaya Sekhar Nagothu.
      pages   cm
   Includes bibliographical references and index.
   1. Food security – Case studies.   2. Food security – Environmental aspects –
   Case studies.   3. Food security – Economic aspects – Case studies.   I. Nagothu,
   Udaya Sekhar, editor of compilation.
   HD9000.5.F59657 2015
   338.1′9–dc23
   2014021701

ISBN: 978-1-138-81701-2 (hbk)
ISBN: 978-1-138-70653-8 (pbk)

Typeset in Baskerville
by Out of House Publishing

Contents

11 The future of food security: summary and recommendations

UDAYA SEKHAR NAGOTHU

Figures

Tables

Boxes

Contributors

Asfaw Adugna is Sorghum Breeder for Africa and works in Advanta Seed International (a UPL Group Company) based in Addis Ababa, Ethiopia.

Robyn Alders is Associate Professor with the Faculty of Veterinary Science, University of Sydney and Director of the Kyeema Foundation.

Brigitte Bagnol is a Social Anthropologist and Research Assistant Professor, Cummins School of Veterinary Medicine at Tufts University, USA and also Research Associate, Department of Anthropology, University of the Witwatersrand, Johannesburg, South Africa.

Thaís Leonardi Bassinello is a Purefood Fellow in Makerere University School of Public Health, New Mulago Hospital, Kampala, Uganda. She is also a PhD candidate at Wageningen University, the Netherlands.

Rachel Bezner Kerr is an Associate Professor in Development Sociology at Cornell University in Ithaca, New York, as well as Adjunct Professor at Western University in London, Ontario.

Jatish Chandra Biswas is a rice nutritionist, and works with Director (Research), Bangladesh Rice Research Institute, Gazipur, Bangladesh.

Ingela T. Flatin is an independent research consultant based in Norway and currently works on food security and nutritional issues.

Sandra Fritz is a research consultant on food security, rural development, agriculture and natural resource management and based in Sydney.

Mohammad Ariful Islam is Senior Agricultural Economist in Bangladesh Rice Research Institute (BRRI), Gazipur, Bangladesh.

Ohnmar Khaing is currently the Coordinator of the Food Security Working Group in Yangon, Myanmar.

Damasa B. Magcale-Macandog is Professor of Ecology at the Institute of Biological Sciences, College of Arts and Sciences, University of the Philippines Los Baños (UPLB), Philippines.

Matthew P. McCartney is Principal Researcher specializing in water and land and agricultural studies in Africa and Asia. He is now head of IWMIs Southeast Asia office, based in Vientiane, Lao PDR.

Crispim Moreira is FAO Representative in Bolivia. He was National Food and Nutrition Security Secretary in the Brazilian Ministry of Social Development and Fight against Hunger during the Government of President Luiz Inácio Lula da Silva.

Halifa Mussa Msami is Principal Veterinary Research Officer and Acting Director, Tanzania Veterinary Laboratory Agency, Ministry of Livestock and Fisheries Development and based in Dar es Salaam, Tanzania.

Karimu Mtambo is the Director of National Food Security in the Ministry of Agriculture Food Security and Cooperatives in Tanzania.

Udaya Sekhar Nagothu is Professor and Director of International Projects at The Norwegian Institute for Agricultural and Environmental Research (Bioforsk), Ås, Norway.

Raj Patel is an Honorary Research Fellow in the School of Development Studies, University of KwaZulu-Natal, Durban, South Africa and also lectures at the University of California, Berkeley. He is currently working with Director Steve James on a book and film about the global food system.

Roberto F. Rañola Jr, is Professor of Resource Economics at the Department of Agricultural Economics, College of Economics and Management, University of the Philippines Los Baños.

Agnes C. Rola is Professor and former Dean of the College of Public Affairs and Development, University of the Philippines Los Baños.

Walfredo R. Rola is Professor and currently the Chairperson of the Department of Community and Environmental Resource Planning, College of Human Ecology, University of the Philippines Los Baños.

Mohammad Abdus Salam is an agricultural economist and works at the Agricultural Economics Division, Bangladesh Rice Research Institute (BRRI), Gazipur, Bangladesh.

Mohammad Abu Bakr Siddique is an agricultural economist and Head of the Agricultural Economics Division, BRRI, Gazipur, Bangladesh.

Mehreteab Tesfai is Senior Research Scientist in the Norwegian Institute for Agricultural and Environmental Research (Bioforsk), Norway.

Zhang-Yue Zhou is Professor and Director for AusAsia Business Research Group at James Cook University.

Preface

Globally, about one billion people suffer from chronic undernourishment, while approximately two billion suffer from micronutrient deficiencies and malnourishment. Hunger is still a perennial problem worldwide, connected to poverty, economic inequality and unjust or inefficient food systems. With 30 per cent more people expected by 2050 and increasing risks from climate change, the world is facing a more challenging food situation than ever before. Everyone is concerned about the same intriguing question: *Where to go from here?* While nobody claims to have found the Holy Grail of food security, debates flare as worldviews clash.

Food security can arguably be approached as a 'wicked problem', because securing a food system that works for all, providing nutritious food in a sustainable manner, is a task embedded in complex interdependencies where the effort to solve one problem may create others, or exacerbate current problems. A greater understanding of food security issues through exploring different country case studies will therefore be useful. This book is thus an attempt to bring together experiences from different countries (China, Philippines, Myanmar, Bangladesh, India, Ethiopia, Tanzania, Malawi and Brazil) in addressing the challenges associated with food security. These experiences are seen through various disciplinary lenses – a main strength of this book. Each of the case studies attempts to analyse different factors (environmental, economic, policy, technology, markets) that have been the most powerful shapers of the food system. The case studies identify interventions at regional, national and local levels that can contribute positively to food security.

I hope that this book will shine some light on the texture of the Gordian knot of food security. Although the book does not propose a single way to slice the knot, it attempts to gain insights into the working of food systems in practice and provides practical steps to move closer to the goal of a sustainable food system.

1 Food security in the context of global environmental and economic change

Ingela T. Flatin and Udaya Sekhar Nagothu

Introduction

According to *The State of Food Insecurity in the World 2012*, almost 870 million people, or about 12.5 per cent of the global population, were chronically undernourished in 2010–12. The vast majority of these, about 852 million, live in developing countries. Up to 2 billion people intermittently lack food security owing to varying degrees of poverty (FAO, WFP and IFAD, 2012). In addition, micronutrient deficiencies, in particular vitamin A, iron and iodine deficiency, often referred to as 'hidden hunger', also affects up to 2 billion people worldwide (WHO, 2002).

While undernourishment has declined in South-Eastern Asia, Eastern Asia and Latin America in the period from 1990/92 to 2010/12, the share of undernourished, however, increased in Southern Asia and sub-Saharan Africa from 32.7 to 35 per cent and 17 to 27 per cent, respectively. Of the 870 million chronically undernourished people, 304 million live in Southern Asia and 234 million live in sub-Saharan Africa (FAO, WFP and IFAD, 2012). These two most vulnerable regions face different challenges. In Southern Asia, although self-sufficient in food, the major challenges are poor access, distribution and malnourishment. In sub-Saharan Africa, where the current population of one billion is projected to double by 2050, increased food production is an additional challenge (UNDP, 2012). The Food and Agriculture Organization (FAO) estimates suggest that undernourishment has evolved in line with global and regional poverty estimates. In developing countries as a whole, undernourishment declined from 23.2 to 14.9 per cent from 1990–92 to 2010–12, while poverty declined from 47.5 to 22.4 per cent (FAO, WFP and IFAD, 2012).

Despite global development and economic growth, the share of undernourished people is still alarmingly high. At the same time, for the first time in history, there are more people that are overweight (around 1.4 billion) than undernourished. The majority of the global population (65 per cent of world population) live in countries where obesity and being overweight kills more people than underweight (WHO, 2013). Overweight people can also face problems of malnutrition and micronutrient deficiencies (Eckhardt, 2006). According to a recent comprehensive global study, obesity is a bigger health crisis globally than hunger and the leading cause of disabilities around the world, with obesity increasing by 82 per cent globally in the past two decades (The Lancet, 2012). The stark contrast between global levels of overweight and under- or malnutrition suggests there are overall, systemic problems with the global food system as a whole. In his book *Stuffed and Starved*, Raj Patel suggests that global undernourishment and obesity are interrelated (Patel, 2007). One important shift in the food security discourse over the years has been from a focus on sufficient calorie intake to nutritional quality (Welch and Graham, 1999; Lang and Heasman, 2003; Carolan, 2013).

FAO projects that by 2050 the global population will increase by over 30 per cent, to 9.1 billion. Nearly all of the population growth will occur in developing countries, many of which are food insecure. In addition, urbanization will continue and income levels will rise. In order to feed this larger, richer, urbanized human population, some experts estimate that global agricultural output must increase by 70 per cent from 2009 to 2050 (FAO, 2009a). Others claim that a focus on increased production is misled as there is currently enough food to feed more than the projected 2050 global population, and that instead the focus should be on creating just and efficient food systems that are sustainable and secure for all people (IAASTD, 2008; Holt-Giménez, 2012; UNCTAD, 2013).

With almost a billion people chronically hungry, growing populations, increasing economic inequity, global warming, environmental degradation, and massive biodiversity loss, securing a food system that works for all is a tall order. It demands nothing short of a new approach to food security.

Food security – the concept

In 1941, the US President Franklin D. Roosevelt held a speech where he spoke of the four freedoms all people in the world should have: freedom of speech, freedom of worship, freedom from want and freedom from fear (FDR library, 2013). In 1943, Roosevelt called a United Nations Conference on Food and Agriculture, and in 1945 the Food and Agriculture Organization (FAO) was established. Roosevelt's 'freedom from want' was translated to mean 'a secure, adequate and suitable supply of food for every man' (Shaw, 2007).

Food security as a concept emerged in the mid-1970s in a context of several incidences of large-scale hunger, which prompted discussions on food supply and sufficiency at the aggregate level (global and national level). The discussion that emerged from the World Food Conference in 1974 had the ambitious goal to eradicate hunger, food insecurity and malnutrition within a decade (FAO, 1999). However, the debate focused on food production and supply, resulting in grand schemes such as the Green Revolution, and neglected sufficiency at the household or individual level, let alone nutritional quality and environmental sustainability. Since then, food security has evolved to incorporate new thinking and perceptions surrounding the causes, including Amartya Sen's analysis of food security as an issue of entitlements and distribution more than merely an issue of production and availability. According to Sen, food security depends on income and political and social power (Sen, 1981).

The World Food Summit in 1996 formulated a definition that is now widely accepted in the discourse:

> Food security exists when all people, at all times, have physical and economic access to sufficient, safe and nutritious food that meets their dietary needs and food preferences for an active and healthy life.
>
> (FAO, 2006a)

This definition later developed to include dimensions of availability, access, utilization and stability (FAO, 2006a), popularly translated into the 3As: *accessibility, affordability and availability*.

It is unlikely that this definition includes full nutritional needs, because, if it does, the FAO estimate of 870 million food insecure people should grow to include the 2 billion people suffering from micronutrient deficiencies (Pinstrup-Andersen, 2009). One might argue that the global obesity epidemic is another case of food insecurity – although in a different vein. Out of the 1.4 billion overweight people, 500 million are obese (WHO, 2013). As an interesting case in point, Townsend *et al.* (2001) found food insecurity and obesity to be positively related in the United States.

An influential paper by Maxwell (1996) outlined three main shifts in the debate on food security since the World Food Conference in 1974: from the global and the national to the household and the individual; from a food first perspective to a livelihood perspective; and from objective indicators to subjective perception. For instance, a household may have the means to acquire the necessary food, but some members of the household might be underfed (for various reasons), or the members may lack knowledge of dietary changes. A simple thing such as lack of nutritional knowledge can lead to deficiencies, as happened in post Green Revolution countries when people changed their staple diets from traditional food grains (millets) and pulses to refined wheat and rice, causing a steep decline in the diet's micronutrient content (Welch and Graham, 1999; Welch, 2002; Graham *et al.*, 2012).

What about people who are 'food secure', but only have access to unclean water and poor sanitation? If food security is supposed to ensure good health and nutrition, policymakers should design interventions to achieve *nutritional security*, guided by measurements of health (Pinstrup-Andersen, 2009). This has broadened the debate on food security to include nutritional security. According to the International Fund for Agricultural Development (IFAD), food security is a necessary but insufficient condition for nutritional security. Nutritional security requires not only access to food but also health care, a hygienic environment, knowledge of personal hygiene and other requirements for a healthy life (IFAD, 2013a).

Maxwell (1996) suggests that there should be no overarching theory of food security, applicable to all situations; rather, policy should recognize the diversity of food insecurity causes, situations and strategies, and relate to particular circumstances. He further states that the character of food insecurity, state capacity and political circumstances are important factors to take into account.

Lang and Barling (2012) conclude that the notion of food security may not be useful or even viable in the new, complex context, quite different to that from which the concept emerged; and not least, because food security can have too many different meanings. They also criticize the accepted FAO definition for lacking any dimension of sustainability, writing: 'a basic truth remains that the only food system to be secure is that which is sustainable, and the route to food security is by addressing sustainability'.

Food security and sustainability

Since *Our Common Future* was published in 1987 (Brundtland, 1987), 'sustainability' has been a key term in the development discourse. The term 'sustainable diets' was introduced in the 1980s, but feeding a hungry world continues to override issues of sustainability (FAO, 2012a). In 2008, the final report of the International Assessment of Agricultural Science and Technology for Development (IAASTD), an independent, multi-stakeholder international assessment of agriculture, concluded that 'business-as-usual in agriculture is not an option', and prescribes an increasing shift towards agroecology and organic practices (IAASTD, 2008). The more recent Trade and Environment Review 2013 concurs, subtitling the report 'Wake up before it is too late: Make agriculture truly sustainable now for food security in a changing climate' (UNCTAD, 2013).

In 2010, FAO arranged a symposium on biodiversity and sustainable diets. The symposium accepted the growing academic recognition of the relationship between current agricultural practices in many parts of the world and environmental degradation and loss of biodiversity, and defined sustainable diets as:

> diets with low environmental impacts which contribute to food and nutrition security and to healthy life for present and future generations. Sustainable diets are protective and respectful of biodiversity and ecosystems, culturally acceptable, accessible, economically fair and affordable; nutritionally adequate, safe and healthy; while optimizing natural and human resources.
>
> (FAO, 2012a)

The symposium concluded that more nutritious diets may reduce dietary impacts on the environment and that a shift to more sustainable diets may trigger upstream effects on the food production (e.g. diversification), processing chain and food consumption patterns (FAO, 2012a). Based on criteria for sustainability, Lang and Barling (2012) suggest that *food security* as a concept may fade into obscurity, replaced by a more all-encompassing term, such as *sustainable food systems*.

In 2009, the UK's Sustainable Development Commission proposed that the government adopt a new definition of food security in terms of genuinely sustainable food systems, the main goal being to 'feed everyone sustainably, equitably and healthily; which addresses needs for availability, affordability and accessibility; which is diverse, ecologically-sound and resilient; and which builds the capabilities and skills necessary for future generations' (SDC, 2009).

This recommendation is part of the emerging human rights and livelihood approaches to food security.

The livelihood, right to food and food sovereignty approaches to food security

Maxwell and Smith note that food insecure groups balance competing needs in a complex way: people may go hungry, up to a point, to meet some other objective. Livelihood approaches place food security in a wider web of human development, justice and environmental issues. The focus is on enhancing people's own abilities to secure their own livelihood in a sustainable manner (Maxwell and Smith, 1992).

Human rights approaches to food security are increasingly becoming common, formulated as a Right to Food. The right to food was already recognized in the 1948 UN Universal Declaration of Human Rights, but the 1996 World Food Summit called for these rights to be more concrete and operational. In 2000, the UN established a mandate for a Special Rapporteur on the Right to Food, and in 2004 the 187 UN member states adopted the Voluntary Guidelines to Support the Progressive Realization of the Right to Adequate Food in the Context of National Food Security. The Right to Food approach encourages countries to be legally accountable to provide their citizens with available, accessible and adequate food (De Schutter, 2010a). Brazil is perhaps the best-known example of a country that has used this approach with great success (Rocha, 2009; Acosta, 2011; FAO, 2011b; Menezes, 2011), adopting a framework law on the right to food in 2006 (De Schutter, 2010a). Under this law, the National Food and Nutritional Security Council was established as a permanent government structure, to ensure proper implementation of the food programmes in the government strategy and to guarantee participation of the people in policy recommendations on food policy (De Schutter, 2010a).

The food sovereignty movement is also gaining ground, connecting food security with justice rather than productivity (Holt-Giménez, 2013; Holt-Giménez and Altieri, 2013). It calls for increased emphasis on agrarian citizenship and ecologically sustainable local food production as a better option than its contrasting dominant model of large-scale, capitalist and export-based agriculture, and emphasizes people to have rights to make and shape food policy themselves (Patel, 2009; Wittman, 2009; Wittman et al., 2010; Holt-Giménez and Shattuck, 2011). The concept 'food sovereignty' was coined by La Via Campesina (the Way of the Peasant), most likely the world's largest transnational social movement, with 200 million members (Vidal, 2013). Food sovereignty focuses on solutions that embed principles of agroecology; social and climate justice and solidarity; a world without violence and discrimination against women; peace and demilitarization; land and territorial rights; seeds; the common lands and water (La Via Campesina, 2013).

From March 2012, after years of privileging the term 'food security', the FAO agreed to introduce the concept of 'food sovereignty' into its public deliberations

(Lawrence and McMichael, 2012). Subsequently, more than 60 members of parliament proposed a new draft law on food sovereignty and food and nutrition security for the right to food in the Dominican Republic in 2013. This was a result of a process that started in 2011 that established an Inter-institutional Committee for Food and Nutrition Security, composed of the Ministries of Agriculture and Health and the Parliamentary Front against Hunger, and with the technical support of FAO, World Food Programme (WFP), Pan American Health Organization (PAHO) and United Nations Development Programme (UNDP) (Latin America Press, 2012). As the concept evolves and gains formal recognition by international agencies and national governments, food sovereignty may become more universally accepted, in both theory and practice.

Forces affecting the global food system: an overview

In their comprehensive, interdisciplinary book, *Food Policy for Developing Countries*, Pinstrup-Andersen and Watson (2011) use Ericksen's (2008) notion of food systems as complex, dynamic systems filled with heterogeneous subsystems affected by nonlinear feedbacks as a basis for their analysis. The nonlinearity of the system's feedback means that a small shock may have one or multiple effects, in contrast to a linear system where effects are always directly proportional to cause. Rather than attempting to isolate and study single causes of food insecurity (e.g. low agricultural output), it is more important to look at forces shaping the food system.

The three main challenges the world will face in the coming decades are population growth, economic growth and climate change (FAO, 2009a; UN, 2010; Nelson *et al.*, 2011). These developments will have a direct impact on food security across the world, in varying degrees (Beddington *et al.*, 2012; Vermeulen *et al.*, 2012). Other factors such as technology, food wastage, land degradation, soil and water scarcity, urbanization, shift in trade patterns, migration of people from rural to urban areas, marginalization of women, and policymaking and political instability will affect food systems. With current trajectories, large regional differences in environmental and economic changes will continue to increase divides between the rich and poor. Coastal and mountainous areas and arid regions will be more vulnerable to future impacts from climate change than other regions. The rural poor and women, in particular in the sub-Saharan Africa and the Asia-Pacific regions, will be most affected. A recent report by Cameron *et al.* (2013) suggests that climate change is an issue of injustice and the likelihood that it might undermine the rights of people, especially the poor, marginalized and vulnerable, and influence future climate negotiations.

Environmental changes and food production

Inefficient food systems (production, distribution and wastage) negatively impact the environment, especially land and water resources, and vice versa (IPCC, 2007). Despite the claims that the Green Revolution lifted millions of poor farmers out of poverty, it has also been widely criticized for causing widespread environmental damage to water bodies, forests and biodiversity due to excessive and inappropriate use of fertilizers and pesticides (Hazell and Haddad, 2001; Mosley, 2003). Environmental impacts of agricultural intensification, although not easily observed, tend to have significant long-term effects on food production and food supply. Increased demand for food will most likely lead to further deforestation, biodiversity depletion and soil erosion, water scarcity and intensified use of fertilizers and chemicals, which may in turn increase emission of greenhouse gases and pollution. According to the IAASTD report (2008), social and economic inequities, political uncertainties and changing environmental conditions demand a new approach to sustainable production and consumption at all levels. There are, nevertheless, enormous opportunities to develop food systems that are more environmentally benign, that can be low-cost and efficient in terms of resource use and productivity if the right political will and resources are available (Government Office for Science, 2011).

Climate change

According to the 5th Intergovernmental Panel on Climate Change (IPCC) report, the continued emissions of greenhouse gases (GHG) due to human influence will cause further global warming and changes in all components of the climate system (IPCC, 2013). Changes are likely to occur both temporally and spatially in temperature; in particular the near-term increases (2016–35) in seasonal mean and annual mean temperatures are expected to be larger in the tropics and sub-tropics. It is more likely that there will be more frequent hot and fewer cold temperature extremes over most land areas on daily and seasonal time scales as global mean temperatures increase. These changes will directly impact food production, in particular beyond 2050 (Thornton and Cramer, 2012; Vermeulen *et al.*, 2012; IPCC, 2013). A systematic review of model-based (simulated) studies of future crop yields in Southern Asia and Africa with high GHG emissions show no impacts on yields of major crops prior to 2050, but significant yield reductions after 2050, especially for maize and sorghum in Southern Asia and wheat, maize, sorghum and millet in Africa (Knox *et al.*, 2011).

According to Bates *et al.* (2008), the most significant consequences of climate change will be the impact on the hydrological cycle, which is already being observed in many parts of the world. Variability in the seasonality of rainfall leads to increased intensive rains, shorter rainy seasons and prolonged dry periods (Gleick, 2010). The 5th IPCC report also indicates that changes in the global water cycle in response to warming in the twenty-first century will not be uniform. The contrast in precipitation between wet and dry seasons and regions will increase, and a shift in the hydrological cycle will make it difficult for farmers and state agencies to plan their farming calendar without adequate weather forecasting in the cropping season (Udaya Sekhar *et al.*, 2012). An estimated 2.3 billion people who live in rural areas and are involved in small-scale agriculture become increasingly vulnerable to food insecurity as their ability to reinvest in farming decreases (Alderman, 2010; Ingram *et al.*, 2010). A recent report by the UNDP in 2013 reveals that climate-related shocks, such as extreme weather events, have destroyed livelihoods and exacerbated Africa's food insecurity, resulting in widespread hunger and poor dietary patterns. As the ability to adapt to climate change differs across regions and households, adaptation measures should be easy to implement and low-cost. Autonomous adaptation measures at the farmer level should be complemented by planned adaptation at the government level (Baethgen, 2010).

The 17th Conference of Parties (COP17) to the United Nations Framework Convention on Climate Change, held in Durban, highlighted climate-smart agriculture (CSA) and its potential to contribute to increased food production, climate change mitigation and adaptation (WFP, 2011). CSA builds on three pillars: (1) sustainably increasing agricultural productivity and incomes; (2) adapting and building resilience to climate change; and (3) reducing and/or removing greenhouse gas emissions, where possible (FAO, 2013). In CSA, the proposed agricultural technology should have minimum impacts on the environment, pose low risks and require low investments, and use site-specific assessments to identify suitable agricultural production technologies and practices (FAO, 2013).

Land and water resources

A number of studies show that the natural resource base needed for agriculture in the tropics is depleting rapidly. In the regions that underwent the Green Revolution, yields have stagnated due to overexploitation of soils. Some scientists believe that poor management and soil fertility depletion is a root cause of food insecurity, particularly in Africa (Oldeman, 1998; Sanchez, 2000). The demands for cereal and meat worldwide will further increase the pressure on land and water resources (IAASTD, 2008).

Global fertilizer use has increased by eight times over the past 40 years, although global cereal production has only doubled during that period. Growth rates in agricultural productivity have recently declined from 2 per cent per year to below 1 per cent (UNCTAD, 2013). It is difficult to increase the productivity unless the soil and water management regimes undergo a radical change in these highly vulnerable regions. A fundamental question is, what kind of agricultural development is most effective to feed the world, and does not add additional stress to the environment and the global climate?

One of the main challenges in sub-Saharan Africa and Southern Asia is to improve the soil fertility and water management on smallholder farms. Smallholders have limited access to capital and inputs such as mineral fertilizers; hence, the alternative is to use locally available resources, which should be encouraged. Improving access to resources, credit and markets, and reducing risks due to extreme weather events can increase productivity and sustainability (World Bank, 2008). A number of low-cost, environmentally benign initiatives including conservation farming, agroecological farming and organic farming are being introduced to increase soil fertility. Some of these initiatives have shown promising results and some have lifted thousands of small farmers out of poverty (Sanchez, 2000). In Zambia, where conservation farming involving minimum tillage, retention of crop residues, crop rotation with legume crops and need-based input application was adopted by thousands of small farmers, the maize yields increased three-fold (Haggblade and Tembo, 2003). Sustainable food production methods that are ecologically efficient and use land, water and other inputs more sparingly and effectively should be central in future agricultural strategies (IAASTD, 2008; EU, 2012). A report submitted by Olivier De Schutter (2011) identifies agroecology as a mode of agricultural development that not only has strong conceptual linkages with the right to food, but also complements conventional agricultural approaches such as breeding high yielding varieties. The report further concludes that necessary policy support, reallocation of resources, capacity building and knowledge development within each country may be needed to boost agroecology at the farm level (De Schutter, 2011).

Access to water and irrigation is a major determinant of land productivity and yield stability (World Bank, 2008). Productivity of irrigated land is twice that of rain-fed land; hence, water conservation and water use efficiency should be in focus in all climate-vulnerable regions. This will be more crucial as climate change leads to uncertainties in rain-fed agriculture that dominates sub-Sahara and parts of Southern Asia. This also applies to other countries in the region that depend on irrigation for food production. As land and fresh water are limited resources, resource-efficient farming will improve the per unit production. Providing secure rights to land and water and recognizing and implementing women's rights will reduce inequalities in distribution and increase efficiency (World Bank, 2008).

Population growth and changing demographic patterns

There are currently three times more people on the earth than in the early 1930s. Population explosion in most countries resulted in agricultural expansion and intensification, deforestation and depletion of soil and water resources. The Food and Agriculture Organization predicts that the global population will reach 9.1 billion by 2050 (FAO, 2009a).

Few others have influenced the discourse on population growth and development as Thomas Malthus (1766–1834). Malthus argued that poverty, malnutrition and disease could be attributed to overpopulation, because while resources grew arithmetically, populations grew exponentially. If human populations were not controlled, they would outpace their local carrying capacity, the capacity of eco-systems or societies to support the local population, leading to catastrophes such as famine, disease and war that would bring the population levels back in balance with its resource base. Malthus did not foresee the grand advances in agricultural technology, and many experts argue that Malthusian theory has been 'foiled again and again' (Trewavas, 2002), with one economist even claiming that population growth is good overall (Simon, 1980). Later demographic experts such as Lochsky (1976) reformulated Malthusian theory, showing fertility as an economic phenomenon. This could explain the reason why family size and income levels are inversely proportional.

The future demographic composition of India and China, with the largest global populations and growing economies, will profoundly affect global food security, both in terms of agricultural productivity and dietary preferences. In particular, the demographic composition and migration from rural to urban areas due to limited non-farm employment and fewer people left in agriculture will have a profound effect on food production and access (Chen, 2007; UN, 2009; UN, 2010). With rapid changes in demographic patterns, women will increasingly play a key role in ensuring food security, and will be better equipped if properly empowered with access to adequate resources.

Economic changes and food consumption patterns

Sustaining the lifestyle of the average American takes 9.5 hectares of land; Britons, 5.3 hectares; Germans, 4.2; and Japanese, 4.9. The world average is 2.7 hectares. China is still below that figure at 2.1, while India and most of Africa (where the populations will grow most) are at or below 1.0 (Pearce, 2009). With the growth of both population and prosperity, especially in developing countries, UNDP warns that the current consumption of minerals, ores, fossil fuels and biomass may triple by 2050, 'far beyond what is likely sustainable' (UNEP, 2011). The planet's resources are already being used faster than they can be renewed. According to World Footprint Network, humanity now uses 1.5 planets to provide the needed resources for use and waste absorption. By 2030, the projection is 2 planets (Global Footprint Network, 2013).

The economic trajectory affects the food system in various ways; some of the most important being a global nutrition transition; a global food system transition; growing economic inequality and new developments such as intensification of biofuel production, food commodity speculation and 'land grabbing'.

The global nutrition transition

Increasing affluence globally has affected the global food system. During the twentieth century, the Western diet increasingly replaced plant foods with animal foods. As large groups of people in the South also increase their purchasing power, diets change here as well. Growth is especially marked in the BRIC (Brazil, Russia, China, India) countries, with the growing urban groups as the most affluent (Smedshaug, 2010). From 1961 to 2009, China increased its per capita meat consumption from 4kg to 59kg and Brazil from 28kg to 72kg (Weis, 2013). The *nutrition transition* typically starts with replacing the root vegetables, pulses and coarse grains with rice and wheat, which in turn are supplemented or replaced by meat and milk products, fresh vegetables, fruit, dietary fats and sweeteners (Drewnowski and Popkin, 1997; Popkin et al., 2012). The shift in food consumption patterns towards livestock products increasingly drives the world food economy (FAO, 2009b). Between 1962 and 2007 global meat production quadrupled, from 71 million tonnes to 284 million tonnes, and by 2050, it is predicted to almost double to about 450 million tonnes (Smedshaug, 2010). The production of milk is also expected to double to 1,043 tonnes by 2050 (FAO, 2006b). Industrial livestock production is expected to account for virtually all of the future growth, which will intensify the demand for industrial grains and oilseed as feed (Weis, 2013).

On the one hand, the actors in the production and value-adding of animal products and animal feed capture economic value in this process; on the other, the environmental implications are serious (Barrett, 2001; FAO, 2006b; McMichael *et al.*, 2007; Jarosz, 2009). Livestock sector growth has been a prime force in deforestation in some countries, and overgrazing in others. In Latin America, around 70 per cent of former forests in the Amazon are now livestock pasture (FAO, 2006b). Animal waste from large livestock operations is a major source of pollution that can create large hypoxic (oxygen depleted) dead zones in coastal areas where polluted rivers run into the sea (Philpott, 2011). The livestock industry also puts pressure on dwindling water resources. In addition, livestock contributes to greenhouse gas concentrations in the atmosphere through methane emissions and nitrous oxide from grazing animals and their waste. The UN report *Livestock's Long Shadow* estimates that the livestock sector contributed 18 per cent of greenhouse gas emissions, which is a higher share than the transportation sector (FAO, 2006b). Another report by the World Watch Institute estimates the true livestock sector emission to be closer to 50 per cent (Goodland and Anhang, 2009). The livestock sector is also a key player in the erosion of biodiversity; 30 per cent of the earth's surface that livestock inhabit was once habitat for wildlife (FAO, 2006b).

World fish[1] supply has grown dramatically in the last five decades, with world per capita food fish consumption increasing from an average of 9.9kg in the 1960s to 18.6kg in 2010 (FAO, 2012c). Aquaculture today provides around half of the global fish supply (FAO, 2012c). Today Asia supplies 89 per cent of the world's farmed fish, with China as the biggest supplier (Bostock *et al.*, 2010). There is widespread agreement that the top potential of marine species was reached some time ago (probably in the 1970s) and is unlikely to change in the next 20 to 30 years (Garcia and Grainger, 2005). FAO estimates that 30 per cent of the fish stocks are overexploited and 57 per cent fully exploited – only 13 per cent of fish stocks are non-fully exploited (FAO, 2012c). To maintain the current level of fish consumption in the world, aquaculture will need to provide an additional 23 million tonnes of farmed fish by 2020. This intensification of aquaculture could lead to degradation of land and marine habitats, pollution from fertilizers and antibiotics, invasive species and greater vulnerability to disease (Nierenberg and Spoden, 2012). Global warming leads to warmer marine and inland waters and is an overarching threat to the future of fisheries, although, as with all global warming, the impact is difficult to predict (Brander, 2007).

Because livestock increasingly feed on grain rather than grazing on marginal lands, many argue that livestock compete with humans for food (Robbins, 2011; Cassidy *et al.*, 2013; Weis, 2013). Around 36 per cent of the world's grain is fed to livestock (Alexandratos and Bruinsma, 2012). Weis argues that in the food security discourse, the 'meatification' of diets is the proverbial elephant – or cow – in the room, which both reflects and exacerbates global inequality (Weis, 2007). Not only do animals increasingly eat food that could have been used for humans, but cycling nutrients through animals to produce meat, eggs and milk in industrial livestock operations is inherently inefficient as most of the energy is used to sustain the animal metabolic processes (Weis, 2013). Transition towards diets higher in animal products in developing countries will have a dramatic impact on the food system.

There is another effect of the nutritional transition in developing countries. There is growing evidence that Western diets rich in animal foods and refined foods and poor in unrefined plant foods (grains, vegetables, legumes, fruits) are unhealthy (Hu, 2003; Campbell and Campbell, 2006; McMichael *et al.*, 2007; O'Hara, 2013; Orlich *et al.*, 2013; Tuso *et al.*, 2013). As people eat more processed foods, animal-based foods, oil and sugar, non-communicable diseases (diseases of affluence – e.g. diabetes, high blood pressure, heart disease, obesity, cancer) become increasingly common. This in turn leads to the paradoxical situation that developing countries may have to increase spending in the health sector to deal with consequences of the richer diets before they have overcome undernutrition; money that could have been used to alleviate poverty (Godfray *et al.*, 2010).

Wahlquist *et al.* (2012) suggest that food policies in Asia should encourage the retention of varied plant-based diets. Several experts claim, based on projections, that plant-based diets may even become necessary on a global scale (Black, 2008; Jägerskog and Jønch Clausen, 2012; Vidal, 2012). Philanthropist Bill Gates sees enormous business opportunities arising in the growing innovation and production of plant-based meats, cheeses and eggs (Gates Notes, 2013), and is investing in companies developing meat mock products such as Beyond Meat and Beyond Egg (Gunther, 2013; Mac, 2013).

The global food system transition

As the developing economies grow, the food systems change dramatically and power shifts down the food system, away from farmers (small farms being replaced by larger ones) to retail, trade, processing and consumer industries (Lang and Heasman, 2003; Patel, 2007; Carolan, 2011). This leads to a situation where corporations play as large a role as governments in shaping food systems (Nestle, 2002; Lang and Heasman, 2003).

Ericksen (2008) outlines the elements of a transition from a 'traditional' to a 'modern' food system as presented in Table 1.1.

A few multinational food companies increasingly drive what people eat globally (Nestle, 2003; Patel, 2007; Stuckler *et al.*, 2012). Stuckler and Nestle (2012) argue that the underlying causes of malnutrition (hunger and obesity) are food systems driven to maximize profits, not to deliver optimal human diets. Processed foods make up three-fourths of world food sales, for which the largest manufacturers hold over a third of the global market. These food companies have legal mandates to maximize the profits of their shareholders (Stuckler and Nestle, 2012). Unhealthy commodities are highly profitable because of their low production cost, long shelf life, and high retail value. Such market characteristics create perverse incentives

Table 1.1 Transition from a 'traditional' to a 'modern' food system.

Food system feature	*'Traditional' food system*	*'Modern' food system*
Principal employment in food sector	In food production	In food processing, packaging and retail
Supply chain	Short, local	Long with many food miles and nodes
Food production system	Diverse, varied productivity	Few crops predominate; intensive, high inputs
Typical farm	Family-based, small to moderate	Industrial, large
Typical food consumed	Basic staples	Processed food with a brand name; more animal products
Purchased food bought from	Small, local shop or market	Large supermarket chain
Nutritional concern	Undernutrition	Chronic dietary diseases
Main source of national food shocks	Poor rains; production shocks	International price and trade problems
Main source of household food shocks	Poor rains; production shocks	Income shocks leading to food poverty
Major environmental concerns	Soil degradation, land clearing	Nutrient loading, chemical run-off, water demand, greenhouse gas emissions
Influential scale	Local to national	National to global

Source: Ericksen, 2008.

for industries to market and sell more of these commodities. Increasingly, markets in developing countries are major areas for expansion (Stuckler *et al.*, 2012).

Processed foods and supermarkets go hand in hand. From the early to mid-1990s, the growth of supermarkets in developing countries increased dramatically (Reardon *et al.*, 2004; Reardon and Hopkins, 2006). Supermarket retailing is growing at 20 per cent per annum in countries such as China, India and Vietnam, a growth that is projected to continue (IAASTD, 2008). Foreign direct investments by transnational food companies in food processing, service and retail have also risen rapidly since the 1980s in developing countries (Hawkes, 2005).

Intertwined with the food system transition is increased concentration of market power, where fewer actors control the market. In 2003, five corporations controlled 60–90 per cent of trade in wheat, maize and rice; three corporations controlled 80 per cent of the banana trade; another three 83 per cent of the cocoa trade; three controlled 85 per cent of tea; and seven firms accounted for 90 per cent of the trade in agro-chemicals (Lang and Heasman, 2003). In *Food Politics*, food policy expert Marion Nestle describes the negative impacts large and increasingly powerful food and agribusinesses have on shaping food systems through advertisement, government lobbying and scientific research, often to the detriment of the public (Nestle, 2003).

Growing economic inequality

Growing national economies embedded in global, more open, markets, combined with rising urbanization can increase the inequality between rural and urban incomes. As an example, in India, the recent economic reforms and subsidies to industry have attracted more investments to the urban areas, which in turn increased the economic divide between urban and rural areas. In Andhra Pradesh, in the decade after 1993, rural income declined by 20 per cent while urban income increased by 40 per cent (Patel, 2007).

The growing and evolving food demands in developing countries can create a greater gap between 'food haves' and 'food have-nots'. Food insecurity correlates with poverty and low incomes. Although real GDP per capita growth in high-income and middle-income countries over the last 40 years or so has outstripped food price growth, it is not the case for low-income countries as a group. For large groups of populations of both urban and rural poor, food is a major proportion of expenditures. For example, in India, Sri Lanka and Nepal, people who live on less than US$1.4 a day used more than 70 per cent of household expenditures for food. Adverse changes in food prices will affect them with greater force (Conceição and Mendoza, 2009). Even in one of the richest countries in the world, the USA, it is estimated that roughly 14.5 per cent of the households, or 50 million people, are defined as food insecure, a situation which is intimately connected to poverty (Coleman-Jensen *et al.*, 2011). Thus, a social justice perspective will be an important component of any food security strategy, in both developing and developed countries.

New developments – biofuels, food commodity speculation and land grabbing

One report estimates that the increased demand for biofuels accounted for 75 per cent increase in food prices in 2008 (Chakrabortty, 2008). The demand for biofuels changed the market by diverting grain away from food for fuel, encouraging farmers to set aside land for biofuel production, and sparked financial speculation in grains (Chakrabortty, 2008; Paramaguru, 2012). As the need for energy increases and oil prices rise, governments pursue clean, renewable sources of energy, leading to a high demand for biofuels. The production of biofuels is often highly subsidized, used as a domestic tool to increase income for local farmers by developed nations (IFPRI, 2008). The issue of biofuel's impact on food security became so critical that FAO set up an expert panel on food security and biofuels, publishing its report in 2013 (HLPE, 2013). As the chairman of the report, M.S. Swaminathan warns: 'if 10 per cent of all transport fuels were to be achieved through biofuels in the world, this would absorb 26 per cent of all crop production and 85 per cent of the world's fresh water resources' (Swaminathan, 2013).

The food crisis of 2008 also reflects the dynamic interdependence between food security and other sectors; especially the tightening links between food, the financial sector and energy demands in a global market (Conceição and Mendoza, 2009). The 2008 food price crisis was unique in that it was possibly the first price crisis greatly affected by a 'financial speculative bubble' in food commodities. After the deregulation of the commodities market in the USA in 2000, massive amounts of novel forms of speculation in commodity derivative markets increased (De Schutter, 2010b). The UNCTAD Trade and Development Report 2009 found that speculation greatly exceeding the liquidity needs of commodity markets to execute the trades of commodity users (i.e. food processors and agricultural commodity importers) was a significant driver of the changes in food prices (UNCTAD, 2009). Because the financial crisis hit the mortgage, credit and real estate markets, money managers fled to commodity markets. In 2003, US$13 billion were invested in commodity index holdings; by 2008, US$317 billion (Kaufman, 2010). There is currently no multilateral framework to respond to global speculation in food prices (IATP, 2009).

Another relatively recent development is that of richer countries investing in land in developing nations to feed their own populations – a phenomenon often termed 'land grabbing'. Food importing countries in Asia and the Middle East are the engines of many of these deals, with Saudi Arabia as one of the most active players (McMahon, 2013). The prime target is Africa, namely countries such as Sudan, Ethiopia, Madagascar, Mozambique, Benin, Tanzania, Sierra Leone and Liberia. These are some of the poorest countries in the world, which all suffer from high levels of malnutrition and food insecurity (McMahon, 2013). Foreign land acquisition in developing countries has amounted, in value, to between five and ten times the level of official development assistance (UNCTAD, 2013). One particular concern is when poor people are forcibly ejected from land they are farming because of these deals (Geary, 2012).

Market trends and trade patterns

The food system is globalized and interconnected. A common argument in support of a globalized food system is that it improves the global efficiency of food production by allowing breadbasket regions to export food to less-favoured regions (Government Office for Science, 2011).

The most influential body in the global market is the World Trade Organization (WTO), whose self-proclaimed primary purpose is to 'open trade for the benefit of all' (WTO, 2013). The General Agreement on Tariffs and Trade (GATT) was signed in 1947 and made an explicit exemption for agriculture, as actors agreed that agriculture could not be treated like other sectors, to protect agriculture from the 'full rigours of the international market' (Healey *et al.*, 1998). The WTO was established in 1995, integrating agriculture more fully into the trade agreements. The philosophy behind this shift was that weak representation of the sector had adverse effects, due to issues of comparative advantage, market instability and effects of protectionism (Healey *et al.*, 1998). The establishment of WTO and the integration of agriculture into its agreements was a turning point in agricultural politics and policies.

One of the main criticisms of WTO and free trade is that the promise of 'levelling playing fields' has not become reality. The average European cow daily receives more in subsidies than the nearly three billion people who live on less than two dollars a day (Wise, 2004). At the same time, high tariffs and other trade barriers keep imports out of developed countries' markets (Watkins and von Braun, 2002). Farmers in the developing world thus compete against farmers in developed countries that spend billions in subsidies on farmers in the agricultural sector; countries with an extensive infrastructure, readily available credit, rich agricultural research traditions, and a strong history of agricultural extension (Carolan, 2011). The result is a global trading system in which success depends less on comparative advantage, as was originally intended, than on comparative access to subsidies. As Watkins and von Braun point out, even though small farmers may be efficient, innovative and competitive, they are not able to compete against the world's richest treasuries (Watkins and von Braun, 2002). Governments in the Global South, farmers' groups and international aid groups have therefore demanded steep cuts in agricultural subsidies in the Global North (Wise, 2004). A projection made by the International Food Policy Research Institute (IFPRI) predicts that if developed countries cease their subsidies to agriculture, developing countries will annually gain US$40 billion (Watkins and von Braun, 2002).

Another concern related to global trade patterns is the growing food dependency of developing countries on affluent nations. The USA was a prominent actor in this shift, illustrated by an often-cited speech made by US Agricultural Secretary John Block in 1986, where he said, 'the idea that developing countries should feed themselves is an anachronism from a bygone era. They could better ensure their food security by relying on US agricultural products, which are available, in most cases, at lower cost' (quoted in Cavanagh and Mander, 2004). Generally, developing countries were overall net agricultural exporters before 1980. Since 1980, however, there has been a trend towards a negative agricultural trade balance. FAO predicts that, as a whole, developing countries will have a net food trade deficit of more than US$50 billion by 2030 (Jones and Elasri, 2010). Chand (2007) points out that trade liberalization, particularly after the implementation of the WTO agreement in 1995, has affected all South Asian countries negatively, except Sri Lanka. It is especially problematic as per capita income in South Asian countries is low, with more than half the household expenditure spent on food. Thus, the majority of people are not able to absorb the fluctuations and shocks in the international market. Chand concludes that these countries need to pursue self-sufficiency, particularly for main staples, to maintain food security until per capita incomes increase (Chand, 2007).

Actors and institutions with more financial- or corporate-based worldviews emphasize the importance of economic growth as well as building and strengthening farmers' roles in the global value chain as innovators, entrepreneurs and businesspeople. For instance, the World Economic Forum in its large-scale New Vision for Agriculture initiative works to develop a shared agenda for action and foster multi-stakeholder collaboration to achieve sustainable agricultural growth through market-based solutions (World Economic Forum, 2013).

A typical approach in strategies that aim for market-based solutions to agricultural innovation is an emphasis on private-public partnerships (PPP). The private sector might aid in research and development, or secure a market for farmers' products, while governments might provide capacity building (Hartwich *et al.*, 2007).

Cross-cutting issues

Farmers, governance, science and technology, gender and civil society are themes that cut across the food system.

Farmers and farmers' organizations

There are around 1.4 billion poor people living in extreme poverty today; 75 per cent live in rural areas with agriculture as their main source of livelihood, especially sub-Saharan Africa and Southern Asia. Globally, there are approximately 2.5 billion people involved in full- or part-time smallholder agriculture, managing an estimated 500 million small farms (IFAD, 2013b). Smallholder farmers produce most of the world's food; an estimated 80 per cent of the food consumed in Asia and sub-Saharan Africa together (IFAD, 2011). Yet, they comprise the majority of the world's undernourished people, and most of those living in absolute poverty (UN Millennium Project, 2005).

Farmers face several overlapping challenges: increasing competition for land and water, increasing influence of and changing markets, rising fuel and fertilizer prices, and climate change. This is extra challenging for smallholders as they are more directly dependent on ecosystem services and are less able to adapt to changing contexts, compared with larger, more resourceful farmers (IFAD, 2013b). Smallholder farmers are also often neglected in policymaking at different levels (Vorley *et al.*, 2012).

Smallholder farmers are gaining policy attention in an era of climate change. IFAD and UNEP concluded in a cohesive report that smallholder farmers are key to increased food security through sustainable agriculture with their vast collective experience and intimate knowledge of local conditions (IFAD, 2013b). Conservation farming, agroforestry, integrated pest management and organic agriculture are all low-cost (although knowledge intensive) measures that have shown considerable positive results (IFAD, 2013b). The United Nations Conference on Trade and Development report *Wake Up Before It's Too Late* (UNCTAD, 2013) urges governments to shift quickly towards farming systems that promote a greater variety of crops, reduce fertilizer use and create stronger links between small farms and local consumers. It is important to recognize that farmers are more than food producers; they are providers and managers of key ecosystem services.

Up until a few generations ago, the vast majority of the world's people were closely connected to farming. Today, urban people are pulled away from those who produce their food, and farmers are more often responding to forces in an increasingly global and complex food system, rather than being primary actors in setting the terms, and becoming increasingly under stress (Tansey and Worsley, 1995; Patel, 2007). For example, Indian farmers facing high levels of debt and a complex political-economic environment are experiencing high rates of suicides. The Center for Human Rights and Global Justice estimates that more than a quarter of a million Indian farmers have committed suicide in the last 16 years (before 2011) – the largest wave of recorded suicides in human history (CHRGJ, 2011). These numbers translate into a suicide every 30 minutes among Indian farmers. Farmers around the world are under stress as the food system changes, favouring larger farms that are better suited to survive and thrive in the international market.

The farmers' movements, as the collective voice of farmers, have always played a central role in the development of food security. They could be small organizations, such as water user associations in India, that are formalized institutions supported by the government and a way to involve farmers in water resource management. Historically, farmers' movements were struggles against local landlords and repressive states, and targets were almost exclusively local. The farmers' movements of the twenty-first century speak up against an unfair food order (Vanhaute and Van Den Abeele, 2013). The modern farmers' movements challenge the predominant neoliberal mode of food production. They take advantage of globalization to network and merge their efforts to work for agrarian justice and sustainable food systems. La Via Campesina is arguably the largest global social movement, representing 200 million peasants, small-scale producers, landless, women, youth, indigenous, migrants, and farm and food workers from 183 organizations and 88 countries (La Via Campesina, 2013). With its focus on food sovereignty, the Campesina are clear that their goal is for people everywhere to have the right to control their own food production and food markets. A key goal is to defend peasant life by constructing, proposing and defending food sovereignty as an alternative model of food and agriculture. To the Campesina, food and farming is much more than producing products for trade; it is a way of life that can meet local and national challenges of poverty, hunger, injustice and environmental degradation, while preserving rural life (Martínez-Torres and Rosset, 2010). Global warming is also on their agenda, as one of their slogans claims: 'Small-scale sustainable farmers are cooling down the earth' (La Via Campesina, 2009).

Governance

One of the principal functions of a government in any political system, yet seldom written into constitutions, is to ensure adequate food for its citizens. Though some countries do have a policy to ensure food security, the implementation is often weak. The majority of the poor and the hungry live in developing countries where the constitution does not provide people the basic right to food, and thus there is a lack of accountability. The combination of rapid population growth, accelerating climate change, and shrinking land, water and energy resources lead to more frequent food shortages (Winkler, 2009). If governments are to be legally accountable for ensuring food security for their people, they must prepare a strategy for increasing domestic production, building adequate food reserves, removing trade barriers and allowing imports when necessary.

Agriculture and food production is not given the same importance it had in the 1970s in many developing countries and investments have considerably decreased (Pardey *et al.*, 2006).

In India, a country that claims to be food self-sufficient, the state runs massive welfare programmes that are poorly implemented and plagued by corruption, leakages, errors in selection of beneficiaries, delays, poor allocations and little accountability. The lapses in implementation were so serious that the Supreme Court of India, in response to a Public Interest Litigation in 2001, directed all state governments to convert the benefits of nine ongoing food-related schemes into 'legal entitlements' and to fully implement these schemes. Despite the court ruling, the poor implementation continued owing to the lack of capacity and structure. The new Food Security bill (2013) in India is a modest initiative attempting to consolidate various food-related programmes and entitlements that have made gradual headway during the last decade (Dreze, 2013). The bill focuses on food grain entitlements, children and pregnant women. However, sceptics of the bill are worried about the enormous resources it would require for implementation, and the challenge in ensuring that the benefits will reach the right beneficiaries (Dreze, 2013). The main difficulty will be to improve transparency in governance at all levels, make bureaucracy accountable and engage civil society in planning and implementation of the programmes. Most developing countries face similar situations as India.

There are a few countries that have been quite successful in addressing food insecurity, Brazil being one of the most cited examples. The *Fome Zero* (Zero Hunger) policy in Brazil was implemented through new channels of popular participation and local democracy, with activities ranging from participatory budgeting to local tripartite social councils (government, private sector and civil society), demonstrating a new form of governance for food security (Rocha, 2009). In addition to prioritizing food access, the strategy also focuses on strengthening family agriculture and income generation. The case of Brazil clearly shows that political will and commitment are key factors to food security. Rocha (2009) credits the Lula government for making *Fome Zero* highly effective and for the transparency adopted in the process towards achieving food security.

Science, technology and innovation

Scientists claim that advancement in science and technology was the main reason for the dramatic increase in food production during the Green Revolution (Swaminathan, 2010). Hundreds of existing agricultural technologies and practices have the potential to boost agricultural yields in the developing world, and the IFPRI has undertaken a massive effort to evaluate these technologies and practices, their risks and benefits and suitability for different conditions. 'Agricultural technologies are really at the heart of food productivity growth,' says Ringler (Ringler, 2012). Technologies to support integrated soil fertility management, integrated water management, high yielding varieties from conventional breeding and genetic modification, all contribute to food security. Improving the nutrient and water use efficiency will be highly relevant in the future, with limited availability of water and nutrients, especially phosphorus. Plant breeding is considered one of the main options to address the demand for more food and nutritious food through biofortification. Artificial photosynthesis and genetically modified crops are being tried out, but there is strong opposition to the introduction of such technologies because of the unforeseen environmental impacts.

Despite massive advancements in science and technology relating to food and agricultural production, including continued yield increases and the development of genetically modified (GM) crop varieties, there remain difficulties in actually applying these innovations in practice, due to lack of policy support, regulation, trade, funding, education and public acceptance (Garvey, 2012). However, small-holder farmers who constitute the majority in developing countries should be able to benefit from the public-private partnerships. Farmers should be able to access and use the technologies without difficulties. There is a need for training and cap-acity building to facilitate farmers to adopt the technologies. Knowledge transfer mechanisms are key for disseminating any new science and technology to farmers (Garvey, 2012).

Gender

In their book *Half the Sky: Turning Oppression into Opportunity for Women Worldwide*, Kristof and WuDunn note that there is an ongoing 'gendercide' of girls in developing nations such as China and India. More girls and women are now missing from the planet, because they are female, than men were killed on the battlefield in all the wars of the twentieth century (Kristof and WuDunn, 2009). Amartya Sen brought the issue into public consciousness when he wrote an essay based on an analysis of the various worldwide sex ratios and concluded: 'A great many more than a hundred million women are simply not there because women are neglected compared with men' (Sen, 1990). In addition to aborting girl foetuses after ultrasound screening, girls also vanish because they do not get the same health care and food as boys. In India, for example, girls between 1 and 5 years are 50 per cent more likely to die than boys their age (Kristof and WuDunn, 2009). Cultures and institutions with stubbornly ingrained patriarchal values discriminate against girls and women in every aspect of life in many developing countries, including food security (Patel, 2012).

Women constitute 43 per cent of the agricultural labour force although, histor-ically, women have not been fully recognized as farmers, a situation which still pre-vails (Jones, 2012). The 'invisibility' of women's contributions in agriculture has been an important hindrance to their participation in decision making (IAASTD, 2008). Women's participation in agriculture has gradually become more visible. One reason is that data collection was previously designed in such a way that undervalued women's participation; but another is that women's participation has both become broader and deeper, as men increasingly migrate to urban areas for work. Often, women's work is combined with care for elders and children and household responsibilities and has been referred to as *women's triple burden* (Moser,

1989). This increasing importance of women in the agricultural sector is often referred to as 'the feminization of agriculture' (Lastarria-Cornhiel, 2006).

Women face a plethora of gender-specific hindrances in decision making about the basic resources for production. Almost everywhere women face greater challenges than men in accessing productive resources (credit, fertilizer, improved seeds), markets (control over products they produce or invest in) and services (extension, capacity building). Women control less land than men and the land they control is often of poorer quality and/or with insecure land tenure (IAASTD, 2008). With less education and less access to extension services, women farmers are less likely to use modern inputs such as improved seeds, fertilizers, pest control measures and mechanical tools. Even when they access credit, they frequently use less and often do not control the credit they obtain. All these factors combine to create a 'gender gap' (FAO 2011a; FAO 2012b). Women are little involved in decision making regarding agricultural technology. In the past, improved technology developed by research and development institutions focused on male workers. The fact that women lag behind in access to and use of agricultural technology can enforce stereotyped gender roles (IAASTD, 2008).

Women are less likely than men to be paid farm labour, and when they are, they are usually employed seasonally or part-time and have lower wages than their male counterparts, even when their qualifications are higher (FAO, 2011a). Women are increasingly valued as labour in agribusinesses as their wages are lower (Lastarria-Cornhiel, 2006). However, because women farmers lack secure control over land, family labour and other resources required to guarantee a reliable flow of produce, they are largely excluded from modern contract farming arrangements (FAO, 2011a). For example, only 10 per cent of the farmers involved in smallholder contract farming schemes in the Kenyan fresh fruit and vegetable export sector are women, and only 1 of a sample of 59 farmers contracted in Senegal to produce French beans for the export sector was a woman (FAO, 2011a).

The yield gap between men and women averages around 20–30 per cent and most research finds that the gap is due to differences in resource use. Closing this gap would decrease global undernourishment by 12–17 per cent, or by 100–150 million people (FAO, 2011a). To achieve this, resources and services must be gender-relevant and responsive, informed by the best and most up-to-date knowledge and information about agricultural development. Agribusiness must also be made aware of the importance of adopting gender-responsive policies, and develop implementation programmes that take account of and reach women (Mehra and Rojas, 2008).

Empowering women in agriculture can increase the resources in the hands of women and strengthen their voice within the household. Increasing women's income will have a positive effect on the food security of a household, when the women retain control over earned money. Women tend to spend their income on issues that benefit the household, especially food, education and health of children (Quisumbing *et al.*, 1995; FAO, 2011a; World Bank, 2011); which is why microcredit schemes such as Grameen Bank focus on women (Yunus, 2011). Educating and empowering girls also decreases population growth, as educated girls tend to have smaller families (Soubbotina and Sheram, 2000; UN, 2011). As an example, the 2011 national demographic survey of Ethiopia found that women with no education had three times as many children (average 5.8 vs 1.9) as those with secondary education (CSA Ethiopia, 2013). As Revenga and Shetty (2012) claim: 'Empowering women is smart economics'.

Civil society

Civil society can be defined as the socio-sphere located between the family, the state and the market, operating beyond the natural confines of national societies, politics and economics (Andheier and Themudo, 2002). Edwards (2000) describes civil society as the arena where people organize because they care enough about a common issue to act collectively, and not for profit or political power. Civil organizations have played important roles in expressing the voices of 'the people', especially those with less power, and historically they often have served to balance the power of the state, and protect individuals from the state's power, or state's failure (Fukuyama, 2001). Today many civic organizations not only balance the power of the state, but increasingly engage in resistance towards the power of the private (corporate) sector and a market economy that has, in the words of Gray *et al.* (2006), 'grown so virtual, large and hyper-real that it actively alienates us'. In *Blessed Unrest*, environmentalist Paul Hawken describes the global movement of civil organizations as the world's immune system, where the activities of hundreds of thousands of non-profit organizations act as humanity's immune response 'to toxins like political corruption, economic disease, and ecological degradation' (Hawken, 2007).

It is difficult to generalize about the role civil society plays in food security as the organizations are vast in number, size, differing aims, structures and con-trasting policies. Different civic organizations also have different linkages to the spheres of market, state and family. At one end of the scale, there are powerful research foundations and institutes like the Rockefeller and Ford Foundations and the International Rice Research Institute that played primary roles in the Green Revolution (Tribe, 1994). Another example is the relatively new, well-endowed Bill and Melinda Gates Foundation, investing large resources in food security in Africa (AGRA – Alliance for a Green Revolution in Africa). At the other end of the scale are women's groups, farmers' associations and various social movements. These may scale up to the state, national or global level, like the global farmers' move-ment La Via Campesina. Other examples are international non-governmental organizations (NGOs), for example, Food First Information and Action Network, working on food security from a justice perspective, and national NGOs such as the Indian M.S. Swaminathan Research Foundation working on food security through agricultural research and capacity building through village knowledge centres.

Brazil's success in dramatically reducing food insecurity is in large part based on civil society demands and participation. In 1993, the National Campaign against Hunger (*Campanha Contra a Fome*) raised awareness of the need to tackle hunger in Brazil and helped establish thousands of collection and food dona-tion committees. The campaign also prompted the government to develop a Hunger Map, as an empirical effort to create policy responses (Acosta, 2011). The citizens' movement led to the establishment of a National Council for Food Security (Consea). When President Lula was elected, he made food secur-ity a top priority and recreated Consea (2003) to consist of 59 members, includ-ing 17 ministers of state and 42 civil society representatives. Several strategic moves show the importance the government gave to civil society participation. First, the chair of Consea was a representative of civil society; second, Consea convened within the premises of the Presidency of the Republic; and third, Consea was defined as a consultative council in charge of giving direct advice to the President of the Republic on policymaking matters and on defining guidelines to ensure the Right to Food. Based on Consea's work, the Right to Food is now institutionalized as a matter of public policy and an obligation of the state (Rocha, 2009).

The global food crisis of 2007/2008 urged the United Nations to make some changes and reformed the Committee on World Food Security (CFS) that was established in 1974 as an intergovernmental body to serve as a forum within the UN system for review and follow-up of food security policies. In 2009, the Committee was reformed to be

> the foremost inclusive international and intergovernmental platform for a broad range of committed stakeholders to work together in a coordinated manner and in support of country-led processes towards the elimination of hunger and ensuring food security and nutrition for all human beings.
>
> (CFS, 2013)

As part of the reform process, CFS established a Civil Society Mechanism (CSM), which is the largest international mechanism of civil society organizations seeking to influence agriculture, food security and nutrition policies and actions – nationally, regionally and globally. The CSM is an inclusive space open to all civil society organizations, with priority given to the organizations and movements of the people most affected by food insecurity and malnutrition, that is, smallholder producers, fishers, pastoralists, indigenous, urban poor, migrants, agricultural workers etc. (CSM, 2013). The CSM arranges an annual forum to prepare for the annual plenary session of the Committee on World Food Security, with participants from a broad range of organizations and regions.

Robert Chambers famously asked: 'Whose reality counts? The reality of the few in centres of power? Or the reality of the many poor at the periphery?' (Chambers, 1995). He concludes: 'the key is to enable them [the poor] to express their reality, to put that reality first and to make it count' (Chambers, 1995). In the same spirit, the strata of civil society that represent the voices of the most mar-ginalized groups play a pivotal role in achieving food security. When these voices are engaged, research methods, agendas and policies in various sectors and at all levels will necessarily change.

Summary

Poverty and hunger are persistent problems in the world today against the backdrop of a growing global population, especially in poor, climate-vulnerable regions, increased social and economic inequity and mounting environmental concerns. It is not far-fetched to describe the world's current state of affairs as a collective crisis. When assessing which path is best to move forward on, it is easy to agree with the IAASTD report (2008) that 'business-as-usual is not an option.'

In many circles (including key institutions like the FAO), there has been a strong focus on increasing food production as a response to global food insecurity. However, it is important to avoid the trap of a one-sided production focus. Almost one billion people remain hungry and two billion malnourished despite the fact that the world currently produces enough calories to feed 12–14 billion people (UNCTAD, 2013). Clearly, there is a great need to support the development of local, national and global food systems that can effectively address problems of poverty and food access in an ecologically, economically and socially sustainable manner for all people. The debate on food security should therefore shift its focus from the traditional productionist discourse towards searching for approaches that create sustainable food systems.

There have been strong voices calling for a New Green Revolution, with a focus on 'sustainable intensification' and expert-driven, costly biotechnological research and development (e.g. genetically modified organisms (GMOs) that promise drought resistance or biofortified staple foods). A wiser call would be for climate resilient food systems that are integrated, diverse and efficient in terms of resource use (with reduced waste in all stages of production and consumption), productivity and environment impact. Perhaps the solutions to hunger and abatement of negative environmental impacts will not lie in one single system, but a combination of systems, sometimes termed an Evergreen Revolution (Swaminathan, 2010) or a Mosaic Approach (UNCTAD, 2013). Carolan suggests that rather than a revolution of any colour, we need Rainbow Evolutions to emphasize local conditions and deflect attention away from magic-bullet solutions (Carolan, 2013).

Finally, there is a need to question the dominant tendency to uncritically accept future demands of increased land grabbing, commodity speculation, biofuel and animal feed production, and global adoption of Western diets high in animal products and post-harvest waste as a given. Systemic policymaking with the overall goal of health for people and planet will necessarily discourage systemic inefficiencies – which means communities and nations must respond appropriately to negative feedback loops. One could argue that the pursuit of sustainable diets and lifestyles can be seen as indicators of progress in itself.

Note

1 Fish here includes the following sub-categories: fin fishes, crustaceans, molluscs, amphibians (frogs), aquatic reptiles (except crocodiles) and other aquatic animals (such as sea cucumbers, sea urchins, sea squirts and jellyfishes).

References

Acosta, A.M. (2011) Examining the political, institutional and governance aspects of delivering a national multi-sectoral response to reduce maternal and child malnutrition. Analyzing nutrition governance: Brazil country report. Institute of Development Studies, UK, online, http://www.ids.ac.uk/files/dmfile/DFID_ANG_Brazil_Report_Final.pdf (accessed 10 August 2013).

Alderman, H. (2010) Safety nets can help address the risks to nutrition from increasing climate variability, *Journal of Nutrition*, 140: 48–52.

Alexandratos, N. and Bruinsma, J. (2012) World agriculture towards 2030/2050: the 2012 revision. ESA Working paper No. 12–03, FAO, Rome.

Andheier, H. and Themudo, N. (2002) Organizational forms of global civil society: implications of going global. In: Glasius, M., Kaldor, M. and Anheier, H. (Eds) *Global Civil Society*, Oxford University Press, Oxford.

Barrett, J.R. (2001) Livestock farming: eating up the environment?, *Environmental Health Perspectives*, 109 (7): 312–17.

Bates, B.C., Kundzewicz, Z.W., Wu, S. and Palutikof, J.P. (Eds) (2008) Climate change and water. Technical paper of the Intergovernmental Panel on Climate Change, IPCC Secretariat, Geneva, 210 pp.

Beddington, J., Asaduzzaman, M., Clark, M., Fernández, A., Guillou, M., Jahn, M., Erda, L, Mamo, T., Van Bo, N., Nobre, C.A., Scholes, R., Sharma, R. and Wakhungu, J. (2012) Achieving food security in the face of climate change. Final report from the Commission on Sustainable Agriculture and Climate Change. CGIAR Research Program on Climate Change, Agriculture and Food Security (CCAFS), Copenhagen, Denmark.

Black, R. (2008) 'Shun meat', says UN climate chief, *BBC News*, 7 September, online, http://news.bbc.co.uk/2/hi/science/nature/7600005.stm (accessed 19 June 2013).

Bostock, J., McAndrew, B., Richards, R., Jauncey, K., Telfer, T., Lorenzen, K., Little, D., Ross, L., Handisyde, N., Gatward, I. and Corner, R. (2010) Aquaculture: global status and trends, *Philosophical Transactions of the Royal Society of London B Biological Science*, 365 (1554): 2897–912.

Brander, K.M. (2007) Global fish production and climate change, *Proceedings of the National Academy of Science, USA*, 104 (50): 19709–14.

Brundtland, G.H. (1987) *Our Common Future*. Report of the World Commission on Environment and Development (WCED) chaired by Gro Harlem Brundtland. Oxford University Press, Oxford.

Cameron, E., Shine, T. and Bevins, W. (2013) Climate justice: equity and justice informing a new climate agreement. Working paper. World Resources Institute, Washington, DC and Mary Robinson Foundation – Climate Justice, Dublin, online, http://www.climatejusticedialogue.org (accessed 2 May 2014).

Campbell, T.C. and Campbell, T.M. (2006) *The China Study*. BenBella Books, Dallas.

Carolan, M. (2011) *The Real Cost of Cheap Food*. Earthscan, New York.

Carolan, M. (2013) *Reclaiming Food Security*. Routledge, London and New York.

Cassidy, E.S., West, P.C., Gerber, J.S. and Foley, J.A. (2013) Redefining agricultural yields: from tonnes to people nourished per hectare, *Environmental Research Letters*, 8: 1–8.

Cavanagh, J. and Mander, J. (Eds) (2004) *Alternatives to Economic Globalization: A Better World is Possible*. Berrett-Koehler Publishers Inc., San Francisco.

CFS (2013) World Committee on Food Security website, online, http://www.fao.org/cfs/en/ (accessed 25 June 2013).

Chakrabortty, A. (2008) Secret report: biofuel caused food crisis. Internal World Bank study delivers blow to plant energy drive, *The Guardian*, 3 July, online, http://www.guardian. co.uk/environment/2008/jul/03/biofuels.renewableenergy (accessed 20 June 2013).

Chambers, R. (1995) Poverty and livelihoods: whose reality counts?, *Environment and Urbanization*, 7 (1): 173–204.

Chand, R. (2007) International trade, food security, and the response to the WTO in South Asian countries. In: Guha-Khasnobis, B., Acharya, S.S. and Davis, B. (Eds) *Food Security: Indicators, Measurement, and the Impact of Trade Openness*. Oxford University Press, Oxford.

Chen, J. (2007) Rapid urbanization in China: a real challenge to soil protection and food security, *Catena*, 69 (1): 1–15.

CHRGJ (2011) *Every Thirty Minutes: Farmer Suicides, Human Rights, and the Agrarian Crisis in India*. Center for Human Rights and Global Justice, NYU School of Law, New York.

Coleman-Jensen, A., Nord, M., Andrews, M. and Carlson, S. (2011) Household food security in the United States, 2010. The United States Department of Agriculture, Economic Research Report No. 125, online, http://162.79.45.209/media/121076/ err125_2_.pdf (accessed 30 July 2013).

Conceição, P. and Mendoza, R.U. (2009) Anatomy of the global food crisis, *Third World Quarterly*, 30 (6): 1159–82.

CSA Ethiopia (2013) Ethiopia 2011 DHS, *Studies in Family Planning*, 44: 233–42.

CSM (2013) International food security and nutrition, Civil Society Mechanism website, online, http://www.csm4cfs.org/about_us-2/what_is_the_csm-1/ (accessed 25 June 2013).

De Schutter, O. (2010a) Countries tackling hunger with a right to food approach. Briefing Note No. 1, May, online, http://www2.ohchr.org/english/issues/food/docs/Briefing_ Note_01_May_2010_EN.pdf (accessed 23 September 2013).

De Schutter, O. (2010b) Food commodities speculation and food price crises. Briefing Note No. 2, online, http://www.srfood.org/images/stories/pdf/otherdocuments/20102309_ briefing_note_02_en_ok.pdf (accessed 23 September 2013).

De Schutter, O. (2011) Agro-ecology and the Right to Food. Report submitted by the Special Rapporteur on the Right to Food to UN Human Rights Council, 20 December, online, http://www.srfood.org/images/stories/pdf/officialreports/20110308_a-hrc-16-49_ agroecology_en.pdf (accessed 3 September 2013).

Drewnowski, A. and Popkin, B.M. (1997) The nutrition transition: new trends in the global diet, *Nutrition Reviews*, 55 (2): 21–43.

Dreze, J. (2013) The food security debate in India, blog, online, http://india.blogs.nytimes. com/2013/07/09/the-food-security-debate-in-india/ (accessed 2 May 2014).

Eckhardt, C.L. (2006) Micronutrient malnutrition, obesity, and chronic disease in countries undergoing the nutrition transition: potential links and program/policy intervention. FCND Discussion paper 213. IFPRI, online, http://www.ifpri.org/sites/default/files/ pubs/divs/fcnd/dp/papers/fcndp213.pdf (accessed 20 June 2013).

Edwards, M. (2000) *NGO Rights and Responsibilities: A New Deal for Global Governance*. The Foreign Policy Centre/NCVO, London.

Ericksen, P.J. (2008) Conceptualizing food systems for global environmental change research, *Global Environmental Change*, 18: 234–45.

European Union (EU) (2012) Sustainable agriculture for the future we want, online, http:// ec.europa.eu/agriculture/events/2012/rio-side-event/brochure_en.pdf (accessed 29 April 2014).

FDR library (2013) FDR and the four freedoms speech, online, http://www.fdrlibrary. marist.edu/fourfreedoms (accessed 24 August 2013).

Food and Agriculture Organization (FAO) (1999) World Food Summit: the world food summit and its follow-up, online, http://www.fao.org/docrep/x2051e/x2051e00.HTM#P45_1647 (accessed 15 August 2013).

Food and Agriculture Organization (FAO) (2006a) Food policy brief, June, Issue 2, online, ftp://ftp.fao.org/es/ESA/policybriefs/pb_02.pdf (accessed 24 June 2013).

Food and Agriculture Organization (FAO) (2006b) Livestock's long shadow: environmental issues and options, online, ftp://ftp.fao.org/docrep/fao/010/a0701e/a0701e00.pdf (accessed 18 July 2013).

Food and Agriculture Organization (FAO) (2009a) How to feed the world in 2050. Report from the high-level expert forum in Rome, 12–13 October, online, http://www.fao.org/fileadmin/templates/wsfs/docs/expert_paper/How_to_Feed_the_World_in_2050.pdf (accessed 20 June 2013).

Food and Agriculture Organization (FAO) (2009b) The state of food and agriculture. Livestock in balance, online, http://www.fao.org/docrep/012/i0680e/i0680e.pdf (accessed 18 June 2013).

Food and Agriculture Organization (FAO) (2011a) The state of food and agriculture 2010/2011. Women in agriculture: closing the gender gap, online, http://www.fao.org/docrep/013/i2050e/i2050e.pdf (accessed 17 June 2013).

Food and Agriculture Organization (FAO) (2011b) Right to food: making it happen, online, http://www.fao.org/docrep/014/i2250e/i2250e.pdf (accessed 30 June 2013).

Food and Agriculture Organization (FAO) (2012a) Sustainable diets and biodiversity. Directions and solutions for policy research and action, online, http://www.fao.org/docrep/016/i3004e/i3004e.pdf (accessed 1 September 2013).

Food and Agriculture Organization (FAO) (2012b) FAO policy on gender equality: attaining food security goals in agriculture and rural development, online, http://www.fao.org/fileadmin/templates/gender/docs/FAO_FinalGender_Policy_2012.pdf (accessed 17 June 2013).

Food and Agriculture Organization (FAO) (2012c) The state of the world fisheries and aquaculture, online, http://www.fao.org/docrep/016/i2727e/i2727e01.pdf (accessed 1 July 2013).

Food and Agriculture Organization (FAO) (2013) Climate-smart agriculture. Sourcebook, online, http://www.fao.org/docrep/018/i3325e/i3325e.pdf (accessed 15 August 2013).

Food and Agriculture Organization (FAO), World Food Programme (WFP) and International Fund for Agricultural Development (IFAD) (2012) The state of food insecurity in the world 2012. Economic growth is necessary but not sufficient to accelerate reduction of hunger and malnutrition. Rome, FAO, online, http://www.fao.org/docrep/016/i3027e/i3027e.pdf (accessed 12 June 2013).

Fukuyama, F. (2001) Social capital, civil society and development, *Third World Quarterly*, 22 (1):7–20.

Garcia, S.M. and Grainger, R.J.R. (2005) Gloom and doom? The future of marine capture fisheries, *Philosophical Transactions of the Royal Society of London B Biological Science*, 360 (1453): 21–46.

Garvey, K. (2012) Global food security: the role of science and technology, 17–19 October, Wilton Park Conference report, WP1189, UK, online, http://www.wiltonpark.org.uk/resources/en/report-pages/2012/wp1189-report (accessed 2 May 2014).

Gates Notes (2013) The future of food, online, http://www.thegatesnotes.com/Features/Future-of-Food (accessed 20 June 2013).

Geary, K. (2012) Our land, our lives. Time out on the global land rush. Oxfam briefing note, online, http://www.oxfam.org/sites/www.oxfam.org/files/bn-land-lives-freeze-041012-en_1.pdf (accessed 24 June 2013).

Gleick, P.H. (2010) Climate change, hydrology, and water resources, *Reviews of Geophysics*, 27 (3): 329–44.

Global Footprint Network, website, online, http://www.footprintnetwork.org/en/index. php/GFN/page/world_footprint/ (accessed 23 June 2013).

Godfray, H.C., Beddington, J.R., Crute, I.R., Haddad, L., Lawrence, D., Muir, J.F., Pretty, J., Robinson, S., Thomas, S.M. and Toulmin, C. (2010) Food security: the challenge of feeding 9 billion people, *Science*, 327: 812–18.

Goodland, R. and Anhang, J. (2009) Livestock and climate change – what if the key actors in climate change are cows, pigs and chickens?, online, http://www.worldwatch.org/ files/pdf/Livestock%20and%20Climate%20Change.pdf (accessed 14 August 2013).

Government Office for Science, London (2011) Foresight. The future of food and farming. Final project report, online, http://www.bis.gov.uk/assets/foresight/docs/food-and-farming/11-546-future-of-food-and-farming-report.pdf (accessed 28 June 2013).

Graham, R.D., Knez, M. and Welch, R.M. (2012) How much nutritional iron deficiency in humans globally is due to an underlying zinc deficiency?, *Advances in Agronomy*, 115: 1–40.

Gray, R., Bebbington, J. and Collison, D. (2006) NGOs, civil society and accountability: making the people accountable to capital, *Accounting, Auditing & Accountability Journal*, 19 (3): 319–48, online, http://www.hapinternational.org/pool/files/ngos,-civil-soc.pdf (accessed 20 August 2013).

Gunther, M. (2013) The Bill Gates-backed company that's reinventing meat, 3 October, *CNN*, online, http://features.blogs.fortune.cnn.com/2013/10/03/bill-gates-backed-company-reinventing-meat/ (accessed 3 November 2013).

Haggblade, S. and Tembo, G. (2003) Conservation farming in Zambia. International Food Policy Research Institute, EPTD Discussion paper No. 108. IFPRI, Washington, DC.

Hartwich, F., Tola, J., Engler, A., González, C., Ghezan, G., Vázquez-Alvarado, J.M.P., Silva, J.A., de Jesús Espinoza, J. and Gottret, M.V. (2007) *Building Public–Private Partnerships for Agricultural Innovation*. Food security in practice, Technical Guide Series. IFPRI, Washington, DC.

Hawken, P. (2007) *Blessed Unrest: How the Largest Social Movement in History is Restoring Grace, Justice, and Beauty to the World*. Viking Penguin, New York.

Hawkes, C. (2005) The role of foreign direct investment in the nutrition transition, *Public Health Nutrition*, 8 (4): 357–65.

Hazell, P. and Haddad, L. (2001) Agricultural research and poverty reduction, 2020 Vision Discussion paper No. 34, IFPRI, Washington, DC.

Healey, S., Pearce, R. and Stockbridge, M. (1998) The implications of the Uruguay round agreement on agriculture for developing countries: a training manual. FAO, Rome, online, http://www.fao.org/docrep/w7814e/w7814e00.htm#Contents (accessed 17 June 2013).

HLPE (2013) Biofuels and Food Security. A report by the High Level Panel of Experts on Food Security and Nutrition of the Committee on World Food Security, Rome 2013, online, http://www.fao.org/fileadmin/user_upload/hlpe/hlpe_documents/HLPE_ Reports/HLPE-Report-5_Biofuels_and_food_security.pdf (accessed 1 September 2013).

Holt-Giménez, E. (2012) We already grow enough food for 10 billion people … and still can't end hunger, *Journal of Sustainable Agriculture*, 36 (6): 595–8.

Holt-Giménez, E. (2013) G-8 leaders: after 20 years it's time to listen to La Via Campesina, 13 June, online, http://www.huffingtonpost.com/eric-holt-gimenez/g-8-leaders_b_3436779.html (accessed 3 October 2013).

Holt-Gimenéz, E. and Altieri, M.A. (2013) Agroecology, food sovereignty, and the new green revolution, *Agroecology and Sustainable Food Systems*, 37 (1): 90–102.

Holt-Giménez, E. and Shattuck, A. (2011) Food crises, food regimes and food movements: rumblings of reform or tides of transformation?, *Journal of Peasant Studies*, 38 (1): 109–144.

Hu, F.B. (2003) Plant-based foods and prevention of cardiovascular disease: an overview, *The American Journal of Clinical Nutrition*, 78 (3): 5445–515.

IAASTD (2008) Synthesis report with executive summary: a synthesis of the global and sub-global IAASTD reports. Edited by McIntyre, B.D., Herren, H.R., Wakhungu, J. and Watson, R.T., Island Press, Washington, DC.

IATP (2009) Commodities market speculation: the risk to food security and agriculture. Institute for Agriculture and Trade Policy, Minneapolis, online, http://www.iatp.org/files/451_2_104414.pdf (accessed 15 August 2013).

Ingram, J.S.I, Ericksen, P. and Liverman, D. (Eds) (2010) *Food Security and Global Environmental Change*. Earthscan, London.

Intergovernmental Panel on Climate Change (IPCC) (2007) Summary for policymakers. In: Solomon, S. *et al.* (Eds) *Climate Change 2007: The Physical Science Basis. Contribution of Working Group I to the Fourth Assessment Report of the Intergovernmental Panel on Climate Change*. Cambridge University Press, Cambridge.

Intergovernmental Panel on Climate Change (IPCC) (2013) Climate change 2013: the physical science basis, online, https://www.ipcc.ch/report/ar5/wg1/ (accessed 2 May 2014).

International Food Policy Research Institute (IFPRI) (2008) Biofuels and food security: balancing needs for food, feed and fuel, online, http://www.ifpri.org/sites/default/files/publications/bioenergybro.pdf (accessed 1 October 2013).

International Fund for Agricultural Development (IFAD) (2011) Viewpoint: smallholders can feed the world, online, http://www.ifad.org/pub/viewpoint/smallholder.pdf (accessed 23 October 2013).

International Fund for Agricultural Development (IFAD) (2013a) Food security: a conceptual framework, online, http://www.ifad.org/hfs/thematic/rural/rural_2.htm (accessed 21 June 2013).

International Fund for Agricultural Development (IFAD) (2013b) Smallholders, food security, and the environment, online, http://www.ifad.org/climate/resources/smallholders_report.pdf (accessed 15 September 2013).

Jarosz, L. (2009) Energy, climate change, meat, and markets: Mapping the coordinates of the current world food crisis, *Geography Compass*, 3 (6): 2065–83.

Jägerskog, A. and Jønch Clausen, T. (Eds) (2012) Feeding a thirsty world: challenges and opportunities for a water and food secure future. Report No. 31. SIWI, Stockholm, online, http://www.siwi.org/documents/Resources/Reports/Feeding_a_thirsty_world_2012worldwaterweek_report_31.pdf (accessed 15 September 2013).

Jones, M. (2012) First Global Conference on Women in Agriculture (GCWA): empowering women in agriculture: rethinking the agricultural needs and actions through the eyes of women, *Food Security*, 4 (2): 305–6.

Jones, W. and Elasri, A. (2010) Rising food prices: causes, consequences and policy responses. In: Karapinar, B. and Häberli, C. (Eds) *Food Crises and the WTO*. Cambridge University Press, Cambridge.

Kaufman, F. (2010) The food bubble: how Wall Street starved millions and got away with it, *Harper's Magazine*, July, pp. 27–34.

Knox, J.W., Hess, T.M., Daccache, A. and Perez Ortola, M. (2011) What are the projected impacts of climate change on food crop productivity in Africa and S Asia? DFID, System review final report, Cranfield University, Bedford, UK.

Kristof, N.D. and WuDunn, S. (2009) *Half the Sky: Turning Oppression into Opportunity for Women Worldwide*. Random House, New York.

Lang, T. and Barling, D. (2012) Food security and food sustainability: reformulating the debate, *The Geographical Journal*, 178 (4): 313–26.

Lang, T. and Heasman, M. (2003) *Food Wars: The Global Battle for Mouths, Minds and Markets*. Routledge, New York.

Lastarria-Cornhiel, S. (2006) Feminization of agriculture: trends and driving forces. Background paper for the World Development Report 2008, online, http://siteresources.worldbank.org/INTWDR2008/Resources/2795087-1191427986785/LastarriaCornhiel_FeminizationOfAgri.pdf (accessed 15 September 2013).

Latin America Press (2012) FAO accepts to debate food sovereignty, 17 May, online, http://lapress.org/articles.asp?art=6630 (accessed 5 August 2013).

La Via Campesina (2009) Small-scale sustainable farmers are cooling down the earth, online, http://viacampesina.net/downloads/PAPER5/EN/paper5-EN.pdf (accessed 15 August 2013).

La Via Campesina (2013) online, www.laviacampesina.org (accessed 14 June 2013).

Lawrence, G. and McMichael, P. (2012) The question of food security, *International Journal of Sociology of Agriculture and Food*, 19 (2): 135–42.

Mac, R. (2013) Bill Gates food fetish: Hampton Creek foods looks to crack the egg industry, 23 November 23, *Forbes*, online, http://www.forbes.com/sites/ryanmac/2013/11/23/bill-gates-food-fetish-hampton-creek-foods-looks-to-crack-the-egg-industry/ (accessed 15 January 2013).

Martínez-Torres, M.E. and Rosset, P.M. (2010) La Vía Campesina: the birth and evolution of a transnational social movement, *The Journal of Peasant Studies*, 37 (1): 149–75.

Maxwell, S. (1996) Food security: a post-modern perspective, *Food Policy*, 21 (2): 155–70.

Maxwell, S. and Smith, M. (1992) Household food security: a conceptual review. In: Maxwell, S. and Frankenberger, T. (Eds) *Household Food Security. Concepts, Indicators, and Measurements. A Technical Review*. UNICEF/IFAD, Online, http://www.ifad.org/hfs/tools/hfs/hfspub/hfs_1.pdf (accessed 20 June 2013).

McMahon, P. (2013) *Feeding Frenzy: The New Politics of Food*. Profile Books, London.

McMichael, A., Powles, J.W., Butler, C.D. and Uauy, R. (2007) Food, livestock production, energy, climate change, and health, *The Lancet*, 370 (9594): 1253–63.

Mehra, R. and Rojas, M.H. (2008) *Women, Food Security and Agriculture in a Global Marketplace*. International Center for Research on Women (ICRW), Washington, DC.

Menezes, F. (2011) Social participation in the zero hunger program: the experience of Consea. In da Silva, J.G., del Grossi, M.E. and de Franca, C.G. (Eds) *The Fome Zero (Zero Hunger) Program – the Brazilian Experience*. FAO/Ministry of Agrarian Development, Brazil, online, http://www.grazianodasilva.org/wp-content/uploads/2011/06/Zero-Hunger-Book-ENGLISH_full.pdf (accessed 24 August 2013).

Moser, C.O.N. (1989) Gender planning in the third world: Meeting practical and strategic gender needs, *World Development*, 17 (11): 1799–825.

Mosley, P. (2003) *A Painful Ascent: The Green Revolution in Africa*. London: Routledge.

Nelson, G.C., Rosegrant M.W., Palazzo, A., Gray, I., Ingersoll, C., Robertson, R., Tokgoz, S., Zhu, T., Sulser, T.B., Ringler, C., Msangi, S. and Yu. L. (2011) *Climate Change: Impact on Agriculture and Costs of Adaptation and Food Security, Farming, and Climate Change to 2050*. IFPRI, Washington, DC.

Nestle, M. (2002) *Food Politics: How the Food Industry Influences Nutrition and Health*. University of California Press, Berkeley.

Nestle, M. (2003) *Safe Food: Bacteria, Biotechnology and Bioterrorism*, University of California Press, Berkeley.

Nierenberg, D. and Spoden, K. (2012) Aquaculture tries to fill world's insatiable appetite for seafood. *Vital Signs*. World Watch Institute, online, http://vitalsigns.worldwatch.org/vs-trend/aquaculture-tries-fill-world%E2%80%99s-insatiable-appetite-seafood (accessed 1 October 2013).

O'Hara, J.K. (2013) The $11 trillion reward: how simple dietary changes can save lives and money, and how we get there. Report for Union of Concerned Scientists, online, http://www.ucsusa.org/assets/documents/food_and_agriculture/11-trillion-reward.pdf (accessed 5 August 2013).

Oldeman, L.R. (1998) Soil degradation: a threat to food security?, *ISRIC*, online, http://www.isric.org/isric/webdocs/docs/ISRIC_Report_1998_01.pdf (accessed 29 April 2014).

Orlich, M.J., Singh, P.N., Sabaté, J., Jaceldo-Siegl, K., Fan, J., Knutsen, S., Beeson, W.L. and Fraser, G.E. (2013) Vegetarian dietary patterns and mortality in adventist health study 2, *JAMA Internal Medicine*, 173 (13): 1230–8.

Paramaguru, K. (2012) Betting on hunger: Is financial speculation to blame for high food prices? *Time Magazine*, 17 December, online, http://science.time.com/2012/12/17/betting-on-hunger-is-financial-speculation-to-blame-for-high-food-prices/ (accessed 19 June 2013).

Pardey, P., Alston, J. and Piggott, R. (Eds) (2006) *Agricultural R&D in the Developing World: Too Little, Too Late?* IFPRI, Washington, DC.

Patel, R. (2007) *Stuffed and Starved: The Hidden Battle for the World's Food System*. Portobello Books, London.

Patel, R. (2009) Food sovereignty, *Journal of Peasant Studies*, 36 (1): 663–706

Patel, R. (2012) The long green revolution, *Journal of Peasant Studies*, 40 (1): 1–63.

Pearce, F. (2009) Consumption dwarfs population as main environmental threat, *The Guardian*, 15 April, online, http://www.guardian.co.uk/environment/2009/apr/15/consumption-versus-population-environmental-impact (accessed 18 June 2013).

Philpott, T. (2011) Your chicken nuggets are killing your crab cakes. *Mother Jones*, 28 July, online, http://www.motherjones.com/tom-philpott/2011/07/chesapeake-dead-zone-agriculture (accessed 18 June 2013).

Pinstrup-Andersen, P. (2009) Food security: definition and measurement, *Food Security*, 1 (1): 5–7.

Pinstrup-Andersen, P. and Watson II, D.D. (2011) *Food Policy for Developing Countries – The Role of Government in Global, National, and Local Food Systems*. Cornell University Press, New York.

Popkin, B.M., Adair, L.S. and Ng, S.W. (2012) Global nutrition transition and the pandemic of obesity in developing countries, *Nutrition Reviews*, 70 (1): 3–21.

Quisumbing, A.R., Brown, L.R., Feldstein, H.S., Haddad, L. and Peña, C. (1995) Women: the key to food security, Food policy report, IFPRI, Washington, DC, online, http://www.ifpri.cgiar.org/sites/default/files/publications/fpr21.pdf (accessed 18 September 2013).

Reardon, T. and Hopkins, R. (2006) The supermarket revolution in developing countries: policies to address emerging tensions among supermarkets, suppliers and traditional retailers, *European Journal of Development Research* 18, 522–55.

Reardon, T., Timmer, P. and Berdegue, J. (2004) The rapid rise of supermarkets in developing countries: induced organizational, institutional, and technological change in agrifood systems, *Electronic Journal of Agricultural and Development Economics*, 1 (2): 168–83.

Revenga, A. and Shetty, S. (2012) Empowering women is smart economics, *Finance & Development*, 49 (1): 40–3.

Ringler, C. (2012) Agricultural technologies, food security or something more, online, http://agrihunt.blogspot.com.au/2012/07/agricultural-technologies-for-food.html (accessed 2 May 2014).

Robbins, J. (2011) *The Food Revolution. How Your Diet Can Help Save Your Life and Our World.* Conari Pess, San Fransisco.

Rocha, C. (2009) Developments in national policies for food and nutrition security in Brazil, *Development Policy Review*, 27 (1): 51–66.

Sanchez, A.P. (2000) Linking climate change research with food security and poverty reduction in the tropics, *Agriculture, Ecosystems and Environment*, 82: 371–83.

SDC (2009) Food security and sustainability, the perfect fit. Sustainable Development Commission position paper, online, http://www.sd-commission.org.uk/data/files/publications/SDCFoodSecurityPositionPaper.pdf (accessed 8 August 2013).

Sen, A. (1981) *Poverty and Famines: An Essay on Entitlements and Deprivations.* Oxford University Press, Oxford.

Sen, A. (1990) More than 100 million women are missing *New York Review of Books*, 37 (20): 61–6.

Shaw, D.J. (2007) *World Food Security: A History since 1945.* Palgrave Macmillan, New York.

Simon, J.L. (1980) Resources, population, environment: an oversupply of false bad news, *Science*, 208 (4451): 1431–7.

Smedshaug, C.A. (2010) *Feeding the World in the 21st Century: A Historical Analysis of Agriculture and Society.* Anthem Press, New York.

Soubbotina, T.P. and Sheram, K.A. (2000) Beyond economic growth: meeting the challenges of global development, World Bank, online, http://www.worldbank.org/depweb/beyond/beyondco/beg_all.pdf (accessed 19 August 2013).

Stuckler, D. and Nestle, M. (2012) Big food, food systems, and global health, *PLoS Medicine*, 9 (6): e1001242. DOI:10.1371/journal.pmed.1001242.

Stuckler, D., McKee, M., Ebrahim, S. and Basu, S. (2012) Manufacturing epidemics: the role of global producers in increased consumption of unhealthy commodities including processed foods, alcohol, and tobacco, *PLoS Medicine*, 9 (6): e1001235. DOI:10.1371/journal.pmed.1001235.

Swaminathan, M.S. (2010) *From Green to Evergreen Revolution.* Academic Foundation, New Delhi.

Swaminathan, M.S. (2013) From Bengal famine to right to food, *The Hindu*, 13 February, online, http://www.thehindu.com/todays-paper/tp-opinion/from-bengal-famine-to-right-to-food/article4409557.ece (accessed 13 September 2013).

Tansey, G. and Worsley, T. (1995) *The Food System: A Guide.* Earthscan, London.

The Lancet (2012) *Global Burden of Disease Study 2010.* The Lancet, online, http://www.thelancet.com/themed/global-burden-of-disease (accessed 15 May 2013).

Thornton, P. and Cramer, L. (2012) Impacts of climate change on the agricultural and aquatic systems and natural resources within the CGIAR's mandate. CCAFS Working paper No. 23. CGIAR CCAFS, Copenhagen.

Townsend, M.S., Peerson, J., Love, B., Achterberg, C. and Murphy, S.P. (2001) Food Insecurity is Positively Related to Overweight in Women, *The Journal of Nutrition*, 131 (6): 1738–45.

Trewavas, A. (2002) Malthus foiled again and again, *Nature*, 418: 668–70.

Tribe, D. (1994) *Feeding and Greening the World: The Role of International Agricultural Research.* CABI, Wallingford.

Tuso, P.J., Ismail, M.H., Ha, B.P. and Bartolotto, C. (2013) Nutritional update for physicians: plant-based diets, *The Permanente Journal*, 17 (2): 61–6.

Udaya Sekhar, N., Gosain, A.K., Barton, D.N., Palanisami, K., Tirupathaiah, K., Reddy, K.K., Stålnacke, P., Deelstra, J. and Gupta, S. (2012) Climate change and impacts on water resources: guidelines for adaptation in India, *Bioforsk*, 7 (173).

United Nations (2009) United Nations. World urbanization prospects. UNDESA, New York.

United Nations (2010) World population prospects: the 2010 revision, UNDESA, New York. United Nations Population Division, online, http://esa.un.org/wpp/unpp/panel_population.htm (accessed 2 May 2014).

United Nations Conference on Trade and Development (UNCTAD) (2009). Trade and Development Report 2009, online, http://unctad.org/en/Docs/tdr2009_en.pdf (accessed 10 August 2013).

United Nations Conference on Trade and Development (UNCTAD) (2013). 'Wake up before it is too late. Make agriculture truly sustainable now for food security in a changing climate.' Trade and Environment Review 2013. United Nations Conference on Trade and Development, online, http://unctad.org/en/PublicationsLibrary/ditcted2012d3_en.pdf (accessed 30 September 2013).

United Nations Development Programme (UNDP) (2012): African Development Report 2012: Towards a Food Secure Future, online, http://www.undp.org/content/undp/en/home/librarypage/hdr/africa-human-development-report-2012/ (accessed 28 April 2014).

United Nations Environment Programme (UNEP) (2011) Decoupling natural resource use and environmental impacts from economic growth, A Report of the Working Group on Decoupling to the International Resource Panel, online, http://www.unep.org/resourcepanel/decoupling/files/pdf/decoupling_report_english.pdf (accessed 3 October 2013).

United Nations Millennium Project (2005) Halving hunger: It can be done, online, http://www.unmillenniumproject.org/documents/Hunger-lowres-complete.pdf (accessed 1 June 2013).

Vanhaute, E. and Van Den Abeele, C. (2013) Peasant movements in the twentieth and twenty-first centuries: from parochial reactions to global struggle? In: Marung, S. and Middell, M.L. (Eds) online, http://www.ccc.ugent.be/file/228 (accessed 20 June 2013).

Vermeulen, S.J., Campbell, B. and Ingram, J.S.I. (2012) Climate change and food systems, *Annual Review of Environment and Resources*, 37: 5.1–5.28.

Vidal, J. (2012) Food shortages could force world into vegetarianism, warn scientists, *The Guardian*, 26 August, online, http://www.guardian.co.uk/global-development/2012/aug/26/food-shortages-world-vegetarianism (accessed 19 June 2013).

Vidal, J. (2013) La Via Campesina's Saragih: we have no choice but to change the system, *The Guardian*, 17 June, online, http://www.theguardian.com/global-development/2013/jun/17/la-via-campesina-henry-saragih (accessed 5 August 2013).

Vorley, B., Cotula, L and Chan, M. (2012) *Tipping the Balance*, Oxfam and IIED Research report, online, http://dlc.dlib.indiana.edu/dlc/bitstream/handle/10535/8729/G03470.pdf (accessed 3 October 2013).

Wahlquist, M.L., McKay, J., Chang, Y.C. and Chiu, Y.W. (2012) Rethinking the food security debate in Asia: some missing ecological and health dimensions and solutions, *Food Security*, 4 (4): 657–70.

Watkins, K. and von Braun, J. (2002) Time to stop dumping on the world's poor. In IFPRI Essays 2002–03, online, http://www.ifpri.org/sites/default/files/pubs/pubs/books/ar2002/ar02.pdf (accessed 3 October 2013).

Weis, T. (2007) *The Global Food Economy: The Battle for the Future of Farming.* Fernwood, Winnipeg.

Weis, T. (2013) The meat of the global food crisis, *Journal of Peasant Studies,* 40 (1): 65–85.

Welch, R.M. (2002) The impact of mineral nutrients in food crops on global human health, *Plant and Soil,* 247: 83–90.

Welch, R.M. and Graham, R.D. (1999) A new paradigm for world agriculture: meeting human needs: productive, sustainable, nutritious, *Field Crops Research,* 60: 1–10.

WFP (2011) Climate-smart agriculture highlighted at the COP 17, online, http://www.wfp. org/stories/ climate-smart-agriculture-csa-highlighted-cop17 (accessed 2 May 2014).

Winkler, J.T. (2009) *The Politics of Global Food Security: Domestic Production, Guaranteed Imports, Enlarged Reserves.* Nutrition Policy Unit, London Metropolitan University, London.

Wise, T. (2004) The paradox of agricultural subsidies: measurement issues, agricultural dumping, and policy reform, Global Development and Environment Institute Working paper No. 04–02, Online, http://www.ase.tufts.edu/gdae/Pubs/wp/04-02AgSubsidies. pdf (accessed 19 June 2013).

Wittman, H. (2009) Reworking the metabolic rift: La Vía Campesina, agrarian citizenship, and food sovereignty, *The Journal of Peasant Studies,* 36 (4):663–706.

Wittman, H.K., Desmarais, A.A. and Wiebe, N. (2010) *Food Sovereignty: Reconnecting Food, Nature and Community.* Food First Books, Oakland, CA.

World Bank (2008) *World Development Report 2008: Agriculture for Development.* World Bank, Washington, DC.

World Bank (2011) World Development Report 2012: Gender Equality and Development, online, http://siteresources.worldbank.org/INTWDR2012/Resources/ 7778105-1299699968583/7786210-1315936222006/Complete-Report.pdf (accessed 19 June 2013).

World Economic Forum (2013) The new vision for agriculture: transforming agriculture through collaboration, online, http://www.weforum.org/issues/agriculture-and-food-security (accessed 17 June 2013).

World Health Organization (WHO) (2002), online, WHO, WFP & UNICEF joint statement, http://www.who.int/nutrition/publications/WHO_WFP_UNICEFstatement.pdf (accessed 1 June 2013).

World Health Organization (WHO) (2013) Obesity and overweight. Fact sheet, online, http://www.who.int/mediacentre/factsheets/fs311/en/ (accessed 1 June 2013).

World Trade Organization (WTO) (2013) About the WTO – a statement by the Director General, online, http://www.wto.org/english/thewto_e/whatis_e/wto_dg_stat_e.htm (accessed 17 June 2013).

Yunus, M. (2011) Micro-credit and women: the Grameen bank experience, *Commonwealth Ministers Reference Book 2011,* pp.1–2, online, http://www.commonwealthministers.com/ images/uploads/documents/CMRB_Yunus_4.pdf (accessed 15 September 2013).

2 Food security in China

Past, present and the future

Zhang-Yue Zhou

Introduction

Food shortages are not uncommon in the history of China and hence the word 'famine' is not new to many Chinese (Lang, 1934; Feng, 1970; Xu, 1996; Yang, 2008). The most recent large-scale famine took place between 1959 and 1962, during which some 37 million people (5 per cent of the population) died of hunger (Yang, 2008). While the horrific experience of the famine cannot be erased from the memories of those who are now in their 50s and above, malnutrition and starvation during the 'Cultural Revolution' period (1966–76) still remains in the minds of the generation who are in their 40s and above.

Today, food supply in China is adequate and easily accessible. Arguably, the past three decades (the early 1980s to date) was one of the best periods in Chinese history so far as food availability is concerned. Thus, examining how China has managed to improve its food availability can be most valuable in generating useful implications not only for China but also for other countries to promote their food security for the future. This chapter examines China's food security practice since the 1950s.

In the following section, we examine China's food security situation since the 1950s, followed by the identification of the key drivers that contributed to its improvement during the past three decades. In the third section, a normative food security framework is used to evaluate the current status of China's food security. Major challenges for China to further improve its food security for the future and influential factors that affect the handling of such challenges are identified and elaborated in the fourth part. And finally, conclusions and implications are provided.

Food security practice in the past

Food scarcity: 1950s–1970s

FAO indicates that prior to the 1980s in China a substantial proportion of the total calorie supply was obtained from foods of plant origin. Such foods largely consisted of grains, chiefly, rice and wheat, the two most important staple foods in China. Table 2.1 confirms that the intake of most other food items was very low

Table 2.1 Per capita consumption of major food items in China (1952–92, kg, selected years).

Year	Grains	Vegetable oil	Pork	Beef and mutton	Poultry	Eggs	Aquatic products	Sugar
1952	198	2.1	5.9	0.9	0.4	1.0	2.7	0.9
1957	203	2.4	5.1	1.1	0.5	1.3	4.3	1.5
1962	165	1.1	2.2	0.8	0.4	0.8	3.0	1.6
1965	183	1.7	6.3	1.0	0.4	1.4	3.3	1.7
1970	187	1.6	6.0	0.8	0.3	1.3	2.9	2.1
1975	191	1.7	7.6	0.7	0.4	1.6	3.3	2.3
1978	195	1.6	7.7	0.8	0.4	2.0	3.5	3.4
1979	207	2.0	10.0	0.8	0.6	2.1	3.2	3.6
1980	214	2.3	11.2	0.8	0.8	2.3	3.4	3.8
1985	252	5.1	13.8	1.3	1.6	4.9	4.8	5.6
1990	239	5.7	16.6	1.7	1.7	6.3	6.5	5.0
1992	236	6.3	18.2	2.1	2.3	7.8	7.3	5.4

Source: Adapted from SSB, 1993 and earlier years.

Note: Grains in the table refer to unprocessed raw grain.

and grain was the major source of food before 1980. Due to the importance of grains to the Chinese, the word 'grain' (in Chinese *pinyin, liangshi*) is more often used than the word 'food' (*shiwu*) in Chinese daily life.[1] As a result, Chinese scientists more often use the term 'grain security' rather than 'food security'. In this chapter, where appropriate, the term 'grain security' will also be used.

Table 2.1 suggests that from the beginning of the 1950s to the end of the 1970s, 'food' was not secure at all. Even in 1978, the per capita availability of most foods was still below the level of 1952. A daily intake of around 0.5kg grain per capita with little other protein and oil foods was far from adequate to supply the needed nutrition, especially for labourers. The author who worked in rural China during the late 1970s still remembers the bitter experiences faced due to food shortages.

One may ask why China's per capita food intake was so low for so long. The following brief account of major events between the 1950s and the 1970s explains why the Chinese did not have enough to eat.

In 1949, China's civil war ended and the Communist Party of China (CPC) came to power. At that time, the country's total grain output was low and many people starved. Boosting grain output became the first priority of the new government. Grain production gradually expanded during 1950–52. However, a large portion of the increased output was consumed by farmers themselves who constituted about 88 per cent of the total population (Table 2.1). This made it difficult for the new government to procure enough grain for distribution to the urban population (Zhao and Qi, 1988).

In 1953, a 'unified grain procurement and sale system' was put into use, which was to procure grain from rural areas and then supply (by ration) to consumers in urban areas; the ration varied according to age, sex and labour strength. The state grain agencies were the sole buyers and sellers in the market. A compulsory procurement quota and a government-set procurement price were the two major instruments to ensure the success of the planned grain purchase. Under this scheme, a grain procurement quota was assigned to each individual farm household with surplus grains. Surplus grain was the quantity left over after a farm household retains grain for home consumption, seed and feed according to standards set by the local governments, and after the farm household pays the agricultural tax. (Paid in kind, this tax accounted for 15.5 per cent of a normal year's grain output in the 1950s, gradually declining until, in 1985, cash was allowed to replace grains in kind, and was eventually abolished in 2006.) The quota generally accounted for 80–90 per cent of the surplus amount produced (Zhao and Qi, 1988).

Farm operations were carried out on a household basis until 1955 when farmers were encouraged, or in many cases coerced, to join cooperatives. Initially, the cooperation was very elementary. During 1955–57, the scope of cooperation was rapidly expanded and become comprehensive. In 1958, almost all farmers joined the People's Commune and farm operations became collectivized. As a result, there were no incentives for individuals to work hard, which in turn resulted in lower agricultural output throughout the country.

During the 1950s, China exported grains despite a shortage in the domestic market (Table 2.2). This was to generate foreign exchange to cover industrial development and military expenses. Following the People's Commune and the Great Leap Forward movements launched by Mao Ze-Dong in 1958, total grain output in 1959 dropped significantly to 170 million tonnes (MT) from the previous high of 200 MT in 1958. It further dropped to 143 MT in 1960, even below that of 1952. During the same period (1952–59), population increased by almost 100 million. The consequence was sharply reduced per capita grain availability. In 1960, per capita grain availability (grain output plus net grain imports divided by total population) dropped to 212kg per person, much lower than the 237kg per person in 1950 (Table 2.2).

Many people starved. Farmers suffered the most. In some places, farmers' harvests were over-procured to feed urban people. Severe food shortage led to the infamous man-made famine in China during which approximately 37 million people died of hunger, most of whom were farmers (Ashton *et al.*, 1984; Kane, 1988; Ding, 1996; Yang, 2008).

During 1960–66, various measures were taken to promote grain production. These included price increase for grains procured under the unified purchase; higher price to farmers who sold grains to the government above their quota; providing farmers with coupons to buy industrial goods as incentives if they sold grains to the government; and reopening rural fairs and allowing farmers to sell grains in the market. By 1966, total grain output reached 214 MT, surpassing its 1958 record.

Just when the grain situation eased, Mao Ze-Dong launched the Cultural Revolution in 1966 that lasted for almost a decade and people all over the country including school students had to take part. Production activities were seriously disrupted including farm production. Grain output stagnated during most of this

Table 2.2 Grain output, net grain imports and per capita grain availability.

Year	Grain output	Net grain imports	Total population	Proportion of rural population	Per capita grain availability
	(MT*)	*(MT)*	*(m)*	*(%)*	*(kg)*
1950	132	−1.16	552	88.8	237
1955	184	−2.05	615	86.5	296
1960	143	−2.65	662	80.3	212
1965	195	3.99	725	82.0	274
1970	240	3.24	830	82.6	293
1975	285	0.93	924	82.7	309
1980	321	11.81	987	80.6	337
1985	379	−3.32	1,059	76.3	355
1990	446	7.47	1,143	73.6	397
1995	467	20.12	1,211	71.0	402
2000	462	−0.48	1,267	63.8	364
2005	484	22.69	1,308	57.0	388
2010	546	64.20	1,341	50.1	455
2012	590	69.54	1,354	47.4	487

Source: Adapted from SSB (2013) and earlier years.

Note: per capita grain availability is obtained by grain output plus net grain imports divided by total population; *MT – million tonnes.

period and even dropped below the 1966 level. During the Cultural Revolution from 1966 to 1976, the first five years showed lower per capita grain availability than that of 1966. It was only marginally higher than the 1966 level in the later five years (Table 2.2).

In the absence of substantial increases in domestic grain production, grain imports from overseas became necessary. During 1971–76, some 12.6 MT were imported. In 1977, per capita grain availability again dropped; a further 12.6 MT of grains were imported in 1977 and 1978.

In addition to the People's Commune, the Great Leap Forward and the Cultural Revolution, there were various other political movements from 1950 until the end of the Cultural Revolution in 1976, when Mao died. With these continuous political movements, the recurrence of food shortage is not surprising. Luckily, in the latter half of the Cultural Revolution, some farmers stopped 'making revolution' and instead produced grains, which led to the slight increase in total grain output as shown in Table 2.2. Otherwise, famine might have again occurred in China during the Cultural Revolution. In short, prior to the 1980s, the Chinese people did not have enough to eat most of the time.

Food abundance: 1980s to date

In 1979, rural economic reforms started. Many controls over farmers were lifted and farmers were allowed to exercise more autonomy. This represented strong

Table 2.3 Output of major agri-foods in China (1978–2012, 1,000 tonnes).

A: Output of major food crops

	Grain	Rice	Wheat	Oil-bearing crops	Sugar crops	Vegetables	Fruits
1978	304,765	136,930	53,840	5,218	23,819	n.a	n.a
1980	320,555	139,905	55,205	7,691	29,113	n.a	n.a
1985	379,108	168,569	85,805	15,784	60,468	n.a	n.a
1990	446,243	189,331	98,229	16,132	72,147	n.a	18,744
1995	466,618	185,226	102,207	22,503	79,401	257,267	42,146
2000	462,175	187,908	99,636	29,548	76,353	n.a	62,251
2005	484,022	180,588	97,445	30,771	94,519	564,515	161,201
2010	546,477	195,761	115,181	32,301	120,085	650,994	214,014
2012	589,580	204,240	121,020	34,368	134,854	708,831	240,568

B: Output of major animal products

	Total meats	Pork, beef & mutton	Pork	Poultry	Poultry eggs	Milk	Aquatic products
1978	8,563	8,563	n.a	n.a	n.a	971	4,590
1980	12,054	12,054	11,341	n.a	n.a	1,367	4,497
1985	19,265	17,607	16,547	1,602	5,347	2,894	7,052
1990	28,570	25,135	22,811	3,229	7,946	4,751	12,370
1995	52,601	42,653	36,484	9,347	16,767	6,728	25,172
2000	60,139	47,432	39,660	11,911	21,820	9,191	37,062
2005	69,389	54,735	45,553	13,442	24,381	28,648	44,199
2010	79,258	61,231	50,712	n.a	27,627	37,480	53,730
2012	83,872	64,059	53,427	n.a	28,612	38,686	n.a

Source: Adapted from SSB, 2013 and earlier years.
n.a. – not available.

incentives to farmers to produce more. As a result, by the early 1980s, grain output increased. In the meantime, China's grain imports also increased. The imported grains were meant to be used for increasing urban distribution, thus enabling farmers to keep more grain for their own needs. The reforms worked and, by 1984, grain was abundant in the country. Per capita grain availability increased rapidly, reaching 397kg per capita and setting a record high.

In 1985, the procurement side of the 'unified grain procurement and sale system' was abolished, replaced with a contractual grain procurement system. This new approach reduced incentives for farmers who produced and sold more grains to the government and led to the overall drop in grain output (Tian, 1990). Consequently, over the following years, various modifications were made to the contractual system. By 1993, grain procurement through contracts was abandoned in many parts of the country. Also in 1993, the 'unified grain sale system' was abolished. From 1994 onwards, urban residents purchased their food grains from the market, and government grain procurement (for reserve purposes) was

Table 2.4 Per capita food consumption in rural and urban China (1978–2012, kg).

	Grains	Vegetables	Cooking oil	Meats	Poultry	Poultry eggs	Aquatic products	Sugar	Alcoholic drinks	Milk and dairy products
Rural										
1978	248	142	1.96	5.76	0.25	0.80	0.84	0.73	1.22	n.a.
1980	257	127	2.49	7.75	0.66	1.20	1.10	1.06	1.89	n.a.
1985	257	131	4.04	10.97	1.03	2.05	1.64	1.46	4.37	n.a.
1990	262	135	5.17	11.34	1.26	2.41	2.13	1.50	6.14	n.a.
1995	259	105	5.80	11.29	1.83	3.22	3.36	1.28	6.53	0.64
2000	250	107	5.45	14.41	2.81	4.77	3.92	1.28	7.02	1.06
2005	209	102	4.90	17.09	3.67	4.71	4.94	1.13	9.59	2.86
2012	164	85	7.80	16.40	4.50	5.90	5.40	1.20	10.00	n.a.
Urban										
1982	145	159	5.78	18.67	2.26	5.88	7.67	2.80	4.48	n.a.
1985	135	144	5.76	19.32	3.24	6.84	7.08	2.52	7.80	n.a.
1990	131	139	6.40	21.74	3.42	7.25	7.69	2.14	9.25	4.6
1995	97	116	7.11	19.68	3.97	9.74	9.20	1.68	9.93	4.6
2000	82	115	8.16	20.06	5.44	11.21	11.74	1.70	10.01	11.55
2005	77	119	9.25	23.86	8.97	10.40	12.55	n.a.	8.85	21.67
2010	82	116	8.84	24.51	10.21	10.00	15.20	n.a.	7.00	18.10
2012	79	112	9.10	24.90	10.80	10.50	15.20	n.a.	6.90	n.a.

Source: Adapted from SSB, 2013 and earlier years.

Note: meats include pork, beef and lamb; n.a. – not available.

also done at market prices. From 1997, the guaranteed procurement of grains at state-set floor prices was introduced for major cereals (such as rice, wheat and maize) in order to encourage farmers to stay in grain production and increase their income. In 1998, the grain harvest was a record high of 512 MT. Grain was easily available in the market with a stable price.

With the economic reforms, while grain output increased, the output of all other foods also increased. Comparing the 1978 and 2012 statistics, the output of some foods doubled (Table 2.3). The increase in the output of sugar crops, vegetables, fruits, meats, poultry and poultry eggs, milk and aquatic products was most significant. However, the increase in production had resulted in high environmental costs.

Increased foods led to increase in per capita consumption of more diverse foods. This then resulted in declining consumption of grains but increased consumption of various other foods (see Table 2.4). The decline in grain intake started earlier in the urban areas. Today, direct grain consumption per person has largely stabilized in urban areas but is still declining in rural areas. On the other hand, the intake of most other foods, such as meat, eggs and aquatic products, has been increasing in both rural and urban areas. The recent decline in dairy food consumption was due to food safety concerns (e.g. melamine-contaminated milk).

From scarcity to abundance: what was the key driver?

Before 1980, food was in seriously short supply and there was not enough food to buy even if one had money (recognizing many people did not have money). Food availability has dramatically improved since 1980, and today one can buy plenty of diversified foods so long as one can afford to. While the percentage of population below the poverty line is still sizeable, few in China today do not have access to some basic foods.[2] So, from food scarcity to food abundance, what was the key driver? The key driver was the removal of controls over farmers on what they could produce and how they should produce it on their farms.

In 1979, the Chinese government officially allowed farmers to practise household-based farming on a trial basis. Farmers in many parts of the country followed suit and it did not take long for many farmers to shift from collective back to household farming. By the end of 1984, almost all farmers had moved back to household-based farming, popularly known as household production responsibility system (HPRS). In essence, farmers had abandoned collective farming and reverted to the household-based farming that had prevailed before the People's Commune.

There was little or even no innovation element in the 'reform': the Chinese government just simply allowed farmers to revert back to the old farming arrangement. Yet, the simple removal of the controls over farmers dramatically lifted food output in China, as shown in Tables 2.2 and 2.3. After the removal of controls, some other factors also joined to contribute to the increase in food output in one way or another. Major factors include: the deregulation of agricultural markets that started in 1985; gradual increase in investment in agricultural research and development (e.g. from ¥0.98 billion in 2000 to ¥2.14 billion in 2006); provision of a floor price for major food crops such as rice, wheat and maize, which started in 1997; and the recently increased agricultural subsidies (from ¥0.1 billion in 2002 to ¥170.1 billion in 2012).

Current status of China's food security

Food supply is plentiful in today's China according to national statistics. However, is food abundance equal to food security? This depends on how the nation defines food security and against which criteria food security is evaluated. This section adopts the widely accepted definition of food security from the 1996 World Food Summit in Rome. The criteria used to evaluate China's current food security status are based on a normative framework (see Figure 2.1) developed by Oshaug et al. (1994). The framework as shown in Figure 2.1 is largely in accordance with the spirit of the definition adopted at the 1996 World Food Summit.

According to Oshaug et al. (1994), adequacy of food supply requires that (1) the overall supply should potentially cover overall nutritional needs in terms of quantity (energy) and quality (provide all essential nutrients); (2) the food should be safe (free of toxic factors and contaminants) and of good food quality (taste, texture, etc.); and (3) the types of foodstuffs commonly available (nationally, in local markets, and eventually at the household level) should be culturally acceptable (fit the prevailing food or dietary culture).

Stability of the supply and access to food refers to environmental sustainability and social stability. Environmental sustainability implies that there is judicious public and community management of natural resources, which have a bearing on food supply. Social stability addresses conditions and mechanisms securing food access. This concerns a just income distribution and effective markets, together with various public and informal support and safety nets. It could be in the form of public social security schemes or in numerous forms of community transactions, self-help and solidarity networks.

According to this normative framework, when addressing food security, attention should be given not only to the features of the food itself, but also to the range of factors determining the security of food supply and access. This framework clearly addresses the sub-goals that must be attained for food security to be achieved as a true development goal. In this framework, each element can be given a precise content in the given situation through the identification of local standards against which deviations can be assessed. Using this analytical framework, the current status of China's food security is evaluated as follows.

Food supply and nutritional adequacy

At the national level, as noted earlier, food supply is abundant. Table 2.3 shows that total output of most food items has continuously increased in the past three

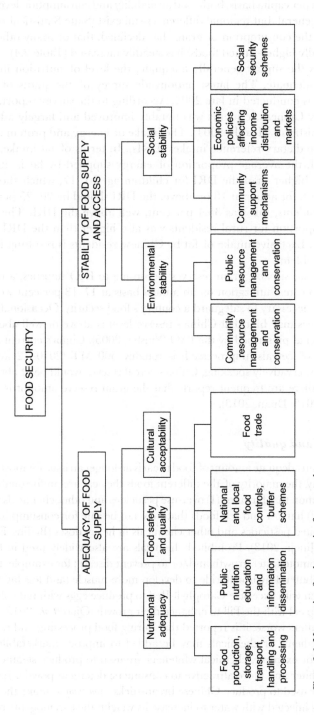

Figure 2.1 Normative food security framework.
Source: Adapted from Oshaug *et al.*, 1994.

decades. On a per capita basis, both food availability and consumption levels have improved in general, but regional differences still exist (State Statistical Bureau, 2013). While the consumption of grains has declined, that of many other food items (especially higher-valued foods) has steadily increased (Table 2.4).

Not only is the supply generally adequate, the level of nutrition intake is also largely adequate. The latest nationwide survey of the status of nutrition intake was conducted in late 2002. According to the survey report, nutrition intake by Chinese residents was notably improved and largely adequate (Chinese Ministry of Health, 2004). The intake of energy and protein is comparable to the dietary reference intakes (DRIs). In terms of fat intake, at the national level, the average proportion of energy supplied by fat is 29.8 per cent. (This is higher than the DRI for children aged 1–17, which should be 25–30 per cent; for adults at 18 or above, the DRI should be 20–25 per cent.) For urban residents, this was 35.4 per cent, well above the DRI. The corresponding proportion for rural residents was also higher than the DRI, being 27.7 per cent. Excessive intake of fat by Chinese residents is resulting in various health problems.

China also has sizeable grain reserves; according to FAO statistics, a ratio of cereal stock to cereal utilization on an annual basis at 17–18 per cent would be the minimum necessary to safeguard a country's food security. Occasionally, government sources may hint that China's reserve level is above or well above this minimum level as prescribed by the FAO (Yinsha, 2005). China's current annual consumption of cereals (unprocessed) is roughly 500 MT (2010–12 average). Therefore, conservatively speaking, China's cereal reserve would be at about 100 MT. In fact, there are frequent reports that the grain reserve amount is far too high (Anon, 2013; Duan, 2013).

Food safety and quality

While having an adequate amount of food to eat is no longer an issue for most people in China today, the majority of the different foods they eat are, unfortunately, not safe. It is common that farmers: (1) over-use pesticides and other chemicals in food production; (2) harvest and sell foods that may not be safe for consumption; and (3) use prohibited pesticides and other chemicals in heavy doses (Beijing Evening News, 2013; Jingji, 2013). Prohibited chemicals are also widely used in feeding animals to promote faster growth and/or to prevent disease; for example, feeding pigs with clenbuterol hydrochloride to develop more muscle (and less fat) tissues; feeding chicken with excessive Carophyll-Red to produce eggs with red yolks; and feeding swamp eel with the Pill to enhance their growth (Qiao et al., 2012).

Making matters worse, it is reported that during food processing and retailing, harmful ingredients or chemicals may be added to improve marketability and profitability. For example, chemical whiteners are used to produce steamed buns which look whiter and more attractive to consumers; detergent powder has been added to flour used to produce Chinese bread-sticks (*you tiao*) to make them look larger; meat is injected with water to increase its weight; the carcinogenic red dye,

Sudan I, is used to make food look attractive; dishes are cooked with oils recycled from drainage; highly poisonous pesticides are used in the production of ham; and we also have witnessed the well-known case where melamine has been added to milk, affecting a large number of babies.

Food adulteration is prevalent in China because: (1) the penalty for producing and selling unsafe foods is too low to deter such very unethical acts; and (2) the surveillance system of the government is weak and corrupt and is not in a position to address such problems. There are other important factors as well. Major ones include: (1) the collapse of social morals, financial gains being the prime motive of business enterprises and individuals; (2) the lack of free press and media, unable to fully trace and report sources of adulterated foods; and (3) local officials do not stop food adulteration in their jurisdiction in order to increase GDP (Duan, 2013).

Cultural acceptability

Cultural acceptability of foods is not a major issue in China. People in China are generally open to eating different foods. A section of Chinese society is also willing to pay for specialized and exotic foods, including wild animals and plants. The market for such rare and exotic foods is increasing rapidly. Chinese consumers care about food appearance, presentation and diversity. Such consumer demand is generally well met by innovative food industries in China.

Environmental sustainability

Environmental sustainability implies that there is judicious public and community management of natural resources, which have a bearing on future food production and supply. Admittedly, China's economic growth has been most impressive over the last three decades. This extraordinary growth, however, has also resulted in serious damage to the quality of land and water and air pollution is also very serious. At the beginning of China's economic take-off in the 1980s, little attention was given to the management of natural resources for sustainable use. Therefore, over the past three decades, the damage to the environment has been dramatic.

Today, environmental degradation in China is serious and widespread. There is no shortage of reports on China's environmental problems. Recently, the Chinese government started to produce environment reports to update the country's overall environmental conditions (Ministry of Environmental Protection, 2013). For example, two central government ministries jointly conducted a nationwide soil pollution survey, which started in 2006 and finished in 2010 and cost about ¥1 billion. However, the survey results have not yet been published (Yuan and Xie, 2012; Li and Xu, 2013).

Not only has environmental pollution caused problems to health (both human and animal, as well as plant health) but it has also resulted in lower food output. According to a report published in 2006, at that time, one-fifth of China's arable land, about 20 million ha, was heavily polluted. As a result, the reduction in grain output was over 10 MT and, in addition, about 12 MT of grains were polluted (Liu, 2006). Since 2006, pollution to the environment has not stopped but unfortunately continued in China. Most firms do not follow the regulations requiring them to treat the pollutants they discharge, as they want to keep their production costs low. Some recent reports indicate that some firms dig wells and inject pollutants into deep soil, causing pollution of underground water (Beijing News, 2013; Dai, 2013).

In addition to pollution, over-extraction of groundwater presents another major problem, especially in northern China, which has now become China's major food producing region. To mitigate the impact of water shortage on future food production in the north, there are plans to convey water from the south to the north via the Yangtze River. However, due to widespread environmental pollution en route from industries, agricultural wastes and domestic sewage, it has been pointed out that by the time the water reaches the north, it would be heavily polluted. Hence, this plan might help to increase water supply in the north but not provide a quality water supply, thus being of limited assistance to sustainably producing quality foods in the north.

Having realized the huge consequences of environmental degradation, there have been increased efforts by the government in recent years to reduce or stop environmental pollution and to rehabilitate the environment. At the community level, efforts to protect the environment are still inadequate and only confined to some small environment-conscious groups. In the foreseeable future, severe pollution to the natural resources will continue to make it very difficult to produce foods that meet safety and quality requirements if the present trends continue. How the damaged environment will further affect the quantity and quality of foods produced in the future remains to be seen. In China, to restore environmental stability and sustainability will take a long time and will continue to be an issue that will haunt the Chinese society for many years to come. But the country cannot wait any longer, and needs to take an integrated approach to address the pollution issues.

Social stability

Social stability addresses conditions and mechanisms securing access to foods. In the past three decades, access to foods experienced a major change. Before the mid-1990s, the 'unified grain sale system' was in operation, under which residents were entitled to buy their ration of grains through government grain shops. In the mid-1990s, the 'unified grain sale system' was abolished and residents started to purchase their grains in the market. Lower income people were provided with financial support. Hence, overall, access to food has been largely ensured for the majority of the people in the country. Extreme nutrition deficiency due to lack of food access has been rare.

However, at the household level, cases exist today where households have difficulties in securing an adequate amount of food. Due to the ever-rising expenses of education, health care and housing, some families have to reduce food consumption

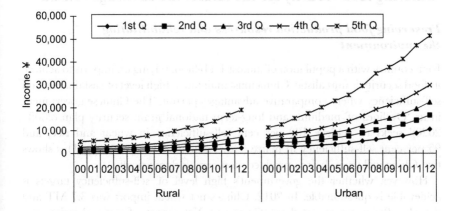

Figure 2.2 Growing income disparities between the rich and poor.
Source: Adapted from SSB, 2012a and SSB, 2012b.

in order to meet other needs. It is also common that in today's China some parents still have to financially support their grown-up children who have little income due to unemployment or very low salary income. The pressure resulting from rising non-food expenditure on low-income households is large and increasing. Unfortunately, due to the high level of inflation, prices for all items, including food, have been rising very quickly in China in recent years.

If family income increases faster than expenditure increases, then the increase in expenditure may not cause major financial difficulties. However, in China, the income gap has been widening between the rich and poor, as well as between rural and urban areas (see Figure 2.2: residents are placed into five quintiles according to their income from low to high).

The growing income inequality as shown in Figure 2.2 is disturbing and is a major cause of concern for social stability. For those low-income residents, especially in rural areas, their income is not sufficient to cover even normal expenditure. Data shows, during the ten years from 2002 to 2011, that for rural residents falling into the bottom 20 per cent (the first quintile), their savings had been negative. Those falling in the second quintile fared slightly better: they had negative savings in only two out of ten years. However, their positive savings in the other eight years were minimal (State Statistical Bureau, 2013).

The above assessment of the current status of food security in China suggests that, at the national level, Chinese people have had sufficient food to eat since the 1980s; however, there are aspects of food security that represent major challenges for China. These include, among others, food safety and quality concerns because of the widespread and prolonged existence of deliberate food adulteration; depletion of and pollution to natural resources impacting on long-term sustainable food production and supply; and growing income inequality undermining social stability and the poor's access to food.

Achieving food security for the future: the challenges ahead

Preserving food production resources and rehabilitating the environment

For a country with a population of almost 1.4 billion, relying on imports to achieve its food security is unrealistic. China must maintain a high level of sustainable food self-sufficiency where comparative advantages permit. The Chinese government in its 'Outlines of medium- and long-term national grain security plan (2008–2020)' seeks to achieve 100 per cent self-sufficiency in wheat and rice, and 95 per cent self-sufficiency in maize (Government of China, 2008). This shows that China will try its best to produce most cereals domestically.[3]

However, whether the government's high level of self-sufficiency targets is achievable is questionable. In 2012, China's net wheat import was 3.7 MT and the self-sufficiency rate was about 97 per cent. Net imports of rice and maize were 2.1 MT and 4.9 MT, with the self-sufficiency rates reaching 99 and 97.5 per cent respectively (State Statistical Bureau, 2013). For soybean, the import was very high, being about 58 MT, and the self-sufficiency rate was only 20 per cent. Of course, one year's trade data is not adequate to infer what will happen in the future. Nonetheless, one thing that is certain is that China's total demand for cereals will continue to increase. China's total population will continue to grow, reaching an estimated peak in about the mid-2030s. The increased demand for cereals as a result of population growth will be partially off-set by the reduced demand for cereals by an increasingly ageing population. However, the income increase will lead to higher per capita demand for cereals, chiefly the derived demand for cereals required for producing livestock products.

Thus, if China wants to achieve a very high level of self-sufficiency in cereal production, it is important to preserve its resources. In the past three decades, land and water resources have been continuously deviated away from agriculture for the purpose of industrialization and urbanization. The future may witness more agricultural resources (chiefly, land and water) being used for non-agricultural purposes on account of the lower comparative advantage of agricultural production. Given the limited natural resources, China has to balance the conflicting needs from agricultural and non-agricultural uses.

Safeguarding the quality of resources is also a vital part of preserving China's food production capacity. Otherwise, some of these resources may become unsuitable for producing foods or could only produce foods of low safety and quality standards. To rehabilitate the environment, China first has to curtail and eventually stop the discharge of pollutants to the environment. This requires (1) firms to treat pollutants before discharge; (2) farmers to adopt a need-based use of agrochemicals; and (3) ordinary citizens to reduce their everyday usage and dispose of waste responsibly.

Awareness education is the key to encouraging Chinese residents to be more environment-conscious and -friendly. Policing environment-unfriendly acts committed by firm owners, factory workers, farmers and the general public is not practical. When residents become conscious about protecting their environment, environmental damage can be reduced.

Unsafe and poor quality foods

To produce and supply safe foods would require stopping inappropriate use of chemicals by farmers and adulteration by food processors. This should be followed by rehabilitation of the environment to ensure that the resources available can produce safe foods. Unfortunately, stopping the production and selling of adulterated foods in China's current social, political and economic environment will not be easy. Further, Chinese consumers are too tolerant of unsafe foods. Every February, two government media agents, *China Net* and *People's Daily*, conduct an internet survey to solicit opinions of the Chinese *netizens* (internet users in China are often referred to as *netizens*) on various issues. The proportion of the respondents who are worried about the safety of foods is as high as 96 per cent. However, only 35 per cent indicated they would do something (e.g. lodge a complaint); and 3 per cent could not care less. The remaining 62 per cent choose to be tolerant because they do not know how to address it (Anon, 2012; Yu, 2013).

Ensuring food safety and quality will continue to be a huge challenge in China for years to come and will require serious reforms and commitment. For example, the Chinese government will have to ensure that food quality and safety surveillance systems function effectively. Furthermore, continuous efforts must be made to reduce, and ultimately eliminate, deliberate food adulteration.

Income inequality

The large and increasing income gap, as shown in Figure 2.2, is a major cause of concern for social stability. In Figure 2.2, the income gap between the top 20 per cent and bottom 20 per cent of consumers is very large. The gap is even larger if the income of the top 5 per cent of the rich is compared to that of the bottom 5 per cent of the poor. According to the China Family Panel Studies (CFPS) conducted by the Institute of Social Science Survey at Beijing University, in 2012 total income received by the bottom 5 per cent of families accounted for 0.1 per cent, while the top 5 per cent of families received 23.4 per cent of the total income of all Chinese families. That is, the income of the top families is 234 times more than that of the bottom families (Du and Shi, 2013).

In 2000, the Chinese government estimated China's Gini coefficient – the Gini coefficient is commonly used as a measure of inequality of income or wealth – to be 0.412, higher than the warning level of 0.4 set by the United Nations. By 2012, it had increased to 0.474. It is crucial that China quickly rectifies the alarming income disparity problem. Unfortunately, effectively increasing the income of rural people and urban low-income people and reducing the income gap does not seem likely in the near future.

Under the Hu-Wen government, a plan to reform the income distribution system was started in 2004 (Qian, 2013). However, because of obstructions by several interest groups, the proposed reforms of the income distribution systems could not be carried out. Without substantial reforms to the current social, economic and political institutional arrangements, reducing China's income inequality to an acceptable level is not possible. This, potentially, has serious implications for food security at the national and household levels. In his last report to the National People's Congress in March 2013, the former Premier Wen Jiabao acknowledged that the income disparity between residents was 'fairly big' (Wen, 2013). However, measures to seriously reduce the gap are yet to be developed and implemented.

Food waste

According to Wang (2010), the amount of food waste from restaurants and other catering facilities and family dining tables each year in China would be sufficient to feed 250–300 million people. There would be less of a burden on the country's natural resources if such wastes could be avoided. Given that China has a large population but limited agricultural resources, curtailing food wastage at all levels 'from farm to the fork' is of great practical significance.

In addition to the direct wastes (post-harvest and after the dinner table), over-consumption due to increased purchasing capacity is increasing, resulting in obesity and health problems. If all such wastes, tangible and intangible, could be reduced or avoided, China would be placed in a much better position regarding its food availability.

Achieving a reduction in food wastes between post-harvest and cooking is relatively easy. But reducing and avoiding food wastes at the table is not as easy. Wasteful practices are partly rooted in the country's culture: when entertaining others, one would show hospitality by displaying a lot of food, be it on public or private occasions. To fix the problem of food waste at the table will not be easy but not insurmountable if serious efforts are made and awareness brought about through public education, especially with schoolchildren. Any effort to reduce food wastage on dining tables and from excessive food intake will help improve China's food availability.

Non-transparency of grain reserve management

Having an adequate amount of grain reserves is necessary for managing a country's food security. In China, the levels of grain reserves are often not disclosed. This may indulge in rent-seeking behaviour, significantly increasing reserve management costs. But, more important, it makes it difficult to stabilize the Chinese grain market as well as the world grain market owing to speculation problems. The Chinese government emphasizes that not disclosing grain reserve information is of strategic significance because of the large population in China. The Indian experience, however, shows otherwise. India also has a large population but the Indian government publicizes the level of its grain reserves to the market on a regular basis (Zhou, 1997; Government of India, 2013). The Indian government also specifies and publicizes minimum buffer norms (in the range of 21.2–31.9

MT depending on the month of the year). If the actual stock was 30 or 40 MT over the norm, the public would protest. In China, there are no government-publicized buffer norms available. Yet, the government seems to be concerned about grain security even though the buffer stock is often well over 100 MT. One of the main reasons for maintaining higher reserves is the lack of transparency in the system (Moli, 2008; Anon, 2009).

China should learn from India's reserve management by bringing transparency to its grain reserve management, which would discourage rent-seeking and speculation. In the meantime, it would help producers and traders from both China and the rest of the world to adjust their production and business activities in response to changes in China's reserve stocks. Making reserve management transparent will: (1) help China to reduce the size of buffer stocks that may not be necessary, thus leading to savings; (2) help China to manage its food security by making use of the world market more effectively; and (3) help other countries to better manage their food security due to information available on China's food demand and supply situations, thereby contributing to global food security. Publicizing buffer norms and the actual levels of grain reserves, and bringing transparency to its grain reserve management, requires changes in the government policy to address issues of corruption.

The need for further political, social and economic reforms

According to the normative framework, if food security is achieved in a country, the food provided to its residents is (1) safe, nutritionally adequate, culturally acceptable, and of an adequate quantity; (2) the provision is sustainable; and (3) access to food is equitable and stable. To achieve food security in accordance with this framework, China has to handle the above-mentioned major challenges successfully. To this end, further changes to the current political, social and economic settings have to be made.

Political reforms: Earlier discussions have frequently pointed out that corruption is the major contributor in China to badly distorting many operations in Chinese society today, including food security. Political reforms are, therefore, necessary to curtail corruption. The process of food security policymaking and the management of reserve stocks should be made transparent, and the bureaucracy should be made accountable to their citizens in providing safe foods. Furthermore, the media should be free to investigate illegitimate doings of any members of society including government officials.

Social and cultural reforms: Some Chinese consumers are willing to pay high prices for various rare food items (not necessarily tasty or nutritious, e.g. shark fins). Such a dietary custom often leads to excessive demand for rare or slow-growing animals and plants. This can result in serious damage to the environment or fast depletion of threatened biospecies, not only in China but also in some other countries that export these rare foods (Fabinyi, 2011). Public education not to eat rare foods is therefore paramount; educating children can be especially effective, teaching them to avoid eating these foods themselves and also to persuade their parents and other family members to do likewise. (Because of the one-child policy, the single child has enormous 'power' to influence the adults' behaviour.) The public should also be educated to reduce or avoid food wastes.

Economic reforms: Cereal production occupies a very important place in achieving China's food security. However, there are two major obstacles for China to continuously produce cereals at a high level. One is that China's comparative advantage in producing cereals is fast vanishing. The other is that the very small farm size significantly restricts land productivity.

It is inevitable that the comparative advantage of grain production declines when other industries become more efficient and profitable. Heavy subsidies are currently provided to encourage farmers to produce more grains, resulting in higher grain prices in China than those on the international market. This is unsustainable. Agricultural research and development can help improve the comparative advantage of grain production and smart investment should be made in this area. At the same time, adequate levels of investment should also be made for extension services.

To overcome the second obstacle, it might be useful to increase the scale of grain production. Research shows that if the scale of grain production per farm is expanded, it follows that higher grain output can be expected. Farmers will also enjoy a higher income (Zhan *et al.*, 2012). To facilitate the farm size to enlarge, significant reforms have to be brought to the current land tenure arrangement. At present, land ownership resides with the 'collectives', from which individual farmers lease land to farm. But in reality, collectives rarely exist. When a farmer's right to farm the land is threatened, no collective will appear to help defend the farmer's interests. Indeed, the collective arrangement has caused a great deal of misery to Chinese farmers over the past decades. Land ownership by the collectives should be abolished, replaced by either private ownership (individual farmers) or public ownership (the state on behalf of the public, which then leases the land to farmers). As such, land consolidation for a greater scale of production will be easier. Experience elsewhere has shown that providing the farmer's right to farm the land is properly protected, whether the land is privately or publicly owned is not critical to agricultural production (Zhou, 2013). However, the collective arrangement has been proven to be most detrimental in rural China.

Conclusions and recommendations

Summary

This chapter examined China's food security practice since the 1950s. It highlighted how China managed to improve its food availability from severe food scarcity to food abundance; it evaluated China's current status of food security; and it identified several key challenges China has to handle in order to further improve its food security for the future.

The fundamental reason that led China to attaining abundant food for its residents was the removal of control over farmers' farming operations. Farmers were allowed to move from collective farming back to individual household-based farming. This gave farmers a strong incentive to work harder, greatly boosting food output.

Following the removal of controls over farmers' farming operations in the early 1980s, several other reforms or policy initiatives were introduced and contributed to the continual improvement of China's food output. These included the removal of controls over agricultural markets, increased investment in agricultural research and development, increased agricultural subsidies, and the implementation of protective floor prices for major cereal crops.

Food availability is unlikely to become a major issue for China in the foreseeable future if there are no large-scale unrests domestically and internationally. In 2012, China produced 590 MT of grains. Net imports of grains were about 70 MT (mostly soybean), accounting for 12 per cent of total output. By the mid-2030s, China's population will have peaked, at about 1,450 million. Assuming by then China can produce 600 MT domestically and have net imports of 100 MT, per capita grain availability will still be comparable to the level of the early 2010s, i.e. close to 500kg per capita. The proportion of imports out of total grain output will be around 17 per cent. Considering that per capita direct grain consumption has been stabilized in urban areas and is declining in rural areas (Table 2.4), in the future, more grains will be used for feed purposes and for food processing.

It is indisputable that, nationally, food is plentiful in China today. Food availability will remain comfortable into the foreseeable future if China's current high level of food output can be sustained coupled with the use of food trade. However, according to the normative framework, food security is not merely about food availability, although the latter is fundamental to the former. Several challenges exist that China needs to overcome in order to further improve its future food security. To handle these major challenges, including widespread unsafe foods, environment degradation and growing income inequality, innovative reforms to current political, social and economic arrangements are necessary.

Recommendations for achieving food security for the future in China

To achieve food security for the present day and for the future, China has to deal with these challenges diligently; only when these challenges are overcome can China claim that it has achieved its food security. Given that almost all these challenges are related to the severe and widespread corruption in the country, the most important course for the Chinese government to follow is to significantly curtail corruption. To achieve this (1) government policymaking processes should be transparent; (2) the bureaucracy should be made accountable to the people; and (3) the media should be free. Without these changes, improvements in various aspects of China's food security, namely, the provision of safe and quality foods, environment sustainability and social stability, are impossible.

Efforts also need to be made in restoring the population's social morals, promoting a culture of fairness and equality, educating the residents to protect natural resources, and encouraging them to avoid food wastage and consume responsibly.

Improvements in these social norms will also help China to achieve better food security for the future.

Policy implications

Examining China's food security practice in the past decades has provided useful lessons and experiences not only for China but also for other countries. One important experience is that removing controls over how farmers should produce on the land is the best support to farmers. China's severe food shortage from the late 1950s until the late 1970s was purely due to policy constraints that controlled what farmers could do to the land. Food supply became abundant after the controls were removed.

Other useful experiences are the deregulation of agricultural markets and increased investment in agricultural research and development. Although it is far from complete, China's deregulation of agricultural markets has helped more efficient allocation of resources, which in turn helped to raise food output level. Experiences elsewhere also show that deregulating agricultural markets helps to improve resource allocation and increase output (Zhou, 2013). Any regulation over agricultural markets, even though it may fulfil some political purposes, is a force that will result in lower agricultural output – ultimately neither in the interest of farmers nor consumers. Needless to say, increased investment in agricultural research and development, when used efficiently, will help agriculture to increase its output.

China's food security practice in the past six decades also points to the need to have governments that are responsible to their citizens if countries want to achieve food security. Otherwise, although improving food availability may be possible, achieving food security, especially a sustained one, is impossible.

Notes

1 Grain in China includes cereals (rice, wheat, maize, sorghum, millet and other miscellaneous grains), tuber crops (sweet potatoes and potatoes only, not including taro and cassava), as well as pulses (soybeans only). The output of tuber crops (sweet potatoes and potatoes) was converted on a 4:1 ratio, i.e. four kilograms of fresh tubers were equivalent to one kilogram of grain, up to 1963. Since 1964, the ratio has been 5:1. The output of beans refers to dry beans without pods.
2 In 1978, the number of people living in poverty was 250 million. By 2010, it reduced to 2.7 million if the per capita annual net income of ¥1,274 was used as the poverty line (in 2010, US$1=¥6.7695; US$0.52 per day equivalent). This poverty line, however, has been criticized by many as being too low. In 2011, a new poverty line of ¥2,300 was set by the Chinese government. With this new line, the population experiencing poverty in 2010 was 128 million (US$0.93 per day equivalent). The majority of the population living in poverty are rural people.
3 Note that the emphasis in the government plan is on 'grain security' not 'food security'. Although non-grain foods are also dealt with in the plan, it is not difficult to sense that what is most important for the Chinese government is to ensure the adequate supply of cereals. Interestingly, the recently passed National Food Security Act of India also has 'its exclusive focus on food grain and cereal availability' (Kumar, 2013).

References

Anon (2009) The real story at China's grain reserve warehouse as told by a warehouse worker: too greedy, online, http://koudai.360.cn/u/18,116401/article_15,3184202. html?s=y# (accessed 23 June 2009).

Anon (2012) Current status of unsafe food problems: 60% choose to tolerate, online, http:// my.icxo.com/41,28579/viewspace-17,16088.html (accessed 3 November 2013).

Anon (2013) What led to excessive grain reserves in China, online, http://cblog.chinadaily. com.cn/blog-14,6420–45,09496.html (accessed 31 October 2013).

Ashton, B., Hill, K., Piazza, A. and Zeitz, R. (1984) Famine in China, 1958–61, *Population and Development Review*, 10: 613–45.

Beijing Evening News (2013) Highly poisonous pesticides are widely available, farmers only eat the vegetables they produce for themselves, online, http://www.chinanews.com/ gn/2013/06-28/49,82205.shtml (accessed 30 June 2013).

Beijing News (2013) Fighting against polluting underground water, online, http://epaper. bjnews.com.cn/html/2013-02/14/content_41,1339.htm?div=-1 (accessed 3 March 2013).

Chinese Ministry of Health (2004) Nutrition and health status of Chinese residents, online, http://news3.xinhuanet.com/forum/2004-10/12/content_20,87980.htm (accessed 30 October 2013).

Dai, J.Y. (2013) Rapid economic expansion and the detrimental impacts on future generations, online, http://www.aisixiang.com/data/61,365.html (accessed 1 March 2013).

Ding, S. (1996) From the Great Leap Forward to the big famine, online, www.cnd.org/ HXWK/author/DING-Shu/zk9601a3-0.gb.html (accessed 15 October 1998).

Du, Q. and Shi, H. (2013) Survey shows the income of top 5% high-income families is 234 times that of bottom 5% low-income families, online, http://news.xinhuanet.com/ world/2013-07/18/c_12,5025474.htm (accessed 13 August 2013).

Duan, Y.W. (2013) *50 Truths that Chinese Economists Dare not Tell You*. 2nd ed. Enrich, Hong Kong.

Fabinyi, M. (2011) Historical, cultural and social perspectives on luxury seafood consumption in China, *Environmental Conservation*, 39: 83–92.

Feng, L.T. (1970) *Food Policies of All Chinese Dynasties*. Jing Xue, Taipei.

Government of China (2008) Outlines of medium- and long-term national grain security plan (2008–20), online, www.gov.cn (accessed 15 December 2008).

Government of India (2013) Economic survey 2012–13 and earlier issues, online, http:// indiabudget.nic.in/ (accessed 31 January 2014).

Jingji, B. (2013) Highly poisonous pesticides are traded without requiring any proof of identity, online, http://news.xinhuanet.com/local/2013-07/15/c_12,5009122.htm (accessed 13 August 2013)].

Kane, P. (1988) *Famine in China, 1959–61: Demographic and Social Implications*. St. Martin's Press, New York.

Kumar, R. (2013) The massive hidden costs of India's food security act, online, http:// www.eastasiaforum.org/2013/11/08/the-massive-hidden-costs-of-indias-food-security-act/ (accessed 11 November 2013).

Lang, J.X. (1934) *History of China's Food Policy*. Commercial Press, Shanghai.

Li, Y.J. and Xu, H. (2013) Results of soil pollution survey remain unpublicised three years after completion; vegetables and rice polluted by heavy metals kept secret, online, http:// www.37ct.com/thread-71,007-1-1.html (accessed 13 August 2013).

Liu, W. (2006) An investigation into groundwater pollution: the public has to be informed of the seriousness of the pollution, online, http://news.xinhuanet.com/ environment/2006-07/07/content_48,03634.htm (accessed 31 January 2014).

Ministry of Environmental Protection (2013) The 2012 China environmental conditions report, Ministry of Environmental Protection, Government of China, Beijing.

Moli, Z. (2008) Empty grain warehouse: reserve grains were stolen from the largest grain warehouse in China's northeast, 4 May, online, http://cache.tianya.cn/publicforum/content/free//12,14420.shtml (accessed 1 June 2009).

Oshaug, A., Eide, W. and Eide, A. (1994) Human rights: a normative basis for food and nutrition-relevant policies, *Food Policy*, 19: 491–516.

Qian, G.L. (2013) Reforms on income distribution must avoid influences of interest groups, online, http://news.xinhuanet.com/comments/2013-01/02/c_11,4224618.htm (accessed 1 August 2013).

Qiao, G.H., Guo, T. and Klein, K. (2012) Melamine and other food safety and health scares in China: Comparing households with and without young children, *Food Control*, 26: 378–86.

State Statistical Bureau (SSB) (1993) *China Statistical Yearbook: Various Issues*. China Statistical Press, Beijing.

State Statistical Bureau (SSB) (2012a) *Yearbook of Price and Urban Income and Expenditure in China: Various Issues*. China Statistical Press, Beijing.

State Statistical Bureau (SSB) (2012b) *Yearbook of Rural Household Surveys in China: Various Issues*. China Statistical Press, Beijing.

State Statistical Bureau (SSB) (2013) *China Statistical Yearbook: Various Issues*. China Statistical Press, Beijing.

Tian, W.M. (1990) Trade-off between stability and efficiency: an empirical study of China's grain procurement system. In: Tian, W.M. (Ed.) (2013), *China's Agricultural Development: Collection of Essays*. China Agricultural Press, Beijing.

Wang, T.A. (2010) Foods wasted each year are enough to feed 300 million people, online, http://www.chinanews.com/gn/news/2010/03-10/21,61052.shtml (accessed 2 August 2013).

Wen, J.B. (2013) Government work report, 5 March, online, http://www.gov.cn/2013lh/content_23,56704.htm (accessed 18 July 2013).

Xu, Z.L. (Ed.) (1996) *Food Economy History of Contemporary China*. Chinese Commerce Press, Beijing.

Yang, J.S. (2008) *Tombstone: The Chinese Famine in the Sixties Documentary*. Cosmos Books, Hong Kong.

Yinsha, J. (2005) Nie Zhenbang: China's level of grain reserves is higher than that stipulated by FAO, online, http://finance.yinsha.com/file/20,0503/20,05030,62219,4810.htm (accessed 10 July 2009).

Yu, Z.G. (2013) What does it mean when 96% of *netizens* are concerned about food safety?, 26 February, online, http://opinion.china.com.cn/opinion_52_65,252.html (accessed 3 November 2013).

Yuan, D.D. and Xie, D. (2012) A national survey on soil pollution was completed two years ago, but the government still does not publish the findings, online, http://news.ifeng.com/shendu/nfzm/detail_2012_12/13/20,137915_0.shtml (accessed 23 February 2013).

Zhan, J.T., Wu, Y.R., Zhang, X.H. and Zhou, Z.Y. (2012) Why do farmers quit from grain production in China: causes and implications, *China Agricultural Economic Review*, 4: 342–62.

Zhao, F.S. and Qi, X.Q. (Eds) (1988) *Grain in Contemporary China*. Chinese Social Sciences Press, Beijing.

Zhou, Z.Y. (1997) *Effects of Grain Marketing Systems on Grain Production: A Comparative Study of China and India*. The Haworth Press, New York.

Zhou, Z.Y. (2013) *Developing Successful Agriculture: An Australian Case Study*. CABI, Oxford.

3 Technological and institutional challenges to food security in the Philippines

Walfredo R. Rola, Roberto F. Rañola Jr, Damasa B. Magcale-Macandog and Agnes C. Rola

Introduction

The food security debate in the Philippines is synonymous with producing enough food, mostly cereals, to meet the country's needs. The current institutional set-up is biased towards food production and less on food accessibility and nutritional balance, including food safety. It has also been the basis of development programs and policies in the Philippines. This is evident to some extent from the Philippines' Agriculture and Fisheries Modernization Act (AFMA) of 1998 whose main goal is to modernize the country's agriculture and fisheries sectors for competitiveness. The AFMA stipulates,

> the State shall promote food security, including sufficiency in our staple food, namely rice and white corn. The production of rice and white corn shall be optimized to meet our local consumption and shall be given adequate support by the State.
>
> (AFMA, 1998)

However, the Act does not specify the important issues of food accessibility and nutritional balance, which constitute essential components of the food security as defined by Pinstrup-Andersen (2009).

With a population growth rate of about 1.9 percent per year, an estimated population of 100 million in 2013, and a limited amount of land available for agriculture, the country needs a paradigm shift in its approach to address the gaps in food security. In an increasing market-based economy, food accessibility is vital to millions of poor households in the country.

This chapter discusses food security in the Philippines from a technological and institutional perspective. To increase production in a limited amount of land is a challenge, unless new technologies and timely investments are made available. Accessing food from other sources will demand more investments and infrastructure. In addition, climate change is currently a serious threat to local food production and supply in the Philippines, which may require adaptation strategies, both technological and institutional, to minimize the negative effects of environment and food security interactions in this changing climate situation.

The organization of this chapter is as follows. The next section discusses the status of food security in the Philippines and the role of past programs in attaining this. The third section presents the threats to long-term food security; this is followed by an analysis of major drivers of food security in the midst of these threats; while the fifth section discusses the initiatives that may trigger the drivers to be effective determinants of food security in the next 20–30 years. The final section offers some brief conclusions, recommendations and policy implications.

Current status of food security in the Philippines

The current status of the country's food security can be described in terms of its food production and consumption trends and an overall assessment of its food self-sufficiency. This section discusses production trends of major food items including *palay* (i.e. the common name for the unthreshed form of rice which is the Filipinos' basic food staple; about 60–65 percent rice can be recovered from *palay* when threshed), corn, root crops, fruits, vegetables, poultry and livestock production among others. Per capita food consumption trends and food self-sufficiency in terms of the food availability and the nutritional requirements are likewise considered key indicators of the current food security status of the country.

Production, consumption and rice self-sufficiency

Food production in the Philippines has shown markedly increasing trends from 1995 to 2011, but only for *palay* and corn (Figure 3.1). Increase in *palay* production was driven largely by the increase in *palay* yield that is mainly due to the new high yielding varieties; while corn production increase was due to the greater land area planted with yellow corn. Expansion of corn cultivation in the uplands was mainly in response to the demand for animal feed, although a very small proportion of area is given over to producing white corn, which is used mainly for human consumption. The area devoted to rice production fell at an average of 2.4 percent per annum during the first half of the 1980s, with the decline primarily noted in marginal, non-irrigated rice farms (PIDS, 2012). As a result, in 1985, the country imported 538,000 tons of rice. The situation improved somewhat in the late 1980s and rice importation decreased. However, in 1990, the country experienced a severe drought; output fell by 1.5 percent, forcing the importation of an estimated 400,000 tons of rice. In 1997–98, the production of both rice and corn decreased, though more significantly for rice, when the country suffered from the effects of the worst drought in history. And in 2010–11, the country was struck by another drought, revealing the vulnerability of the rice sector to extreme climate events (Rola *et al.*, 2012).

There was no increase in production patterns of other crops, such as fruits, vegetables and root crops (as illustrated in Figure 3.1), demonstrating insufficient technology and absence of land expansion regarding these crops. On the other hand, livestock production increased from 1995 to 2009 by about 60 percent, or

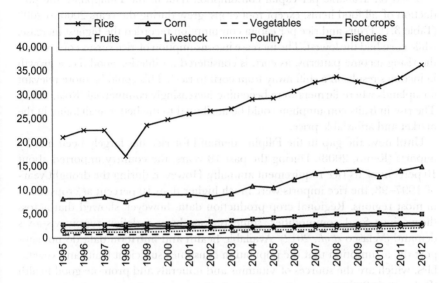

Figure 3.1 Production trends, by commodity (in 1,000 metric tons), 1995–2012.
Source: Based on data from DA-BAR, 2007.

Table 3.1 Per capita consumption (kg) and total consumption (metric tons), 2000 and 2009.

Item	Per capita consumption (kg)		Total consumption (thousand MT)	
	2000	*2009*	*2000*	*2009*
Rice	103.16	119.92	7,892.16	11,059.66
Corn	18.57	18.61	1,420.68	1,716.31
Vegetables	13.53	16.15	1,035.10	1,489.44
Root crops	11.43	10.44	874.44	962.83
Fruits	58.01	81.74	4,438.00	7,538.50
Livestock	20.79	22.86	1,590.52	2,108.27
Poultry	10.92	13.81	835.42	1,273.63
Fisheries	9.59	13.63	733.67	1,257.03

Source: Adapted from Velasco *et al.*, 2012.

Note: Population in 2000: 76,504,077; in 2009: 92,225,319.

an annual increase of about 4 percent per year, while poultry production increased by 6 percent per year during the period 1995–2010. Much of the increase in the livestock production can be attributed to increasing livestock intensity per unit area. Contract growers for these industries also contributed to this increase. Furthermore, fisheries production also increased almost two-fold from 1995 to 2010, mostly because of the aquaculture industry expansion.

Based on available per capita consumption data in the Philippines, the production of all food items, except root crops, grew during the years 2000 to 2009 (Table 3.1). Fruits and rice per capita consumption recorded the highest increase, while corn had the lowest. The increase in consumption of rice versus corn reflects the rising income patterns, as corn is considered an inferior good (i.e. a growth in incomes results in a shift away from corn to rice). This could be more relevant for uplands where farmers were becoming increasingly commercial (Rola, 2011). The rise in fruits consumption could be attributed to the better availability in the market and affordable price.

Until now, the gap in the Filipino demand for rice has largely been met by imports (Remo, 2008). During the past 18 years, the country imported about 10 percent of its rice requirement annually. However, during the drought years of 1997–98, the rice imports were much higher than 10 percent as crops failed in most regions. Regional crop production data, however, showed that across the various food commodities, some regions have a deficit supply vis-à-vis demand (Velasco *et al.*, 2012). Available health and nutrition data do not support the assumption that the population consumes sufficient fruits and vegetables, which are the sources of vitamins and minerals and promote good health (Pedro *et al.*, 2006).

Furthermore, Food and Nutrition Research Institute (FNRI) data reveal that while the country has a sufficient supply of food, which meets the recommended dietary allowance of the population, the subsistence incidence or the proportion of the population below the food per capita threshold is estimated at roughly 15 percent, thus concluding that a significant proportion of the country's population is food insecure (Velasco *et al.*, 2012). Many are without access to food, despite the seemingly self-sufficiency in food supply. Studies also show that many Filipinos are nutritionally insecure (Pedro *et al.*, 2006). This is reflected in different forms – i.e. undernutrition, micronutrient deficiencies, overnutrition or obesity and other chronic nutrition-related diseases. Micronutrient deficiencies (iron, vitamin A and iodine) are also prevalent across different population groups. The proportion of households meeting energy adequacy in 2008 decreased from that of 2003. In terms of nutrient intake, the decline in the proportion of households meeting adequacy in iron was also statistically significant (Pedro *et al.*, 2006).

Thus, while there is an observable level of sufficiency in food security within the country, nutrition insecurity at the household level prevails. One of the reasons for such a scenario could be the lack of an integrative program that links food production plans with nutrition security programs (Velasco *et al.*, 2012). Velasco and colleagues used a systems approach to study food and nutrition security in the Philippines. The authors were guided by a systems framework where opening up opportunities to all players in the agriculture sector can empower the sector. The system starts with good governance of both the resources and the markets, oriented towards empowerment of the agriculture sector and eventually attaining food availability and nutrition security. The system is based on policy subsystems dealing with access to resources, markets, food availability and nutrition security. Overarching these policy systems are efficient and effective institutions. The study showed that institutions themselves were disconnected from one another, and there was no coherent policy that jointly addresses food and nutrition security in the country.

Programs that contributed to food security in the Philippines

The Philippine government has historically embarked on addressing national food security through the adoption of globally introduced food production technologies, particularly the high yielding varieties (HYVs) developed by the Philippine-based International Rice Research Institute (IRRI). In later years, the sustainability issues of the Green Revolution technology came to the fore, inspiring the Philippines to embark on organic agriculture. To complement the effort to address food security through food production, the government also initiated a number of programs and policies. Foremost of these were the: (1) Comprehensive Agrarian Reform Program (CARP) to promote equitable access to land, increase productivity and incomes in rural areas, and transform farmer-beneficiaries into self-reliant entrepreneurs; (2) initiation of several banking and credit programs such as the creation of the Land Bank of the Philippines (LBP), the largest single source of credit to small farmers and fishers; (3) innovations in agricultural extension; and (4) creation of the Philippine Crop Insurance Program to provide insurance protection for the country's agricultural producers, particularly subsistence farmers, during extreme weather events.

Technology programs

THE GREEN REVOLUTION

In the mid-1960s, there was growing recognition of potential hunger in the developing world if innovative technology was not going to respond to the food needs of an increasing population. The Green Revolution was launched globally, which referred to the sequence of research, development and technology transfer initiatives to generate varieties of seeds, fertilizers, pesticides, infrastructure and technology, to achieve a sustainable agriculture to save billions of people from famine, hunger and malnourishment (Hazell, 2009). It prioritized development of new varieties of maize, wheat and rice (HYVs) that yielded more than the traditional varieties. One of the significant observations about HYVs is that they are only able to surpass the yields produced by traditional varieties if there is sufficient irrigation, pesticides and fertilizers.

To promote the technology package, the Philippines designed a credit and extension program called the Masagana 99 to encourage farmers to use the necessary inputs to produce approximately 4.9 metric tons per hectare (ha). The program involved a delivery system with a package that included high yielding rice varieties, fertilizer, credit and other modern inputs (Alix, 1979). The advent of the Green Revolution resulted in an increase of *palay* production from 3.7 to 7.7 million tons in the two decades of the 1960s and 1970s (FAO,

1979), averting the possible hunger that might have happened with the use of traditional varieties alone.

Because of the Green Revolution, the dependency on chemical fertilizers, pesticides, herbicides and other petroleum products dramatically increased and hindered the relatively poorer rice farmers (e.g. upland and small lowland rice farmers) from participation in the program. Later research showed, however, that fertilizers indeed had a negative impact on the environment (Pingali *et al.*, 1990) and pesticides had negative effects on farmers' health (Rola and Pingali, 1993).

SUSTAINABLE AGRICULTURE THROUGH ORGANIC FARMING

The organic agriculture program was promoted to minimize use of chemicals in agriculture, which later on was supported by the Organic Agriculture Act of 2010. In this law, it is envisioned that at least 5 percent of Philippine agricultural farm areas will practice organic farming by 2016. However, farmers do not favor organic agriculture, because it is labor intensive, lacks a market, and the regulations are strict (Rola, 2013b).

On the other hand, the few farmers who do use organic techniques claim that there is long-term sustainability in terms of soil and biodiversity conservation (Rola, 2013b). Indeed, there is a conflict with the way the goal of food security in the Philippines was defined and how sustainable agricultural resources are used. The government needs to formulate policies and programs that can support the different dimensions of food security. Investments into research of varieties that are both high yielding and respond to an organic farming system will be the challenge. Non-government organizations are active in the promotion of organic agriculture.

Institutional reform programs

COMPREHENSIVE AGRARIAN REFORM

The Philippines initiated a number of programs and policies that were responsible to ensure food security throughout the country. These programs included the Comprehensive Agrarian Reform Law (CARL) in 1988 that instituted the Comprehensive Agrarian Reform Program (CARP), which aimed to promote equitable access to land, to increase productivity and incomes in rural areas, and to transform farmer-beneficiaries into self-reliant entrepreneurs (Peñalba *et al.*, 2009). The Philippines' Department of Agrarian Reform (DAR) was responsible for the distribution of private and government-owned lands and settlement areas while the Department of Environment and Natural Resources (DENR) was involved in the distribution of public lands and stewardship contracts in forest areas. The CARP was tasked to provide the delivery of basic services (capacity building, credit and marketing assistance, farm infrastructure, etc.) needed to transform the beneficiaries into efficient agricultural producers and entrepreneurs.

The new landowners were not given the required support services despite the CARP program initiatives, thus resulting in below optimum yields (Rola *et al.*,

1998). To remedy this, the Agrarian Reform Community (ARC) development approach was conceptualized to allow for the convergence of the necessary support services (Peñalba, 2006). In order to increase farm productivity, agrarian reform beneficiaries (ARBs) were trained to enhance their knowledge and skills on entrepreneurship, application of modern technology, organization management, and mediation and conciliation of agrarian conflicts.

After almost 21 years of implementation, it was found that CARP resulted in a significant positive social and economic transformation of the direct beneficiaries, at both the household (ARB) and community levels (ARCs) according to Peñalba *et al.* (2009). However, the level of productivity was not significantly influenced by the massive distribution of agricultural land to landless tenants and farm workers, mainly because of the lack of access to capital to purchase inputs by the agricultural smallholders.

CREDIT PROGRAMS FOR FARMERS

To address the lack of capital for inputs, the Philippine government promoted a policy environment that encouraged more participation of formal banking institutions in lending to the agriculture sector, particularly to smallholders in agriculture. Institutions such as the Agricultural Credit Policy Council (ACPC) were tasked with designing, developing and implementing innovative financing programs in partnership with finance institutions. Despite these initiatives, about 94 percent of agricultural loans still come from commercial banks. The credit programs mostly focused on linking producers to markets and processors, and strengthening cooperatives and local government units. However, due to bureaucratic procedures, smallholders were discouraged from approaching formal banking institutions and therefore faced difficulties in accessing credit facilities. In proportion to the total amount of loans granted by all banks, the share of the agriculture sector was only 3–4 percent (Corpuz and Paguia, 2008). There are a number of reasons for this, such as the acceptability of farmlands as collateral, the poor credit standing of many farmers, the inherent risks in agricultural projects and the high costs of lending and borrowing, among others.

Another important credit program is the Agro-Industry Modernization Credit and Financing Program under the Integrated Rural Financing (IRF). It is a wholesale lending program for small-scale farmers and fishers, which combines the delivery of credit services with institution-building. The IRF encourages the formation of farmer groups or cooperatives that can access credit. At the same time it provides training to the members of cooperatives in program monitoring and evaluation systems, bookkeeping, credit management, financial management and leadership (Corpuz and Paguia, 2008).

Notwithstanding a number of well-intentioned credit programs, productivity (especially in rice) remained low especially because of poor access to these programs by small-scale farmers (Castillo *et al.*, 2012). Furthermore, farmers were discouraged by too much paperwork and the high level of transaction costs involved in the follow-up of the loan requirements. In addition, loan payments were not timely, which meant that farmers sought the help of private sources despite high interest rates.

NEW INNOVATIVE PROGRAMS IN AGRICULTURAL EXTENSION

Since 1992 the agricultural extension system has followed the political decentralization where local governments are responsible for this role. Location-specific and participatory approaches are used to disseminate new technologies. The new community-based participatory action research was introduced to improve farming systems and technologies for specific micro agro-climatic environments targeting location-specific research and extension. This downstream program focuses on technology verification, adaptation, demonstration and dissemination of improved technologies suitable for particular localities and communities. Its main responsibility is to convert technology into knowledge for action. The grant provided by the program is aimed at enhancing 'the role of RD&E [research, development and extension] through technology transfer to improve [the] production management system', developing 'strategies for effective integration of support services for enterprise and agribusiness development'; and institutionalizing 'active community participation in the overall management of farm and coastal resources for enterprise and agribusiness development' (DA-BAR, 2007). The effectiveness of this program is yet to be evaluated.

THE PHILIPPINE CROP INSURANCE PROGRAM

Recently, a new crop insurance program to help farmers especially in coping with climate variability and change was introduced by the Philippine Crop Insurance Corporation. The Corporation was tasked to provide insurance protection to the country's agricultural producers, particularly the subsistence farmers, against loss of their crop and non-crop agricultural assets because of risks from natural calamities such as typhoons, floods, droughts, earthquakes, volcanic eruptions, plant pests and diseases and/or other perils.

The rice crop insurance program has encouraged farmers to increase their investments in rice production inputs since they are covered by the crop insurance programs in cases of crop failures due to natural risks. Research also showed that farmers with crop insurance had less income loss than those without crop insurance (Rola, 2013a). Such insurance initiatives directly or indirectly contributed to reduce income loss, hence contributing to food security of farm households in the Philippines.

Major threats to food security in the Philippines

Threats to food security globally are well recognized. First, the high crop yields of the 1970s did not continue, because inputs became expensive and chemicals applied to crops such as rice contributed to environmental degradation (Pingali et al., 1990). Land degradation and soil nutrient depletion became serious

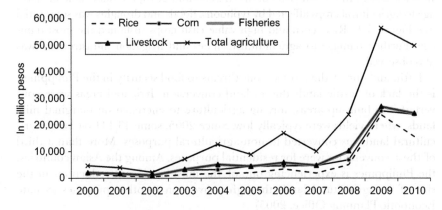

Figure 3.2 Damage to Philippine agriculture from natural calamities, 2000–10.
Source: Based on data from Israel and Briones, 2012.

problems in many regions in India that witnessed the Green Revolution (Shiva, 1991). Similar trends were also observed in the Philippines, as fragile coastal and hilly environments were brought under farming.

Second, upland agricultural resource degradation was also observed. Evidence from the literature revealed that agriculture to agriculture externality (upland soil erosion–reservoir sedimentation–loss in irrigable area) increased, but other upland activities such as mining were also responsible for soil erosion (Rola *et al.*, 2009; Rañola *et al.*, 2012). Shively and Coxhead (2004) identified hillside soil erosion and downstream sedimentation as among the most significant agricultural external-ities facing developing countries today. As Gerpacio *et al.* (2004) noted, soil erosion was a common problem in these upland areas planted with corn on account of their naturally hilly topography.

Third, the degradation of the Philippine coastal resources has been quite rapid. Only 4–5 percent of the Philippine coral reefs remain in excellent condition; the rest are depleted due to the impact of human activities. With more than 70 percent of the nation's mangrove forests converted to aquaculture, logged or reclaimed for other uses the fragile mangrove habitat – vital for fisheries and coastal protec-tion – remains threatened. During the 1990s, the annual losses in fish exports were around US$30 million due to red tides (harmful algal blooms largely caused by increasing pollution loads) (World Bank, 2005).

Fourth, tropical storms and droughts and the climate change in general are threats to food security. There are about 790,000 ha of potential sites for natural disasters in the Philippines, of which 80 percent are agricultural lands (Godilano, 2004). The cost of damage caused by weather and climate-related disasters is substantial. In a decade, from 2001 to 2012, the country was hit by a total of 184 typhoons, making an average of 18 typhoons per year. Droughts occurred in the Philippines in 2007 and 2011 affecting almost all regions in Luzon (Israel and

Briones, 2012). In the ten years between 2000 and 2010, the total value of damage to agricultural crops affected by typhoons, floods and droughts was substantial (see Figure 3.2). Rice, corn and high-value cash crops sustained the most damage. Further, damage to agricultural facilities and irrigation infrastructure was also observed.

Fifth, and one of the most serious threats to food security in the Philippines, is the lack of fertile lands due to land conversion. Irrigated areas were converted into built-up areas, forcing agriculture to encroach on marginal hilly lands, where yields were typically low. Since 2005, some 43,141.64 ha of agricultural land was converted to non-agricultural purposes. More than a third of these conversions were for residential purposes. Among the Asian countries, the Philippines is experiencing one of the most significant reductions in the size of its agricultural lands through conversion to other purposes (Senate Economic Planning Office, 2005).

Last, the fragmented institutional set-up of agricultural extension bodies has also contributed to the nation's food insecurity (Velasco *et al.*, 2012). With devolution, the local government determines what programs should be prioritized and what plans to implement. This could be problematic as local chief executives may have different priorities other than those identified in the AFMA, or pursued by the national government or needed by the community. In addition, within and among the different levels of the local government, there are various conceptualizations of the goals and corresponding strategies of agricultural modernization, which further complicates the matter. This problem can be attributed to the lack of a shared framework for extension, which could have been formulated by an apex agency that provides policy and programmatic direction.

Major drivers of food security in the Philippines

Given the threats above, and the growing population, the country is doubly challenged to address food security. The authors feel that among the major drivers of food security are: forthcoming improvements in science and technology that will be able to produce HYVs that are both environmentally friendly and resistant to extreme climatic events; research in post-harvest technologies; a strong extension system that will bring these technologies to where they are needed; a good market infrastructure for more efficient distribution of food, and better livelihood opportunities for poor households in order to access the food market; and a high awareness about good nutrition for households to make informed choices on cheap and highly nutritious foods.

In this section, we discuss drivers of food security from the perspective of (1) food production and availability, backed by increased investments in research and development, extension and other infrastructure; (2) food accessibility through efficient markets and welfare programs; and (3) food consumption through nutrition awareness and education.

Investments in agricultural research and other infrastructure

Since 2006, there has been an increased trend in the Department of Agriculture (DA) budget in terms of share in the total government budget. However, it was observed that the regional distribution of the Agriculture and Fisheries Modernization Program (AFMP) fund allocation was rather unequal. Almost two-thirds of the funds were allocated to the central offices of DA and DAR (69.4 per cent of total AFMP). In addition, a mere 4 percent was allocated directly to DA and DAR regional offices, where most of the implementation happens (Lange, 2009).

The DA records also show that the share of the AFMP's budgetary allocation for post-production facilities and other infrastructure increased between 2006 and 2010. In spite of this improvement in budgetary allocation, the country is still deficient in drying and storage facilities in major rice production areas in terms of both quantity and capacity. Although there are net surpluses of rice mills in the country, some regions, including top rice producing regions, had recorded deficits in units and capacities in rice mills.

A substantial and sustained budget in research will be needed for both hard infrastructure and technologies. In the face of climate change, crop modelling and climate model scenarios are powerful tools in forecasting simulated crop yields and developing early warning systems to mitigate the impacts of natural calamities on agricultural crops and aquatic resources. Priority technology research will include those that can make the nation adapt to climate changes and those that can minimize losses due to post-production processing and spoilage.

An efficient market system

Agricultural marketing policies and systems play a very important role in reducing food insecurity and poverty in developing countries. Agricultural marketing includes:

> (a) the performance of physical and institutional infrastructure to transfer farm products from the farmers to consumers; (b) the discovery of prices at different stages of marketing; and (c) the transmission of price signals in the marketing chain specifically from consumers to farmers.
>
> (Acharya, 2001)

In the Philippines, according to the National Food Authority, there are a number of factors that account for the failure of marketing programs to encourage participation from farmers. One is the 'lack of post-harvest facilities and poor infrastructure support for value-adding activities and transport of agricultural products' for farms located far from trading centers. Another major factor is the 'lack of advocacy and farmers' immediate need for cash'. The third is the 'lack of timely marketing information and training'. These include 'timeliness of information and the ability to analyze the information' as well as 'technological literacy' (EFSIM, 2009).

In a country like the Philippines that is frequently visited by typhoons, knowledge of market networks (both local and international) would be important to identify the geographic areas that have access to food supplies and thus precisely identify the most affected areas. However, focusing only on those areas that are directly affected by typhoons could seriously underestimate the number of food insecure households. Those most affected could be outside the areas that are directly affected by adverse climatic events since these areas could be suffering from reduced rainfall and production. 'Markets help trace out the effects and impacts of stresses and shocks and more precisely define needs and appropriate responses' (FEWS, 2009).

On the other hand, in the coastal areas, poverty is exacerbated by high losses and spoilage due to improper handling of fish catch, possibly affecting as much as 25 to 30 percent of total catch. Possibly 40 percent of all marine landings are discarded on account of spoilage from lack of a post-harvest infrastructure such as cold storage and poor roads that contribute to inefficient marketing and a reduction in the value of fish. It is estimated that if such infrastructures were in place, the savings in post-harvest losses might even wipe out the fish supply deficiency of the country, allowing self-sufficiency to be attained (World Bank, 2005).

Nutrition awareness through education

A balanced nutritional intake of food at the individual and household levels is an important element of food security. Towards this end, a nutrition education program called the Barangay [village] Integrated Development Approach for Nutrition Improvement (BIDANI) is being implemented through major Philippine State Universities and Colleges (SUCs). The program assists local leaders on how to implement their plans with the end goal of household nutrition improvement (BIDANI, 2012).

BIDANI collaborates with local government units in program planning through a participatory, multisectoral, integrated, systematic and holistic approach. An evaluation of BIDANI in the pilot areas showed an observed 50 percent reduction in malnutrition that was a direct effect of improvement in energy and protein intake and health status of the family (BIDANI, 2012). Food consumption was raised by increasing food production at household level and generating higher family incomes (Eusebio *et al.*, 1989). The household beneficiaries' income increased at an average of approximately 60 percent; the number of nutritionally normal pre-schoolers increased by 32 percent; the number of children immunized by 118 percent; the household using water sealed toilets by 9.5 percent and those using blind drainage by 137 percent. Of significance also is the attainment of maximum awareness and participation of (village) people in development projects and activities (Retuerma, 1989). BIDANI is now a component of the Philippine Plan of Action for Nutrition for building capacities of local governments to integrate nutrition into local development programs.

Major initiatives adopted to address food security in the Philippines

The Philippines has attracted several international agencies to finance programs and projects that relate to food security. Among these are the Canadian International Development Agency (CIDA) and the World Bank. Locally funded programs are more sustainable. In the villages, non-government organizations (NGOs) are actively promoting programs for providing better market access to increase income opportunities, especially for the poorer households.

Food staples sufficiency program

The Philippines is implementing the Food Staples Sufficiency Program until 2016, to achieve self-sufficiency in food staples where farmers benefit from rising standards of living. Food staples refer to rice and other staples including white corn, root crops and plantain. Additional funds have been provided in 2013 to relevant departments to support this program.

The Food Staples Sufficiency Program is anchored on improving farm productivity and making the Filipino farmer globally competitive. To achieve these targets, various strategies have been identified and put in place to include: (1) sustaining research and development in new varieties and crop management; (2) promoting mechanization of on-farm and post-harvest operations; (3) enhancing effectiveness and delivery of extension services; (4) increasing yield growths in rain-fed areas; (5) harnessing the potential of high-elevation and upland rice ecosystems; (6) enhancing economic incentives and enabling mechanisms; and (7) managing food staples consumption towards a more diversified diet (PIDS, 2012).

This program veers away from the previous programs that focused mostly on rice. There are other sources of nutritious foods and local and indigenous species that are promoted for both production and consumption. This type of strategy also takes into account the extreme weather events, and thereby substitutes foods (e.g. root crops) that are not as vulnerable to the weather conditions.

Promoting highland agriculture

Upland agriculture will expand because of the conversion of lowlands into built-up areas. Several major ongoing programs fund road infrastructure, irrigation facilities and sustainable technology research and extension. For example, the International Fund for Agricultural Development (IFAD) and Asian Development Bank (ADB) loan grant to the Department of Agriculture is financing a major program – the Cordillera Highland Agricultural Resource Management Project (CHARMP 2) – for the period 2009–15 (ADB, 2008). Its purposes are to (1) increase farm family income of the rural poor in target areas; (2) improve land tenure security; (3) ensure food security; and (4) conserve highland forests and watersheds based on sustainable practices. An equally important accomplishment of these projects to date has been the improvement of upland farming practices to safeguard the fragile upland environment and to encourage farmers towards sustained crop production in the Cordillera highlands. It will be interesting to see the outcomes of these initiatives after project completion in 2016.

Market and other institutional reforms

The Canadian International Development Agency (CIDA), through the Canadian Cooperatives Association (CCA), provided a financial grant to implement the Sustainable Livelihoods through Cooperatives project for the period 2011–15. The project aims to promote the cooperative model to support economic growth and improve food security in communities. There are notable achievements that relate to food security including (1) an increase in entrepreneur productivity and incomes by improving their knowledge and skills in business planning, marketing and agriculture; (2) assistance to women microenterprise groups to gain access to business skills development programs and services offered by national and local governments and link to finance, technology and markets; (3) provision of business support services such as improved connections to domestic and international markets; (4) access to finance; (5) and better product quality and packaging support to organic rice, sugar cane and seaweed farmers' microenterprises. While the CIDA support has made some notable achievements, its extent is fragmented, indirect and minimal in terms of addressing food security issues (Trade and Development Canada, 2013).

The Philippines' National Food Authority (NFA) has the responsibility to maintain stability of rice supply and price through the procurement of paddy from individual farmers and their organizations; buffer stocking; processing activities; dispersal of paddy and milled rice to strategic locations; and the distribution of the staple grain to various marketing outlets at appropriate times of the year. The stabilization function of NFA intends to protect both rice producers and consumers by setting and defending reasonable floor and ceiling prices to influence domestic price levels. Studies on the rice price stabilization job of NFA indicate that it did indeed stabilize the market price of milled rice (Chupungco, 1991). Bordey and Castaneda's (2011) study also showed that NFA's ceiling price (retail price) ably controlled the price of milled rice from 1990 to 2010. Unfortunately, while NFA's success in keeping milled rice prices down has favored the consumers, low *palay* prices have made *palay* production less profitable to smallholders.

The private sector also plays an active role in marketing in the Philippines. These include cooperatives composed of independent growers, small-scale farmers and input/service providers – e.g. the cooperative in northern Mindanao where buyers include local traders, fast food chains, processors, hotels and restaurants, supermarkets and consolidators. Their strategy is to utilize the modern market chain of organizing growers and businesses to facilitate the market. Growers are organized into clusters that commit to collective marketing. This approach not only ensures the quality but also the quantity (economic volumes), competitive pricing and reliability (good organizing). Growers are trained to enter into cluster agreements that consider quality, volume and delivery schedule, contingency supply and operational flow (ESFIM, 2009). The sustainability of the operations is not as well secured if farmers are unable to meet the contracted quantity and quality. Some farmers who sell to this cooperative withdrew because they were not paid promptly (Rola, 2011).

Some cooperatives are so successful that they have expanded agribusiness operations from grains marketing to pork production, operation of agri-stores, and farm mechanization service and trading centers. A major scheme of the cooperative is to deal directly with institutional buyers (e.g. Institutionalized Procurement Program tie–up with NFA) since it offers additional incentives and fewer handling and transporting costs. The cooperative, although already successful in its present ventures, has been adding value to its agri-products – especially corn, promoting internet-based marketing to save on cost, and encouraging farmers to organize and venture into contract-growing (ESFIM, 2009).

Environmentally sustainable food production technologies / strategies

Given the scarcity of lowland areas for cultivation, it is imperative to look at the uplands as potential agricultural land. In the uplands, development and use of soil conservation and erosion free technologies has also seen major investments in both research and extension in recent years.

Agroforestry

Agroforestry serves as the most promising alternative in rehabilitating denuded lands and at the same time developing the countryside through the active participation and cooperation of upland farmers. In the case of smallholder farms in Mindanao Island, agroforestry systems were found to be useful and provided staple foods such as rice and corn for household consumption, and stable access to food from the sales of timber, tomatoes, bananas and other fruits harvested on the farm (Magcale-Macandog et al., 2004; Pulhin et al., 2008). Intercropping with bananas was found to be highly profitable and ranked as the number one perennial fruit crop on agroforestry farms. Small-scale farmers harvested bananas twice a month and about 80 percent of banana production was sold to market, providing a steady source of cash for the households. Timber trees also served as a 'green bank' providing savings for future major expenses such as schooling and house construction.

Sustainable fisheries strategies

A sizable percentage of the population derives their livelihoods and nutrition from fisheries and aquaculture. Hence, it is important that the country manages its coastal and off-shore habitats to protect biodiversity, at the same time providing options for the poor households to carry out fisheries and aquaculture. In the process, the country has started to take measures for the protection of coastal resources through (1) establishing effectively managed Marine Protected Areas (MPA) and forming MPA networks in ecologically connected and critical areas; (2) co-managing with local communities of these areas to allow them to benefit from these resources by promoting and introducing innovative and sustainable financing schemes; (3) introducing efficient regulatory options, such as an effective fishing license system that would control access to fishing areas and use of fishing gears; (4) establishing limits to individual catch, and setting ecosystem boundaries and parameters of fisheries; and (5) reducing erosion and degradation of critical estuarine habitats as well as restoring or rehabilitating other important coastal ecosystems, especially coral reefs to improve fish stocks and fisheries yields. In addition, the local livelihoods of communities can be addressed by providing alternative livelihoods that conserve coastal resources as well as reducing population pressure through improved reproductive health practices (World Bank, 2005). The MPAs need investments and proper monitoring and regulation to achieve the set goals. There are other conflicting interests such as commercial fisheries, shipping and off-shore gas exploration that may hinder the progress of the MPAs.

Other programs

The World Bank with other small donors also supported food security programs in the Philippines including the Food Crisis Response Development Policy Operation Supplemental Financing Program and the Global Food Crisis Response Program Development Policy Operation. The purpose of the former is to lessen the impact of recent typhoons. The program aims to ensure financial assistance and a tracking expenditure system for immediate reconstruction, especially for agricultural infrastructures and areas (World Bank, 2005; World Bank, 2013). This type of program only addresses calamity-related (e.g. typhoon) assistance and does not present a long-term solution to directly address food security issues.

As observed, international aid in general is fragmented and not sustainable. The main effort has to come from the government and local initiatives supported by the private sector.

Conclusions, recommendations and policy implications

This chapter has addressed several programs, threats and initiatives towards food security amidst increasing population growth, climate change and other shocks. This section offers conclusions, together with recommendations and policy implications that the authors feel are priority areas.

Conclusions

Food security programs in the Philippines have been successful at the national level. However, this food security status has not been translated into household nutrition security. Some factors that contributed to this state are (1) prevalent poverty incidence and an alarming population growth in the country; (2) inequitable distribution of goods through weak marketing system; and (3) weak institutional set-up to deliver the food security programs. Threats to future food production include the environmental degradation of agricultural land and aquatic resources, impact of climate change and the conversion of agricultural lands to other uses.

Despite these threats, certain drivers can be manipulated for food security attainment. These include sustained investments in research and development, strategies for more efficient markets, and nutrition awareness through education. Mechanisms for implementation of these drivers include government, non-government and the private sectors, besides the international donors.

Recommendations and policy implications

Need for a national land use plan

There are current policies to protect conversion, especially of rice lands, but they are not consistently implemented. The following measures could help to protect agricultural lands: (1) develop a legal framework to declare all rice lands as protected and enforce the law properly; (2) tax idle lands in order to urge landowners to put their agricultural lands to productive use; (3) change implementing rules and regulations of the Agriculture and Fisheries Modernization Act to allow the sharing of proceeds from idle land tax to municipalities; and (4) make some improvements to the land reclassification process which is the first step towards land use conversion.

A proposal was filed in Congress to prohibit conversion of agricultural lands to other uses. The bill 'provides for a strict prohibition of land use conversion of prime agricultural lands and other non-prime agricultural lands until Congress shall have enacted a national land use plan'. The aim of the prohibition is to 'stop the decimation of prime lands as a way of protecting agriculture, the farmers as well as the environment' (Beleo, 2010).

Strengthening agricultural extension system

Exploring new approaches to deliver extension, credit, insurance and other services is warranted. Currently there are several actors in the extension system: public sector based at the national, provincial and municipal governments; and private sector and civil society sector, including NGOs and academe. A more holistic approach is needed to the contribution of the different sectors and players and to prioritize them based on their importance and contribution.

With devolution of powers, the local government now determines which programs are to be prioritized and what plans to implement. In addition, within and among the different levels of the local government, there is a different conceptualization of the goals and corresponding strategies of agricultural modernization. Between levels of the government, the national offices do not have administrative links with the local government units whose loyalty is normally with the local chief executive. The provincial office does not have administrative control over the municipal agricultural officers who are directly under the control of the mayor. With the separation of the extension workers from the subject matter specialists, there are problems in the research–extension linkage. This proves detrimental to the municipal offices that may have prioritized food security but do not have the technical capacity to deliver the programs because research specialists remain with the national office. This institutional constraint needs to be addressed to make agricultural extension more effective.

To counter these problems, the national government should provide strategic and policy directions in extension complementary to the food and security goals. The provincial agriculture office should take the lead in planning, coordinating and supporting municipal agriculture plans to ensure that they contribute to the vision of the province and to the national goals. The provincial agriculture office has the relative advantage in planning for agroecological zones that cut across municipal political boundaries. As a start, the provincial agriculture office can come up with programs for implementation in the municipalities through catalytic funding accessed from the national government or other donors. Extension should also transcend its agricultural focus and respond to a wider range of needs by offering services that promote the well-being of rural people (Baconguis, 2010), including information on nutrition security.

Strengthening the marketing system

A number of strategies have been proposed and implemented to improve the efficiency of the marketing system. These include the provision of infrastructures such as rural roads in agricultural production areas to reduce the cost of transporting farm products (Acharya, 2001). While this has been a major government program, there are still many other areas where the cost of transporting goods is quite high because of the scarcity or absence of good farm-to-market roads.

A second market-related issue is improvement of post-harvest facilities and training of farmers in post-harvest handling of farm products. The minimum facilities should include physical facilities for drying, cleaning, sorting, grading and packaging; and covered sheds, storage facilities and warehouses including multi-channel and multi-purpose cold stores in the market yards. This could be a joint activity of the private sector and government, especially in training related to post-harvest handling.

Third, transportation of perishable commodities (e.g. with refrigerated vans) from one market to another should also be provided. It will also be important to encourage the involvement of the private sector or farmers' cooperatives in this and in handling food grains and various functions of marketing for these to reach inaccessible areas.

Last, it would be important for government to encourage grading, standardizing and monitoring quality standards at all the stages in the marketing chain. The undertaking or promotion of studies relating to changes in farm incomes, real prices of food, physical losses in the marketing chain, malpractices in the marketing system and other major concerns should be carried out. In this connection, there is a need to collect, compile and disseminate market and outlook information. Linkages between all levels in the market hierarchy (e.g. through telephones, internet connections) should likewise be developed.

Promoting an integrative approach for food and nutrition security

Through the BIDANI program discussed above, it is expected that the issue of nutrition security can be significantly addressed and may partly reduce the over-reliance of the Philippine government on major staples such as rice and corn in terms of food use for food security. In the Philippines, calorie deficiency is found to be a major contributor to nutritional deprivation. While production of other cereals such as corn and starchy root crops should be continuously promoted, the ultimate goal should be the improvement of the overall diet of the entire household in view of the intra-household food distribution. Food production programs should be continued as the food and nutrition insecure households tend to benefit from them. The planting of fruits and vegetables should be emphasized, as the consumption of these foods has been consistently low. Moreover, the production and consumption of various foods as substitutes for rice as the staple can be done, but their cultural acceptability and palatability to the Filipino taste must be carefully studied. Some foods are nutritious but are not widely consumed as the people are not used to eating them and/or the price is high, as in the case of brown rice. In addition, increased food consumption should be encouraged to meet the recommended energy and nutrient intake, as well as dietary diversification to include food items rich in iron, folate, vitamin A and iodine together with the foods that promote absorption of these nutrients.

In planning for food security, the Department of Agriculture should consider the nutritional requirements of the population. Nutrition security would, however, imply that household food security would have to be addressed and not just national, regional or provincial food security, as is presently the case. There are several other challenges such as improving the database at the municipal level on the population demand for specific foods that will promote nutrition security. Convergence of institutions delivering services for food and nutrition is of paramount importance.

References

Acharya, S.S. (2001) Agricultural marketing in Asia and the Pacific: issues and priorities. Proceedings of the mini roundtable meeting on agricultural marketing and food security organized by the Regional Office for Asia and the Pacific (RAP) of FAO in Bangkok 1–2 November, online, http://www.fao.org/docrep/006/ad639e/ad639e05.htm (accessed 28 August 2013).

AFMA (1998) Agriculture and Fisheries Modernization Act, 1998, online, http://nafc.da.gov.ph/afma/primer_en.php (accessed 9 July 2013).

Alix, J.C. (1979) The impact of the Masagana 99 program on small farmer production and income in the Philippines. FAO workshop on small farmer development, Bangkok, Thailand, January, FAO, Rome.

Asian Development Bank (ADB) (2008) Japan support Philippines' drive for food security, online, http://www.adb.org (accessed 29 July 2013).

Baconguis, R.D.T. (2010) Issues and challenges in the governance of the Philippine agricultural extension system, UPLB Professorial Lecture, Operations Room, Administration Building, University of the Philippines, Los Baños, 6 December.

Beleo, S. (2010) Solons moves to prohibit conversion of agricultural lands into other uses, online, http://www.congress.gov.ph/press/details.php?pressid=4042 (accessed 3 June 2013).

BIDANI (2012) The BIDANI strategy: about us, online, http://bidaniaboutus.wordpress.com/2012/10/16/the-bidani-strategy/ (accessed 7 August 2013).

Bordey, F.H. and Castaneda, A. (2011) Rice science for decision-makers, Technical report, Philippine Rice Research Institute, Philippines, 2 (3), ISSN 2094-8409.

Castillo, E.T., Dumayas, E.E. and Zapata, N.R. Jr (2012) Institutional partnership for loans delivery. In: Rola, J.E. *et al.* (Eds) *Partnership for Food Security*. DABAR, Quezon City and University of the Philippines, Los Baños, Laguna.

Chupungco, A.R. (1991) Agricultural price and marketing: some policy issues. In: Librero, A.R. and Rola, A.C. (Eds) *Agricultural Policy in the Philippines: An Analysis of Issues in the Eighties*. University of the Philippines, Los Baños, Laguna.

Corpuz, J. and Paguia, F. (2008) Rural credit success stories: the case of the Philippines and selected Apraca member countries. Presented during the Regional Consultation on World Development Report and Preparation for the 2008 IFAP World Farmers Congress, 16 April, AIM Conference Center, Makati City, Philippines, online, http://www.acpc.da.gov.ph/ACPC Paper/Rural Credit Success Stories.pdf (accessed 9 July 2013).

Department of Agriculture Bureau of Agricultural Research (DABAR) (2007) Guidelines for availing CPAR grants for the DA-RFUs/BFAR-ROs (RIARCs/RFRDCs), online, http://www.bar.gov.ph/downloadables/brochures/cpar_guidelines_rfus.pdf (accessed 9 July 2013).

ESFIM (2009) Report on ESFIM workshop on agricultural commodity marketing programs and issues, 26–27 February, Metro Manila, Philippines, online, http://www.esfim.org/wp-content/uploads/PHILIPPINES_Report_Workshop_ESFIM1.pdf (accessed 31 July 2013).

Eusebio, J., Beghin, I., Stuyot, P.V.D., Kusin, J., Greindl, I., Redondo, S., Dacanay, E. and Dacanay, R. (1989) Evaluation of impact of *Barangay* (village) integrated development approach for nutrition improvement (BIDANI) of the rural poor. RTPFNP Monograph Series, Issue No. 12. Regional Training Program on Food and Nutrition Security, College of Human Ecology, University of the Philippines, Los Baños, Laguna.

FEWS net (2009) Markets, food security and early warning reporting. USAID's FEWS NET Markets Guidance, No. 6, October, online, http://www.fews.net/sites/default/files/MT_Guidance_Markets,%20Food%20Security%20and%20Early%20Warning%20Reporting_No%206_En.pdf (accessed 24 June 2014).

Food and Agriculture Organization (FAO) (1979) Rice paddies, online, http://en.wikipedia.org/wiki/Green_Revolution (accessed 13 November 2013).

Gerpacio, R.V., Labios, J.D., Labios, R.V. and Diangkinay, E.I. (2004) *Maize in the Philippines: Production Systems, Constraints, and Research Priorities*. CIMMYT, Mexico.

Godilano, E.C. (2004) Geospatial technology in disaster prediction and agriculture and natural resources management. Bureau of Agricultural Research, Department of Agriculture, online, http://www.bar.gov.ph/downloadables/2004/Disaster_Leyet.pdf (accessed 16 August 2013).

Hazell, P.B.R. (2009) Transforming agriculture: the green revolution in Asia. Ch. 3 International Food Policy Research Institute, Discussion paper. Washington, DC, IFPRI, online, http://www.ifpri.org/sites/default/files/publications/oc64ch03.pdf (accessed 24 June 2014).

Israel, D.C. and Briones, R.M. (2012) Rice self-sufficiency in the Philippines: is it feasible? PIDS Policy Notes No. 2012-12. p. 1–4. Philippine Institute for Development Studies, Makati City, ISSN 0115-9097.

Lange, A. (2009). Philippines: A Study on Results Based Planning in the Philippine Rural Development Sector. Project Number: 41060 April 2009. Background Paper for ADB TA 7190-PHI: Harmonization and Development Effectiveness. Makati City.

Magcale-Macandog, D.B., Rañola, F.M., Rañola, R.F., Ani, P.A.B. and Vidal, N.B. (2004) Enhancing the food security of upland farming households through agroforestry in Claveria, Misamis Oriental, Philippines, *Agroforestry Systems*, 79 (3): 327–42.

Pedro, M.R.A., Benavides, R.C. and Barba, C.V.C. (2006) Dietary changes and their health implications in the Philippines. The Double Burden of Malnutrition Case Studies from Six Developing Countries series, online, http://www.fao.org/docrep/009/a0442e/a0442e0p.htm (accessed 22 June 2013).

Peñalba, L.M. (2006) Support service delivery for program beneficiaries development. In: GTZ, *The Comprehensive Agrarian Reform Program: Scenarios and Options for Future Development*. DAR-German Technical Cooperation (GTZ).

Peñalba, L.M., Gordoncillio, P.U., Paunlagui, M.M. and Rola, A.C. (2009) Rural-based asset reform in the Philippines: recommendations for future directions, General Assembly of the National Academy of Science and Technology (NAST), Taguig City.

Philippine Institute for Development Studies (PIDS) (2012) Rice self-sufficiency = no rice imports: is it really feasible? Philippine Institute for Development Studies, Makati City, ISSN 0115-9097.

Pingali, P.L., Moya, P.F. and Velasco, L.R.I. (1990) The post green revolution blues in Asian rice production: the diminished gap between experiment station and farmer yields, IRRI Social Sciences Division Paper No. 90–01, University of Philippines, Los Baños, Laguna.

Pinstrup-Andersen, P. (2009) Food security: definition and measurement, online, http://www.iica.int/Esp/organizacion/LTGC/Documentacion/BibliotecaVenezuela/Boletines/2009/n4/foodsecurity-Springer-articulo2.pdf (accessed 7 June 2013).

Pulhin, J.M., Dizon, J.T. and Cruz, R.V.O. (2008) Tenure reform and its impacts on the Philippine forest lands. Paper presented on the 12th Biennial Conference of the International Association of the Study of Commons, 14–18 July, University of Gloucestershire, Cheltenham, UK.

Rañola, R.F. Jr, Macandog, D.M. and Rola, W.R. (2012) Crafting UPLB's integrated research, development and extension programs in the upland areas to address food security, UPLB Centennial Professorial Lecture, 29 March, University of Philippines, Los Baños, Laguna.

Remo, A.R. (2008) Marcos' Masagana 99 made RP rice exporter self-sufficient. *Philippine Daily Inquirer*, online, http://newsinfo.inquirer.net/inquirerheadlines/nation/view/2008 0426-132782/Marcos-Masagana-99-made-RP-rice-exporter-self-sufficient (accessed 4 November 2013).

Retuerma, B.O. (1989) Evaluation of the BU-BIDANI pilot project, *Research and Development Journal*, 6: 68–76.

Rola, A.C. (2011) An upland community in transition: institutional innovations for sustainable development in rural Philippines. Southeast Asia Regional Center for

Graduate Study and Research in Agriculture (SEARCA) and the Institute of Southeast Asian Studies (ISEAS), Singapore.

Rola, A.C. (2013a) Factors affecting farmers' participation in the Philippine Crop Insurance Corporation rice insurance program and the effects of the insurance program in reducing income losses of the rice farmer-participants in selected lakeshore municipalities in Laguna, wet season 2012. Unpublished undergraduate thesis, University of the Philippines, Los Baños.

Rola, A.C. (2013b) Environmental and health impacts of organic rice production. Progress report submitted to the DABAR, Quezon City, Philippines.

Rola, A.C. and Pingali, P.L. (1993) *Pesticides, Rice Productivity and Farmers' Health: An Economic Assessment.* World Resources Institute, Washington, DC.

Rola, A.C., Provido, Z.S., Olanday, M.O., Paraguas, F.J., Sirue, A.S., Espadon, V.M. and Hupeda, S.P. (1998) *Making Farmers Better Decision-makers through the Farmer Field School.* SEARCA, Laguna.

Rola, A.C., Rabang, M.J.M., Paunlagui, M.M. and Rodriguez, C.E. (2012) Towards rice sufficiency in southern Tagalog and the Bicol regions: a trends analysis. In: Rola, A.C. and Paunlagui, M.M. *Policy Perspectives for Food Self-Sufficiency at the Regional Level: Southern Tagalog and the Bicol Regions.* University of the Philippines, Laguna.

Rola, A.C., Sajise, J.A.U., Harder, D. and Alpuerto, J.M. (2009) Soil conservation decisions and upland corn productivity: a Philippine case study, *Asian Journal of Agriculture and Development*, 6 (2): 1–19.

Senate Economic Planning Office (2005) Requisites of a land use policy: policy insights (PI-05-05), online, http://www.senate.gov.ph/publications/PI 2005–09 Requisites Land Use Policy.pdf (accessed 12 December 2013).

Shiva, V. (1991) The Green Revolution in the Punjab, *The Ecologist*, 21 (2): 57–60.

Shively, G. and Coxhead, I. (2004) Conducting economic policy analysis at a landscape scale: examples from a Philippine watershed, *Agriculture, Ecosystems and Environment*, 10 (4): 159–70.

Trade and Development Canada (2013) News Releases – 2013, online, http://www.acdi-cida. gc.ca/acdi-cida/acdi-cida.nsf/vWNR-Eng?OpenView&RestrictToCategory=2013 (accessed 13 November 2013).

Velasco, L.R.I., Rola, A.C., Lantican, F.A., Amit, M.G.C., Carada, W.B., Cortes, D.T., Javier, A.B., Paunlagui, M.M. and Talavera, M.T.M. (2012) Agenda for action for food and nutrition security in the Philippines: a systems perspectives and convergence initiatives. UP Policy Paper Award, University of the Philippines, Los Baños, Laguna.

World Bank (2005) Philippines environment monitor 2005: coastal and marine resource management, online, http://documents.worldbank.org/curated/en/2005/12/7129749/philippines-environment-monitor-2005-coastal-marine-resource-management (accessed 7 August 2013).

World Bank (2013) World Bank projects in the Philippines, online, http://web.worldbank.org/external/projects/main?pagePK=51351038&piPK=51351152&theSitePK=40941&projid=P113492 (accessed 17 January 2014).

4 A country in rapid transition

Can Myanmar achieve food security?

Matthew P. McCartney and Ohnmar Khaing

Introduction

Myanmar was a major exporter of rice (up to about 3 million tonnes of milled rice per year) from 1921 to 1941 and was known as Asia's 'rice bowl'. Since it gained independence from British rule in 1948 and despite changes in political and economic systems, agriculture has remained the most important sector in the economy and rice remains the country's most crucial agricultural commodity. Today, Myanmar is self-sufficient in basic food (i.e. rice and fish) at the national level and, though no longer a leading rice producer, the country continues to export food, primarily rice and beans to China (Dapice, 2013). However, hunger, undernourishment and malnutrition affect large segments of Myanmar's population and food insecurity at the household level is a serious problem among the poor (UNDP *et al.*, 2011).

Although China, India and the member states of the Association of Southeast Asian Nations (ASEAN) continued full commercial engagement, over the past three decades economic development in Myanmar was constrained by harsh sanctions imposed by the USA and milder sanctions imposed by the European Union and Japan. However, the economic failure of Myanmar since independence is, to a large extent, the consequence of failed policies since 1962, arising from the Burmese Way to Socialism programme. These ultimately forced Myanmar to apply to the United Nations for status as a least developed country in 1986. The international sanctions were introduced after 1988 when the Burma Socialist Program Party collapsed and the army seized power, forming the repressive State Law and Order Restoration Council, which abolished the 1974 constitution and brutally suppressed opposition. Sanctions included bans on investment in state-owned enterprises and targeted trade bans, as well as the suspension of non-humanitarian development programmes. Moreover, neither the World Bank nor the Asian Development Bank (ADB) would extend credit to Myanmar (Hadar, 1998; Bajora, 2013; BCN, 2013).

United Nations agencies, including the Food and Agriculture Organization (FAO) and the United Nations Development Programme (UNDP), as well as the Japan International Cooperation Agency (JICA), supported development of rural Myanmar throughout the period of sanctions. However, support was provided mainly in the form of assistance that can best be compared to humanitarian aid as no capacity building of government officials was allowed by donors. Inflows of official development assistance were low and the sanctions, in combination with government policies and lack of professional capacity, resulted in a much slower development progress in Myanmar than in its neighbouring countries. The UNDP Human Development Index – based on measures of life expectancy, literacy and standard of living – places Myanmar in the bottom quarter (149 out of 186) of countries surveyed (UNDP, 2013). Food security at the household level remains elusive, particularly in rural areas, and without significant improvement Myanmar will fail to achieve the Millennium Development Goal (MDG) of halving the proportion of people suffering from hunger by the year 2015 (FAO, 2011).

Expectations of the political and economic reforms after the November 2010 elections are high and some predict that Myanmar could become the next 'rising star' in Asia if it can successfully leverage its rich endowments such as natural resources, labour force and geographic advantage (i.e. on account of its strategic location between the region's two economic giants, China and India) (ADB, 2012a). Annual GDP growth was estimated to be 4.6 per cent for the period 2002–10 (IMF, 2012), increasing to 6.5 per cent in 2012/13 and projected to be 6.8 per cent in 2013/14 (World Bank, 2013). However, as experience from other fast-growing economies shows, economic growth alone is rarely inclusive enough to lift the majority of the rural poor out of poverty (Burnley, 2011). Moreover, the challenges to be overcome in the case of Myanmar in terms of creating unity in one of the most diverse populations on Earth are tremendous. The risk remains that, even if the expectations for economic growth are realized, the poor and marginalized ethnic minority groups will remain food insecure. Clearly more focused interventions that target the poorest and most vulnerable are necessary, not least to secure social inclusion and in turn political stability, and should be part of overall development strategies to achieve food security at all levels.

This chapter presents an overview of food security issues in Myanmar. The next section provides background and describes trends in poverty and food security in recent years. The third section describes the complex and interlinked drivers and challenges to food security in the country. The fourth and fifth sections describe the government programmes, strategies and policies to address food security, and the role being played by non-government actors, respectively. And the final, sixth section draws conclusions and makes some recommendations.

Poverty and food security in Myanmar

Overview

Myanmar remains a largely agrarian society. Approximately 80 per cent of the population lives in rural areas. Agriculture comprises 25–35 per cent of GDP and accounts for more than 60 per cent of total employment (ADB, 2012b; Kudo *et al.*, 2013). Rice is the major crop, grown on approximately half the total cultivated area of 12.44 million ha of which 2.97 million ha (i.e. 24 per cent) is officially irrigated. Official statistics indicate that, since 1961, both the area (ha) under rice

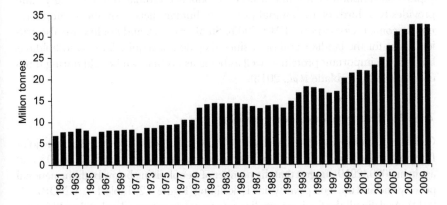

Figure 4.1 Total rice production in Myanmar, 1961–2010.
Source: Adapted from FAOSTAT, 2012.

and the average productivity (tha^{-1}) have increased significantly. As a result, total production has risen (Figure 4.1). The increase has been particularly noticeable since 1998, when the government started to liberalize the agriculture sector. However, the official government figures are controversial and considerable uncertainty remains over how much rice is actually produced. The United States Department of Agriculture (USDA) estimates much lower total production which, if correct, means average countrywide rice yields have declined from about 3 tha^{-1} between 1985 and 2000, to about 2.7 tha^{-1} now (Dapice *et al.*, 2010). Notwithstanding this uncertainty, the government intention is to significantly increase rice production and to reinstate Myanmar as a major global rice producer.

Other important crops in Myanmar are maize, black gram, green gram, groundnut, onions and sugar cane. Cotton, sesame, jute and wheat are also grown in some places. As well as rice, Myanmar is a major exporter of beans and pulses and agricultural products provide 25–30 per cent of the value of the country's exports (Kudo *et al.*, 2013).

Fish and fish products (i.e. small fresh fish, dried fish, fish paste and fermented fish) are second only to rice in the diets of Myanmar people and fisheries play an important role in both food security and income generation, particularly in the Ayeyarwady and Tanintharyi regions. It is estimated that fisheries (marine, inland and aquaculture) directly employs more than 3 million people, with 12–15 million people benefiting from the fisheries sector. There is relatively little information available on the patterns of consumption, inter-regional differences, availability and types of fish consumed but total national fish production is estimated at approximately 3.2 million tonnes with aquaculture being the fastest-growing sector (FAO, 2009). The Ayeyarwady River capture fishery provides food security and employment benefits for millions and is perhaps of a similar magnitude to the Mekong River which currently supports the world's largest inland fishery. Per capita consumption of fish and fisheries products is estimated to be 23kg y⁻¹ and provides two-thirds of the animal protein in human diets. Fish and shrimp have now become major exports (FAO, 2005). Small livestock and poultry are also critical assets for the landless and poor since they do not require large land holdings but provide important protein as well as being assets that can be sold during times of hardship (Haggblade *et al.*, 2013).

Trends in poverty and food security

Official statistics derived from a survey of more than 18,000 households, in the joint Integrated Household Living Conditions Assessment, conducted in 2004/05 and again in 2009/2010, suggest that the number of people living below both the national poverty line and the food poverty line is declining (Figure 4.2; Table 4.1) (UNDP *et al.*, 2011). As defined, the food poverty line represents an extreme level of hardship: it is the amount required to meet household nutritional requirements assuming that all household income is spent on food. The poverty line makes an allowance for non-food expenditure. The incidence of food poverty was estimated to be 47 per cent in 1990 (ADB, 2012a). Currently, 26 per cent of Myanmar's households live below the national poverty line, and 5 per cent live below the official food poverty line (UNDP *et al.*, 2011). Other reports suggest poverty rates are much higher, of the order of a minimum of 50 per cent of households (Wilson and Wai, 2013).

Most poverty and food poverty is concentrated in rural areas, in geographic areas dominated by ethnic minorities, and among landless and functionally landless households. Rural areas account for 87 per cent of total food poverty. The greatest poverty and food poverty incidence are in Chin, Rakhine, Tanintharyi, Shan and Ayeyarwady states and in absolute terms the four major contributing states are Ayeyarwady, Mandalay, Shan and Rakhine (Table 4.1). Together these four states account for over half of total poverty and around two-thirds of the total food poverty in Myanmar. Since 2005, overall poverty and food poverty have declined with the downward trend occurring in almost all states and regions, though in many the changes are not statistically significant (UNDP *et al.*, 2011). More detailed analyses of the survey data found that:

- transitory poverty (i.e. those falling in and out of poverty) affects close to three times the number of households in chronic poverty (i.e. permanently poor);
- generally poverty is not a consequence of economic inactivity but rather is a consequence of low returns from economic activities;
- around 54 per cent of poor household members are engaged in agricultural activities;
- most land is cultivated by small-scale farmers, with the average farm size of poor farmers at 1.78 ha;
- landlessness is a significant phenomenon affecting 24 per cent of those whose primary economic activity is agriculture and is much higher among the poor (34 per cent) than the non-poor (19 per cent).

(UNDP *et al.*, 2011)

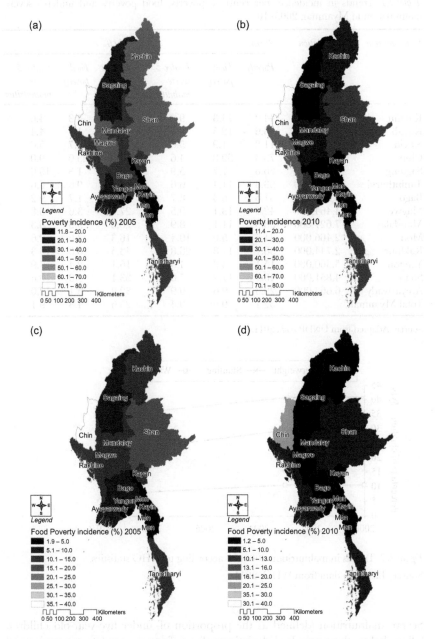

Figure 4.2 Incidence of poverty and food poverty in the states/divisions of Myanmar, 2005 and 2010.

Source: Based on data from UNDP *et al.*, 2011.

Table 4.1 Trends in incidence (per cent) of poverty, food poverty and under-5 severe malnutrition in Myanmar, 2005–10.

State/division	Population	2005			2010		
		Poverty	*Food poverty*	*Under-5 severe malnutrition*	*Poverty*	*Food poverty*	*Under-5 severe malnutrition*
Kachin	1,270,000	44.2	14.3	9.0	28.6	4.3	4.6
Kayah	259,000	33.6	12.5	3.5	11.4	1.2	4.4
Kayin	1,431,377	11.8	1.9	5.8	17.4	1.7	5.6
Chin	480,000	73.3	39.8	4.6	73.3	25.0	9.0
Sagaing	5,300,000	26.6	7.7	5.9	15.1	1.3	10.6
Tanintharyi	1,356,000	33.8	11.4	6.6	32.6	9.6	6.6
Bago	5,099,000	31.6	6.3	8.7	18.3	1.7	9.2
Magwe	4,464,000	42.1	13.1	9.5	27.0	3.6	6.8
Mandalay	7,627,000	38.9	11.1	8.9	26.6	5.3	6.3
Mon	2,466,000	21.5	5.0	10.4	16.3	3.6	2.6
Rakhine	2,744,000	38.1	11.8	26.8	43.5	10.0	16.3
Yangon	5,560,000	15.1	3.9	4.5	16.1	2.4	7.9
Shan	4,851,000	46.1	17.2	7.6	33.1	9.0	10.6
Ayeyarwady	6,663,000	29.3	9.6	9.9	32.2	6.1	12.0
Total Myanmar		32.1	9.6	9.4	25.6	4.8	9.1

Source: Adapted from UNDP *et al.*, 2011.

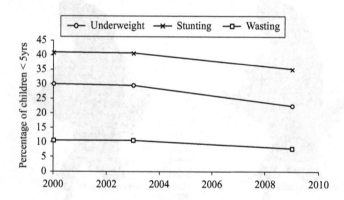

Figure 4.3 Trends in malnutrition 2000–09 according to WHO statistics.
Source: Based on data from WHO, 2011.

Severe malnutrition (defined as the proportion of under five-year-old children falling below three standard deviations of a reference population norm) stood at 9.1 per cent in 2010, a non-statistically significant decline from the 2005 level of 9.4 per cent (Table 4.1). Malnutrition was greater among the poor than the non-poor and greater in rural than in urban populations (UNDP *et al.*, 2011). Overall, official statistics have shown limited improvements in rates of stunting and undernourishment (Figure 4.3).

Major drivers of food insecurity in Myanmar

There are a number of complex and interlinked drivers (i.e. institutional, technological and policy related) that constrain the achievement of household-level food security throughout Myanmar. Geographic, social and economic factors indicate that food insecurity and malnutrition are determined by where people live, the livelihoods they pursue and the extent to which they are able to benefit from the economic growth that Myanmar is experiencing.

Poverty

In many rural areas, food insecurity is aggravated by low wages and incomes. According to the last agricultural census (2003) only about 40 per cent of rural households produce crops primarily for sale and the remaining 60 per cent produce mainly for subsistence. Low agricultural productivity translates into low levels of value added per worker: crop yields are generally below those of neighbouring countries and consequently average annual per capita farm earnings in Myanmar (US$194) are significantly lower than in those countries (c.f. Vietnam = US$367; Cambodia = US$ 434 and Thailand = US$ 706) (Haggblade *et al.*, 2013). Casual labour provides the most important income for landless rural households. Although daily rates vary greatly, values are typically in the range US$1.75–3 per day, with women typically receiving lower wages than men (Haggblade *et al.*, 2013).

Pronounced seasonality of agricultural employment, scarcity of alternatives and low wages constrain annual earnings and result in a high proportion of the rural population living under the poverty line. In addition to lower levels of land ownership, poor rural households typically own less livestock and have less access to credit. Lower income and fewer assets mean that poor households are less able to cope with seasonal and periodic health and weather shocks. As a result, the average rural household has adequate food supplies for only ten months of the year (LIFT, 2012). Poor rural families spend over 70 per cent of their income on food and one-third of rural households borrow at some point in the year to buy food (LIFT, 2012).

Poor nutrition

In Myanmar, low dietary diversity is as major a contributor to malnutrition as insufficient caloric intake (Wilson and Wai, 2013). There is heavy reliance on rice throughout the country, with low awareness of nutrition and nutritional aspects of food, including lack of knowledge on the need for a balanced diet and good food preparation. FAO estimates that carbohydrates (primarily from rice) constitute 67 per cent, and protein (primarily from fish) makes up 11.4 per cent of the average diet (Wilson and Wai, 2013). Five major undernutrition issues have been identified by the National Nutrition Centre: protein energy malnutrition; iodine deficiency disorders; vitamin A deficiency; iron deficiency anaemia; and vitamin B1 deficiency. These problems are exacerbated by high disease burden in a country where, until recently, only 0.5 per cent of GDP was spent on health services (Stads and Kam, 2007). Lack of education, poor infant and young child feeding, as well as poor sanitation, also contribute (Wilson and Wai, 2013).

Access to land

As noted above, limited access to land correlates with poverty and vulnerability to food security. As a result of lower incomes and higher poverty rates, landless households are more likely to go hungry and borrow to purchase food. In addition, because land serves as collateral in informal lending, landless households typically have less access to credit. Nearly 50 per cent of rural households are landless (Wilson and Wai, 2013) (Box 4.1; Table 4.2). This problem is exacerbated by the lack of land tenure guarantees for small-scale farmers, and, in recent years, by the expansion of agribusiness and associated 'land grabbing' by both domestic and foreign enterprises (FSWG, 2011). Although the exact information is difficult to obtain, it is estimated that over the last 20 years 'several hundred thousand hectares across Myanmar have been allocated to hundreds of companies and converted into a variety of cash crop plantations' (Talbott *et al.*, 2012). Furthermore, the previous military regime identified 6.5 million ha of national land suitable for cropping (notably rubber plantations) and animal husbandry as part of its agricultural commercialization policy. If fully implemented this could mean potentially millions of people are dispossessed of land (Talbott *et al.*, 2012).

Box 4.1   Landlessness in Myanmar

In Myanmar, distribution of cultivable land is highly skewed. Although estimates of landlessness differ widely – 30 per cent (FAO, 2005); 30–50 per cent (Okamoto, 2008); 24 per cent (UNDP *et al.*, 2011) – most available evidence suggests that approximately 50 per cent of all rural households have no land use rights to cultivable land. The highest rates of landlessness occur in the Delta region. In the Dry Zone and Uplands, land pressure is less, but nevertheless the share of landlessness is still 26–43 per cent. Of the total 6.5 million rural households in Myanmar, approximately 3 million were landless during the 2003 agricultural census and another 0.5 million held tillage rights on holdings of less than 0.4 ha, a level commonly associated with functional landlessness.

Source: Haggblade *et al.*, 2013.

Conflict

Mutual distrust and conflict over natural resources, including gold, gems and timber, have characterized the history between the rulers of Myanmar – primarily of Burmese background (approximately 69 per cent of the country's population) – and many of the 135 other ethnic groups that comprise the nation. Since independence, successive central governments have fought numerous ethnic and political rebellions. In recent years, some 25 different ethnic groups have signed

Table 4.2 Land size distribution in rural Myanmar, 2011.

Size of landholding (hectares)	Percent of rural households		
	Delta / coastal	Dry Zone	Uplands
0	72	43	26
<2	7	37	63
2–4	9	12	9
>4	12	8	2
Total	100	100	100

Source: Adapted from LIFT, 2012.

ceasefire agreements with the government. However, ethnic strife continues to be a major destabilizing factor within the country and a key factor undermining food security.

Conflict disrupts economic activities and undermines food security in numerous ways. Both displaced and non-displaced communities are badly affected (WFP, 2013). In addition to large-scale displacement and the loss of productive assets – including fields, livestock, fish and shrimp farms, farm and fishing equipment, as well as livelihood-supportive infrastructure – restrictions to movement (e.g. curfews) and limited access to markets and surrounding natural resources, reduce the ability of non-displaced households to produce food and restrict income-generating opportunities (Poe, 2011). Internally displaced people living in camps face considerable difficulties in accessing livelihoods such as fishing and farming and are often completely reliant on assistance from friends/relatives, religious institutions, the government or non-governmental organizations (NGOs). Declining purchasing power leaves many unable to afford basic food needs and makes it difficult for farmers to pay back loans taken to purchase agricultural inputs (WFP, 2013).

Climate and extreme events

Myanmar has many poor people with low adaptive capacity. These people are vulnerable to environmental shocks such as droughts, floods and extreme weather conditions. The climate in Myanmar is monsoonal with rainfall occurring predominantly between June and October. Inter-annual variability is high, and erratic rainfall, drought and floods are common phenomena. The lack of infrastructure and measures to cope with rainfall and hence water variability limits production to one crop per year throughout much of the country (Box 4.2). Semi-frequent natural disasters, such as cyclone Nargis which overwhelmed coastal regions in May 2008, can have devastating impacts not only on lives (138,000 casualties) and infrastructure (economic damage estimated at US$4.1 billion) but also agricultural production (ESCAP, 2011). Exposure to natural disasters, such as flooding and landslides, regularly lead to transitory food insecurity either directly by damaging shelter and agricultural land of affected households or by limiting physical access and thereby increasing local food prices (Poe, 2011). It is anticipated that as a consequence of climate change, rainfall variability and the frequency of droughts and floods may increase in the future (Lwin, 2002; ADB, 2012a).

Box 4.2   Water access in Myanmar's Dry Zone

The Dry Zone is part of the central plain of Myanmar. It spreads across three divisions, Sagaing, Mandalay and Magwe, with a population of 14.5 million. Mean annual rainfall in the Dry Zone is lower than in the rest of the country, ranging from 500 to 1000mm. Due to the two major rivers, the Ayeyarwady and Chindwin, flowing through the region, annual per capita water availability is actually very high, of the order of 25,000m^3. The problem is the variability in water resources. The rainfall is highly seasonal, varies significantly from year to year and is typically very different even in villages located close together.

It is the insufficient storage capacity and irrigation infrastructure in appropriate locations, as well as poor management of the existing infrastructure, that means farmers cannot access water when they need it in the dry season. Access to safe and reliable water, not just for agriculture (including livestock), but also for domestic use, is widely acknowledged to be a key constraint to livelihoods and food security in the region. In the wet season flooding is often a problem. Improving water management and access would reduce risk, help stabilize agricultural productivity, increase the resilience of households, improve food security and contribute to poverty reduction. What is needed, in order of priority, is:

- improved dry season water supplies sufficient (as a minimum) for domestic uses and livestock
- sufficient water to enable irrigation during the wet season (i.e. to overcome short dry spells)
- protection against flooding
- sufficient water to enable irrigation during the dry season.

Achieving water security, in the order outlined above, requires progressively increased investment in both the hydraulic and the institutional infrastructure needed to store, convey and manage water effectively.
Source: McCartney *et al.*, 2013.

Water availability and access

Since 1988, the government has made considerable efforts to increase water utilization in agriculture and provision of formal irrigation is a priority. Across Myanmar, a total of 233 dams and weirs have been constructed, 327 pumping stations have been built and 8,032 tube wells installed (FAO, 2011). The total irrigated command area in 2009–10 was approximately 2.33 million ha, approximately 20 per cent of the total agricultural area. However, irrigation efficiency and effectiveness are low. A government report released by the Auditor-General's Office in 2012 found that nationally 67 river water pumping stations have achieved 16.3 per cent of their target, providing water to 48,833 acres out of the 299,895 acres originally planned and that some reservoirs and diversion dams could not supply water at all (Johnston *et al.*, 2013).

Analyses suggest that this does not, on the whole, reflect a physical shortage of water but is the consequence of a complex set of factors. Typical problems include: (1) considerable losses due to canal seepage; (2) poor canal and embankment construction and maintenance; (3) sediment deposition in the canals; (4) insufficient drainage that causes waterlogging and, in places, build-up of soil salinity; and (5) poor timing in relation to the delivery of water. These factors adversely affect crop yields, with significant implications for the farmers' food security and livelihoods as well as the economic viability of the schemes. Approximately 201,000 ha of the official total irrigated area is by 'lift' irrigation with water pumped primarily from rivers. A major constraint to these schemes is lack of electricity to operate the pumps partly because supply is insufficient but also because the cost of electricity is too high (Anderson Irrigation, 2012).

This situation resembles the problem of poor performance in irrigation systems observed in many other places, linked to a vicious cycle of bad construction, deferred maintenance and premature rehabilitation (Johnston *et al.*, 2013). In such a situation, improving the performance of formal irrigation infrastructure through rehabilitation will only address the symptoms, rather than tackle the roots of the problem.

Poor seed quality and post-harvest losses

Agricultural yields are adversely affected by poor seed quality. In Myanmar currently there is little use of certified seeds. Many farmers rely on open pollinating varieties for extended periods but many seed lines are old, with the result that they have accumulated significant pest and disease problems (Dapice *et al.*, 2011). Post-harvest losses of rice are also high as a consequence of shattering and general spoilage and waste at the farm level, reduced milling yields and grain quality reduction during processing. The losses result in lower quality rice for consumption or sale, smaller returns for farmers and greater pressure on the environment as farmers try to compensate by growing more. There is little information on the extent of such losses in Myanmar but, typically, losses in South and South-East Asia are 10–25 per cent (IRRI, 2013).

Land degradation

Land degradation is widespread and ongoing in Myanmar with significant impacts on agricultural production (through loss of topsoil, low nutrient status), loss of productive land (through gullying and loss of vegetation cover), and impacts on infrastructure (silting up of ponds, sedimentation in canals, damage to pumps from high sediment loads in water) (Johnston *et al.*, 2013). The main causes of land degradation are, inter alia, demographic pressure, expansion of agricultural land, overgrazing, shifting cultivation, illicit logging and excessive use of fuelwood, and installation of industrial plants and mining. Myanmar's forest cover and quality have steadily declined over the last 30 years. Forest cover decreased from 61 per cent of the land area in 1975 to less than 48 per cent in 2005. Between 1990 and 2005, Myanmar lost on average 465,000 ha per year (i.e. 18 per cent of its total forest cover in just 15 years) (Htun, 2009).

Natural processes in vulnerable (i.e. marginal) farming areas (uplands and drylands, estimated to be 33 per cent of the country's total cultivated area in 2008) are aggravated by human interventions. In the uplands, shifting cultivation is the major agent of forest loss. Growth in the upland human population is a key pressure that is closely correlated with land degradation and changes in land productivity. From 1980 to 2008, the upland population increased by 7 million to 17.5 million people, or about 30 per cent of the national population (ADB, 2012b). In 2002, the government established the Highland Reclamation and Cultivation Committee with a mandate to replace shifting cultivation with terrace farming. It is not clear how effective this has been. Soil salinity is a problem in some places (e.g. the Dry Zone and Rakhine state). The decline in rice productivity suggested by the USDA production figures as cited earlier in this chapter are consistent with comments from farmers about increasing pest problems, 'tired soils' and growing problems with diseases and weeds (Dapice *et al.*, 2010).

Research and extension

Links between extension services and farmers are weak and severely restricted by funding constraints, which means that transport and field allowances are minimal. A recent investigation found that 'extension of agricultural advice is virtually nonexistent' (Anderson Irrigation, 2012). Furthermore, the predisposition – rooted in two generations of command and control management – to instruct rather than listen to farmers, and the primary focus on production targets (particularly for rice) further reduces the impact of the extension services on improving farm incomes and poverty alleviation (Haggblade *et al.*, 2013).

Another hindrance is the lack of agricultural research. In 2003, Myanmar spent only US$8 million on agricultural research. This equates to just US$0.06 for every US$100 in agricultural output and is among the lowest in the world. It compares to an average of US$0.41 and US$0.53 per US$100 in Asian countries and in all developing countries globally, respectively (Stads and Kam, 2007). The Department of Agricultural Research (DAR) under the Ministry of Agriculture and Irrigation (MOAI) is the principal government agency conducting agricultural research and development. Low salaries in the civil service make attracting and retaining well-qualified research staff difficult, particularly given increasing opportunities in international organizations, NGOs and the private sector. Staff turnover is a major problem and, in comparison to neighbouring countries, the proportion of postgraduate qualified government research staff in DAR is very low (Stads and Kam, 2007).

DAR focuses on increasing crop production through improved seed, crop management and crop protection; and cropping systems tailored to suit the country's varied agroecological zones (Stads and Kam, 2007). However, it currently conducts no breeding research on improved varieties of green or black gram despite these being among the country's most valuable exports (Haggblade *et al.*, 2013). Rice research, which accounts for 25 per cent of all research on crops (Stads and Kam, 2007), has focused primarily on hybrids rather than the promotion of classic improved varieties. Given the high costs and low value of hybrids, adoption rates are low: just 1 per cent of paddy area is currently under hybrids (Xe, 2011). Although in the long term they may prove to be viable in some areas, a mix of conventional breeding and hybrids would probably offer the most rapid pathway to productivity gains. Investment in publicly funded plant breeding and agronomic research is particularly critical because the majority of planted area in Myanmar is given over to self-pollinated crops (i.e. rice and pulses), for which there is little incentive for the private sector to invest. Raising productivity in livestock and fisheries similarly requires public investment (Haggblade *et al.*, 2013).

Transport infrastructure

Myanmar currently ranks lowest in the ASEAN region in quality of transport infrastructure (ADB, 2012a). The potential of the main rivers to provide cheap transport is high but the management of links between water, rail, road and air transport are not well developed. Investment in recent years has focused primarily on major highways and rail links. However, for the benefits of these to be realized in rural areas there is need to also increase access for regional towns and local communities (ADB, 2012a).

Indebtedness and lack of access to credit

Many of Myanmar's farmers are in debt and face extreme difficulty paying off existing loans. Although there has recently been a doubling of the loan ceiling for farmers (World Bank, 2013), they can still only access relatively small amounts of money from official banks at reasonable interest rates (8 per cent per annum) and are often forced to borrow money at much higher rates (5–10 per cent per month) from unofficial lenders (Haggblade *et al.*, 2013). As a result, they often have to sell their crops immediately after harvesting – when prices are low – in order to pay back loans as quickly as possible. It is speculated that this is one cause for the high levels of landlessness (Box 4.1). Although landless households do not have loans for production, they are frequently forced to borrow simply to buy food (Dapice *et al.*, 2011).

Government programmes, strategies and policies

The country's rich agricultural resources, abundant water and favourable climate provide enormous potential for growth and poverty reduction if successfully harnessed. Since the majority of the poor live in rural areas in Myanmar, growth in the agricultural sector would benefit the rural poor more than growth in other sectors (World Bank, 2008; Stuart, 2011). Currently, the government prioritizes agriculture and rural development as drivers of economic growth and broad-based development (ADB, 2012a). The government expects the agriculture sector to ensure food security, increase foreign exchange earnings through exports and promote rural development.

Starting in 1962, the Government of Myanmar exercised tight control over production and marketing of major food crops. For rice, the production quota assigned to farmers was between 1.5 and 2.1 tha^{-1} and farmers were supposed to surrender all harvest except that for their own consumption and seed paddy. Since 1988, the government has liberalized the agricultural sector (starting with pulses) by reducing the role of public procurement, loosening restrictions on the distribution of fertilizers and pesticides, permitting the export of agricultural produce by the private sector and encouraging private sector investors. The private sector has been permitted to export rice since December 2007. By 2011, the government had sold all its rice mills and removed all restrictions on private sector trade and export for both pulses and rice. With oilseeds, cotton and sugar, reforms have been slower but the private sector is playing an increasingly greater role (Haggblade *et al.*, 2013). In 2013, the Ministry of Commerce reconstituted the Myanmar Agricultural and Farm Produces Trading Department as the Trade Promotion Department. The ministry announced that this was intended to streamline the department's procedures in preparation for the country's active participation in ASEAN Free Trade Agreements from 2015 (World Bank, 2013).

Land reform

The new Farmland Law passed in the summer of 2012 replaced the Land Nationalization Law of 1953 that made all land the property of the state and made private land ownership and transfers illegal (Oberndorf, 2012). The new law permits the transfer and mortgaging of land tillage rights but the government retains state ownership and control of all agricultural land. The law lacks clarity and tenure security for farmland remains weak: smallholder farmers remain vulnerable to dispossession of their land use rights and the government retains control over some production decisions. The law does not cover customary tenure or include internationally recognized protection standards, such as 'free, prior and informed consent' (a right for indigenous peoples under international law). This can be particularly damaging for women who tend to have less formal ownership of assets, including land. Moreover, loopholes in new land and foreign investment laws allow investments in land to be prioritized and approved if they are in the national economic interest. Thus, farmers still lack complete land tenure and continue to be subject to government's crop prescriptions and production quotas (Oberndorf, 2012). These contrast with Vietnam where more clearly defined land rights in the 1980s were critical to boosting farm productivity and transforming the country into a global exporter of rice, coffee and cashews (Hiebert and Nguyen, 2012).

Investment in agricultural production

In recent years, the government has made considerable investments to increase agricultural production, particularly rice. Much of the capital investment has been in irrigation and flood defence infrastructure. The government's Agriculture Long-term Plan (2001–31) aims to provide irrigation water through construction and rehabilitation of reservoirs, watershed management, water harvesting techniques and utilization of groundwater. In some places, they are also providing pumping equipment to farmers. However, typically, only 15–35 per cent of irrigated areas are double cropped and the benefits to be gained from irrigation remain constrained by a variety of factors including: (1) government policy that mandates the production of paddy in much of the irrigated lands; (2) failure to integrate irrigation development with other agricultural policies (e.g. pricing of agricultural products, cost of inputs like fertilizers, pesticides and seeds); and (3) insufficient power supplies and the high cost of electricity in pumped schemes (Johnston *et al.*, 2013).

A seed law was enacted in 2011 and came into force in January 2013. Its objectives are to encourage: (1) the use of quality seed in the production of crops; (2) the development of seed business by providing incentives to private seed growers and seed companies; and (3) the revitalization of development cooperatives and seed business associations. In addition, an awareness programme to reach farmers and private business has been established (Oo and Shwe, 2013).

Rural development

Recently, the Ministry of Livestock, Fisheries and Rural Development launched a Strategic Framework for Rural Development, the objective of which is to reduce poverty in areas of high poverty incidence. Over a period of 30 months, it seeks to deliver development assistance to 3 million rural poor with the intention of enabling them to rise above the official poverty line by increasing per capita income. Twenty-eight districts have been selected for which development benefits are to be sought in a variety of ways, through both district and township investment funds that cover among other things: (1) enhancing income-generating opportunities; (2) upgrading village infrastructure; (3) restoring ecological stability and productivity; (4) improving community resilience and adaptive capacity to mitigate the risks of climate change and social conflicts; (5) promoting investment in sustainable land-based economic development; (6) enhancing rural communities' access to public services, including agricultural extension; (7) improving market linkages and value chain development. An Agriculture and Rural Development Sector Working Group has been established under the chairmanship of the Director General of the Department of Agriculture (MOAI) and is co-led by FAO and the United States Agency for International Development (USAID).

Nutritional security

In the past, the Government of Myanmar has focused to a large extent on increasing food availability and access but there has been much less emphasis on nutrition and health. Nevertheless, Myanmar became a signatory of the World Declaration on Nutrition and the Plan of Action on Nutrition at the International Conference on Nutrition in December 1992. There is a National Plan of Action for Food and Nutrition. This was initiated in 1994 and has been updated several times subsequently. It comprises four main pillars: (1) household food security; (2) food quality and food safety; (3) improved nutrition-related health care services; and (4) prevention of malnutrition and promotion of nutrition activities (WHO, 2012). As part of this Plan, the National Nutrition Centre has established a national surveillance system, which includes the monitoring of hospital cases arising from nutritional deficiency, an assessment of household food intake in regional and state capitals, and regular food and nutrition surveys. However, to date there has been little reporting of either the findings of the surveillance or the effectiveness of any of the measures taken.

In May 2013, the Government of Myanmar became a signatory of the Scaling Up Nutrition (SUN) programme, a global movement for action and investment to improve maternal and child nutrition. The initiative is a joint programme involving various UN agencies, UNICEF, FAO, Word Food Programme (WFP) and World Health Organization (WHO) and international NGOs, Save the Children, Action Contre La Faim and Hellen Keller International. Intended to accelerate efforts in increasing child nutrition – one of the MDGs for which progress in Myanmar is deemed insufficient – the SUN initiative will be integrated into the National Plan of Action for Food and Nutrition (UNICEF, 2013).

Non-government actors

The shift towards democracy provides significant opportunities for non-government actors, both national and international, to contribute towards the many issues that affect food security in Myanmar. In recent years, the humanitarian 'space' has opened up significantly both in terms of where in the country NGOs can operate and the government's willingness to collaborate with development actors. Similarly, re-engagement in the global economy provides opportunities for the private sector which, if carefully directed, has the potential to deliver huge economic benefits to those currently food insecure and living in poverty. However, the transitions required are complex and very challenging. Close coordination is required if these transformations are to successfully benefit the poor and setbacks are to be avoided.

International non-governmental organizations

In the aftermath of cyclone Nargis, numerous international NGOs (INGOs) gained access to Myanmar and were involved in the provision of humanitarian assistance and relief efforts. Many of these INGOs continue to have a presence; it is estimated that at least 65 INGOs are currently operating in the country (Saha, 2011). These organizations are increasingly shifting to longer-term development assistance, providing services and technical support across a range of sectors including agriculture, education and health, with varying degrees of success.

In the past, because of the sanctions many donors refused to support any work with the government. Consequently, INGO interventions were largely independent of the government. Donor attitudes are changing and with the easing of sanctions and the recognition that sustainable development is dependent on government involvement, there is increasing willingness to work with government departments. Virtually all the INGOs in Myanmar operate under a framework agreement (i.e. Memorandum of Understanding or Letter of Agreement) with a government ministry. Similarly, the government appears to be increasingly willing to work with INGOs.

A recent study concluded that in addition to significant political reform, aid effectiveness could be enhanced by increasing aid levels (with a focus on more long-term, development-focused funding), continuing dialogue with the government to improve humanitarian access, building local capacity, improving donor coordination and generating better data (Saha, 2011).

Civil society

The democratic transition in Myanmar has resulted in the country being more receptive to civil society efforts, with many new civil society groups being formed in recent years. Most local civil society groups are not officially registered, so it is difficult to estimate their numbers. However, international organizations observe a rise in the numbers of local groups and their level of activity (Saha, 2011). Farmer groups and farmer associations, including those contributing to the management of irrigation systems, are important civil society forums that have an important role to play in implementing national agricultural production and food security strategies.

Several forums exist for INGOs and civil society to collaborate, coordinate and pursue joint action. These include the Food Security Working Group (FSWG), which comprises 165 NGOs (local and international), community-based organizations and individuals, providing a platform for members to collectively learn, share and advocate on issues relating to food security in the country. As such, the FSWG has an important contribution to make in integrating the initiatives of a wide range of actors in the field of food security.

Private sector

Large-scale investments in land and agriculture are growing in Myanmar, encouraged by the government's strategy to attract new investors and modernize the agricultural sector. This includes private traders who, since the withdrawal of state marketing companies for agricultural products, have emerged to serve as market intermediaries in the wholesale and export of agricultural products (Haggblade *et al.*, 2013). It also increasingly includes foreign investments (Box 4.3). Such investments provide significant opportunities to increase productivity but also carry considerable risk, because they may not accept social and environmental responsibilities. Single farmers, as individual actors, have very little power and can rarely compete with large-scale agribusiness, with the result that supply chains are often dominated by large investors who have the power to set prices and dictate terms to smaller producers. As has been well documented elsewhere, wealth that is generated in local value chains but not captured by poor communities can deepen poverty and exacerbate inequalities. Ignoring these inequalities will increase the dependency of small-scale farmers on large-scale agriculture, reinforcing their inability to access profitable markets (Burnley, 2011).

Box 4.3   Foreign direct investment (FDI) law

Myanmar's Foreign Investment Law was passed in November 2012 and new regulations to supplement and operationalize it were passed in March 2013. Where previously foreigners had been prohibited from investing in sectors that 'could be carried out by citizens' and could 'affect the natural environment and public health', the new regulations permit up to 20 per cent foreign ownership in a range of sectors including cultivation, livestock and fisheries. As such, the law indicates Myanmar's new openness to foreign investment. However, there remain concerns around its capacity to ensure that basic social and environmental requirements are addressed and the most vulnerable protected.

Under the law significant decision-making power is given to the Myanmar Investment Committee over investments and the conditions under which they may proceed. This includes the power to decide social and environmental provisions, as well as broad decision-making power over land investment. It is not clear how these decisions relate to existing land laws (including customary ownership) or to bodies controlling land allocation decisions. The law currently lacks any reference to the need to balance the benefits of investment against social and environmental safeguards and concerns over 'land grabbing' are widespread.

Source: Burnley, 2013; World Bank, 2013.

Donors and international financial institutions

A large number of donors are once again active in Myanmar, including bilateral agencies, the UN system and multilateral funds. International financial institutions (IFIs) (i.e. the World Bank and Asian Development Bank) have also recently re-engaged. Donor priorities and commitment in Myanmar are still very fluid. Most donors have only just developed country strategies or are in the process of doing so. Until recently emergency aid, democracy, human rights, education and health were key priorities. However, in part because the Government of Myanmar stressed the importance of efforts to reduce poverty through agricultural development during the first Development Cooperation Forum in January 2013, agricultural development and food security are likely to play a more prominent role in donor investments in the future. Both the ADB and USAID have recently commissioned diagnostic studies of the agricultural sector (ADB, 2013; Haggblade *et al.*, 2013) and the World Bank is presently undertaking a food security analysis. Of the three multidonor trust funds currently operating in Myanmar, the Livelihoods and Food Security Trust Fund (LIFT) focuses on poverty and hunger eradication, notably by supporting agricultural production and strengthening the capacity of local partners to support livelihoods and food security initiatives.

Conclusions

As this chapter has described, the overall food and nutrition situation in Myanmar is complex, dynamic and subject to many positive and negative influences. In the future, as Myanmar opens up and transitions to a fully democratic country, it will be exposed to far-ranging changes in the global and regional geopolitical and socioeconomic environment (ADB, 2012a). To optimize development possibilities, progress from least developed country status and improve the well-being of its people, Myanmar needs to strategically plan to embrace the opportunities and curtail the threats that these changes will present.

Prevailing high levels of household food insecurity as well as the significant environmental pressures that Myanmar's present growth pattern is creating suggest that current economic growth is neither sufficiently inclusive nor sustainable in the long term. Ultimately, both are constraints to progress. Myanmar's future depends in large measure on stewardship of its natural resources and greater inclusiveness of its citizens in the benefits from resource exploitation (ADB, 2012a).

The size of the agricultural sector combined with the predominantly rural population and the currently small size of the manufacturing and service sectors make a strong case for the centrality of rural-based agriculture-led development to a successful strategy of poverty reduction and increased food security (UNDP *et al.*, 2011). The Government of Myanmar must urgently transform the agricultural sector to simultaneously reduce poverty, improve household food and nutrition security and reduce environmental degradation. No single policy instrument will suffice. Rather, improving food security outcomes will be dependent on a mix of policies that promote higher household incomes, improve education on, and awareness of, better uses of food and nutrition, and are able to tackle the specific constraints of the poorer and more vulnerable segments of the predominantly rural population that incur high expenditure on food.

Recommendations for the future

The following are some possible approaches for unleashing the potential for growth in the smallholder agricultural sector and improving household food security.

Build resilience and improve agricultural performance

• *Improve land access and farmer decision making*: Land access is currently a highly contentious issue in Myanmar. The Government of Myanmar must ensure that the land rights of communities and small-scale producers are protected against damaging large-scale land acquisitions (Burnley, 2011). As evidenced by other countries in the region, clarifying land tenure arrangements and allowing farmers to select the crops they want to grow (e.g. relaxing 'rice first' policies) would significantly improve long-term efforts to modernize and raise the productivity of Myanmar's agricultural sector. Resolution of the many ongoing conflicts surrounding land is also critical. The government needs to put in place a coherent legal framework for land use and gradually transfer authority to resolve land disputes to the judiciary (Hiebert and Nguyen, 2012; Haggblade *et al.*, 2013).

• *Invest in agricultural water management and irrigation*: Investments in water control in both rainfed and irrigated systems will be critical for Myanmar to reduce the risks from climate change and increase agricultural productivity. For rainfed agriculture, simple technologies that enhance infiltration and water retention in the soil profile can stabilize and increase crop yields. Examples vary from place to place but the most promising include reduced tillage, zero tillage, mulching, various types of planting basin and bunds, and ways to reduce soil erosion. It may also include the use of different (low-water requirement) crops. For irrigated agriculture, clearly there is a need to address issues hampering the performance of existing systems based on in-depth research before investing in new development. Opportunities for using groundwater should be investigated. Improving livestock access to water, reducing the distance that animals have to walk to water sources, can significantly improve animal well-being and increase productivity.

• *Invest in and reform agricultural support institutions*: In recent decades, the Government of Myanmar has chronically underinvested in agricultural research, extension and education. Current uncertainties in basic agricultural and natural resource statistics make it difficult to evaluate the likely food security implications of different policy options. Basic monitoring and improvements in data quality are essential to guide policy and improve decision making. Furthermore, investment in research, extension and education needs to be substantially bolstered to build and retain adequate human capital and ensure that sufficient resources (e.g. in terms of vehicles, cell phones and basic research facilities) are available to provide services to farmers. All the support institutions require restructuring to replace command and control systems with more participatory farmer-centred approaches. This should include: (1) improving links between farmers, researchers and extension staff so that practical problems relevant to farmers are addressed; and (2) investing in human capital to ensure that contemporary skills are available to meet the needs of a new era of participation and engagement (Haggblade *et al.*, 2013).

• *Invest in infrastructure*: Rural transport (roads, rail and river) and telecommunications are essential for the development of efficient input supply systems, access to agricultural markets and extension. To make up for decades of underinvestment, the government needs to substantially increase funding for rural transport and telecommunication links and, to take advantages of its strategic location, improve international border crossings.

- *Improve access to good seed and reduce post-harvest losses*: There is considerable scope to increase production and productivity through both use of better seeds and reduction of post-harvest losses. However, comprehensive analysis of the key issues around these constraints is necessary to inform the design of effective strategies to improve both.
- *Invest in climate monitoring and warning*: Given the unpredictability of monsoon rainfall and likely increased frequency of extreme events, improved capacity to monitor and forecast weather patterns (e.g. using contemporary satellite-based technology) and provide early warning of floods and droughts is essential for Myanmar to properly manage its water resources and agriculture in the future (Haggblade *et al.*, 2013). Properly designed, such a system would greatly facilitate both water resource and agricultural planning and would easily justify both the financial and human resources required to establish and maintain it.
- *Promote smallholder agriculture*: Donors and IFIs can shape the direction of agricultural development in Myanmar by ensuring that aid supports small-scale farmers and strengthens their ability to engage with markets. Donors need to harmonize their efforts and work closely with the government, civil society and the private sector to ensure that national policy is explicitly aimed at supporting small-scale farmers. IFIs should ensure their technical advice helps the government develop policy to support growth through small-scale agriculture. Crucially, donors and IFIs providing assistance should guarantee that any engagement on agricultural or private sector development is clearly linked to the protection of rights.

Improve nutrition and health outcomes

- *Promote basic health and nutrition*: Initiatives that promote basic health and nutrition should be integrated into new programmes aimed at improving agricultural sector growth and/or enhancing food security, including the recently launched rural development programme as well as future LIFT initiatives.
- *Improve national safety nets and food reserves*: Myanmar has contributed to the ASEAN+3 Emergency Rice Reserve (APTERR). However, as part of the current food security-related policies, the Government of Myanmar should consider further developing a national rice reserve and seed programme. Investment in a new generation of clearly mandated, well-governed and efficient emergency food and seed reserves – involving the participation and oversight of smallholder farmers and civil society – can be effective (ActionAid, 2011).
- *Improve rural financial systems*: To reduce debt and help farmers recapitalize, consideration should be given to providing them with cash grants or extending assistance in other forms that reduce the costs of cultivation and increase productivity (e.g. by providing mechanical rice tillers or wells/ponds for irrigation) (Dapice *et al.*, 2011). Considerable improvements could also be made by enabling loan repayments some time after the harvest date to facilitate

farmers' ability to sell their crops at a time of their choosing. Over the long term, efforts to build up credit systems and institutions to provide rural households with finance at reasonable rates will require institutional development (Haggblade *et al.*, 2013).

*   *Protect wild fisheries and enhance aquaculture*: Opportunities for improving fisheries' operations need to be investigated to make informed decisions about how best to sustainably develop Myanmar's fisheries in the future. For example, there is potential for stocking or strategic feeding in some natural water bodies and reservoirs. The development of small-scale fish ponds (less than 60 m^2) has proved a highly successful contribution to the livelihoods of poor rural families in neighbouring countries and, because the fish ponds require relatively little land and small initial investment, they could provide opportunities for the landless in Myanmar. Another possibility for investigation is to enhance rice-fisheries, which are also seen to be successful in some neighbouring countries, although these can limit opportunities for rice intensification (FAO, 2003).

It is clear from the divergent list of possible opportunities above that traditional governance approaches focused on single issues will be insufficient for the complexities and uncertainties underlying food insecurity in Myanmar. In the future, better integrated social mechanisms and coordination/collaboration across sectors, as well as between government, development partners, civil society and the private sector, are required to ensure successful outcomes.

References

ActionAid (2011) No more food crises: the indispensable role of food reserves, online, http://www.actionaid.org/sites/files/actionaid/polcy_briefing_-_the_role_of_food_reserves.pdf (accessed 14 December 2013).

Anderson Irrigation (2012) Increasing the efficiency and effectiveness of pumped irrigation schemes in the Central Dry Zone of Myanmar. Working paper No. 3: Agriculture. Livelihoods and Food Security Trust Fund/UNOPS/Water Resources Utilization Department, Yangon, Myanmar.

Asian Development Bank (ADB) (2012a) Myanmar in transition: opportunities and challenges. ADB, Mandaluyong City, Philippines, online, http://www.adb.org/publications/myanmar-transition-opportunities-and-challenges (accessed 15 December 2013).

Asian Development Bank (ADB) (2012b) Environment analysis. Interim Country Partnership Strategy 2012–14: Myanmar. ADB, Mandaluyong City, Philippines, online, http://www.adb.org/documents/myanmar-interim-country-partnership-strategy-2012-2014 (accessed 15 December 2013).

Asian Development Bank (ADB) (2013) Sector assessment (summary): agriculture and natural resources. Interim Country Partnership Strategy, 2012–14: Myanmar. ADB, Mandaluyong City, Philippines, online, http://www.adb.org/documents/myanmar-interim-country-partnership-strategy-2012-2014 (accessed 15 December 2013).

Bajora, J. (2013) Understanding Myanmar. Council on foreign relations, online, http://www.cato.org/publications/trade-policy-analysis/us-sanctions-against-burma-failure-all-fronts (accessed 13 September 2013).

BCN (2013) EU sanctions, online, http://www.burmacentrum.nl/bcn-in-english/english/eu-sanctions (accessed 13 September 2013).

Burnley, J. (2013) A new dawn for equitable growth in Myanmar? Making the private sector work for small-scale agriculture. Oxfam issue briefing, online, http://www.oxfam.org/sites/www.oxfam.org/files/ib-equitable-growth-myanmar-040613-en.pdf (accessed 22 January 2014).

Dapice, D.O. (2013) Rice policy in Myanmar: it's getting complicated. Harvard Kennedy School. Ash Center for Democratic Governance and Innovation, online, http://www.ash.harvard.edu/extension/ash/docs/RicePolicy.pdf (accessed 12 December 2013).

Dapice, D.O., Vallely, T.J., Wilkinson, B. and Montesano, M.J. (2010) Revitalizing agriculture in Myanmar: breaking down barriers, building a framework for growth. Harvard Kennedy School. Ash Centre for Democratic Governance and Innovation, online, http://www.ash.harvard.edu/extension/ash/docs/burma.pdf (accessed 13 September 2013).

Dapice, D.O., Vallely, T.J., Wilkinson, B. and McPherson, M. (2011) Myanmar agriculture in 2011: old problems and new challenges. Harvard Kennedy School. Ash Center for Democratic Governance and Innovation, online, http://www.ash.harvard.edu/extension/ash/docs/myanmar1111.pdf (accessed 13 September 2013).

ESCAP (2011) Statistical yearbook for Asia and the Pacific 2011, ESCAP, Bangkok, online, http://www.unescap.org/stat/data/syb2013/ (accessed 25 November 2013).

FAO (2003) Myanmar aquaculture and inland fisheries. RAP publication 2003/18: FAO Regional Office for Asia and the Pacific. Bangkok, online, http://www.fao.org/docrep/004/ad497e/ad497e00.htm (accessed 23 October 2013).

FAO (2005) Myanmar agricultural sector review and investment strategy. FAO Regional Office for Asia and the Pacific. Bangkok, online, http://www.mm.undp.org/content/dam/myanmar/docs/Publications/PovRedu/MMR_FA1_InvestStrategyReview.pdf (accessed 23 October 2013).

FAO (2009) Digital agricultural atlas of the union of Myanmar. Linked from FAO geonetwork, FAO Regional Office for Asia and the Pacific. Bangkok, online, http://dwms.fao.org/atlases/myanmar/atlas_en.htm (accessed 15 October 2013).

FAO (2011) Myanmar and FAO. Achievements and success stories. Rome, online, http://www.fao.org/fileadmin/templates/rap/files/epublications/MyanmaredocFINAL.pdf (accessed 5 February 2013).

FAOSTAT (2013) Food and Agriculture Organization Statistics, online, http://faostat.fao.org/ (accessed 23 October 2013).

Food Security Working Group (FSWG) (2011) Upland land tenure security in Myanmar: an overview, online, http://www.myanmarfswg.net/land%20tenure%20briefing%20paper-eng.swf (accessed 24 September 2013).

Hadar, L.T. (1998) US sanctions against Burma: a failure on all fronts. Trade policy analysis, online, http://www.cato.org/publications/trade-policy-analysis/us-sanctions-against-burma-failure-all-fronts (accessed 13 September 2013).

Haggblade, S., Boughton, D., Denning, G., Kloeppinger-Todd, R., Cho, K.M., Wilson, S., Wong, L.C.Y., Oo Z., Than, T.M., Wai, N.E.M.A., Win, N.W. and Sandar, T.M. (2013) A strategic agriculture and food security diagnostic for Myanmar, online, http://fsg.afre.msu.edu/Myanmar/myanmar_agricultural_sector_diagnostic_july_2013.pdf (accessed 12 November 2013).

Heibert, M. and Nguyen, P. (2012) Land reform: a critical test for Myanmar's government. (9 November 2012). CSIS Center for Strategic and International Studies, online, http://csis.org/publication/land-reform-critical-test-myanmars-government (accessed 21 August 2014).

Htun, K. (2009) Myanmar forestry outlook study. Asia Pacific Forestry Sector Outlook Study II. Working Paper No. 07, APFSOS II/WP/2009/07, FAO, Bangkok, online, http://www.fao.org/docrep/014/am252e/am252e00.pdf (accessed 13 October 2013).

International Monetary Fund (IMF) (2012) Article IV Consultation with Myanmar, online, http://www.imf.org/external/pubs/ft/scr/2013/cr13250.pdf (accessed 22 January 2014).

Johnston, R., Ameer, R., Balasubramanaya, S., Dousangsavanh, S., Lacombe, G., McCartney, M., Pavelic, P., Senaratna Sellamuttu, S., Sotoukee, T., Suhardiman, D. and Joffre, O. (2013) Identifying priority investments in water in Myanmar's Dry Zone. Report to Livelihoods and Food Security Trust Fund /UNOPS 52 pp., online, http://lift-fund.net/downloads/Component%203%20Final_19Aug13.pdf (accessed 18 September 2013).

Kudo, T., Kumagai, S. and Ishido, H. (2013) Agriculture plus: growth strategy for Myanmar Agriculture. IDE Discussion paper No. 421, online, http://www.ide.go.jp/English/Publish/Download/Dp/421.html (accessed 23 October 2013).

LIFT (2012) Baseline survey results, online http://archive.lift-fund.net/downloads/LIFT%20Baseline%20Survey%20Report%20-%20July%202012.pdf (accessed 23 April 2013).

Lwin, T. (2002) The climate changes over Myanmar during the last decades, economic and social commission for Asia and the Pacific, *Water Resources Journal*, ESCAP, June, Bangkok: 95–106.

McCartney, M.P., Pavelic, P., Lacombe, G., Latt, K., Zan, A.K., Thein, K., Douangsavanh, S., Balasubramanya, S., Ameer, R., Myint, A., Cho, C., Johnston, R. and Sotoukee, T. (2013) Water resources assessment of the Dry Zone of Myanmar. Report to Livelihoods and Food Security Trust Fund/UNOPS 48 pp., online, http://publications.iwmi.org/pdf/H046133.pdf (accessed August 20 2013).

Oberndorf, R. (2012) Legal review of recently enacted farmland law and vacant, fallow and virgin lands management law. Land Core Group of the Food Security Working Group, online, http://www.forest-trends.org/documents/files/doc_3274.pdf (accessed 23 February 2014).

Okamoto, I. (2008) *Economic Disparity in Rural Myanmar*. National University of Singapore Press.

Oo, T.H. and Shwe, T.M. (2013) Position paper on the seed industry. Role of seed in transforming agriculture in Myanmar, online, http://www.slideshare.net/resakssasia/the-seed-sector-in-myanmar-tin-maung-shew-tin-htut-oo (accessed 12 December 2013).

Poe, C.A. (2011) Food security assessment in northern Rakhine state. World Food Programme, online, http://reliefweb.int/sites/reliefweb.int/files/resources/Full_Report_288.pdf (accessed 18 February 2014).

Saha, S.R. (2011) Working through ambiguity: international NGOs in Myanmar. The Hauser Center for Non-profit Organizations. Harvard University, online http://www.hks.harvard.edu/var/ezp_site/storage/fckeditor/file/pdfs/centers-programs/centers/hauser/publications/reports/myanmar_report_final_version_2011_09_08.pdf (accessed 22 February 2014).

Stads, G.J. and Kam, P.S. (2007) Myanmar: agricultural science and technology indicators country brief No. 38, International food Policy Research Institute, Washington, DC, online, http://www.ifpri.org/sites/default/files/publications/myanmar_cb38.pdf (accessed 13 January 2014).

Stuart, E. (2011) Making growth inclusive. Some lessons from countries and the literature. Oxfam research report, online, http://policy-practice.oxfam.org.uk/publications/making-growth-inclusive-some-lessons-from-countries-and-the-literature-128736 (accessed 22 January 2014).

Talbott, K., Waugh, J. and Batson, D. (2012) Sharing the wealth: Burma's post-military rule and natural resource governance. *Small Wars Journal*, online, http://smallwarsjournal. com/jrnl/art/sharing-the-wealth-burma%E2%80%99s-post-military-rule-and-natural-resource-governance (accessed 24 September 2013).

United Nations Children's Fund (UNICEF) (2013) Myanmar pledges stronger combat against child malnutrition, online, http://www.unicef.org/media/media_69183.html (accessed 14 December 2013).

United Nations Development Programme (UNDP), Ministry of National Planning and Economic Development, UNICEF and SIDA (2011) Integrated household living conditions survey in Myanmar (2009–10): poverty profile. Yangon, Myanmar, online, http://www. mm.undp.org/content/myanmar/en/home/library/poverty/publication_1/ (accessed 23 April 2013).

United Nations Development Programme (UNDP) (2013) Human development report 2013: the rise of the south: human progress in a diverse world, online, http://hdr.undp. org/en/2013-report (accessed 22 January 2014).

Wilson, S. and Wai, A. (2013) Food and nutrition security in Myanmar. Working paper prepared for USAID, online, http://fsg.afre.msu.edu/Myanmar/myanmar_background_paper_4_food_security.pdf (accessed 13 December 2013).

World Bank (2008) *World Development Report 2008: Agriculture for Development*, online, http:// siteresources.worldbank.org/INTWDR2008/Resources/2795087-1192111580172/ WDROver2008-ENG.pdf (accessed 21 August 2014).

World Bank (2013) Myanmar economic monitor, online, http://www.worldbank.org/ content/dam/Worldbank/document/EAP/Myanmar/Myanmar_Economic_Monitor_October_2013.pdf (accessed 22 January 2014).

World Food Programme (WFP) (2013) Rapid assessment of non-displaced populations in Sittwe township, online, http://documents.wfp.org/stellent/groups/public/documents/ ena/wfp254681.pdf (accessed 22 February 2104).

World Health Organization (WHO) (2012) Policy – national plan of action for food and nutrition, online, https://extranet.who.int/nutrition/gina/en/node/8781 (accessed 14 December 2013).

World Health Organization (WHO) (2013) Nutritional landscape information system, online, http://www.who.int/nutrition/nlis/en/ (accessed 24 September 2013).

Xe, F. (2011) Hybrid rice R&D programme at IRRI, online, http://www.unapcaem.org/ Activities%20Files/A1112sanya/irri.pdf (accessed 13 February 2013).

5 Implications of climate change, population and resource scarcity for food security in Bangladesh

Mohammad A.B. Siddique, Jatish C. Biswas, Mohammad A. Salam and Mohammad A. Islam

Introduction

Bangladesh is one of South Asia's poorest countries and has the highest population density and malnutrition rates in the world. Geographic and climatic features, coupled with its social and economic changes make Bangladesh highly vulnerable to risks from climate change. The ever-increasing frequency of floods, droughts and cyclones have, during the last two decades, caused severe economic damage and have impaired the livelihoods of millions of poor households. The emerging and exacerbating impacts of global climate change severely threaten people's food security, especially the poor and marginal sections of the society (World Bank, 2013). The impacts of climate change on food production are global concerns, but they are greater for countries such as Bangladesh because agriculture is the largest sector of its economy (Basak *et al.*, 2010). Agriculture is dominated greatly by rice cultivation and crop diversification is still rather limited in Bangladesh. Although the aggregated food supplies are adequate at the macro level, a number of factors in Bangladesh prevent a vast majority of poor households or individuals from accessing food (IFPRI, 2013). Landless farm laborers and casual fishers are the most vulnerable and food insecure groups. Moreover, these groups have deteriorating access to increasingly scarce natural resources, especially water and land.

In spite of the constraints, Bangladesh has made notable progress in agricultural development and domestic food production over the past three decades. This was mainly due to growth in agricultural productivity combined with macroeconomic stability, liberalization of markets and economy (FAO, IFAD and WFP, 2013). The country meets its food demand mostly from domestic production and to some extent supplemented by imports, development aid and national food reserves. Nevertheless, there are large regional variations in poverty and food insecurity in this small densely populated country. Although fighting food and nutrition insecurity is high on the government's agenda, progress is poor, and it remains a hurdle for Bangladesh to become a middle-income country (BBS, 2011).

This chapter will focus on main challenges and potential strategies for attaining food security in Bangladesh. The central issues addressed in this chapter are: (1) the current food security status and challenges; (2) the major drivers to food insecurity; (3) the responses to reduce food insecurity; and finally (4) conclusions and policy recommendations.

The food security status

Population, food production and availability

The population in Bangladesh is estimated at 146.1 million, sharing about 147,570 square kilometers (BER, 2010), and is projected to reach 230 million by 2050 (Streatfield and Karar, 2008). As a result, the population density will increase, land per capita will decrease significantly and the total food demand will increase. Total demand for rice by 2050 will increase by 56 percent compared to 2001 (Mukherjee *et al.*, 2011). This will amount to more than 55 million tons of rice to feed its people by the year 2050. The demand for maize will increase by ten times and that of wheat will be doubled by 2050. With the expanding middle-income households, fish and meat consumption is expected to increase by around 150 percent. Non-grain crops, such as potato, which can be a substitute for rice in the future, will increase by more than 200 percent and other animal products such as milk and eggs will increase by more than 500 and 200 percent, respectively (Mukherjee *et al.*, 2011).

On the production front, total annual rice and wheat production increased from less than 10 million tons in the early 1970s to more than 33 million tons by 2009/10. There has also been a substantial improvement in the overall availability of food as shown in Table 5.1.

Although domestic production of food grains persistently increased since the 1970s, imported food grains constituted a significant proportion of total availability in the country. Moreover, while government imports were significant during the 1990s, the private imports increasingly dominated total import over the years (FPMU, 2008).

In the recent past, the country was a net importer of rice (FPMU, 2008). However, no rice has been imported since 2010; instead, scented rice exports increased from Bangladesh (Pavel, 2013). This scenario might change in the future because of population and economic growth, along with natural calamities and impacts of climate change and variability. Currently, food expenditure accounts for almost 54 percent of total household expenditure in Bangladesh and, in the rural areas, it accounts for nearly 60 percent (WFP, 2013).

Although total per capita food consumption increased between 1991/92 and 2005, the per capita calorie consumption slightly decreased during the same years for rural and urban households but then increased from 2005 to 2010 (Table 5.2). This trend may be attributed to compositional changes in food consumption in the form of substitution of lower calorie intensive foods to higher calorie intensive foods. Consumption of cereal foods, especially rice, decreased in both rural and urban areas during the same period.

Assuming food consumption is more or less directly proportional to calorie intake, the upper income groups of households consume excessive calories compared to the physiological norm of calorie intake as shown in Table 5.3 (Talukder, 2008). The disparity was more pronounced for urban than for rural households, with the lowest income groups consuming as low as 0.622kg daily compared to 1.403kg by the highest income groups, showing that income and amount of food consumed are directly proportional.

Table 5.1 Rice and wheat production and availability in Bangladesh.

Year	Gross domestic production (MT)	Net domestic production (MT)	Private import (MT)	Public distribution (MT)	Internal procurement (MT)	National availability (MT)	Per capita availability	
							kg/yr	oz/day
1	2	3	4	5	6	7=3+4+5–6	8	9
1991/92	19,317	17,385	0	2,345	1,016	18,714	166	16
2000/01	26,758	24,082	1,063	1,774	1,088	25,831	197	19
2009/10	33,158	29,179	2,899	1,961	805	33,234	225	21

Source: Adapted from FPMU, 2013.

Table 5.2 Per capita calorie and protein intake by rural and urban households.

Survey year	Calorie intake (kcal/cap/day)			Protein intake (g/cap/day)		
	National	Rural	Urban	National	Rural	Urban
2010	2,318	2,344	2,244	66	65	69
2005	2,239	2,253	2,194	63	62	65
2000	2,240	2,263	2,150	63	62	65
1995/96	2,244	2,251	2,209	65	64	68
1991/92	2,266	2,267	2,258	63	62	65

Source: Adapted from HIES, 2010; BBS, 2011.

Table 5.3 Per capita daily food intake (kg) as influenced by monthly household expenditure.

Monthly household expenditure group (Tk.)	Per capita daily food intake (kg)		
	National	Rural	Urban
Less than 750	0.727	0.744	0.622
1,500–19,999	0.791	0.796	0.760
10,000–12,999	1.198	1.249	1.094
Above 20,000	1.432	1.478	1.403

Source: Adapted from Talukder, 2008.

Current utilization of food is governed by a number of factors such as people's food preferences, crops grown, general health status and the overall conditions under which food is prepared and consumed. This becomes important as processed food items dominate the market and the nutritional value is compromised to improve the taste and presentation. Even in countries such as Bangladesh, supermarket chains and multinational companies have started to dominate the markets in recent years, and they may not prioritize nutrition over profits, taste and presentation.

Agriculture sector contribution to food production

Agriculture provides almost 43.6 percent employment of total labor force (BBS, 2009), and it contributes about 20 percent (BER, 2012) to the total gross domestic product (GDP) as a whole, of which the crop sector alone provides about 11 percent. During the last decade, the GDP has grown at the rate of 5.5 percent, especially towards the end. Since 2003/04, growth has hovered around or above 6 percent per year (MoF, 2010). During the same period, agricultural GDP has grown at a moderate rate of only 3.4 percent (Asaduzzaman et al., 2010). The overall annual growth rate in agriculture was 3.4 percent during 1997–2011. During the same period, GDP from livestock, fisheries and forestry increased at annual rates of 4.3, 3.4 and 4.7 percent, respectively. Currently, rice accounts for 92 percent of the total food grain production and is grown on approximately 11.25 million ha, covering about 82 percent of the total cropped land (BBS, 2011). According to the latest estimation made by BBS (2011) per capita rice consumption is about 166kg/year. The increase in rice output over the last quarter of the century was mainly due to cultivation of the dry season irrigated *boro* rice (December/January to April/May) crop. The area expansion under *boro* was at the cost of *aus* rice cultivation (March/June). Area under rainfed *T. aman* rice cultivation (July/August to November/December) has generally remained static.

The other main reason for the increase in rice production is the introduction of high yielding varieties. During the green revolution, the Bangladesh Academy for Rural Development imported IR8 seeds (1967/68) from the International Rice Research Institute and introduced those to the farmers in *boro* and *aus* seasons. For the *T. aman* season, IR20 was the first high yielding rice variety grown in Bangladesh. Since then widespread adoption of high yielding varieties released by the Bangladesh Rice Research Institute has significantly helped to solve the food crisis in the country. Rice production currently is increasing by more than 400,000 tons annually in contrast to the growing population of 1.8 million per year (Hossain *et al.*, 2007). There is, however, a large gap between the current actual yields and the potential yield per hectare in rice. The gap is mainly attributed to lack of timely access to technology, inputs, low market prices, poor investments and extension services.

The area indices constructed for different food grains showed an overall increasing trend for *boro* rice, total rice and maize area with respect to their corresponding base period (1971–75). This is due to the decrease in area under *aus* rice, *T. aman* and wheat, and a significant shift to *boro* rice and maize cultivation in Bangladesh (Islam *et al.*, 2011). Although the share in value added for paddy has somewhat fallen and those of the so-called minor crops – potato, other vegetables and fruits – has increased, several other crops have lost share, including pulses and oilseeds. Incentives for irrigation and fuel and agricultural research have in a way encouraged production of *boro* rice. But, cultivation of *boro* rice is mostly dependent on groundwater resource and thus competes with other crops such as pulses, vegetables and oils. As a result, the country depends on large imports of pulses and oilseeds to meet the demand.

In Bangladesh, post-harvest losses are quite significant due to poor storage facilities at the various stages, which is a serious problem. The government needs to store huge quantities of foods particularly cereals to meet the requirement of public food distribution and stabilization of market prices. Loss of nutritional value from improper storage, processing and cooking methods is also quite serious (Baqui, 2005). For vegetables, fruits and spices, the major storage losses occur at the farmers' level. Lack of good processing facilities affects physical and chemical properties of food and thus reduces the quality of the available food.

Fisheries and livestock production

Fisheries

Fisheries in Bangladesh provides livelihood to approximately 1.28 million fishers, 3.08 million fish farmers and 0.44 million fish and shrimp seed collectors who live and trade in the country primarily at the subsistence level (DoF, 2009). The marine and coastal capture fisheries sector is the only primary source of income and nutrition for over 0.48 million households and 2.7 million family members in the coastal area of Bangladesh (DoF, 2009). Therefore, it is important to keep these small-scale fisheries sustainable. Water pollution, salinity, reduced water supply during the dry season, flooding in the wet season and eutrophication are the greatest challenges for the fisheries sector in Bangladesh. Nitrogen and phosphorus coming from agricultural run-off, sewage and the burning of fossil fuels are responsible for eutrophication, which greatly impairs fish production in the inland fresh water bodies and delta areas. Increased eutrophication of water bodies in Chittagong and Khulna, two major fish producing regions, means gradual loss of coastal mangrove vegetation causing ecological imbalance and health hazards to the population concomitant with its adverse effect on the economy of the country (Linda *et al.*, 2012). At present, there is no consolidated effort to protect the coastal fisheries and agriculture in Bangladesh.

Farmers practice pond embankment and fencing by net to protect fish from floods and overflow of rainwater. They are advised to harvest pond fish before periods of drought, and in commercial farming to manage water supply in peak periods. Measures such as enhancement of fish production through aquatic vegetation shelter in ponds, deeper re-excavation, changing species of fish, polycultures and introduction of saline tolerant species and establishment of fish sanctuary may increase aquaculture production. Bangladesh has established fish sanctuaries and executes a ban on fishing during the reproduction period of commercial fishes, but due to lack of proper monitoring it is difficult to implement the ban.

Livestock

The current contribution of the livestock subsector to overall GDP is about 2.73 percent, which is 17.15 percent of agricultural GDP. It has been estimated that by the year 2025 the demand for milk, eggs and meat will increase by 6, 5.2 and 5.6 percent, respectively (Karim, 2009). These rates are well above the recent production and consumption growth rates. Only the present growth of poultry and egg production is relatively close to these projections. The growth rate for poultry is expected to be 4.41 percent and for sheep and goats would be around 1.99 percent. Livestock population in general is decreasing in many parts of the country because of reduced grazing land; the country will therefore have to depend on imports to meet the increasing demand for beef consumption. Moreover, climate change impact can introduce vector-borne diseases and attack of parasites and transmission of new livestock diseases (Thornton and

Herrero, 2008). Livestock requires a quick response during flood and post flood rehabilitations. It is necessary to transfer small ruminants and poultry from flood and cyclone affected areas to high land and make shelter sheds to reduce losses during hazards. Although there are some disaster shelters, these are used mainly for human beings and are not adequate for livestock as well. Feed preservation and preventive measures for disease control during the hazards should be ensured to reduce further losses in the most vulnerable areas.

Major drivers of food insecurity

Poverty and regional inequality

In South Asia, poverty and economic inequality are one of the main reasons for food insecurity. Low-income levels restrict the poor to purchase necessary foods at prevailing market prices, especially those who may not have access to land for their own cultivation or may lack the required assets or access to credit to help cope with difficult times (WFP, 2013). Almost 40 percent of rural Bangladeshis live on less than US$1.25 per day and 60 percent of that income is spent on food (IFPRI, 2013). Lack of assured employment and income is the principal driver of undernutrition and malnutrition for approximately 65.3 million people in the country who live under the poverty line (WFP, 2013). Almost 45 percent of the country's population is now food insecure (less than 2,122 kcal/person/day) and nearly 23.9 percent of the population is severely food insecure (consuming less than 1,805 kcal/person/day). The estimation does not take into account the nutritional value of the diet, but is based on a per capita calorie intake per day, which may not fit the FAO definition of food security. However, both rural and urban poverty in general decreased from 1991/92 to 2010, as measured by the cost of basic needs (CBN) method (Table 5.4). Using the upper poverty line, the poverty rate at national level was estimated to be 56.6 percent in 1991/92 and decreased to 31.5 percent in 2010.

Households that are poor lack the resources to acquire sufficient and nutritious food, and are likely to be food insecure; people who are food insecure may have to sell or consume their productive assets to satisfy their immediate food needs. This undermines their longer-term income potential and development, and they may become even poorer thus trapped in a vicious circle. Although Bangladesh has achieved overall progress in poverty reduction, there remains widespread poverty and hunger at national and regional levels. There are also marked variations in poverty incidence between rural and urban parts of Bangladesh.

Other factors, such as gender disparities in food distribution, also contribute to high malnutrition levels in Bangladesh. Within households, children, the disabled, pregnant women, nursing mothers and the elderly face relatively higher nutritional risks than other members in the household. Over 60 percent of all pregnant and lactating women have insufficient calorie intake, which can lead to malnourished children. More than 90 percent of rural Bangladeshis do not get enough vitamin A (IFPRI, 2013). And iron deficiency – which can cause anemia

Table 5.4 Head count rate of incidence of poverty, 1991/92–2010 (CBN method).

Residence	Upper poverty line					Lower poverty line				
	2010	2005	2000	1995/96	1991/92	2010	2005	2000	1995/96	1991/92
National	31.5	40.0	48.9	50.1	56.6	17.6	25.1	34.3	35.1	41.0
Rural	35.2	43.8	52.3	54.5	58.7	21.1	28.6	37.9	39.4	43.7
Urban	21.3	28.4	35.2	27.8	42.7	7.7	14.6	20.0	13.7	23.6

Source: Adapted from HIES, 2010.

and the risk of death in childbirth – is also very high, especially for women of reproductive age.

Food security in the country is characterized by considerable regional variations. Factors such as a tendency to natural disasters, distribution and quality of agricultural land, access to education and health facilities, level of infrastructure development, employment opportunities, and dietary and caring practices provide possible explanations for this. Disaster vulnerability is driven by high population density along the country's coast and around the large river deltas. Over 80 percent of the population is potentially exposed to floods, earthquakes and droughts and more than 70 percent to frequent cyclones (NPDM, 2010). The poorest sub-districts, namely Mymensingh, Netrakona, Bandarban and Rangamati, and districts with more than one million people living in extreme poverty including Sirajganj, Naogaon, Bogra, Mymensingh and Chittagong all have the highest food insecurity.

Food contamination and adulteration is becoming another major challenge in Bangladesh. Poor household males were observed to have greater deficiency in minerals (calcium, magnesium and potassium) and trace elements (such as iron, copper and zinc) than non-poor household males (Islam *et al.*, 2013). According to the study, about 94 percent of males from poor households and 78 percent of males from non-poor households have cadmium intake above the provisional tolerable weekly intake (PTWI). Puffed rice, a popular food item in Bangladesh, had more elevated concentrations of sodium, potassium, iron, manganese and aluminum than normal rice (Islam *et al.*, 2013). Arsenic, another toxic element, gets into the human body mainly through rice irrigated with arsenic-contaminated water (usually surface water). Therefore, cultivating rice using arsenic-contaminated water should, in fact, be banned in the country.

Climate change and natural resource scarcity

A number of studies have shown that Bangladesh is one of the most vulnerable countries to climate change and variability impacts. Temperature ranges from 36.7 to 40.6°C and from 10 to 27.5°C during summer and winter seasons, respectively (Khan *et al.*, 2011). According to the 5th Intergovernmental Panel on Climate Change (IPCC) report, average temperatures will increase by 1.8 to 3.4°C by 2050.

The IPCC forecast that global warming will result in sea level rises of between 0.18 and 0.79m, which could increase coastal flooding and saline intrusion into aquifers and rivers across a wide belt of southern Bangladesh, although most of the area is protected by polders (MoEF, 2008). There will be erratic rainfall coupled with a shorter monsoon period and slightly higher rainfall in the winter season (IPCC, 2013). This will result in more frequent droughts and scarcity of fresh water that will create further challenges to agriculture and food production in the country. Droughts have a direct impact on water availability, land degradation, livestock population, employment and health. It was estimated that about 17 percent of a wet season crop could be lost because of drought in Bangladesh (NPDM, 2010). The northwestern regions of Bangladesh are particularly vulnerable to droughts, significantly affecting crop yields (Mahatab and Karim, 2002).

Temperature and rainfall changes can affect *T. aman* rice that is totally dependent on seasonal rainfall. Under a moderate climate change scenario, it is predicted that *aus* (summer rice) production would decline by 27 percent while wheat production would be reduced to 61 percent of its current level (Karim *et al.*, 1998). Water scarcity might force farmers to reduce the area under *boro* (dry season irrigated rice) crop cultivation. In the case of severe drought, forced by a change of temperature of +2.0°C and a 10 percent reduction in precipitation, run-off in the Ganges, Brahmaputra and Maghna rivers would be reduced by 32, 25 and 17 percent, respectively (Mirza and Dixit, 1997). This would limit surface irrigation potential in the drought-vulnerable areas, thus challenging the national food security program.

On the other hand, prolonged floods would tend to delay *T. aman* planting. Loss of *boro* crop from flash floods has become a regular phenomenon during the months of June to November over recent years. Evidence shows that the food availability and accessibility is poorer in flood prone areas than for the average national rural level. This has considerable effects on the health and productivity of the people in the region already affected by extreme weather events.

Both *T. aman* and *boro* outputs are volatile, but with lower magnitude in the case of *boro* rice. *T. aman* rice output is highly volatile due to its susceptibility to natural hazards such as flash flood, storm and drought resulting in a significant reduction in output (BER, 2012). The nature of volatility of *boro* output is just the opposite of *T. aman*, with changes mostly on the positive side. In fact, the positive *boro* output change often counterbalances the negative output changes in *T. aman* (BER, 2012). Absence of abiotic and climatic stresses during *boro* season makes the environment conducive to attaining higher yields in this season, and hence efforts to increase and sustain *boro* rice production is favorable for Bangladesh, the disadvantage being a less diversified crop production. If the current rice production meets the demand, increasing crop diversity should be given high priority.

Developing stress-tolerant and short-duration rice varieties to boost *T. aman* production could be another option. Achieving a higher output is also possible by focusing on regions where crop agriculture has comparatively lagged behind, particularly in southwest Bangladesh. It has been observed that all districts showing low yields of rice are in the south-western region, particularly along the coast;

while those showing more than 2.5 metric tons of yield per hectare fall in Jessore, Kushtia, Chittagong, Comilla, Dhaka and Mymensingh districts. Major challenges to crop yields in the coastal districts are salinity during the dry period, waterlogging and drainage congestion in many areas and the storm surges during cyclones, which make agriculture riskier. Considering all the direct and induced adverse effects of climate change on agriculture, one may conclude that crop agriculture and communities would be even more vulnerable in Bangladesh in a warmer world (WB, 2000).

Seasonal food insecurity, locally called *monga*, is also prevalent in ecologically vulnerable and economically weaker regions of northwestern Bangladesh, primarily because of poor employment and income deficiency before *T. aman* is harvested. It mainly affects those rural poor whose only source of income is directly or indirectly based on agriculture. Providing diversified livelihoods, improving rural infrastructure and reducing vulnerability may help to improve the food and nutritional security in the vulnerable regions of the country.

Land will be one of the most limiting factors in countries such as Bangladesh due to urbanization and increasing demand. Improved soil and water management thus is crucial to reduce the vulnerability owing to droughts and increased land and water use efficiency. Measures to increase on-farm water conservation and short-duration or drought tolerant varieties should be introduced to conserve the soil moisture in the drought prone regions. Higher discharge and low drainage capacity combined with increased backwater effects would increase the frequency of devastating floods under climate change scenarios.

Price shocks

Increase in the price of food grains is a very sensitive matter for countries such as Bangladesh where more than 50 percent of the people spend about two-thirds of their income on purchasing food. The prices of rice, wheat, coarse grains and oilseed crops almost doubled between 2005 and 2011 and increased further in early 2012, putting pressure on the middle and lower income groups' household budgets. A report (*Daily Star*, 2011) showed that a 10 percent increase in food price had actually pushed a large number of people from the marginal to below the poverty line in Bangladesh. The price hike in 2013 has pushed an even larger portion of the lower-middle class to stand in the open market sale line to procure cheaper rice. High food prices lower the purchasing power of a nominal income household and therefore affect expenditure decisions. Since nominal wage rates tend to adjust to price increases only after a time lag, and even then often only partially, price inflation leads to decline in real wages, which again lowers consumption and reduces economic growth (FPMU, 2013). In addition, price inflation hollows out the real value of savings, which may lead to lower investment, thus further compromising economic growth. As a result of diminished real income, households may respond to higher food prices by reducing consumption, thereby falling into the undernutrition category, and/or adjusting their consumption bundle, as a response to changed relative prices.

For the urban poor, the impacts will be strongly negative, as an even higher share of their limited income will be required to purchase food. This increase in agricultural commodity price therefore has a significant consequence on the general public and is also a cause of food insecurity and hunger both temporally and spatially in Bangladesh.

Responses to food insecurity

Agricultural subsidies and food production

Farmers are squeezed by both higher input and energy costs and price fluctuations in national and international markets. The Government of Bangladesh provides a number of subsidies to support farmers and sustain food production. Fertilizer subsidies represent the largest element of public expenditure in agriculture and play a significant role in boosting food production in the country. In fact, fertilizer subsidies doubled in the years 2007/08 to 2011/12 and accounted for 4.3 percent of total government spending. With substantial reallocation, the share of subsidies for urea went down to only one-third of the total subsidy, compared to 89 percent in 2007/08. While urea subsidies were cut by a quarter, non-urea subsidies increased by 12 times. The reallocation of subsidies, combined with price dynamics on international markets, have driven changes in absolute and relative prices of the four main fertilizers. Farmers need to improve the current fertilizer use efficiency that is possible through soil testing and soil mapping of individual farms, and to apply the required amount of fertilizers and supplement with organic and microbial fertilizers wherever possible. This helps in reducing the amount of chemical fertilizers applied, costs to farmers and further environmental impacts.

The distribution of subsidy for agricultural inputs steadily increased over the years 2001–13. In the year 2011/12, farmers also received irrigation subsidies. In addition, in pursuit of self-sufficiency in food grains production and to make the best use of all government-sponsored facilities, in 2010 the government launched the new helpline Agricultural Input Assistant Card and Cash Assistance Program to assist the farmers in cash and kind. Under this program, farmers receive money from the banks as a cash subsidy to buy diesel and other inputs. For drawing subsidies and monetary transactions, farmers can easily open a bank account with a very nominal initial deposit, affordable even to very poor households. The policy for input subsidization is to keep the cost of production low for the food grain producers, so that they do not get discouraged from growing food grains on account of liquidity constraints and otherwise high prices of inputs as well as fluctuating market prices. But the big question is, do subsidies in Bangladesh promote sustainable agricultural growth?

Food prices in Bangladesh are very unstable and fluctuate violently, fall in the post-harvest months and increase later in the year. Stabilizing prices may secure farmers' incomes as well as sustain production. Several measures could be considered to help farmers to get a better share of the sale price, which include: (1) fixation of minimum support price by the government; (2) purchase of the commodity if price falls below that level; and (3) development of warehouse facilities for post-harvest storage.

The internal public procurement of food grains from domestic production is a major method of the government's price intervention policy. This policy can achieve the following objectives such as: (1) stabilizing internal food grains prices; (2) encouraging production through price incentives to the rice growers; (3) preventing the smuggling of food grains across the border; and (4) ensuring adequate supplies for the public food grains distribution system. The procurement price is normally announced by the government before the harvesting of major crops. Farmers usually fail to take such benefit directly because they do not meet the required standards and, in the process, middlemen get the benefits.

Public measures to improve food and nutrition security

The government has initiated a number of measures to address food and nutrition security. Some government programs provide poor people with in-kind or cash transfers to supplement food acquisition capacity. There are other programs such as the Food for Asset Creation (FFA) where rice is provided that makes up about 60 percent of the food given through Income-Generating Vulnerable Group Development (IGVGD). Food provided through Food Security Vulnerable Group Development (FSVGD) is almost entirely micronutrient-fortified wheat flour (Ahmed *et al.*, 2009). The IGVGD participants receive food transfers on a monthly basis, while food transfers under the FSVGD are less regular. Cash payments were observed to be irregular in all three programs. The main reasons for the irregularity of cash transfers to FSVGD participants are often due to: (1) delays in fund release from donor to the Government of Bangladesh (GoB); and (2) irregular flow of funds from the Bangladesh Bank to local commercial bank branches. The GoB operates an open market sales system to face sudden supply shortages of the general consumers' daily essentials such as coarse rice, pulses, edible oil, onion and garlic.

The GoB also implements a number of safety net programs through various ministries, state divisions and sometimes in collaboration with international donor organizations. The social safety net program for the elderly (i.e. Old Age Allowance Scheme) has been found moderately useful in fulfilling various needs of elderly people. The support, albeit small, provides the recipients with a sense of security as well as empowerment. In the past, it enhanced not only food security but also, to a certain extent, mobility, medical care, access to credit and respect from family members (Bhattacharjee *et al.*, 2012). Short-term or seasonal programs provide poor households with quick or emergency cash or food support to minimize the impact of natural disasters. Food for Work and Cash for Work are the short-term programs.

There are some long-term programs that offer both cash and food support throughout the year: the Employment Generation Program for the Poorest (EGPP), Vulnerable Group Development (VGD) and Vulnerable Group Feeding (VGF) are long-term programs. The EGPP specifically addresses seasonal vulnerability and is one of the largest public safety net programs in Bangladesh. Initiated in 1975, as a relief program for families affected by natural calamities, the EGPP program today exclusively targets rural women, integrating food security and nutrition with development and income generation. This program in a way addresses the overall food security dimension and empowers women in the household. In 2005/06 alone, some 750,000 ultra-poor rural women received support from EGPP. The VGD program operates through two components: Income Generation for Vulnerable Group Development (IGVGD), which covers 85 percent of total VGD beneficiaries; and Food Security for Vulnerable Group Development (FSVGD), covering 15 percent of VGD beneficiaries. These programs need to be strengthened as they contribute to food security at the household level for the poorest sections of society.

The Rural Maintenance Program (RMP) is another example of government support to improve food security, originally introduced in 1983 by the international non-governmental organization (NGO) CARE and is now under the Ministry of Local Government, Rural Development and Cooperatives. In February 2002, the GoB and the WFP together introduced a new program, entitled Integrated Food Security. The purpose of the program is to allocate resources to the most food insecure areas in the country as identified by vulnerability analysis and mapping and to target ultra-poor individuals living in these areas. The Integrated Food Security program has three components: food for asset creation (FFA), community nutrition initiative, and training and nutrition centers (Ahmed *et al.*, 2009). FFA participants receive food and cash compensation for infrastructure development work at various times of the year.

The FFA component has been designed to promote human and capital resource development for the ultra-poor by providing awareness and training in legal, social, health and nutrition issues by enabling participants to work for community infrastructure development and productive asset creation. The Local Government Engineering Department under the Ministry of Local Government Rural Development and Cooperatives coordinates FFA activities. Both women and men participate in FFA, but at least 70 percent of the participants must be women. User committees are formed from among the participants and the committees are responsible for organizing village-based micro planning to identify participants in FFA activities. Participants in the FFA component receive both food and cash compensation subject to the amount of work done within the program.

A study by the International Food Policy Research Institute (IFPRI) demonstrates that, out of four programs (IGVGD, FSVGD, FFA, and RMP), transfer, as a percentage of household expenditure, is highest for FFA, at 38.2 percent, followed by RMP (30.2 percent), IGVGD (15.5 percent), and FSVGD (15.0 percent) (Ahmed *et al.*, 2009). The same study reported that among the four programs, FFA has shown the best results and targeted, helping to lift 72 percent of its beneficiaries above the poorest 10 percent of the population. Using data from the Household Income and Expenditure Surveys (HIES) 2000 and 2005, Khandker *et al.* (2011) found that VGF decreased poverty among its beneficiaries, and programs such as FFW reduced both seasonal and chronic poverty (Table 5.5).

Table 5.5 Bangladesh's major safety net programs.

Programs	Beneficiary group	Requirement	Cash/kind	Key features
Rural Maintenance Program	Women able to work	Work	Cash	Public works program; average payment of Tk. 43 per day
Primary Education Stipend Project	Households	Schooling	Cash	Program to promote school enrollment and attendance, reduce dropout rate
Female Secondary School Assistance Program	Households	Schooling	Cash	Program to promote and encourage continuing education for females
Old Age Allowance	Households with elderly members unable to work without pension or income	No work requirement	Food grain	Allowance to reduce vulnerability of households with elderly members in non-municipal areas; average payment is Tk. 165 per month
Food for Work (FFW)	Individuals able to work	Work mostly in infrastructure development	Food grain	Food transfer program to reduce food vulnerability among the poor; in 2003, provided food in exchange for some 75 million hours of work
Test Relief	Individuals able to work	Works related to cleaning ponds and bushes	Food grain	Food transfer program to reduce food vulnerability among poor individuals and households in rural areas; much smaller program than FFW
Vulnerable Group Development (VGD)	Households	No work requirement	Food grain	Food transfer program that trains vulnerable groups in life and work skills; since June 2004 had provided food to some 480,000 households
Vulnerable Group Feeding (VGF)	Households	No work requirement	Food grain	Food transfer program that offers post-disaster food relief to selected households; during the 1998 flood, about 6 million households benefited
Gratuitous Relief	Households	No work requirement	Food grain	Key government food transfer program offering vulnerable groups immediate, short-term relief following natural and other disasters; much smaller program than the VGD or VGF

Source: Adopted from Khandker et al., 2011.

Research and development of new crop varieties

Empirical evidences indicated that investment in crop research in Bangladesh has a high pay-off, although the allocation of funds for agricultural research is only about 0.32 percent of agricultural GDP (Ministry of Food, 2013). Thus, there exists potential for investing more in agricultural research. There is a 1–2 tons/ha rice yield gap between the potential and actual yields on the farmers' fields. Similar magnitudes of yield gap are also evident in the case of wheat, potato, maize and vegetables. Improving yield levels will ultimately help to ensure food security.

Research programs are in the process of developing new crop varieties that can adapt to drought and salinity. Various national institutes have undertaken research to develop stress-tolerant and short-duration rice crop varieties. These varieties are popular across the country and have contributed to sustaining rice production, despite the adverse climatic conditions.

With the rapid adoption of modern rice varieties, its total production has increased greatly. During 1972–80, the share in total production was only 29 percent, but by the year 1980/1985, it increased to 41 percent and further triggered to 65 percent during 1991–95. However, the share of modern rice to total production has jumped to nearly 90 percent by 2008/09, implying a highly impressive contribution of the diffusion of modern rice technologies in Bangladesh. Since the 1970s, the adoption of high yielding modern varieties (MVs) has led to a 3.5 fold increase in total production in the recent years. The dissemination of MVs was accelerated by the Department of Agricultural Extension (DAE), NGOs and farmer-to-farmer contact. Conducive irrigation and fertilizer policies helped further adoption of MVs resulting in higher yields and national production, but indiscriminate use of fertilizers has had negative effects on soils and water bodies, leading to pollution.

Together with the development of new crop varieties, the farmers need to practice sustainable soil and land management measures to cope with salinity and drought (e.g. the use of ash and an additional 20kg/ha potash in the field to sustain rice production in saline areas). Farmers are also adopting some innovative practices (namely, zero tillage, priming of seeds during sowing, mulching, relay cropping, dry seeding, rainwater harvest, etc.) in the drought prone areas, and zero tillage (the *sorjan* system) of floating bed agriculture, etc. in flood prone and the salinity/tidal surge areas of Bangladesh. However, farmers need continuous support through targeted training, capacity building and inputs to adopt the new crop varieties and technologies over a wide area. Private sector investments should be encouraged in the agriculture sector to facilitate future growth.

Public sector research-extension linkages are governed by some formal regulations, and the technology dissemination process in the public sector is considered rather protracted, which explains why it takes much longer than expected to reach the end users. The NGO sector can directly contact the researchers and demonstrate the tried and tested technologies for validation. A good example, after the storm *Sidr* in southern Bangladesh when there was a serious damage of assets and crops, is how NGOs provided financial and technological intervention packages to restore the victims' livelihoods. NGOs developed local entrepreneurs for providing land preparation and irrigation services to the farmers through their microcredit programs. There is also a need to screen out and improve rice varieties for lower uptake of arsenic and cadmium by grains.

Improved seeds/supply of quality inputs to improve productivity

Quality seed is a key element for enhancing the production of a crop. The Government of Bangladesh considers the seed sector a main priority to boost production levels. The National Agricultural Extension Policy (NAEP, 2012) emphasizes the development of quality seeds by proposing to encourage the private sector in undertaking breeding programs and to import foundation/breeder seeds for notified crops. Moreover, it calls for a strengthening of the seed certification process, in order to support the private sector which endeavors to meet the increasing demand for quality seeds.

Over the past decade, multiple activities have been undertaken with the support of numerous development partners such as Australia, Belgium, Denmark, Germany, the Netherlands, the USA, the EU and the FAO. The key government agencies involved in food production are the Bangladesh Agricultural Development Corporation (BADC), the Bangladesh Agricultural Research Institution (BARI), the Bangladesh Rice Research Institute (BRRI) and the Department of Agricultural Extension. Among them, BADC remains the largest national producer of foundation seeds, producing quality seeds for rice, wheat, maize, jute, vegetables, spices, potato, pulse and oilseeds, through seed multiplication farms and 75 contract growers' zones. In 2011, BADC set a target to produce 143,000 tons of seeds including 91,000 tons of rice seeds. Against that target of production, 131,000 tons of seeds were actually distributed (BER, 2011).

With more than 100 companies, over 8,000 registered seed dealers and thousands of farmers contracted to produce seed, the private sector has been expanding its presence from high-value vegetable seeds to include rice and maize hybrids. This demonstrates the importance of private sector and public-private partnerships in ensuring food production and food security in the country. Moreover, at least 20 NGOs have been increasingly involved in seed production and distribution as part of their relief and livelihood promotion interventions. The Bangladesh Rural Advancement Committee (BRAC) has become a major stakeholder in the sector through one seed company, 23 seed producing farms and one agricultural research center, having an annual capacity to produce 5,200 tons of certified quality seeds of hybrid maize, rice, onion, pulses, oil crops and potatoes (Ministry of Food, 2013).

As part of its commitment to promote climate resilient agricultural practices in Bangladesh, the International Finance Corporation (IFC) is working with four large private seed companies to demonstrate the business case for stress-tolerant seeds. IFC aims to support farmers in adapting to climate change as well as strengthening food security and social inclusion by increasing the production, distribution and adoption of stress-tolerant seed varieties; and by involving rural women in seed production in remote areas and linking them to the seed supply chain (IFC Bulletin, 2012). However, these efforts are not adequate and need to be up-scaled to other regions.

Technology options

The overall potential of agro-processing is huge for countries like Bangladesh and it has not yet been properly utilized. Agro-processing can reduce wastage, enhance food security, improve livelihoods for the poorest and empower women through simple technologies for dehydration, pickling, bottling, pulping and preparing preserves and relishes from a variety of vegetables and fruits. As part of the nutrition improvement strategy through agro-processing, FAO's Integrated Horticulture and Nutrition Development Project (IHNDP) developed and promoted a wide range of processed foods at household and community levels (FAO, 2007) reaching a total of 31,400 men and women.

Rural credit

The Bangladesh Bank has expanded credit supply in recent years, with disbursements in 2011/12 showing an increase of 8 percent over the previous year, in line with inflation. Targeting smallholder farmers' and sharecroppers' cultivation under 200 decimals (247decimals = 1hectare), the Bank provided 5 billion taka (Tk.) to BRAC's *Borga Chashi Unnayan* Program, which provides agricultural credit at 5 percent interest rate, through village organizations that manage the credit and promote savings (Ministry of Food, 2013). Loan duration varies between six and ten months; one-third of the loan is repaid in monthly installments and the remainder at the end of the cropping season or just after harvest. With the credit scheme's rising popularity, the number of beneficiaries grew from 238,071 in 2010 to 578,210 in 2013 (Ministry of Food, 2013).

A recent study found that access to formal credit significantly correlates to agricultural production and food security, particularly for marginal and smallholder farmers (Ministry of Food, 2013). Farmers borrowed for advanced *boro* rice production, where irrigation and other input costs surpass equity financing. Home-based and commercial poultry, fishery and livestock rearing often seek bank credit for financing the activities.

Conclusions and recommendations

Measures to promote food production

Modern science and technology, if properly used, offers tremendous opportunities for improving the food security status of current and future generations. This should be accompanied by capacity building and inputs to be made readily available to farmers. A sustainable growth pattern is important for Bangladesh to meet the future challenge of increased production and food security. Faced with the challenges of increasing population, limited availability of agricultural land and water resources and increasing food prices, the country needs to adopt a multi-pronged strategy to deal with the situation. It can start by taking measures towards increasing productivity: diversifying to other crops, learning from recent experiences in rice production and cutting down on significant post-harvest yield losses. Diversification of the food basket to attain self-sufficiency in non-cereal food grains for improving nutritional value is needed. The various levels of government, NGOs and local community in Bangladesh should cooperate and establish participatory governance to address food insecurity issues. They should develop tangible technology options to ensure food production. Some of the recommendations to increase food production are discussed below. They begin with measures that government agencies and farmers have to adopt to address climate change impacts.

- In the flood prone regions of Bangladesh, the Water Development Board and local governments should engage in the construction of embankments with adequate sluice gates to protect agricultural lands and vulnerable farming communities.
- In other areas, the government should take up the excavation and re-excavation of canals, ponds, ditches and the construction of sluice gates on the canal outlets. Construction of water reservoirs where possible and improving irrigation facilities in the northwestern region will help in the expansion of irrigated agriculture.
- Local government, NGOs and community can develop a contingency plan for the planting of deep-rooted trees and fruit plants on embankment areas and newly formed land to protect them from cyclones, tornadoes and storm surges. Social and community forestry programs should be intensified, involving village councils and local people.
- Research and innovation are needed to promote climate-smart farming systems, changes in cropping practices and irrigation methods. Production technologies need to be developed to adapt and mitigate climate change impacts, especially drought- and saline-tolerant rice and other crop varieties. Special emphasis should also be given to develop high yielding deep-water rice varieties.
- Improving access to technology and information should be a priority for the government. This can be done by modernizing extension services across the country and use of advanced communication technologies including mobile phone services to disseminate information to farmers.

On the market front, farmers should be ensured minimum prices for their produce. Though the government has initiated some measures, they are not adequate to protect small-scale farmers from market fluctuations. Improving the market environment calls for various measures, for example: (1) the development of market infrastructure, storage and movements for private trade; (2) provision of incentives for the private sector, such as non-discriminatory credit; (3) enforcement of quality standards; (4) and selective non-distortionary public food market intervention for price stabilization. Agriculture in the future should attract more investments from both government and private agencies.

The production of oilseeds, pulses and other crops should be encouraged in the country to meet the current demand and to reduce imports. This is possible in the dry zones where water scarcity is an increasing problem and rice cultivation is no longer advisable in such regions. Dissemination of quality seeds of improved crop varieties other than rice is a key element for enhancing a diversified production. Initiatives to produce quality seed and its distribution have to be intensified at a fair price, taking into consideration the purchasing power of farmers. Good seed should be made readily available for farmers located in the vulnerable regions prone to droughts and floods. Vertical or pyramid culture for vegetable production is gaining popularity in the southern saline and flood prone belt of Bangladesh. This is positive and such measures should be encouraged.

Improvement of adaptive capacity of the farming community is required primarily to develop resilience. Soft measures including training, education and alternative means of livelihood system are effective to a large extent besides technological and institutional support.

Measures to promote food access and nutritional security

The Government of Bangladesh has implemented a number of programs to increase the food availability and access for the poorer sections of society, which have been discussed earlier in the chapter. However, there is a need to improve the efficiency and transparency of these programs. The right beneficiaries should be targeted and quality of food grains provided through these programs should be improved.

Access to food can also be improved through government strategies such as providing supplementary nutrition to children (such as midday meals in schools) and pregnant women, the provision of unemployment and pension benefits and development of food banks and food distribution systems for the indigent people (safety nets). By implementing these programs properly, the country can, to a large extent, effectively address food insecurity (Fatima, 2012). Efficient local and regional food markets will ensure an unhindered flow of goods and services across time and space.

Improving nutritional security in Bangladesh should start by diversifying its food basket to attain self-sufficiency in the non-cereal food grains. At the same time, the government should encourage consumption of diversified foods through change in diets to ensure nutritional quality at the household level (Akanda, 2010). It is a known fact that proper nutrition and human health depend on the production and availability of a diversified food basket.

To some extent, encouraging home gardens in rural areas can improve the household dietary patterns. The country can improve utilization of diversified foods through targeted campaigning and educating the people on nutrition and health. Improving knowledge on food-based nutrition (right methods of cooking, balanced diet from locally available food) will help the poor households' access to nutritious food. Careful promotion of fortified foodstuffs can also be done as this provides a proven and cost-effective strategy for dealing with micronutrient deficiencies.

Ready access to credit is relevant for small-scale farmers, especially in periods of droughts and floods, in order to cope with losses. Access to credit has also made the lease of additional land possible and helped communities to expand non-farm activities, as well as overall social development (Ministry of Food, 2013).

Policy interventions

The goal of the first National Food Policy, which was adopted in 1988, was to achieve food security for all people by increasing food production and attaining self-sufficiency. The declared goal of food policy is to ensure food security for all people at all times. Food policy in the Bangladesh context is a multisectoral issue involving several ministries and agencies, who, through their respective programs and strategies, aim to achieve the common goal of establishing a food security system. Formulation of an effective integrated food and nutritional security policy was therefore a matter of utmost importance for Bangladesh. As a consequence, the Comprehensive Food Security Policy for Bangladesh (CFSPB) started in Bangladesh in 2002 but its implementation has been weak. Through this policy, a high priority is given to strengthen and harmonize the government's efforts to ensure food security for all. It was initiated by revisiting all existing related policies and strategies addressing food security in the country. Moreover, the Country Investment Plan (CIP) of Bangladesh is a result-based tool aiming to improve food security in a comprehensive manner. The CIP was prepared by the GoB involving a wide range of ministries, agencies and departments, with the Food Planning Monitoring Unit (under the Ministry of Food and Disaster Management) playing a coordination role. The current policies and programs offer immense opportunities for the country to improve the food security situation in the country. The government and Bangladeshi people must rise to the occasion and use the opportunities to fight food insecurity in the coming years.

References

Ahmed, A.U., Quisumbing, A.R., Nasreen, M., Hoddinott, J.F. and Bryan, E. (2009) Comparing food and cash transfers to the ultra-poor in Bangladesh. International Food Policy Research Institute, Washington, DC. 20006–1002, *Research Monograph*, 163: 1–224.

Akanda, A.I. (2010) Rethinking crop diversification under changing climate, hydrology and food habit in Bangladesh, *Journal of Agriculture and Environment for International Development*, 104 (1–2): 21.

Asaduzzaman, M., Ringler, C., Thurlow, J. and Alam, S. (2010) Investing in crop agriculture in Bangladesh for high growth and productivity and adaptation to climate change. Prepared for the Bangladesh Food Security Investment Forum, 10 May, p. 6.

Bangladesh Bureau of Statistics (BBS) (2009) Statistical Year Book of Bangladesh, Statistics Division, Ministry of Planning, Government of the People's Republic of Bangladesh, Dhaka, p. 69.

Bangladesh Bureau of Statistics (BBS) (2011) Statistical Year Book of Bangladesh, Statistics Division, Ministry of Planning, Government of the People's Republic of Bangladesh, Dhaka, pp. 49, 59, 128.

Bangladesh Bureau of Statistics (BBS) (2012) Statistical Year Book of Bangladesh, Statistics Division, Ministry of Planning, Government of the People's Republic of Bangladesh, Dhaka, p.128.

Bangladesh Economic Review (BER) (2010) Bangladesh Economic Review, Finance Division, Ministry of Finance, Government of the People's Republic of Bangladesh, Dhaka.

Bangladesh Economic Review (BER) (2011) Bangladesh Economic Review, Ministry of Finance, Government of Bangladesh, Dhaka, p. 82.

Bangladesh Economic Review (BER) (2012) Bangladesh Economic Review, Finance Division, Ministry of Finance, Dhaka, pp. 18, 78.

Baqui, M.A. (2005) Post-harvest processing, handling, and preservation of agricultural products: its present status and future challenges in Bangladesh, FMPHT Division, Bangladesh Rice Research Institute (BRRI), Gazipur, pp. 10.

Basak, J.K., Ali, M.A., Islam, M.N. and Rashid, M.A. (2010) Assessment of the effect of climate change on *boro* rice production in Bangladesh using DSSAT model, *Journal of Civil Engineering*, 38 (2): 95–108.

Bhattacharjee, M.K, Hasan, M.K, Mahmuda, A. and Khan, A. (2012) Impact of social safety net programmes on elderly people in rural areas, Bangladesh Academy for Rural Development, Kotbari, pp. 24–5.

Daily Star (2011) Food price hike: role of government, online, http://archive.thedailystar. net/newDesign/news-details.php?nid=170979:18 (accessed 2 May 2014).

Department of Fisheries (DoF) (2009) Fishery, Statistical Yearbook of Bangladesh, Department of Fisheries, Bangladesh, Dhaka, p. 42.

Fatima, S. (2012) Bangladesh – striving for food security, online, http://www.saglobalaffairs. com/ back-issues/1319-bangladesh-striving-for-food-security.html (accessed 2 August 2013).

Food and Agriculture Organization (FAO) (2007) Experience of integrated horticulture and nutrition development in food-based nutrition strategies in Bangladesh, Regional Office for Asia and the Pacific, Bangkok: pp. 1–68.

Food and Agriculture Organization (FAO), IFAD and WFP (2013) The state of food insecurity in the world 2013: the multiple dimensions of food security, FAO, Rome, pp. 29–31.

Food Planning and Monitoring Unit (FPMU) (2008) Food balance sheet of Bangladesh. Food Planning and Monitoring Unit, Dhaka, p. 2.

Food Planning and Monitoring Unit (FPMU) (2013) Food balance sheet of Bangladesh. Food Planning and Monitoring Unit, Dhaka, pp. 2–3.

Household Income and Expenditure Survey (HIES) (2010) Report of the household income and expenditure survey 2010. Statistics Division, Bangladesh Bureau of Statistics, Ministry of Planning, Dhaka, p. 61.

Hossain, M., Lewis, D., Bose, M.L. and Chowdhury, A. (2007) Rice research technologies progress and poverty: the Bangladesh case. In Adato, M. and Meinzen-Dick, R.S. (Eds) *Agricultural Research, Livelihoods and Poverty: Studies of Economic and Social Impact in Six Countries*. The Johns Hopkins University Press, Baltimore: 56–102.

IFC (2012) Agri-seed: making Bangladesh's agricultural sector more sustainable, online, http://www1.ifc.org/wps/wcm/connect/tops_ext_content/ifc_external_corporate_ site/ifc+sustainability/sustainable+business+advisory+services/project+examples/ sba-project-agriseed (accessed 15 June 2013).

Intergovernmental Panel on Climate Change (IPCC) (2013) Climate change: the physical science basis, approved summary for policymakers. Working Group I Contribution to the Fifth Assessment Report, Twelfth Session of Working Group 1. IPCC Report 5, pp. 1–36.

Islam, M.A., Quyaum, M.A. and Salam, M.A. (2011) Long-term growth analysis of food grains in Bangladesh. Internal review report, Agricultural Economics Division, BRRI, Gazipur.

Islam, M.R., Jahiruddin, M., Islam, M.R., Alim, M.A. and Akhtaruzzaman, M. (2013) Consumption of unsafe foods: evidence from heavy metal, mineral and trace element contamination. Report presented in the national food policy capacity strengthening programme and implemented by the FPMU, Ministry of Food and FAO, Dhaka.

Karim, Z. (2009) Climate change inputs on Bangladesh: policy, strategy and management interventions. Presented at the Consultative Workshop on Climate Change Impacts on Agriculture and Food Security, Organized by Ministry of Agriculture, Government of the People's Republic of Bangladesh in Collaboration with the FAO at CIRDAP Auditorium, Dhaka.

Karim, Z., Hussain, Sk. G. and Ahmed, A.U. (1998) Climate Change Vulnerability of Crop Agriculture. In: Huq, S., Karim, Z., Asaduzzaman, M. and Mahtab, F. (Eds) *Vulnerability and Adaptation to Climate Change for Bangladesh*. Kluwer Academic Publishers, Dordrecht.

Khan, M.S., Sen, R., Noor, S., Naser, H.M. and Alam, M.K.M. (2011) Soil, water and climate related constraints for crop production in Bangladesh. In: Lal, R., Sivkumar, M.V., Fiaz, S.M.A., Rahman Mustafizur, A.H.M. and Islam, K.R. (Eds) *Climate Change and Food Security in South Asia*. Springer Dordrecht, Heidelberg and London.

Khandker, S.R., Khaleque, M.A. and Samad, H.A. (2011) Can social safety nets alleviate seasonal deprivation? Evidence from Northwest Bangladesh Agriculture and Rural Development Team; World Bank, Washington, DC.

Linda, A.D., Johnson, D.S., Warren, R.S., Peterson, B.J., Fleeger, J.W., Fagherazzi, S. and Wollheim, W.M. (2012) Loss of salt marsh bodies due to constant enrichment of nutrients (eutrophication), *Nature*, 490: 388–92.

Mahatab, U. and Karim, Z. (2002) *Natural Hazards in Bangladesh*. 1st ed. Bangladesh Agricultural Research Council (BARC), Dhaka.

Ministry of Environment and Forests (MoEF) (2008) Bangladesh Climate Change Strategy and Action Plan 2008. Ministry of Environment and Forests, Government of the People's Republic of Bangladesh, Dhaka: pp. 25, 68.

Ministry of Finance (MoF) (2010) GDP, Saving and Investment. Bangladesh Economic Review, Finance Division, Dhaka.

Ministry of Food (2013) Monitoring Report. Food Planning and Monitoring Unit, Ministry of Food, Dhaka. pp. 39–51.

Mirza, M.M. and Dixit, A. (1997) Climate change and water management in the GBM basins, *Water Nepal*, 5 (1): 71–100.

Mukherjee, N., Choudhury, G.A., Khan, M.F.A. and Islam, A.K.M.S. (2011) Implications of changing consumption pattern on food security and water resources in Bangladesh, Third International Conference for Water and Flood Management, 8–10 January, BUET, Swasti Printers, Dhaka (2): 731–7.

National Agricultural Extension Policy (NAEP) (2012) National Agricultural Extension Policy, Ministry of Agriculture, Government of the People's Republic of Bangladesh. Dhaka, p. 46.

National Plan for Disaster Management (NPDM) (2010) National Plan for Disaster Management, Disaster Management Bureau, Disaster Management and Relief Division, Government of the People's Republic of Bangladesh, Dhaka, p. 103.

Pavel, E.H. (2013) Great success by the government in agriculture sector, *Daily Janata*, 3 July, p. 5.

Streatfield, P.K. and Karar, Z.A. (2008) Population challenges for Bangladesh in the coming decades, *Journal of Health Population and Nutrition*, 26 (3): 261–72.

Talukder, R.K. (2008) Food security in Bangladesh: national and global perspective. Paper presented at the 13th National Conference and Seminar on Climate Changes: Food Security in Bangladesh. Bangladesh Agricultural Economist Association, 30 August, Dhaka: pp. 12.

Thornton, P. and Herrero, M. (2008) Climate change, vulnerability and livestock keepers: challenges for poverty alleviation. Proceedings of the Conference on Livestock and Global Change, 17–20 May, Tunisia, Hammamet, pp. 1–33.

World Bank (WB) (2000) Bangladesh: climate change and sustainable development. Report No. 21104-BD, Rural Development Unit, South Asia Region, World Bank, Dhaka, p. 95.

World Bank (WB) (2013) World Bank Group–Bangladesh: country program snapshot, World Bank, South Asia Region, Dhaka.

World Food Program (WFP) (2013) Food security atlas, online, http://www.foodsecurityatlas. org/bgd/ country/availability (accessed 18 March 2013).

6 Food security in India

The need for sustainable food systems

Udaya Sekhar Nagothu

Introduction

Throughout the history of human existence, food and water have held centre stage in the development of civilizations. India, the second most populous country in the world, must provide food security to more than a billion people under challenging conditions, and while meeting the export demand. The country recorded an overall economic growth rate of 8 per cent from 2007 to 2012, despite the global recession (Gulati *et al.*, 2012). However, during the same period the agriculture sector underperformed with a growth rate of only 2.8 per cent. The agriculture sector is fundamental to India's economy. Over 55 per cent of the population depend on agriculture for their livelihoods and agriculture contributes about 18 per cent of the country's GDP (GoI, 2013). More than 80 per cent of farm holdings in India are less than 2 hectares and more than 60 per cent of farmers operate on less than 1 hectare (GoI, 2007). Hence, any underperformance in agriculture will impact the livelihoods of millions of rural households in the country. The various agricultural development strategies adopted by the government since the 1950s have no doubt contributed to agricultural growth and food production at the macro level, but without significantly improving nutrition or reducing poverty at the household level. Estimates show that 22 per cent of the population in India is still undernourished (FAO, 2011). Throughout the world, India has the highest number of children suffering from malnutrition. Hence, there is a clear disconnect between economic growth, agricultural performance and food security indicators. According to Sen (1981, 2009), lack of entitlements and poverty are some of the main reasons for hunger and malnutrition in India. Social and economic institutional arrangements in India largely determine an individual's access to food and nutritional security (Pritchard *et al.*, 2014).

In recent years, the importance of addressing nutrition and poverty has been recognized. The government has recently initiated large-scale food and nutrition programmes targeting pregnant women, children and the poor across the country. In July 2013, India introduced the Food Security Act, a landmark legal measure that makes the government accountable to make food accessible to every citizen in the country (Swaminathan, 2013). There are both critics as well as supporters of this new policy. The impact of this new policy on the country's food and nutrition security status in the coming years will be a telling outcome of the government's level of commitment to food security and capacity to ensure good governance.

This chapter provides an overview of the current food security status in India and future directions. It will not be possible to detail all of the elements of food security; the aim is to cover the most relevant issues. The next section explores the key factors that impact the current food security (food production, access and nutrition) status in India. Factors including science and technology, demography, climate change, globalization and trade, inequality and poverty, and their implications on food and nutrition security are discussed. The third section describes the recent policy measures and the challenges and opportunities they provide for achieving food security. The last section presents future needs and recommendations for moving towards a sustainable food systems approach in India.

Food security status in India

Food production: from a food deficit to a food surplus country

India has experienced high levels of food insecurity during the post-independence period in the 1950s when the country was deficit of food grains. This prompted the government to explore new science and technologies to grow more food in order to fight hunger in a predominantly rural economy. High yielding varieties of wheat and rice were introduced and farmers across the country were given subsidized seeds, fertilizers and free power to boost production. At the same time, heavy investments were made to build large dams and irrigation infrastructure, to improve agricultural research and education and to develop agricultural extension services. As a result, by the mid-1970s, India was one of the first countries to benefit from the Green Revolution (Pingali, 2012). Although the population doubled from the early 1950s to 70s, food production tripled, and the dire predictions of a Malthusian famine were belied. As a result of technology interventions, there was a significant shift in the food supply function, contributing to a fall in real food prices. But, the growth in the agriculture sector during the Green Revolution was confined to irrigated and more favourable areas and it did not make much impact in the poorer, rainfed areas in the country. By the mid-1980s, the country started to export food. Currently, India is more or less self-sufficient in cereals, but has a deficit of pulses and oilseeds (Dev and Sharma, 2010).

The crop-livestock systems developed in many Indian states as an outcome of the Green Revolution. In fact, these systems grew out of farmers' own initiatives. Basu and Scholten (2012) analysed the linkage between India's Green Revolution and White Revolution and how the crop-livestock interactions developed and benefited rural communities. As a consequence, a number of dairy cooperatives were established in several states formalizing these systems. Notably, women in many states such as Gujarat, Andhra Pradesh and Tamil Nadu benefited from the expansion of the country's dairy industry because it provided supplemental income through selling milk to the dairy cooperative outlets that were established within the villages. With the expansion of irrigation during the 1980s, the production of other crops such as cotton, sugarcane, fruits and vegetables also increased significantly.

All along, the country remained democratic, and successive elected governments since 1947 were guided by the five-year plans which focused on different areas of development. Agriculture and food production was no doubt the priority of the government until the 1980s. There were limitations and negative impacts of the Green Revolution and the need for alternative solutions was recognized (Pingali, 2012). The civil society and non-governmental organizations played an important role in challenging the government promoted models of growth. Expansion of the area under agriculture since the early 1950s also led to large-scale deforestation and loss of biodiversity. Poor land management, over-reliance on chemical fertilizers to maintain soil fertility, deforestation and fewer investments in soil and water management led to large-scale erosion and soil loss. Crop diversity was reduced and the majority of cultivated land was mostly dominated by rice, wheat and maize. The cultivation of millets that were traditionally grown in rainfed areas, and far superior to rice or wheat from a nutritional point of view, was drastically reduced.

By the mid-1990s, the productivity of major cereal crops stagnanted and it was also the time when investments in agriculture were reduced as spending in other sectors gained momentum. A Government of India (2007) report pointed out that deceleration in the growth of agricultural output (from 3.3 per cent in 1980/81 to 2 per cent in 1994/95) had not been witnessed for over 50 years. Other allied sectors including livestock, fisheries and horticulture also experienced negative growth. These growth rates were lower than those in the rural population and the agricultural workforce, implying that per capita income in agriculture was declining. The report further outlined some of the main reasons for stagnation including mining of nutrients, loss of soil fertility, neglect of micronutrients, soil and water erosion, decline in surface and groundwater irrigation, urbanization and shrinking of agricultural land, and volatility in food prices. In some areas, the water withdrawal was far above the water recharge thereby depleting the water table and reducing crop productivity. Water use efficiency remained low (35–40 per cent) and efforts to increase it were initiated through nationwide programmes. Though several watershed programmes were implemented across the country, lack of integration and scattered implementation did not improve water availability for smallholders.

The lower levels of crop production and income plus the volatility of markets affected smallholders, making them more vulnerable to risks and forcing them into irrecoverable debts. In recent years, farmer suicides have become frequent in India due to increased environmental and economic related risks in agriculture (Munster, 2012). The institutional arrangements to cover risks are weak; smallholders and crops such as rice in general are not covered by crop insurance schemes. Overall experience since the Green Revolution has shown that the production pathway followed by the country to achieve self-sufficiency in food production was not sustainable (Dev and Sharma, 2010). India is now at a crossroads and needs to choose the right path as it moves forward in its efforts to achieve a sustainable food production mode. In the process, factors such as demography, climate change, globalization and trade, and inequality and poverty will challenge the future of food security. Some of these factors are briefly discussed below.

Demography

The current population of India is estimated at about 1.27 billion people and expected to reach 1.68 billion by 2050 if the current growth rate continues (WPS, 2013). The demographic changes have already had a profound effect on India's food security in terms of the amount of food produced and consumed. These changes are likely to continue in the future. It is expected that if the current economic and population growth continues in the same manner, the country will have to significantly increase its food production by 2050. A review by Shetty (2002) examined the demographic changes in the population with consequent effects on the population pyramid, the rapidity and rates of urbanization, changes in lifestyles in urban and rural communities and the impact on health in urban communities. The impacts from population increase in India will also be felt at the global level, as India is one of the major exporters of food grains. The current demographic patterns indicate a bulge in the nation's productive population and labour force that will have both positive and negative implications for food security. India cannot afford to see a further increase in population with the shrinking of its natural resources.

Climate change and variability

Climate change will have serious consequences for a country like India where agriculture is highly dependent on monsoon rainfall (Singh and Sontakke, 2002). The 5th Intergovernmental Panel on Climate Change (IPCC) report indicates that changes in the global water cycle in response to the warming in the twenty-first century will not be uniform (IPCC, 2013). As a result of climate change there will be increased intensive rains, shorter rainy periods and prolonged dry periods. A shift in the hydrological cycle will disrupt the farming calendar. This will be more serious in rainfed areas where the majority of farmers operate in smallholdings (less than 2 ha) and are relatively more vulnerable to extreme weather, especially droughts and prolonged dry periods. Sanghi and Mendelsohn (2008) have estimated that under moderate climate change scenarios, there could be about a 9 per cent decline in farm-level net revenues in India. They further argue that temperature changes will have a more profound effect on farm values and net revenues than rainfall patterns. According to Bates *et al.* (2008), the most significant consequences of climate change will be the impact on the hydrological cycle and the availability of fresh surface and ground water resources. In India, 85 per cent of fresh water is used for irrigation and hence any change in the hydrological cycle will have a direct impact on food production.

The poor, women and children will be highly sensitive to climate change as they are more vulnerable from a livelihood/income perspective; they have less resilience and adaptive capacity (Pritchard *et al.*, 2014). How small farmers will adjust and adapt to climate change will largely determine the future of agriculture in India. The first National Action Plan on Climate Change (NAPCC) was released in 2008 and promotes climate change mitigation and adaptation through sustainable development. This is an important step showing India's commitment to adapt to climate change. Agriculture and water are two key areas that will be given importance in the adaptation strategies.

Under the NAPCC, eight national missions were developed targeting the vulnerable sectors. Among these, the National Mission for Sustainable Agriculture and the National Water Mission have been identified as critical, since they affect millions of small-scale farmers and their livelihoods, a sector highly vulnerable to climate change and food insecurity (GoI, 2008). The Agriculture Mission's objective is to devise strategies to make agriculture more resilient to climate change. This, as envisaged in the Mission document, should be made possible through developing new varieties of crops, alternative climate-smart cropping systems, integrating traditional knowledge and practice systems, information technology and automatic sensor systems for climate monitoring and forecasting, new credit and insurance mechanisms, and capacity building. Most of these actions will have to be initiated in states that have different geophysical features where climate change as a consequence may act differently. The National Water Mission objective is to improve water use efficiency by 20 per cent, explore the possibilities of basin-level management strategies in Indian rivers and capacity building options. Further, these missions are to be supported by other inputs from the fields of information technology and biotechnology. Smallholders need help in the form of credit, inputs, insurance and early warnings to adapt to climate change (Udaya Sekhar *et al.*, 2012).

Globalization and trade

A strategy for food security should not preclude external trade in food. Trade may take place on the margin and according to need: exports in surplus situations and imports in deficit periods. In order to compete in a liberalized trade regime, there is need for a paradigm shift to achieving efficient growth from the current status. At the same time, efficient use of resources, including land, water and chemical inputs, is essential for sustainability (GoI, 2007). With globalization, trade in food commodities is bound to increase and India will be one of the major exporters to other nations. In 2012/13, cereal exports were around 24 million tonnes; 50 per cent of it was rice, 27 per cent wheat and the rest were coarse grains like corn, sorghum and others (Sood, 2013). Trade will influence the future food production patterns of the country.

Efficiency in the entire value chain of food grains is low; for example, marketing, processing and transport facilities are not very well developed in India and there is room for improvement. Most grain is stored as buffer stocks in government-owned warehouses and the rest privately. In the former, significant losses occur due to pests and diseases during storage and transport. Small-scale farmers in particular do not have good storage facilities. Storage prices are too high and farmers cannot afford to use the services. Private investments in cold storage and grains transport are increasing in some states but it does not serve the interests of smallholders. The agricultural markets in general are not well developed in many states and farmers are not assured of minimum prices for most crops except wheat, rice and some commercial crops such as cotton and tobacco. Owing to various market imperfections, there is a strong asymmetry in transmission of price between retail and wholesale level and farm level (GoI, 2007).

Food access and nutrition: implications of inequality and poverty

India has more undernourished people in the world than any other country (FAO, 2011). The Green Revolution successfully increased agricultural productivity, but it was not the panacea for solving the myriad of poverty, improving food access and nutrition problems facing the poor in India. The less-favoured rainfed areas and smallholder farmers in these areas did not realize the benefits of Green Revolution, and this is where the higher levels of malnutrition and poverty can be observed today (Fan and Hazell, 2001). The regional differences have subsequently led to inter-regional disparities within the country. In some states such as Orissa, Bihar and Chhattisgarh, the undernutrition problems of poverty and food insecurity are alarmingly high when compared to other states. The spatial or geographical inequality of this problem also means unequal life opportunities for future generations. In India, agriculture and food is a 'state subject', meaning that state or provincial governments are primarily responsible for policies and priorities that impact poverty and food security. The federal nature of Indian political structure further creates problems for achieving a uniform food security status across the country.

It was estimated that a 1 per cent increase in agricultural value added per hectare leads to a 0.4 per cent reduction in poverty in the short run and 1.9 per cent reduction in the long run, the latter arising through the indirect effects of lower food prices and higher wages (Ravallion and Datt, 1996). Where agricultural growth was not targeted towards the poor there was no poverty reduction (Dev, 2008). According to Pingali (2012), inequitable land distribution, insecure land tenure rights, lack of access to credit and markets, lack of pro-poor policies and fewer employment opportunities in the villages contributed largely to the persistence of poverty. This prompted large-scale migration from villages to nearby towns and cities in search of employment as a strategy for poverty reduction and securing food. This was more dominant in the states such as Bihar, Orissa and Chhattisgarh. For many households, migration did not really improve their food security situation. On the contrary, it increased the problems at the household level. Increased migration from rural to urban areas and fewer people left in the agriculture sector will seriously impact future food security in developing countries (Chen, 2007; UNPD, 2010). In India, it is mostly men that migrate to urban areas in search of employment leaving behind the women who have to bear the burden of the household and also take part in farming activities, without the necessary rights to land, access to resources, knowledge and skills. Both increased population and migration impact India's food and nutritional security.

Access to food and malnutrition varies greatly between different economic and social groups in India. Landless households suffer more than those who own land, women suffer more than men do and rural areas in general suffer more than urban areas. The social and geographical segregation has direct implications for livelihood opportunities and food security (Pritchard *et al.*, 2014). According to Bhutta *et al.* (2004) the strong incidence of gender undernutrition is a core characteristic of food insecurity in India. This is due to low social status, lack of awareness and a low literacy rate among women. Jose (2011) recognizes the complexity involved in gender and malnutrition due to high levels of inequality between men and women.

The level of malnutrition in India is almost double those of many countries in Africa (Dev and Sharma, 2010). This status is contrary to the commitments made by the Government of India in 2000 as it signed onto the Millennium Development Goals (MDGs) to 'eradicate extreme poverty and hunger' and 'to halve the proportion of the people who suffer from hunger by 2015'. The Green Revolution's contribution towards nutritional security has been very uneven and poor. Although overall calorie consumption increased, dietary diversity decreased for many poor people and malnutrition (in particular micronutrient deficiency) remains a serious issue in India (Shetty, 2002). One out of every three children suffers from malnutrition. According to Kumar and Kumar (2013), 47 per cent of children were malnourished in 2005/06 and both stunting (46 per cent of children) and wasting (16 per cent of children) are serious problems among children under five years. This is primarily due to a lack of proper nutritious diets during their early age (the first 1,000 days after their birth). These problems will significantly impact their growth, development and life expectancy. Malnutrition in children is not affected by insufficient access to food alone; it is also influenced by lack of access to proper health and sanitation services, inadequate care provided to child and pregnant mother, and other political, cultural and social reasons (UNICEF, 2012). Although considerable stunting has been observed in children from households with higher economic status, the prevalence of child stunting and being underweight in the household quintile with the lowest 'wealth' score is more than twice that in the highest quintile (Svedberg, 2008). Girls in India are more at risk than boys because of their lower social status. Consequently, the difference between quintiles was also observed with reference to female education and malnutrition. This indicates there are reasons other than income and education that contribute to malnutrition in India.

Poverty further reduces households' ability to access qualified child and maternal health care. Svedberg (2008) reported that low income constrains the household's ability to purchase high-nutrient food items such as meat, fruits and vegetables, which are invariably more expensive than cereals. Poverty and lack of purchasing power have been identified as two major factors responsible for low dietary intake and malnutrition (Kumar and Kumar, 2013). As the majority of the poor (73 per cent) who suffer from malnutrition live in rural areas where agriculture is the main occupation, augmenting incomes from agriculture can impact nutritional outcomes of rural households (Haddad, 2000). In summary, persistence of malnutrition is mainly explained by modest poverty reduction despite high economic growth; low productivity and income growth in the agricultural sector, which employs 54 per cent of the Indian labour force; and the lack of good governance.

Malnutrition, to a large extent, can be avoided by providing a balanced nutritious diet with all the necessary micronutrients for overall body growth at the right age. Shortage of micronutrient-dense foods and high prices relative to staples is one of the reasons for decreased consumption (Bouis, 2000; Kataki, 2002). In India, an inverse relationship can be seen between the increase in price of legumes and decline in pulse consumption across all income groups. This is because of a decline in the production of pulses (major source of protein in India), which the country currently imports to meet the market demand. Traditionally pulses and other nutrient-rich crops were produced on part of the land as rotational or intercrops by smallholders for household consumption, but gradually they were displaced by cereals that are supported by subsidies (Welch and Graham, 2000).

Government programmes and policies

Poor policies, lack of long-term planning, inefficient bureaucracy, corruption, lack of accountability and constraints within the social structure have been largely responsible for food insecurity in India. These largely explain why, despite the implementation of so many rural programmes during the last three to four decades – such as *Jawahar Rojgar Yojana* and the National Rural Landless Employment Guarantee Programme to provide employment to the poor and landless – progress has not been proportional to the investments made.

This section will provide a snapshot of four important interventions made by the government to address food and nutrition across the country (agricultural subsidies, rural credit, Public Distribution System and the Food Security Act), gaps in the approaches and lack of outreach at different levels. Massive investments were made in these programmes, which aimed to improve food security directly or indirectly since the 1950s. Until the 1980s, the five-year plans allocated adequate amounts of budget to cover agricultural subsidies and promote food production. From the 1990s, emphasis was put on improving food access and nutrition through other programmes. Achieving food and nutrition security was one of the major objectives of the 9th Five-Year Plan 1997–2002.

Agricultural subsidies

Until the 1980s, most policies and programmes were aimed at promoting food production in India. The government started to subsidize food production from the 1960s. In 1995/96, the food subsidies amounted to 0.5 per cent of the GDP (GoI, 1997). Agricultural subsidies have been mostly in the form of subsidized fertilizers, free electricity and irrigation. They played an important role in the early phase of agricultural development by addressing market failures and promoting new technologies (Fan *et al.*, 2008). The subsidies' benefits were evident from the increased yields of major cereals, especially rice and wheat, during the Green Revolution (Sharma, 1982; Gupta, 1984). The yields subsequently stagnated and by the mid-1990s the productivity of some regions even decreased. At the same time, critics argued that subsidies have led to overuse of water, power and fertilizers, and reduced crop diversity in many parts of the country. According to Gulati (2007), the government should invest in improving rural infrastructure rather than provide subsidies; whereas others recommend that subsidies should be given only to selected farmers who actually need them in order to prevent the decline in agriculture production and income (Kaur and Sharma, 2012).

Rural credit facilities

India's cooperative credit structure is one of the largest of its kind in the world and services farm input distribution, crop production, processing and marketing. The cooperative credit structure never realized the enormous potential within its reach (Shah *et al.*, 2007). Some of the initiatives such as the Integrated Rural Development Programme (IRDP) and the National Bank for Agriculture for Rural Development (NABARD) were targeted specifically towards rural areas and the agriculture sector. The IRDP was launched in 1980, aimed to cover all the districts in the country and reduce poverty through provision of micro-loans and creating household assets. The NABARD was started in 1982 to facilitate credit flow to agriculture and allied sectors. By the 1990s, rural banks were set up across the country (35,000 rural bank branches) to serve the people in the villages. From 1971 to 1991, the share of the informal sector decreased (from 75 to 25 per cent) and that of the formal sector doubled (Shah *et al.*, 2007). This was a positive trend for smallholders and the poor who had to pay high interest on loans from informal moneylenders. However, by the 1990s, the government phased out rural credit provision because of other priorities and some argue that this shift affected agricultural growth (Binswanger *et al.*, 1993). Although the growth of microfinance institutions and self-help groups with NABARD has strengthened in rural areas over the last decade, these organizations need training to improve operations, both for the organizations themselves and for the farmers who use these services. Access to microfinance should also broaden to include, for example, non-traditional crops, agribusiness, natural resources conservation, micro-irrigation, and nutrition programmes. Lessons from the past are important while devising new credit programmes for the rural poor in the future.

Targeted Public Distribution System

One of the major initiatives launched by the government to improve access to food in India is the Public Distribution System (PDS). It is jointly managed by the central and state governments, the former managing procurement, storage and transport, and the latter responsible for identifying the target beneficiaries, food distribution and maintenance of the fair price shops. Initially, rice, wheat, sugar and kerosene were distributed to almost 330 million people (Kattumuri, 2010) under this programme. PDS was basically started on the basis that food distribution could improve food access and nutrition. It is the largest government programme targeting the poor and uses about 5 per cent of the central government expenditure (Kochar, 2005). After implementing it for a few years, the government realized that the system was not functioning as expected, by targeting the poorest. It was reorganized in the mid-1990s and renamed the Targeted PDS (TPDS). The TPDS differentiated the below and above poverty line households and introduced a dual price system that was not present in the earlier system. In the process, about 65.2 million households were categorized as below poverty line households who are entitled to receive food at below market prices. The government food reserves had to be expanded to feed the TPDS beneficiaries. In 2012, the TPDS incurred an expenditure of US$16.67 billion, an increase of more than 25 times since 1992, without showing a proportionate decrease in the numbers of undernourished.

Though the intentions of the programme to address food security and malnutrition are good, it encourages corruption at several stages. The system does not provide legal protection to the poorest who are often discriminated against and not given an equal and fair share in food and employment (Thorat and Dubey, 2012). In some cases, food grains that are meant for distribution to the poor are diverted to other purposes (Khera, 2011). The low price difference between market grains and TPDS grains does not compensate for the low quality of the latter, thereby leading to low take-up among beneficiaries (Nagavarapu and Sekhri, 2011). In addition, inaccessibility of the shops and limited awareness of intended beneficiaries of their rights also prevents them from collecting grains. According to Kochar (2005), the TPDS subsidy had only a marginal impact on the calorie intake of rural households, mainly because only a small proportion of households bought a small share of their monthly rice and wheat requirements from the fair price shops. The TPDS will continue under the purview of the new National Food Security Act.

The National Food Security Act

In September 2013, the landmark National Food Security Act (the Act) was approved by the parliament to support a massive food safety net programme. The Act seeks, according to its preamble, to 'provide for food and nutritional security by ensuring access to adequate quantity of quality food at affordable prices to people'. It will cover almost 820 million people (75 per cent of the rural and 50 per cent of the urban population) who will receive 5kg of food grains each month at a subsidized price (FSP, 2013). The existing Targeted Public Distribution System (TPDS) is already enormous and faces many challenges. The new Act is considered by many as an important step in India's fight against hunger (Swaminathan, 2013). But much debate has been generated regarding the sustainability of the programme in the long run (Kishore *et al.*, 2013). The Act will identify households as either covered or uncovered based on data provided by the states. It depends on whether states will be able to provide proper data and how the households will be classified. Under this Act, millets and sorghum will be added to the distribution of rice and wheat, at very nominal prices. Extremely poor households will get an additional 10kg of grains per month under a special scheme (the *Antyodaya Anna Yojana*). But the costs of implementing this Act will be enormous, not only due to the costs of grains themselves, but also the costs of distribution centres and the bureaucracy involved in monitoring.

The programme is ambitious in its reach and commitment yet it relies on existing inefficient institutions. The Act has provisions to prevent leakages and track the movement and distribution of grains, but Acts need to be put in practice, otherwise they may not make much difference. Bulk procurement of food grains to accommodate distribution can affect prices in the open markets. Critics are of the opinion that it would be better if these costs were diverted towards improving rural and urban infrastructure, generating employment, investing in agriculture or even providing cash transfers to the needy households.

Towards sustainable food systems: recommendations for the future

Since the 1950s, we have seen both positive and negative influences of various interventions by the government to address food security (Thorat and Dubey, 2012; Swaminathan, 2013). As the economy keeps growing and population continues to expand, the future of food security will be profoundly influenced by the way food is produced and consumed. India needs to plan strategically to explore the existing opportunities and optimize development options to improve the food security situation in the future. There is an urgent need to check the population growth through mass campaigns, public awareness and education programmes. Since the majority of the population in India are still rural based, agriculture should be profitable to attract rural youth to take up farming as an occupation.

The high level of malnourishment on the other hand is an ironic situation, given the positive growth and vast natural and human resources India has at its disposal. This suggests that the economic growth has not been inclusive, but biased towards urban rich and middle class and the elite. Further, high geographic and social disparities in food security indicate that future policies and programmes should be targeted and need based. The country's growth pattern so far has seriously depleted natural resources and is no longer sustainable. Some of the development trends and their impacts or effects are summarized in Table 6.1.

From the standpoint of human well-being, the purpose of food is to maintain balanced nutrition and health. Unfortunately, the past initiatives in India used crop yield as an indicator for agricultural performance. In the process, the food-nutrition-health disconnect widened. Under the current agricultural growth paradigm, we see fewer crops beings produced and consumed. This trend definitely has to be reversed in India, which has varied agro-climatic zones and the potential to produce diverse nutritious foods (millets, legumes, tuber crops, fruits and vegetables). Rather than focusing on yield indicators, the focus should be shifted

Table 6.1 Development trends and impacts on agriculture and food systems in India.

Development trends	Impacts
• Government policies and programs to promote agriculture growth and employment and reduce food insecurity since the 1950s.	• Overall increase in food production; smallholders and rural poor marginalized; growth pattern promoted geographical and social disparities; overall hunger index has improved, but the number of people suffering from undernutrition and malnutrition remains high.
• Improvement in agricultural research and technology; provision of subsidies; investments in irrigation and extension services during 1960s and 70s; cereal grain crops like rice, wheat and maize favoured.	• Productivity of rice, wheat and maize dramatically increased; food self-sufficiency at the macro level attained; cultivation of traditional crops like millets and legumes reduced; crop diversity and traditional agro-ecosystems neglected.
• Population growth in India since the 1950s; pressure on land and water resources; increased demand for food.	• Agriculture expansion, deforestation, depletion of land and water resources; loss of biodiversity.
• Trade and liberalization of food commodities; dominance of multinational food chains; more demand to produce food.	• Growth of agribusiness; employment for rural youth; smallholders marginalized; local foods and local farmer markets replaced by processed foods and multinationals.
• Economic growth and urbanization; change in consumption patterns.	• More demand for meat and milk products; more pressure on land and water resources; diversion of productive land for urban and industrial use (special economic zones).

Source: Author's own analysis.

towards health- and sustainability-based indicators (Popkin, 2003). In the next section, attempt will be made to provide pointers to some of the critical elements that would help to secure the food security needs of the country based on the assessments and arguments provided in the chapter. The recommendations and lessons can also be useful to other countries in the region.

Recommendations

Sustainable agricultural growth and food production

• *A green economy model combined with inclusive growth* according to eminent scientist Swaminathan (2010; 2012; 2013) is the way forward to address food insecurity in India. Green agricultural systems can meet the future needs of nutrition but they need to be: (1) biodiverse, meaning that agricultural systems and landscapes must grow diverse crops, multiple varieties, have an integration of crop and livestock systems, conserve local species and varieties; (2) use local resources; (3) adopt resource-conserving systems adapted to the local ecology and new science; (4) eco-friendly; (5) climate-smart and smallholder focused

(Giovannucci *et al.*, 2012). It is possible to combine large-scale production systems that focus on major cereal production with green agricultural systems that are targeted towards providing diverse nutritious crops and ecosystem services within the different agro-climatic zones of the country. There is no single solution possible for a vast and diverse country like India. A mosaic of options has to be put together depending on the agro-climatic region, opportunity and risks.

- *Empower smallholders, women and the poor* and ensure that they are included in the future initiatives to improve food security. This has been one of the major constraints in India and a reason for food insecurity. To promote green agricultural systems obviously requires a focus on rural areas and smallholders who constitute the majority of farm households in the country. Providing need-based support (credit, technology, capacity building, marketing, storage, sanitation, drinking water) to smallholders and women can play a key role in reducing food insecurity (Giovannucci *et al.*, 2012). The technologies and new science have to be easily adaptable by them; e.g. water conservation using farm ponds that are locally designed and low-cost; cultivating and marketing traditional millets (that are adaptable to dry regions), legumes, fruits and vegetables.

- *Reinvest in land and water resources* that are basic to food production. Conservation of these resources should be one of the top priorities of farmers and government agencies. It is difficult to increase productivity unless the soil and water management regimes undergo a radical change. India has in the past tried to implement large-scale soil and water conservation projects, but the results were poor despite huge investments made in these projects. Instead, low-cost, environmentally benign initiatives (e.g. zero tillage, soil mulching, agroforestry) can be introduced to increase soil fertility. In dry regions, simple soil and water conservation measures can improve soil moisture and can support crop production on small farms. The solutions have to be localized and integrated with land management, agroforestry and animal husbandry. In the future, the government should consider targeting regions where agriculture performance is poor.

- *Promote low-cost and small-scale irrigation systems* that are environmentally friendly. India so far has focused on big dams and large-scale irrigation projects which have no doubt contributed positively to growth. However, the efficiency of these systems across the country is low and needs improvement. In the future, India cannot afford big dams due to high costs and maintenance. To move towards green farming systems, small-scale sustainable irrigation systems could be more appropriate. At the farm level, efficient cropping systems along with high-efficiency water use should be introduced (e.g. system of rice intensification, alternate wetting and drying irrigation in rice). There is potential to improve rainwater harvesting at the farm level and it does not require big investments.

- *Reinvest in extension services*: though reforms have been made during the 1990s, the agricultural extension services need further changes in order to suit the shift towards sustainable agricultural intensification. The Agricultural Technology Management Agency, a model introduced by the central government in 2005–06 to operate in all districts in the country, is a good initiative for integrating extension programmes across line departments such as animal husbandry, fisheries and forestry; and linking research and extension units within a district. Similarly, the *Krishi Vigyan Kendra*'s 529 centres countrywide also provide valuable training to farmers based on on-farm research. The current systems primarily focus on on-farm activities and a few crops, but farmers require information for the whole food and agriculture value chain (Glendenning *et al.*, 2010). The private sector e-Choupal initiative and other similar models also tried to include prices and accessing markets. The current systems should be decentralized, more participatory and need based for better results (Katharina, 2008). Farmer-based organizations and self-help groups are key organizations to make extension demand-driven. In small groups, it is easier to get feedback on the information needs of the members (Swanson, 2006). Use of information and technology tools is gaining importance in recent years; they can reduce costs and time by providing timely information.

- *Invest in rural infrastructure* including rural sanitation, drinking water, rural roads, education and health facilities during the course of future development initiatives. One of the most dismal records India has relates to sanitation and health. During the 1990s, the Integrated Rural Sanitation Programme and the Rural Water Supply and Sanitation Programme were launched to improve the rural sanitation and drinking water facilities. However, these programmes need modifying to include the poor who often lack the land on which to construct the toilets; and other problems are more social in nature, as different social groups are not used to sharing public facilities. Private investments to improve rural and urban sanitation facilities should be encouraged. Numerous studies have established a positive relationship between rural infrastructure and development, especially roads, in reducing rural poverty through productivity growth, increasing non-agricultural employment and higher wages (Fan *et al.*, 2008). Improving rural road networks also facilitates the marketing of agricultural commodities through faster mobility.

- *Improve storage and marketing facilities*: storage facilities, especially for smallholders, should be improved, because this will enable them to store grains not only for their own consumption but also to sell at a later stage when the market prices are favourable. Storage helps stabilize the crop's market price. Simple and low-cost devices such as metal silos, solar bins and other traditional storage facilities should be made accessible in rural areas. In some areas, common cold storage facilities can be provided where small-scale farmers can share the space. This is where the private sector can invest and help farmers to realize the benefits of marketing and eliminate intermediaries. The growth in agribusiness, storage, processing and transport should be prioritized to reduce losses and increase the market value of the food commodities. This will make a significant contribution to the income of smallholders in the country. A typical approach in strategies that aim for market-based solutions to agricultural innovation is an emphasis on private-public partnerships. The private sector could help in research and development, or market farmers' products, while the government could carry out capacity building (Hartwich *et al.*, 2007). The government needs to introduce special measures to protect small farmers from market fluctuations.

- *Adaptation to climate change* is necessary to reduce vulnerability due to climate change and increase resilience of smallholders and the poor. State governments need support to develop comprehensive adaptation and policy frameworks as a follow-up of the NAPCC. Some of them have initiated measures but require technical expertise, especially in terms of integrating adaptation technologies with larger development programmes, training in climate and hydrology modelling, interpretation of scenarios and further up-scaling. Private investments have to be encouraged to support climate-smart farming systems wherever possible. Capacity building of farmers and officials regarding climate change risks and adaptation should be adopted in all districts within the country.

- *Export and import policies* should be framed considering the long-term implications of food trade on small farmer's livelihoods and income, pressure on natural resources and opportunity costs. Trade in food grains can be a viable option for a country such as India that has the potential and technology to produce more. Trade policies should not undermine the current nutrition indicators in the country.

- *Promote innovative research integrating agriculture, nutrition and environmental management* and at the same time targeting the problems of smallholders will contribute significantly towards smallholder involvement in sustainable agriculture intensification and increasing a productivity that is currently stagnated. Farmer-to-farmer learning has proven to be highly effective in disseminating research results. Lead farmers in villagers should be linked with research and used as a means to upscale research results wherever possible. Research should cater with diverse technologies suitable in different socioeconomic and ecological contexts.

Improving food access and nutrition

- *Revise and increase efficiency, accountability and transparency* of the government policies and programmes. The TPDS and the Food Security Act of 2013 are steps that the country has taken to improve rural employment, reduce poverty and improve food security in the country. However, there are several flaws in the programmes as discussed earlier in the chapter, and revisions should be made to target the socially and economically weakest sections of society. States have to take primary responsibility in implementing the programs if they are interested in realizing the benefits. The nutritional aspect of food security has not been adequately emphasized in the new Food Security Act.

It is a critical time for India to prioritize food access, nutrition and health in the development programmes. Now, while the Act is fairly new, it is time for policymakers to recognize the weaknesses of the programme and modify it to suit the dietary needs of different target groups and agro-climatic zones of the country. Diversification of foods would strengthen the agriculture-nutrition link and also create demand for growing different crops. India will not be able to meet its commitments made towards the MDGs, in particular, the commitments to reduce hunger and malnutrition, unless it takes the right and timely measures.

- *Improve the diversity of food basket with vegetables, pulses, millets, fruits and other crops* that are important sources of critical micronutrients (such as iron and vitamin A). They should be re-introduced as part of farming systems across the country. This is possible to some extent by supply of seeds and inputs to grow these crops. At the same time, traditional farmers' markets can offer cheap, locally produced and nutritious diverse foods to residents at the village level. Local village councils can play an important role in taking responsibility for organizing the markets and necessary programmes to curb malnutrition. Unless priority is given to eradicate malnutrition in the country through large-scale campaigns and programmes addressing the different causes of malnutrition, progress cannot be made. Improvement in dietary patterns, health and sanitary conditions and providing clean drinking water should be the goal of the programmes. The solutions have to be based on locally driven initiatives, using local resources and involving local people.

- *Nutrition-focused outreach* through innovative interventions to high-risk families, especially children under two years of age and pregnant women (pre- and post-care), will significantly reduce malnutrition levels in the country (Bajpai and Dholakia, 2011). Interventions through counselling, regular monitoring, awareness programmes and home-based actions can strengthen targeted approaches. Awareness should start at primary and secondary schools through courses on food and nutrition issues.

- *More structural and functional integration* is necessary at all levels between the ongoing initiatives including the Integrated Child Development Services programme, the Targeted Public Distribution System and the Midday Meal Scheme among others, addressing food and nutrition security, poverty and health. This should in turn be supported by dynamic leadership to run the programmes effectively. The Prime Minister's National Council meeting on India's Nutrition Challenges in 2010 was an important step that recognized the need for integration and consolidation of programmes related to health and nutrition. The recommendations from the meeting need to be followed up. Similar efforts in Brazil have paid off where an independent body oversees the various issues related to food and nutrition security. In the future, structural changes are needed in the way the system is operated in order to increase transparency, efficiency and desired outcome.

Final remarks

Mahatma Gandhi, the Father of the Nation in the 1940s, rightly said, 'Unsustainable lifestyles and unacceptable poverty should become problems of the past, to achieve harmony with nature and with each other'. India has not paid adequate attention to those words, and its policies by and large have promoted unsustainable lifestyles and growth models since the 1950s. The future of food and nutrition security in India depends very much on how the natural resources are managed and how the poorest sections of society are fully covered in food and employment policies and programmes. The predominantly rural population that is dependent on agriculture for their livelihood indicates that special efforts have to be made to increase growth in agriculture sustainably, reduce poverty and improve food security in rural areas. The country needs a paradigm shift where future growth should be inclusive and sustainable. It is a big challenge to make changes in the current system, but at the same time, it is a window of opportunity to combine the goals of better food, healthy environment and reduced poverty. Strong policy support, transparency, accountability and effective implementation of the policies are definitely needed to ensure food security for millions of people suffering from hunger and malnutrition in the country. Targeted efforts, investments and regular monitoring should follow to ensure smooth implementation of the new policies to address food security in the country.

Food security policies should include legal protection against discrimination of the rural poor, smallholders and women. At the same time, practical steps have to be taken to ensure them equal and fair shares in food and employment programmes. Such an approach would help reduce poverty at an accelerated rate (Thorat and Dubey, 2012). Aside from more food production, policies and programmes should also recognize the importance of food access, nutrition and health outcomes to be achieved within a sustainable food systems approach.

References

Bajpai, N. and Dholakia, R.H. (2011) Improving the integration of health and nutrition sectors in India, online, http://globalcenters.columbia.edu/content/improving-integration-health-and-nutrition-sectors-india (accessed 30 April 2014).

Basu, P. and Scholten, B.A. (2012) Crop-livestock systems in rural development: linking India's green and white revolutions, *International Journal of Agricultural Sustainability*, 10 (2): 175–91.

Bates, B.C., Kundzewicz, Z.W., Wu, S. and Palutikof, J.P. (Eds) (2008) Climate change and water. Technical Paper of the Intergovernmental Panel on Climate Change, IPCC Secretariat, Geneva, p. 210.

Bhutta, Z.A., Gupta, I., d'Silva, H., Manandhar, D., Awasthi, S., Hossain, S.M.M. and Salam, M.A. (2004) Maternal and child health: is South Asia ready for a change?, *British Medical Journal*, 328: 816–19.

Binswanger, H.P., Khandker, S.R. and Rosenzweig, M.R. (1993) How infrastructure and financial institutions affect agricultural output and investment in India, *Journal of Development Economics*, 41: 337–66.

Bouis, H. (2000) Improving human nutrition through agriculture: the role of international agricultural research, *Food Nutrition Bulletin*, 21: 550–67.

Chen, J. (2007) Rapid urbanization in China: A real challenge to soil protection and food security, *Catena*, 69 (1): 1–15.

Dev, S.M. (2008) *Inclusive Growth in India: Agriculture, Poverty, and Human Development*. Oxford University Press, New Delhi.

Dev, S.M. and Sharma, A.N (2010) Food security in India: performance, challenges and policies, Oxfam India Working Paper Series, September, 01WPS-VII.

Fan, S. and Hazell, P. (2001) Returns to public investments in the less-favoured areas of India and China, *American Journal of Agricultural Economics*, 83: 1217–22.

Fan, S., Gulati, A. and Thorat, S. (2008) Investment, subsidies and pro-poor growth in rural India, *Agricultural Economic*, 39 (2): 163–70.

Food and Agriculture Organization (FAO) (2011) Food security statistics, online, http://www.fao.org/economic/ess/ess-fs/ fs-data/ess-fadata/en/ (accessed 21 April 2014).

Food Security Portal (FSP) (2013) Updated: will India's food security bill help or hurt?, online, http://www.foodsecurityportal.org/will-indias-national-food-security-bill-help-or-hurt (accessed 28 April 2014).

Giovannucci, D., Scherr, S.J., Nierenberg, D., Hebebrand, C., Shapiro, J., Milder, J. and Wheeler, K. (2012) Food and agriculture: the future of sustainability (March 1, 2012). The Sustainable Development in the 21st century (SD21) Report for Rio+20, New York: United Nations, online, http://ssrn.com/abstract=2054838 or http://dx.doi.org/10.2139/ssrn.2054838 (accessed 30 April 2014).

Glendenning, C.J., Babu, S. and Asenso-Okyere, K. (2010) Review of agricultural extension in India: are farmers' information needs being met?, online, http://www.ifpri.org/sites/default/files/publications/ifpridp01048.pdf (accessed 30 April 2014).

Government of India (GoI) (1997) 9th Five-Year Plan, vol. II: Agriculture, Irrigation, Food Security and Nutrition, online, http://planningcommission.nic.in/plans/planrel/fiveyr/9th/vol2/v2c4-3.htm (accessed 28 April 2014).

Government of India (GoI) (2007) Report of the Steering Committee on Agriculture and Allied Sectors for the Formulation of the 11th Five-Year Plan, online, http://planningcommission.nic.in/aboutus/committee/strgrp11/str11_agriall.pdf (accessed 27 April 2014).

Government of India (GoI) (2008) National Action Plan on Climate Change, online, http://pmindia.nic.in/climate_change.php (accessed 30 April 2014).

Government of India (GoI) (2013) Advance Estimates of National Income, 2012–13, Ministry of Statistics and Program Implementation, online, http://pib.nic.in/newsite/erelease.aspx?relid=92062 (accessed 27 April 2014).

Gulati, A. (2007) Investment, subsidies and pro-poor growth in rural India, *Economic and Political Weekly*, 18 (3).

Gulati, A., Ganesh Kumar, A., Shreedhar, G. and Nandakumar, T. (2012) Agriculture and malnutrition in India, *Food and Nutrition Bulletin*, 33 (1): 74–86.

Gupta, A. (1984) Impact of agricultural subsidies, *Economic and Political Weekly*, 39 (4): 48–53.

Haddad, L. (2000) A conceptual framework for assessing agriculture-nutrition linkages, *Food and Nutrition Bulletin*, 21: 367–73.

Hartwich, F., Tola, J., Engler, A., González, C., Ghezan, G., Vázquez-Alvarado, J.M.P., Silva, J.A., de Jesús Espinoza, J. and Gottret, M.V. (2007) Building public–private partnerships for agricultural innovation. Food Security in Practice Technical Guide Series, IFPRI, Washington, DC.

Intergovernmental Panel on Climate Change (IPCC) (2013) Working Group I contribution to the IPCC 5th Assessment Report Climate Change 2013: The Physical Science Basis, Summary for Policymakers, online, http://www.climatechange2013.org/ images/ uploads/ WGIAR5-SPM_Approved27Sep2013.pdf (accessed 21 April 2014).

Jose, S. (2011) Adult under-nutrition in India: is there a huge gender gap?, *Economic and Political Weekly*, 46 (29): 95–102.

Kataki, P.K. (2002) Shifts in cropping system and its effect on human nutrition: Case study from India, *Journal of Crop Production*, 6:119–44.

Katharina, R. (2008) Reforming the agricultural extension system in India, online, http://www.ifpri.org/publication/reforming-agricultural-extension-system-india (accessed 30 April 2014).

Kattumuri, R. (2010) Food security and the targeted public distribution system in India, online, http://indiagovernance.gov.in/files/Food_Security_Public%20distribution.pdf (accessed 29 April 2014).

Kaur, R. and Sharma, M. (2012) Agricultural subsidies in India, boon or curse, *Journal of Humanities and Social Science*, 2 (4): 40–6.

Khera, R. (2011) Trends in diversion of grain from the public distribution system, *Economic and Political Weekly*, 46 (21): 106–14.

Kishore, A., Joshi, P.K. and Hoddinott, J. (2013) A Novel Approach to Food Security, online, http://www.ifpri.org/gfpr/2013/indias-right-to-food-act (accessed 29 April 2014).

Kochar, A. (2005) Can targeted food programs improve nutrition? An empirical analysis of India's public distribution system, *Economic Development and Cultural Change*, 54 (1): 203–5.

Kumar, P. and Kumar, H.V. (2013) Food security and nutritional scenario of India: an overview, *Journal of Agriculture and Veterinary Science*, 2 (5): 28–39.

Munster, D. (2012) Farmers' suicide and the state in India: conceptual and ethnographic notes from Waynad, Kerala, *Contributions to Indian Sociology*, 46 (1–2): 181–208.

Nagavarapu, S. and Sekhri, S. (2011) Who is targeted by India's targeted public distribution system?, online, http://www.stanford.edu/group/SITE/archive/SITE_2011/2011_segment_2/2011_segment_2_papers/nagavarapu.pdf (accessed 29 April 2014).

Pingali, P.L. (2012) Green revolution: impacts, limits, and the path ahead, online, http://www.ncbi.nlm.nih.gov/pmc/articles/PMC3411969/ (accessed 27 April 2014).

Popkin, B.M. (2003). The nutrition transition in the developing world, *Development Policy Review*, 21 (5–6): 581–97.

Pritchard, B.R., Sekher, A., Parasuraman, M.S. and Chouthani, C. (2014) *Feeding India: Livelihoods, Entitlements and Capabilities*. Routledge, London: 153–61.

Ravallion, M. and Datt, G. (1996) How important to India's poor is the sectoral composition of economic growth? *World Bank Economic Review*, 10: 1–25.

Sanghi, A. and Mendelsohn, R. (2008) The impacts of global warming on farmers in Brazil and India, *Global Environmental Change*, 18: 655–65.

Sen, A.K. (1981) *Poverty and Famines: An Essay on Entitlements and Deprivations*. Oxford University Press, Oxford.

Sen, A.K. (2009) *The Idea of Justice*. Harvard University Press, Cambridge, MA.

Shah, M., Rao, R. and Vijay-Shankar, P.S. (2007) Rural credit in 20th century India: an overview of history and perspectives, online, http://www1.ximb.ac.in/users/fac/Shambu/Sprasad.nsf/dd5cab6801f1723585256474005327c8/e78490ff090249d06525730c0030abf9/$FILE/Mihir%20Shah_rural_credit__April_2007__epw.pdf (accessed 30 April 2014).

Sharma, V.K. (1982) Impact of agricultural subsidies on national income and agricultural production, *Economic and Political Weekly*, 47 (7): 66–71.

Shetty, P.S. (2002) Nutrition transition in India, *Public Health and Nutrition*, 5: 175–82.

Singh, N. and Sontakke, N.A. (2002) On climate fluctuations and environmental changes of the Indo-Gangetic plains, India, *Climatic Change*, 52: 287–313.

Sood, J. (2013) Grain glut: India faces a surplus of food grains, is exporting a good option?, online, http://www.downtoearth.org.in/content/grain-glut (accessed 28 April 2014).

Svedberg, P. (2008) Why malnutrition in shining India persists?, online, http://www.isid.ac.in/~pu/conference/dec_08_conf/Papers/PeterSvedberg.pdf (accessed 28 April 2014).

Swaminathan, M.S. (2010) *From Green to Evergreen Revolution*. Academic Foundation, New Delhi.

Swaminathan, M.S. (2012) Green economy and inclusive growth, online, http://www.uncsd2012.org/content/documents/Plenary3%20Day1%20M%20S%20Swaminathan%20Whole.pdf (accessed 30 April 2014).

Swaminathan, M.S. (2013) From Bengal famine to right to food, *The Hindu*, 13 February, online, http://www.thehindu.com/todays-paper/tp-opinion/from-bengal-famine-to-right-to-food/article4409557.ece (accessed 13 September 2013).

Swanson, B. (2006) The changing role of agricultural extension in a global economy, *Journal of International Agricultural and Extension Education*, 13 (3): 5–17.

Thorat, S. and Dubey, A. (2012) Has growth been socially inclusive during 1993/94–2009/10, *Economic and Political Weekly*, 48 (10): 43–54.

Udaya Sekhar, N., Gosain, A.K., Barton, D.N., Palanisami, K., Tirupathaiah, K., Reddy, K.K., Stålnacke, P., Deelstra, J. and Gupta, S. (2012) Climate change and impacts on water resources: guidelines for adaptation in India, Bioforsk report No. 7 (173), Ås, Norway.

United Nations Children's Fund (UNICEF) (2012) Nutrition, online, http://www.unicef.org/india/children_2356.htm (accessed 28 April 2014).

United Nations Population Division (UNPD) (2010) World population prospects: the 2010 revision, online, http://esa.un.org/wpp/unpp/panel_population.htm (accessed 17 April 2014).

Welch, R.M. and Graham, R.D. (2000) A new paradigm for world agriculture: productive, sustainable, nutritious, healthful food systems, *Food and Nutrition Bulletin*, 21: 361–6.

World Population Statistics (WPS) (2013) India Population, 2013, online, http://www.worldpopulationstatistics.com/india-population-2013/ (accessed 28 April 2014).

7 Status and trends of food security in Ethiopia

Mehreteab Tesfai, Asfaw Adugna and
Udaya Sekhar Nagothu

Introduction

Agriculture has been the backbone of the Ethiopian economy for centuries and contributes nearly 85 percent of the employment, 50 percent of gross domestic product (GDP) and 90 percent of foreign exchange earnings (Abate, 2006; Rashid, 2010). Furthermore, about 90 percent of the agricultural output comes from smallholder farms characterized by low-input and low-output production farming systems with heavy dependence on rainfall (Devereux, 2000; Abebaw *et al.*, 2010). The erratic nature of rainfall, prolonged droughts and dry spells coupled with poor agricultural practices, has degraded the agricultural land resulting in poor soils and low productivity (Abebaw *et al.*, 2010). On top of this, political instability and inappropriate past government policies, combined with limited availability and use of modern technology inputs, has weakened the agricultural sector leading to serious food insecurity in the country (Amsalu, 2012). Over the past four decades, Ethiopia has been hit by four major famines in 1971–75, 1984–85, 1999–2000 and 2002–03 that have cost the lives of more than a million people (van der Veen and Gebrehiwot, 2011).

On the other hand, Ethiopia is endowed with rich natural resources, as evident from the nine major perennial rivers including the Blue Nile, fertile agricultural lands in the western and southern parts of the country, mineral resources and, above all, its human resources. Ethiopia ranks first in the numbers of livestock in Africa, and it is the second most populous country in Africa next to Nigeria (Gelan, 2007) and the most populous landlocked nation in the world (USAID and EFMH, 2012). The current population is estimated to be 85 million and is projected to reach 130 million by the year 2030 (CSA, 2007). Ethiopia remains one of the poorest countries in the world (UNDP, 2006a) where food is insecure for 52 percent of the rural and 36 percent of the country's urban population (FDRE, 2002; Adenew, 2004). Many Ethiopians live in conditions of hunger with an average daily energy intake of 2,097 kcal/capita/day, and with about 37 percent prevalence of undernourishment (van der Veen and Gebrehiwot, 2011).

The Ethiopian agricultural sector experienced short-sighted agricultural policies during the past military regime (i.e. the Derg). During the Derg government (1974–91), land was declared to be public or state property, and farmers were deprived of land use rights (Gutema, 2001). According to the World Bank (1987) report, excessive market regulation through compulsory quota deliveries by farmers at below market prices was one of the most serious shortcomings of the agricultural policy of the military regime. There was a near total neglect of small-holder producers, with focus given only to collective and large-scale state farms. Private sector development was plagued by insecurities and free market operations were largely undermined (Gutema, 2001).

After 1991, the new government within the Federal Democratic Republic of Ethiopia (FDRE) introduced a free market economy and adopted economic lib-eralization policies. These new policies gave farmers the opportunity to diversify their incomes. Farmers were free to sell their products based on market prices (Amsalu *et al.*, 2007). Over the past two decades, there has been an increased recognition of the importance of developing new food security interventions in Ethiopia.

The objective of this chapter is to review the status and trends of food security in Ethiopia by analyzing the main challenges to food insecurity, programs and policy measures to improve food security during 1993–2013, and finally to draw some conclusions and policy implications.

Major drivers of food insecurity

The major drivers impacting food security and the various measures taken are discussed in the following sections.

Climate and extreme weather events

Extreme weather events, particularly droughts, have contributed to several famines in Ethiopia over the past 40 years (Tadege, 2007). Major droughts in Ethiopia occurred in 1971–75, 1984–85, 1999–2000 and 2002–03, but almost every year since 1980 at least some parts of the country have been affected by drought. The percentage of people affected by drought has increased from 4 percent to over 19 percent (i.e. ≥13 million people) between 1973 and 2003 (Lebeda *et al.*, 2010). It has been observed that households affected by at least one drought face 20 percent lower per capita food consumption over the same period (Dercon *et al.*, 2005). The 1984–85 drought had a tragic result exacerbated by the unwillingness of the previous military government to accept food aid and the slowness of the donor response (del Ninno *et al.*, 2007). During the 2002/03 cropping season, drought affected over 10 million people in Ethiopia. The percentage of Ethiopian population at risk of droughts, floods and extreme temperature was about 3.3 percent in 2009 (FAO, 2013). Even during the non-drought years, agricultural production satisfies only about 80 percent of the national food requirements.

To address the impacts caused by extreme weather events, the Government of Ethiopia (GoE) designed a National Adaptation Program of Action (NAPA), which was submitted to the United Nations Framework Convention on Climate Change

(UNFCCC) Secretariat in 2007. The NAPA has been updated and replaced by Ethiopia's Program of Adaptation to Climate Change (EPACC). This is also a program of action aimed at building a Climate Resilient Green Economy (CRGE) through adaptation at sectoral, regional and local community levels (Cesár and Ekbom, 2013). The GoE cannot support the programs on its own. Investments have to be generated from various sources including the private sector. Capacity building at different levels, especially farmers, should be prioritized at the same time for better adoption of the climate resilient measures.

Land degradation

Several studies have examined the impacts of land degradation (soil, water, vegetation), particularly in the highlands of Ethiopia (e.g. Bewket and Sterk, 2002; Amsalu and de Graaff, 2006). One of the most serious impacts has been on crop production to the extent that average yields of cereals seldom exceed 1 ton/ ha even during good years. With the current pace of soil loss at an average of 137 tons/ha/year on cultivated slopes (IFPRI, 2010) and sometimes reaching as high as 300 tons/ha/year (Philor, 2011), soil erosion is expected to reduce per capita income in the highlands by ≥30 percent (Bewket and Sterk, 2002). Soil fertility is one of the key factors to drive Ethiopia's growth and food security (IFPRI, 2010). Assuming an average soil depth of 60 cm, Hurni (1993) predicted that most of the cultivated slopes in the highlands of Ethiopia would be entirely stripped of the soil mantle within 150 years if no conservation measures are taken. Under such conditions, food security cannot be achieved without restoring the land resources and improving soil fertility and water management. Although the GoE has recognized the threat of rapid land degradation, previous soil and water conservation programs have not been very successful (Bewket and Sterk, 2002; Amsalu and de Graaff, 2006), since land degradation cannot be addressed just by implementing biophysical conservation measures. Other socioeconomic and political factors (such as land tenure policies, incentives and land use conflicts) equally need to be addressed. To combat land degradation and its consequent impacts on food security, the government launched the MERET program in the early 1990s.

The MERET program

The acronym 'MERET' means 'land' in Amharic (Nedessa and Wickrema, 2010). This Managing Environmental Resources to Enable Transitions program was supported by the World Food Program (WFP) (MoFED, 2002) and operated in five regions of Ethiopia in 72 food insecure districts (DRN-ADE-BAASTEL-ECO-NCG, 2004). The objective of the program was to increase incomes for the poor through asset creation and rehabilitation of degraded agricultural lands using Food for Work. The MERET program had a measurable impact on food security among some of Ethiopia's poorest communities. For instance, in the period 1994–2002, the program assisted 1.4 million food insecure people in over 800 communities and landless households benefited from their direct participation in food-for-assets activities. The program covered almost 20 percent of the 5 million chronically food insecure people in Ethiopia. The following were the major results observed due to MERET (DRN-ADE-BAASTEL-ECO-NCG, 2004):

- A 40 percent decrease in food shortage duration from five to three months per year;
- About 60 percent of the beneficiaries reported an increase in the number of meals per day;
- 72 percent experienced an income increase from the sale of different agricultural products;
- 73 percent of families had more money to spend on education, health and clothing;
- 84 percent reported a 150–400 kg increase in crop production per year per household;
- 85 percent indicated an improved ability to cope with drought;
- 88 percent reported that their livelihoods had improved.

According to Nedessa and Wickrema (2010), the biggest positive impact of MERET was building community capacity and empowerment, but the greatest challenges were to reduce social and cultural barriers such as the prohibition of free grazing.

Inappropriate policies (land tenure, settlement program, land acquisition, food aid)

Land tenure

It is believed that one of the major causes of land degradation and food insecurity in Ethiopia has been the insecure land tenure system (UNDP, 2006b). As specified by the Ethiopian Constitution, the government remains the only landowner, and local governments are required to adhere to this statute in the design of land reforms. Thus, land is a domain of the state by law. The government holds land tenure rights, and land sales and mortgages are outlawed (von Braun and Olofinbiyi, 2007). Consequently smallholder farmers do not feel a sense of ownership of their farmland (Gebreselassie, 2006), and refrain from investing long-term structures on their plots of land, which otherwise could reduce erosion and rehabilitate their lands (Dorosh and Rashid, 2013). Recently, the farmers in the four regional states (i.e. Amhara, Oromia, SNNP and Tigray) received certificates of land acknowledging their user rights to ensure tenure security, thereby contributing to increased agricultural productivity and food security (MoFED, 2007; César and Ekbom, 2013). The current land tenure system offers opportunities for land distribution or redistribution, land transfer to family members based on inheritance, and rent or lease land to other farmers and/or investors (Zewdu and Malek, 2010). There are lessons to learn from the past soil and water conservation programs in the country and their implications. For example, accountability and responsibility rests neither with the farmer nor with the community to repair the hillside terraces constructed across the highlands of Ethiopia once the food/cash for work program was over. In fact, by not maintaining these infrastructures, soil erosion has increased and land degradation has been even more severe in those areas.

Settlement program/villagization

Resettlement programs and forced villagization were implemented during the military regime (Derg) in response to the famine that occurred in the mid-1980s (Gutema, 2001). Under the program, hundreds of thousands of people were forced to move from degraded areas in the northern part of Ethiopia to the fertile lands in the west (Gutema, 2001). Prefeasibility land use studies on the suitability of the area for agriculture and human settlement were not carried out. Even the local indigenous people were not well aware of the incoming people. The new climate, agricultural system, culture and language were all challenges for the new forced settlers to adapt to and cope with in the new environment. Because the plot allocated for a farm household was inadequate, the farmers tended to resort to cutting trees and selling them as firewood in order to supplement their income and satisfy consumption needs. Lack of suitable land use planning led to over-cultivation and overgrazing rather than providing new opportunities and livelihoods. Moreover, the increased use of wood for new house construction and firewood further contributed to rapid deforestation and consequent land degradation in the new settlement areas (Gutema, 2001). Since the Derg regime was toppled by the Ethiopian People's Revolutionary Democratic Front (EPRDF) in 1991, most people have returned to their original locations. Those who remained behind are still facing challenges to sustain their livelihoods (Gutema, 2001).

Large-scale acquisitions of land

With the goal of increasing national food security, the government launched a new form of transferring fertile agricultural lands to foreign investors, often in long-term leases to develop extensive commercial farms (Graham *et al.*, 2011; Vhughen and Gebru, 2012). As a result, in recent years, Ethiopia has leased more than 3 million hectares of land (a large proportion in Gambella, Benshangul-Gumuz and Oromia regions) to foreign investors with the stated aim of enhancing food security (Graham *et al.*, 2011), but has instead focused on a foreign exchange-based food security strategy (Lavers, 2012). Unfortunately, the farmland leased to foreign investors is being used to produce cash crops for export rather than to enhance staple foods for local consumption. Many believe that such large-scale land acquisitions will expose the local population to even greater food insecurity, since the rural poor could be evicted or lose the traditional rights to access land, water and other related resources in their areas (Graham *et al.*, 2011; Lavers, 2012).

Food aid

Comprehensive information is lacking with regard to the actual amount of food aid donated to Ethiopia as the type of food aid delivery system differs from donor to donor. For instance, the food aid donated from the USA is often in-kind, whereas the European Commission (EC) donates cash. As Clay *et al.* (1999) reported, annual cereal food aid ranged from 200,000 to 1.2 million tons between 1985 and 1996. This was equivalent to 3.5 percent (in 1985) and 26 percent (in 1996) of the total national cereal production. Figure 7.1 compares the annual grain production and food aid distribution in Ethiopia between 1995 and 2007. In 1999, 2000 and 2002, the food grain aid distribution was much greater than the local production, but was lower in the rest of the years. The largest food aid distribution was in 2002 (approximately 19 million MT) because of the severe drought that affected millions of people.

Food aid has been given in different forms such as food-for-work, food-for-assets and school feeding. In 2008, Food-for-Peace (FFP) responded with more than 1 million MT of food aid for the Horn of Africa countries of which 71 percent (735,140 MT) was donated to Ethiopia (USAID-USDA, 2008). In 2011, Ethiopia received the highest proportion (19 percent) of the 55 percent food aid received by the top eight recipient countries (WFP, 2012). However, from a nutrition point of view, the food delivered to Ethiopia (e.g. in 2006) from USA and EC was deficient in vitamin A and iodine (Doak *et al.*, 2008). Many scholars believe that food aid dependency has crippled people's motivation to work hard (Gelan, 2007). A popular saying in Ethiopia was 'It does not matter if it is raining here, what matters is if it is raining in Canada' (Devereux, 2000). Depending on food aid will rather encourage people and government officials to externalize responsibility and/or accountability and consequently delay seeking long-term solutions to food insecurity, while more and more people continue to suffer (Gebreselassie, 2006).

Learning from the past military government policy failures in addressing food security, the FDRE formulated a new National Food Security Strategy (NFSS) and later a Productive Safety Net Program.

National food security strategy

In 1996, a food security strategy was adopted for the first time to attain food security for 5 million chronically food insecure people and another 10 million who are badly affected by food shortages in drought years (MoFED, 2006). The NFSS was updated in 2002, focusing on increasing the availability of food through domestic production, ensuring access to food for food deficit households, and strengthening institutional emergency response capabilities (FDRE, 2002). Ethiopia's food aid program states that no able-bodied person should receive food aid without working in a community development project in return (Clay *et al.*, 1999; Jayne *et al.*, 2001). Under the program, food aid was mobilized for over 5 million people every year in the period 1994–2003. Cognizant that decades of food aid have had no discernible impacts on reducing food insecurity, rural

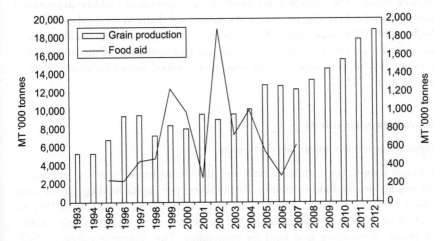

Figure 7.1 Annual cereal production (1993–2012) and food aid distribution (1995–2007) in Ethiopia.
Source: Adapted from Rashid and Lemma, 2011 and FAO, 2013.

poverty and vulnerability, there was a need for a new approach that could address the structural problems underlying Ethiopia's food insecurity and this program is the Productive Safety Net Program.

Productive Safety Net Program

A Productive Safety Net Program (PSNP), the largest safety net program in sub-Sahara Africa (SSA), which targets about 7.3 million food insecure households, was launched in 2005 by the GoE to provide 'predictable transfers to meet predictable needs' of chronically food insecure people in chronically food insecure districts (Sabates and Devereux, 2010). The PSNP provides support to create productive and sustainable households, community assets and incomes that can contribute to large-scale rehabilitation of severely degraded areas (FDRE, 2012). In this context, the PSNP employs an approach of 'predictable transfers to meet predictable needs' to tackle chronic food insecurity and break Ethiopia's dependence on food aid once and for all. There was a consensus that the PSNP represents a significant improvement over previous relief programs and is a positive step towards finding long-term solutions to Ethiopia's food insecurity (Shoham, 2007). The 2002 impact assessment study showed that participants of the PSNP gained increased production, enhanced income, improved livelihoods and increased ability to cope with drought (DRN-ADE-BAASTEL-ECO-NCG, 2004). The school feeding program is one of the PSNP interventions. During 2008–09, total food distribution under school feeding programs averaged only 6,590 tons. This is small compared to the needs of the whole country where almost 14.5 million children between the ages of 7 and 14 are enrolled in schools. Even if only poor children are covered under the school feeding programs, the additional demand for food could be as high as 568,000 tons per year. This is a large demand for a justifiable intervention, which not only keeps children in school and increases the nation's future labor productivity, but also contributes to generate local food processing sectors (Rashid and Lemma, 2011).

Socioeconomic forces

Population growth and pressure on land resources

Ethiopia's rapid population growth and the demographic patterns are major driving factors for food insecurity. For instance, per capita holdings under crop production were reduced all over the country from 0.5 ha per person in 1960 to 0.21 ha per person in 1999 (Amsalu, 2012), on account of the increasing number of people demanding new land for cultivation. The synergetic effects of high population pressure on the land leads to declining agricultural productivity and eventually increased food insecurity. The population policy is aimed at balancing the trade-offs between the high population growth rate and the national food production growth rate through birth control and limiting family size, while sustaining the natural resource base (ENPP, 1993). The country's family planning program is generally reported to be successful in reducing the rate of population growth (UNFPA, 2012). For instance, prevalence of modern contraceptives increased from 6.3 to 27.3 percent between 2000 and 2011 (USAID and EFMH, 2012; UNFPA, 2012).

Food prices

The soaring food prices in Ethiopia in 2007–09 adversely affected Ethiopia's food economy and still continue to do so. During the 2008 food crisis in Ethiopia 'food prices rose so fast from 83 percent to 184 percent' across several cereal markets (Minot, 2010). Ulimwengu *et al.* (2009) used pre-crisis survey data to simulate the calorie loss expected for Ethiopians and concluded that a 50 percent increase in food prices would result in calorie consumption decline from 7 to 25 percent, suggesting that rural areas would be harder hit by food insecurity. Alem and Söderbom (2011) reported calorie losses due to food prices increased in urban Ethiopian settings and demonstrated that consumption growth for households with meagre assets was lowest during periods of rapid food price increases. Hence, poor households in urban and rural Ethiopia were more affected by rapidly rising food prices. In response to the elevated food prices, the government tried to intervene by stopping the export of major food grains, and by importing and distributing reasonably priced wheat and palm oil. Despite these measures, the nominal price of the major grains in the cities showed unprecedented increase, for example in the case of the native annual cereal, *tef (Eragrostis tef)*, by 500–600 percent during the past ten years. *Tef* is being exported in the form of *injera* (a local food) as the export ban does not prohibit processed products (Demeke and Marcantonio, 2013). The rise in the nominal price forced the government to implement an urban food rationing program in April 2007 (Rashid and Negassa, 2011).

Inadequate use of agricultural inputs

Ethiopian agriculture has been unable to produce sufficient quantities to feed the country's rapidly growing population (Kassa, 2004), even during the good rainfall years, because of low agricultural productivity. One of the main causes of low agricultural productivity is inadequate application of agricultural inputs such as improved seeds, livestock breeds, fertilizers and other yield enhancing climate-smart agricultural technologies including effective rainwater management and irrigation practices. For example, improved varieties of maize and wheat seeds were used in only 4 percent of the total cropped area (USAID-COMPETE, 2010). There are a range of improved agricultural technologies developed by the different research and higher learning institutions within the country (Abate, 2006). While some of these technologies are promising, they have not been made available to farmers, or farmers do not have the capacity to grow them mainly due to the country's weak agricultural extension services.

Weak agricultural extension services

The absence of effective linkages among agricultural research, extension systems and farmers has repeatedly been reported as one of the major reasons for the low productivity of Ethiopian agriculture (FDRE, 1999; Kassa, 2003). Having realized this wide gap, the government established the Agricultural Technical Vocational Education and Training Centers under the five-year Growth and Transformation Plan. This is also to strengthen the Agricultural Development-Led Industrialization (ADLI) strategy under the Plan for Accelerated and Sustained Development to End Poverty (PASDEP) through which thousands of development agents were trained. Accordingly, in each peasant association (locally called *Kebele*) three development agents were assigned in three fields of agricultural sciences, namely plant science, animal science and natural resources conservation, to train farmers about modern agricultural extension packages. To further assist, thousands of farmers' training centers were established. Through a loan from the World Bank in the form of an agricultural research and training project and rural capacity building project, a number of agricultural researchers, teachers and experts were also trained.

In 1993, the FDRE formulated and adopted ADLI and three poverty reduction strategy programs in which agriculture was seen as the primary engine of indus-trial development and economic growth (Amsalu *et al.*, 2007).

The agricultural development-led industrialization (ADLI)

The ADLI is one of the long-term development policies to reduce poverty and to achieve sustainable and faster economic growth. Its objective is to strengthen the linkages between agriculture and industry and thereby increasing the productivity of small-scale farmers, expanding large-scale and private commercial farms, and reconstructing the manufacturing sector in such a way that it can use the country's human and natural resources effectively. The smallholder farmers' productivity was mostly targeted through the diffusion of fertilizers and improved seeds, as well as the establishment of credit schemes. In addition, expansion of the road system and improvement of primary education and water supply were also adopted to improve food systems in the country (FDRE, 1994). The government offered seasonal credit services for the farmers to purchase inputs such as seeds and chemical fertilizers. Nonetheless, the number of participating farm households in the credit scheme seldom exceeded 37 percent of the estimated 75 million farmers in the country (Belshaw and Coyle, 2001).

Poverty reduction strategy programs

Poverty is endemic to Ethiopia (Doocy *et al.*, 2005). The causes of poverty are several, including environmental degradation, underdeveloped production technologies and poor services (IFAD, 2012). Today about 30 percent of the Ethiopian population lives below the poverty line (FDRE, 2012). To alleviate poverty, the government has developed three poverty reduction strategy programs:

- the Sustainable Development and Poverty Reduction Program (SDPRP) (2002–05);
- the Plan for Accelerated and Sustained Development to End Poverty (PASDEP) introduced in 2006 to tackle the Millennium Development Goals (MDGs) (Brown and Teshome, 2007);
- the Growth and Transformation Plan to be implemented during 2011 to 2015, aimed at meeting the MDGs by registering an average yearly economic growth of 14.9 percent (Amsalu, 2012).

In terms of sectoral coverage, the PASDEP is more comprehensive than the SDPRP (MoFED, 2007). During SDPRP the Ethiopian economy showed negative real GDP growth rate of 3.3 percent in 2002/03 due to drought, followed by strong positive performance of 11.9 percent in 2003/04 and 10.6 percent in 2004/05, which in turn resulted in 6.4 percent annual real GDP average growth (MoFED, 2006). Positive growth at the national level, although encouraging, is not necessarily a good indicator of food security at the household level across the country.

Food security assessments

Food security is a complex, multidimensional issue that embraces four key dimensions: food availability, access to food, food utilization and food stability. Each dimension of food security is analyzed in the following sections through a

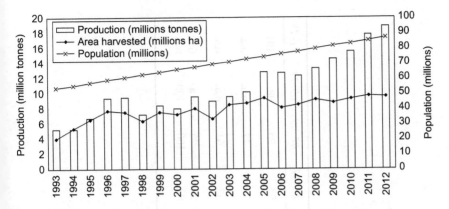

Figure 7.2 Cereal production and population growth in Ethiopia, 1993 and 2012.
Source: Adapted from FAO, 2013.

set of key indicators which are relevant to the Ethiopian conditions and for which long-term data are available.

Food production and availability

According to Figure 7.2, a positive trend in cereal grain production was observed from 1993 to 2012 at the national level. Since 1993, the total area under cereal crops has doubled (i.e. from 4 to 9.5 million ha). Between 1996 and 2012, total cereal production doubled from about 9.5 to 19 million tons, suggesting that productivity increased from 1.2 to 2 t/ha mostly due to programs introduced by the government. Production varied significantly within and between the cereal producing areas of Ethiopia and also varied between years because of droughts and other related factors. On average, the cereal production growth rate was +7.8 percent per annum (ranging between −24.2 and +39.2 percent).

However, between 1993 and 2012, the population growth was linear with an average growth rate of 2.7 percent per annum (Figure 7.2). The population has increased from 53.5 to 86.5 (by 30 million) during the past 20 years and is projected to reach 130 million by 2030 (CSA, 2007). This implies that there will be a greater demand for food in the country.

Dietary energy supply adequacy

Overall, the average dietary energy supply adequacy has risen from 73 percent to 101 percent between 1993–95 and 2011–13 (Table 7.1). However, the percentage of dietary energy supply adequacy is still lower than the SSA average (i.e. 111 percent). One of the reasons could be that most of the people living in the northern and eastern parts of Ethiopia consume more *tef* and sorghum respectively, which

Table 7.1 Food availability indicators based on 3-year averages for Ethiopia (1993–2013).

	93–95	95–97	97–99	99–01	01–03	03–05	05–07	07–09	09–11	11–13
Dietary energy supply adequacy (%)	73	77	80	83	87	90	93	95	98	101
Energy supply derived from cereals, roots and tubers (%)	82	82	82	82	81	79	79	77	n.a.	n.a.
Protein supply from plant origin (g/capita/day)	43	47	48	51	54	56	58	61	n.a.	n.a.
Fat supply (g/capita/day)	16.3	16.3	16.3	17.3	19.7	21.7	22.7	25	n.a.	n.a.
Value of food production (International $ per capita)	67	76	75	78	87	93	97	100	109	n.a.

Source: Adapted from FAO, 2013. n.a. – not available.

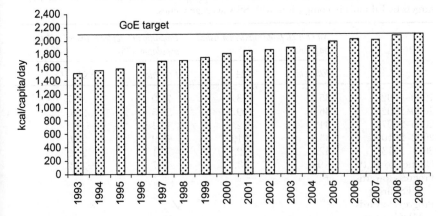

Figure 7.3 Average dietary energy intake (kcal/capita/day) in Ethiopia, 1993–2009.
Source: Adapted from FAO, 2013.

contain lower calories (336–339 kcal/100g) compared with maize (365 kcal/100g) (Dejene and Lemlem, 2012). Maize is predominantly grown and consumed in the southern and south-western part of Ethiopia (Jayne and Molla, 1995).

Figure 7.3 shows a gradual increasing trend of calorie intake from 1,500 to 2,100 kcal/capita/day in 2009. The minimum requirement set by the Food and Nutrition Board (2002) of the International Organization for Migration for dietary food intake of calories is 2,100 kcal/capita/day and this level is also the government's target (MoFED, 2002) which was therefore met in 2009 at the national level. However, the average calorie intake varies among the nine administrative regions of Ethiopia. In 2005, the average calorie intake was lower than 2,100 kcal/capita/day for the residents in the cities of Addis Ababa and Dire-Dawa, Amhara, Afar, and Tigray regions. Whereas, for the regions of Oromia, Somali, Benshagul-Gumuz, SNNP and Harari, where more root and tuber crops are consumed, it was more than the 2,100 calorie/capita/day intake (CSA, 2012).

Share of dietary energy supply from cereals, roots and tuber

The share of dietary energy supply from cereals, roots and tubers slightly declined from 82 percent to 75 percent between 1993–95 and 2008–10, as shown in Table 7.1. This could be because the major source of energy for most of the Ethiopians comes from cereals, which account for about 60 percent of total calorie consumption (Rashid, 2010).

PROTEIN AND FAT SUPPLY

According to Table 7.1, the national average protein supply from plant origin has increased from 43 to 63g/capita/day between the periods of 1993–95 and

Table 7.2 Prevalence of undernourishment and progress towards the WFS and the MDG targets by Ethiopia in comparison with SSA average values.

	Number of people undernourished (millions)		Proportion of undernourished in total population (%)	
	Ethiopia	SSA	Ethiopia	SSA
1990–1992	35.5	173.1	71.0	32.7
2000–2002	36.0	209.5	53.5	30.6
2005–2007	34.5	212.8	45.4	27.5
2008–2010	33.2	221.6	40.9	26.6
2011–2013	32.1	222.7	37.1	24.8
Change so far (%)	−9.6	28.7	−47.7	−24.2
Progress towards WFS target	+	−		
Progress towards MDG target			✓	✕

Source: Adapted from FAO, 2013.

Notes: +/−: Number reduced/increased by more than 5%, respectively.
✓: Target is expected to be met by 2015 or prevalence <5% based on exponential trend on all data between 1990–92 and 2011–13.
✕: Progress insufficient to reach the target if prevailing trends persist.

2008–10. On a regional scale in SSA, the average protein supply has also shown a small increase from 52 to 59g/capita/day by the end of 2008–10. The average supply of protein derived from animal origin in Ethiopia has also increased, but by a smaller amount from 5 to 8g/capita/day between 1993–95 and 2008–10. However, protein supply from animal products is smaller than the SSA average, that is, 11–13g/capita/day (FAO, 2013). During 1993–2010, the average fat supply in Ethiopia ranged from 16.3 to 26.3g/capita/day, which is much lower than the SSA average range of 43.9 to 50.3g/capita/day (FAO database, 2013). Livestock meat and fish are more expensive foods and thus consumed less frequently by the majority of poor people in Ethiopia.

Although cereal food production per capita increased from about 0.16 to 0.22 tons (between 1996 and 2012: see Figure 7.2), people's dietary demand for energy, protein and other essential minerals are not sufficiently met from agriculture, food imports or emergency aid. Hence, the availability dimension of food security still remains a problem in Ethiopia.

Access to food

Table 7.2 presents a comparison between Ethiopia and sub-Saharan Africa, in terms of the number of people undernourished and progress made towards MDG and World Food Summit (WFS) targets. FAO and national statistics show that Ethiopia has made very little progress in reducing the number of undernourished people (i.e. only by 9.6 percent) using the 1990–92 baseline data. The country is expected to meet the MDG target, but most likely not the WFS target.

Table 7.3 Access to food indicators, 3-year average values for Ethiopia, 1993–2013.

	93–95	95–97	97–99	99–01	01–03	03–05	05–07	07–09	09–11	11–13
Prevalence of food inadequacy (%)	78	71	67	62	58	55	52	50	46	44
Paved roads over total roads (%)	15.0	15.5	15.3	13.3	12.0	12.9	11.0	13.7	n.a.	n.a.
Road density (km road per 100 km²)	2.55	2.12	2.16	2.59	2.85	3.07	3.84	4.02	4.02	n.a.
Domestic food price level index	1.66	1.74	1.69	1.77	1.61	1.76	1.8	1.87	1.9	1.87
Depth of the food deficit (kcal/capita/day)	623	565	537	496	452	418	391	370	335	314

Source: Adapted from FAO, 2013.

Table 7.3 presents key indicators used to assess the physical and economic access to food in Ethiopia during 1993–2012.

Physical access to food

In general, the road density in Ethiopia has increased from 2.55km to 4.02km per 100km^2 between 1993 and 2010, whereas the percentage of paved roads over the total roads has slightly dropped from 15 percent to 13.7 percent between 1993 and 2009 (Table 7.3). The improvements in the country's road network both within and to the neighboring countries will indirectly facilitate marketing and food access in the drought prone and remote areas of the country. In this regard, efforts are required to increase the percentage of paved roads – <20 percent at present (Rancourt *et al.*, 2013) – as well as road density in both surplus producing and in food deficit areas in order to expedite the distribution, marketing and ready access to food. The country has also established dry ports at Semera in the Afar region and Mojo in Oromia to minimize the cost of port warehouses in Djibouti.

Economic access to food

The food price index in Ethiopia showed an increase from 1.66 to 1.87 between 1993 and 2013, which is close to the average index of SSA (i.e. 1.95). Between March and September 2008, the cereal price index increased by about 172 percent. In this period, the food prices for cereals more than doubled and prices for non-food items rose by 27 percent (Admassie, 2013). The surge in food prices was caused mainly by domestic imbalance of supply and demand for food. The global financial and economic crisis in 2007–08 had minor impact on the domestic food price crisis, but the soaring food prices negatively affected the food security situation so that an additional 6.4 million people were pushed into the food insecurity zone and became dependent on emergency food assistance (HLTF, 2009). To address the prevailing food crisis during 2007–08, the government released emergency food grain reserves, imported and distributed wheat at subsidized price, banned the export of staple cereals, removed value-added and turnover taxes on food items (Admassie, 2013), re-introduced urban food rationing and informally suspended local procurement by WFP and others (Demeke and Marcantonio, 2013). Such *ad hoc* measures can partly address food shortages in the short term, but the country needs to set up long-term food reserves that can buffer food shortages and famines.

During the past 20 years, the deficit in calorie intake in Ethiopia has been significantly reduced from 623 to 314 kcal/capita/day but food insecurity is still a threat to the poor households (Table 7.3). It is noteworthy that the food deficit rate in Ethiopia is still higher than the SSA average, despite progress made in fulfilling the minimum dietary energy requirements of 2,100 kcal/capita/day (Figure 7.3) on a countrywide scale. However, high food availability by itself does not always guarantee high food security. Certain population groups suffer from acute undernourishment, despite abundant food supplies (FAO, 2013).

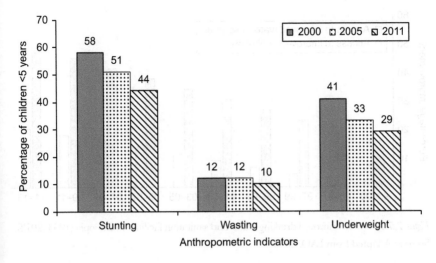

Figure 7.4 Trends in nutritional status of Ethiopian children under the age of five.
Source: Adapted from CSA, 2012.

Food consumption and utilization trends

Ethiopia has an enormous diversity in food utilization and consumption habits. The five major cereals (*tef*, wheat, maize, sorghum, and barley) and a non-cereal enset (*Ensete ventricosum*) are the major staple food crops (Dorosh and Rashid, 2013). In addition, fruits, vegetables and livestock food products are also common in the traditional diets of Ethiopian society.

Children's nutritional status

Trends in the nutritional status of children for the years 2000, 2005 and 2011 are shown in Figure 7.4 using the anthropometric indicators of stunting, wasting and underweight. For the purpose of comparison, the data for 2000 and 2005 were recalculated using the new World Health Organization (WHO) standard reference population to make it comparable to the results of the 2011 Ethiopian Demography Health Survey (EDHS). There was a downward trend in the proportion of children stunted and underweight over the three EDHS surveys in 2000, 2005 and 2011. Stunting prevalence decreased by 7 percent (i.e. from 58 percent to 51 percent) between 2000 and 2005 and by an additional 7 percent to 44 percent between 2005 and 2011 (CSA, 2012). The decline in the proportion of stunted Ethiopian children shows improvement in chronic malnutrition over the past 11 years.

A similar pattern was also observed for the proportion of children underweight, which dropped by 8 percent from 2000 to 2005 and by an additional 4 percent from 2005 to 2011. The prevalence of wasting children under the age of five

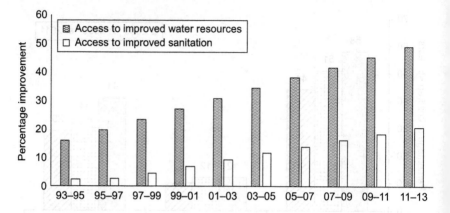

Figure 7.5 Access to improved drinking water and sanitation facilities in Ethiopia (1993–2013).
Source: Adapted from FAO, 2013.

remained constant between 2000 and 2005, but then slightly decreased by 2 percent between 2005 and 2011.

Access to improved drinking water and sanitation

The percentage of population having access to improved drinking water resources and sanitation has increased between 1993 and 2013 (Figure 7.5). However, this improvement is still lower than the SSA average (62.7 percent) registered in 2013 (FAO, 2013). Today, more than 50 percent of the Ethiopian population does not have access to clean and safe drinking water and about 80 percent does still not have access to improved sanitation facilities.

The situation is similar over the entire region of SSA. Concerted efforts are needed to improve access to both clean drinking water and sanitation facilities. Improvements in sanitation facilities contribute to clean and safe drinking water supplies as well as to safe and healthy food nutrition.

Food stability

The determinants for food stability are vulnerability and shocks that are assessed through a suite of indicators as presented in Table 7.4.

Vulnerability

The key indicators to assess the vulnerability of food instability that are relevant to Ethiopian conditions are the cereal import dependency ratio and the percentage of arable land equipped for irrigation development.

$$Cereal\ import\ dependency = \frac{Cereal\ imports}{(Cereal\ production + Cereal\ import - Cereal\ export)} \quad [1]$$

This indicator [1] is a proxy to measure the cereal self-sufficiency of a country and the potential impact of shocks in the international trade market (FAO, 2013). Table 7.4 shows a slight decline in the cereal import dependency ratio (i.e. from 11.3 percent during 1993–95 to 10.1 percent during 2007–09) with the exception of a slight increase (i.e. 12.4 percent) in 2001–03 (drought years). This implies that imported cereals constituted only 10 percent in 2007–09 and that the remaining 90 percent of the cereal food requirement was fulfilled by domestic production (Table 7.4). Broadly speaking, the country depends little on imported cereal food, with the exception of emergency food aid sought during droughts. The situation in Ethiopia regarding the cereal dependency ratio was better than for the entire SSA, which ranged from 16.7 percent to 21.5 percent between 1994–96 and 2008–10 (FAO, 2013). This could be explained by increased growth in agriculture and measures taken by the government to encourage local grain markets through blocking of food exports.

In Ethiopia, only about 2.9 percent and 2.1 percent of the total arable land had irrigation facilities in 1993–95 and 2009–11, respectively (Table 7.4). Agriculture in Ethiopia is largely dependent on rainfall which is highly vulnerable due to climate change and variability. Local adaptation measures to conserve soil and water in the form of farm ponds, bunds and agroforestry can help to reduce risk from climate and extreme weather. In 2006, over 200,000 farmers practiced rainwater harvesting in the entire country through the PSNP to increase the size of irrigated land (MoFED, 2006).

Shocks

The key indicators used for assessing shock-induced food instability are domestic food price volatility index, per capita food production variability, and per capita food supply variability. The domestic food price volatility index compares the variations of the domestic food price index over time and reflects the food demand and supply situation in a country. Table 7.4 shows the volatility of the domestic food price index in Ethiopia that varied from 48.9 to 100.6 between 1993 and 2013. This implies that average food prices have doubled in the last 20 years. Domestic food prices in Ethiopia are highly volatile as a result of high food supply variability as shown in Table 7.4.

The per capita food production variability during the past 20 years ranged from 1.3–7.8. The lowest variability in the net food production value (1.3) was recorded in 2007 when domestic food production declined. On the other hand, the highest net food production value (7.8) was registered in 1995 when national food production was relatively higher than the previous years (Figure 7.1). The food supply variability ranged from 5.2 kcal/capita/day in 2003–05 to 29.7 kcal/capita/day in 2009–11

Table 7.4 Food stability indicators, 3-year average values for Ethiopia, 1993–2013.

	93–95	95–97	97–99	99–01	01–03	03–05	05–07	07–09	09–11	11–13
Cereal import dependency ratio (%)	11.3	5.0	5.9	11.0	12.4	9.8	6.0	10.1	n.a.	n.a.
Arable land equipped for irrigation (%)	2.9	2.9	2.9	2.8	2.8	2.5	2.2	2.1	2.1	n.a.
Domestic food price volatility index	48.9	22.4	33.3	24.9	84.0	67.6	56.8	91.6	97.4	100.6
Food production variability (per capita)	2.6	7.8	5.8	5.6	4.1	3.6	3.3	1.3	3.3	2.0
Food supply variability (per capita)	n.a.	20.6	22.6	22.0	13.8	5.2	17.2	23.5	29.7	n.a.

Source: Adapted from FAO, 2013.

(Table 7.4). The cause for high food supply variability (i.e. 29.7 in late 2008) may be explained by the surge of domestic food prices at that time which persuaded poor people to consume cheaper and less nutritive foods. On the other hand, the low food supply variability (i.e. 5.2 in 2003–05) was mainly due to the effects of drought. During food deficit, government interventions of banning the export of food items and of importing selective staple foods help to stabilize food supply variability, though there are reports of smuggling *tef* abroad (Demeke and Marcantonio, 2013).

Conclusions and recommendations

Conclusions

This chapter discussed the main drivers of food insecurity and analyzed the data on key indicators of food availability, accessibility, utilization and stability. Most of the analysis focused on government policy and programs between 1993 and 2013, as most of the measures to address food security were initiated during this period. Despite the efforts, food insecurity remains a challenge. The severe land degradation, rapid population growth rate and climate change have exacerbated the problem of food insecurity in Ethiopia. The lack of clarity in land tenure is a factor that needs immediate attention in Ethiopia, as we have seen that farmers are not motivated to make long-term investments if they do not have entitlements to land. The ongoing large-scale land leasing to private investors will make matters worse, and perhaps it will not serve the food security needs of the country and the rural poor.

Future prospects for food production in Ethiopia are not encouraging if they follow the current trend of low application of agricultural technology. The mid-range emissions' scenario of the Intergovernmental Panel on Climate Change (IPCC) model predicts that temperatures in Ethiopia are expected to increase by 0.9–1.1°C by 2030, 1.7–2.1°C by 2050 and 2.7–3.4°C by 2080, accompanied by a small increase in average annual precipitation, as well as a sharp decline in rainfall during Ethiopia's summer period (June to September), especially in the southwestern and central parts of the country (NMA, 2007). As a result, droughts are expected to become more frequent and intense, with corresponding negative impacts upon agriculture, incomes and food security (Held *et al.*, 2012).

Recommendations and policy implications

The 'business-as-usual' agricultural practices will no longer improve national and/ or household food security under the future climate change scenario for Ethiopia. Thus, a paradigm shift to climate-smart agricultural practices is required in the Ethiopian agricultural system. Ethiopia's future agricultural development and food security will depend, to a great extent, on its ability to tackle the following three challenges:

1   the move towards sustainable, ecological and climate-smart agriculture underpinned by science-based knowledge and modern use of technologies and inputs;

2   the need to promote the production of staple foods and other foods to reduce
     Ethiopia's reliance on foreign food aid;
3   in the long term, a structural transformation towards a greener economy that
     is based less on agriculture and more on diversified, higher value-added ser-
     vices and sustainable industries.

Measures to be taken in the short to long-term plan to achieve food security in
Ethiopia are suggested as follows:

Measures in the short term (2015–20)

•   continuing conservation measures to rehabilitate degraded agricultural lands
    and establish wooded lots and community forest plantations; protecting and
    re-establishing forests for their economic and ecosystem services; construction
    of feeder roads;
•   increasing application and availability of modern agricultural inputs through
    establishment of credit schemes and implementation of climate-smart agri-
    cultural technologies including effective rainwater management;
•   increasing investments in irrigation infrastructure, and cultivating more land
    under water and energy saving irrigation systems;
•   promoting effective agricultural product value chain and reduce post-harvest
    losses through improved access to markets;
•   support to the new land tenure policy which is under implementation in four
    regions of Ethiopia and expand it to other regions;
•   undertaking prefeasibility land use studies and consultation of the indigenous
    people prior to implementing large-scale acquisition of land and settlement
    programs.

Measures in the long term (2015–25)

•   improving education especially on vocational fields and strengthening cap-
    acity of research facilities in higher learning institutions and national agricul-
    tural research centers;
•   strengthening linkages among agricultural research centers, extension ser-
    vices and farmers;
•   strengthening linkages between agriculture and industry by increasing the
    productivity of small-scale farmers and private sectors;
•   strengthening national capacity to manage climate induced crises by building
    national food reserves and using effective early warning systems;
•   improving access to potable water to increase the percentage of population
    with access to clean and safe drinking water from 50 percent at present to
    75 percent by 2025;
•   improving sanitation facilities in towns and cities to increase percentage of
    population having access to these facilities from 20 percent at present to
    50 percent by 2025;

- expanding electricity generation from renewable sources of energy for domestic and regional markets and modern energy-efficient technologies in transport, industrial sectors, and buildings;
- promoting sustainable family planning program in the households through awareness raising and training.

References

Abate, T. (2006) Focusing agricultural research to address development needs: the way I see it. In: Abate, T. (Ed.) *Successes with Value Chain, Scaling up and Scaling out Agricultural Technologies in Ethiopia*. EIAR, Addis Ababa.

Abebaw, D., Fentie, Y. and Kassa, B. (2010) The impact of food security program on household food consumption in north-western Ethiopia: a matching estimator approach, *Food Policy*, 35: 286–93.

Adenew, B. (2004) The food security role of agriculture in Ethiopia, *Journal of Agricultural and Development Economics*, 1: 138–53.

Admassie, A. (2013) The political economy of food price: the case of Ethiopia. WIDER Working Paper No. 2013/001, Helsinki, Finland: United Nations University, UNU-WIDER, World Institute for Development Economic Research, online, www.wider.unu.edu (accessed 30 November 2013).

Alem, Y. and Söderbom, M. (2011) Household-level consumption in urban Ethiopia: the effect of a large price shock, *World Development*, 40 (1): 146–62.

Amsalu, A. (2012) Eradicating extreme poverty and hunger in Ethiopia: a review of development strategies, achievements, and challenges in relation with MDG1. NCCR North-South Dialogue 45 Working Paper, Special Research Project 4 – Beyond the MDGs. Bern, Switzerland: NCCR, North-South, online, http://www.cde.unibe.ch/CDE/pdf/01.pdf (accessed 15 February 2014).

Amsalu, A. and de Graaff, J. (2006) Farmers' views of soil erosion problems and their conservation knowledge at Beressa watershed, central highlands of Ethiopia, *Agriculture and Human Values*, 23: 99–108.

Amsalu, A., Stroosnijder, L. and de Graaff, J. (2007) Long-term dynamics in land resource use and the driving forces in the Beressa watershed highlands of Ethiopia, *Journal of Environmental Management*, 83: 448–59.

Belshaw, D. and Coyle, E. (2001) *Poverty Reduction in Ethiopia and the Role of NGOs: Qualitative Studies of Selected Projects.* Overseas Development Institute, London.

Bewket, W. and Sterk, G. (2002) Farmers' participation in soil and water conservation activities in the Chemoga watershed, Blue Nile basin, Ethiopia, *Land Degradation and Development*, 13 (3): 189–200.

Brown, T. and Teshome, A. (2007) Implementing policies for chronic poverty in Ethiopia. Background paper for the Chronic Poverty Report 2008–09, Chronic Poverty Research Center and ODI, online, http://www.chronicpoverty.org/uploads/publication_files/CPR2_Background_Papers_Brown-Teshome.pdf (accessed 10 January 2014).

Central Statistical Authority (CSA) (2007) National Population Statistics. Addis Ababa, Ethiopia: Federal Democratic republic of Ethiopia, Central Statistical Authority, online, http://unstats.un.org/unsd/censuskb20/Attachment489.aspx (accessed 15 December 2013).

Central Statistical Authority (CSA) (2012) Ethiopia Demographic and Health Survey 2011, Addis Ababa, Ethiopia and Calverton, Maryland, USA: Central Statistical Agency and

ICF International, online, http://www.usaid.gov/sites/default/files/documents/1860/ Demographic%20Health%20Survey%202011%20Ethiopia%20Final%20Report.pdf (accessed 10 November 2013).

Cesár, E. and Ekbom, A. (2013) Ethiopia environmental and climate change policy brief. Sida's Helpdesk for Environment and Climate Change, SLU, Sweden, 32 pp., online, www.sidaenvironmenthelpdesk.se (accessed 31 January 2014).

Clay, D.C., Molla, D. and Habtewold, D. (1999) Food aid in Ethiopia: a study of who needs it and who gets it, *Food Policy*, 24: 391–409.

Dejene, K.M. and Lemlem, S.M. (2012) Integrated agronomic crop managements to improve tef productivity under terminal drought. In: Rahman, I.M.M. and Hasegawa, H. (Ed.) *Water Stress*. ISBN: 978-953-307-963-9, online, http://www.intechopen. com/books/water-stress/integrated-agronomiccrop-managments-to-improve-tef-productivity-under-terminal-drought (accessed 20 November 2013).

del Ninno, C., Dorosh, P.A. and Subbarao, K. (2007) Food aid, domestic policy and food security: Contrasting experiences from south Asia and sub-Saharan Africa, *Food Policy*, 32: 413–35.

Demeke, M. and Di Marcantonio, F. (2013) Analysis of incentives and disincentives for tef in Ethiopia. Technical Notes Series, MAFAP, FAO, Rome, online, http://www.fao. org/fileadmin/templates/mafap/documents/technical_notes/Ethiopia/ETHIOPIA_ Technical_Note_TEFF_EN_Jan2013.pdf (accessed 10 January 2014).

Dercon, S., Hoddinott, J. and Woldehanna, T. (2005) Shocks and consumption in 15 Ethiopian villages, 1999–2004, *Journal of African Economics*, 14 (4): 559–85.

Devereux, S. (2000) Food insecurity in Ethiopia: a discussion paper for DFID, IDS, Sussex, online, http://www.addisvoice.com/wp-content/uploads/2010/03/FoodSecEthiopia4. pdf (accessed 15 November 2013).

Doak, C., Subran, L., Marapin, S. and Ponce, M.C. (2008) Assessing the quality of food aid deliveries. A WFP project supported by the EC and Canada, VU University Amsterdam, online, http://www.wfp.org/fais/sites/default/files/Report%20of%20Nutritionist%20 2%20March%202009.pdf (accessed 15 January 2014).

Doocy, S., Teferra, S., Norell, D. and Burnham, G. (2005) Credit program outcomes: coping capacity and nutritional status in the food insecure context of Ethiopia, *Social Science & Medicine*, 60: 2371–82.

Dorosh, P.A. and Rashid, S. (2013) Food and agriculture in Ethiopia: progress and policy challenges, IFPRI Issue brief 74, Washington, DC, online, http://www.ifpri.org/sites/ default/files/publications/ib74.pdf (accessed 5 December 2013).

DRN-ADE-BAASTEL-ECO-NCG (2004) Joint evaluation of effectiveness and impact of the enabling development policy of the WFP: Ethiopia Country Study, vol. I, online, www.edpevaluation.com (accessed 30 December 2013).

Ethiopia National Population Policy (ENPP) (1993) National Population Policy of Ethiopia, Addis Ababa, Ethiopia, Office of the Prime Minister, online http://www.un.org/popin/ regional/africa/ethiopia/policy/ (accessed 25 November 2013).

Federal Democratic Republic of Ethiopia (FDRE) (1994) An economic development strategy for Ethiopia, Addis Ababa, Ethiopia.

Federal Democratic Republic of Ethiopia (FDRE) (1999) Agricultural Research and Training Project: Ethiopian Research-Extension Farmer Linkages Strategy, vol. I, Addis Ababa, Ethiopia.

Federal Democratic Republic of Ethiopia (FDRE) (2002) Food Security Strategy, Addis Ababa, Government of Ethiopia.

Federal Democratic Republic of Ethiopia (FDRE) (2012) Productive Safety Net Program, Addis Ababa, Government of Ethiopia.

Food and Agriculture Organization (FAO) (2013) The state of food insecurity in the world: the multiple dimensions of food security, Rome, online, http://http://www.fao.org/economic/ess/e ss-fs/ess-fadata/en/ (accessed 29 November 2013).

Food and Nutrition Board (2002) *Dietary Reference Intakes for Energy, Carbohydrate, Fiber, Fat, Fatty Acids, Cholesterol, Protein, and Amino Acids.* National Academy Press, Washington, DC.

Gebreselassie, S. (2006) Food aid and small holder agriculture in Ethiopia: options and scenarios. A policy paper for the future agricultures consortium workshop, IDS, online, http://www.future-agricultures.org/pdf%20files/SG_paper_1.pdf (accessed 30 December 2013).

Gelan, A.U. (2007) Does food aid have disincentive effects on local production? A general equilibrium perspective on food aid in Ethiopia, *Food Policy*, (32): 436–58.

Graham, A., Aubry, S., Künnemann, R. and Suárez, S.M. (2011) The role of the EU in land grabbing in Africa – CSO Monitoring 2009–10. Advancing African Agriculture: The Impact of Europe's Policies and Practices on African Agriculture and Food Security. Paper presented at the International Conference on Global Land Grabbing, 6–8 April, IDS, Sussex.

Gutema, B.B. (2001) Food insecurity in Ethiopia: the impact of socio political forces. Development research series, research centre on development and international relations. Working paper No. 102, Aalborg University, Denmark, online, http://vbn.aau.dk/files/33641604/DIR_wp_102.pdf (accessed 30 October 2013).

Held, D., Nag, E-M. and Roger, C. (2012) The governance of climate change in developing countries. A Report on the International and Domestic Climate Change Policies in China, Brazil, Ethiopia, and Tuvalu, STIN, France.

HLTF (2009) Ethiopia: Full country visit report. Coordination team of the UN System High-Level Task Force on the Global Food Security Crisis, online, http://un-foodsecurity.org/sites/default/files/Ethiopia_Sept09.pdf (accessed 10 December 2013).

Hurni, H. (1993) Land degradation, famine, and land resource scenarios in Ethiopia. In: Pimentel, D. (Ed.) *World Soil Erosion and Conservation. Cambridge Studies in Applied Ecology and Resource Management.* Cambridge University Press, Cambridge.

International Food Policy Research Institute (IFPRI) (2010) Fertilizer and soil fertility potential in Ethiopia: constraints and opportunities for enhancing the system. Working paper, July, online, http://www.ifpri.org/sites/default/files/publications/ethiopianagsectorwp_soil.pdf (accessed 10 December 2013).

International Fund for Agricultural Development (IFAD) (2012) Enabling poor rural people to overcome poverty in Ethiopia. October, Addis Ababa, Ethiopia, online, www.ruralpovertyportal.org (accessed 10 December 2013).

Jayne, T.S. and Molla, D. (1995) Food security research project: toward a research agenda to promote household access to food in Ethiopia. Working paper 2, Food Security Research Project, Ministry of Economic Development and Cooperation, Addis Ababa, online, http://fsg.afre.msu.edu/ethiopia/wp2.pdf (accessed 5 December 2013).

Jayne, T.S., Strauss, J., Yamano, T. and Molla, D. (2001) Targeting of food aid in rural Ethiopia: chronic need or inertia?, *Journal of Development Economics*, 68: 247–88.

Kassa, B. (2003) Agricultural extension in Ethiopia: the case of participatory demonstration and training extension system, *Journal of Social Development in Africa*, 18 (1): 49–83.

Kassa, B. (2004) Management of droughts and famines in Ethiopia, *Journal of Social Development in Africa*, 19 (1): 93–127.

Lavers, T. (2012) 'Land grab' as development strategy? The political economy of agricultural investment in Ethiopia, *The Journal of Peasant Studies*, 39 (1): 105–32.

Lebeda, P., Chambers, Z., Destrée, A., Doležal, J., Lukáš, I., Marčík, F., Maritz, C. and Milerová-Prášková, D. (2010) *Ethiopia's Food Insecurity: Europe's Role within the Broader Context of Food Flows, Climate Change and Land Grabs*. Glopolis, Prague.

Minot, N. (2010) *Transmission of Food Price Changes from World Markets to African Markets and its Effect on Household Welfare*. IFPRI, Washington, DC.

MoFED (2002) Ethiopia: Sustainable Development and Poverty Reduction Program, Addis Ababa, Ethiopia, online, http://siteresources.worldbank.org/INTETHIOPIA/Overview/20207639/2002_07_prsp.pdf (accessed 10 December 2013).

MoFED (2006) Building on progress: a plan for accelerated and sustained development to end poverty 2005/06–2009/10, vol. I, September, Addis Ababa, Ethiopia, online, http://www.afdb.org/fileadmin/uploads/afdb/Documents/Policy-Documents/Plan_for_Accelerated_and_Sustained_(PASDEP)_final_July_2007_Volume_I_3.pdf (accessed 30 November 2013).

MoFED (2007) Building on progress: a plan for accelerated and sustained development to end poverty, Annual progress report 2005/06, Addis Ababa, online, http://cooperacionetiopia.files.wordpress.com/2011/01/pasdep-annual-progress-report-2005-2006.pdf (accessed 30 November 2013).

Nedessa, B. and Wickrema, S. (2010) Disaster risk reduction: experience from the MERET project in Ethiopia. In: Omamo, S.W., Gentilini, U. and Sandstrom, S., *Revolution: From Food Aid to Food Assistance: Innovations in Overcoming Hunger*. WFP, Rome, online, http://documents.wfp.org/stellent/groups/public/documents/newsroom/wfp225646.pdf (accessed 5 December 2013).

NMA (2007) Climate change: National Adaptation Programme of Action of Ethiopia, Addis Ababa, Ethiopia, online, http://unfccc.int/resource/docs/napa/eth01.pdf (accessed 10 December 2013).

Philor, L. (2011) Erosion impacts on soil and environmental quality: vertisols in the Highlands Region of Ethiopia, University of Florida, Florida.

Rancourt, M., Bellavance, F. and Goentzel, J. (2013) Market analysis and transportation procurement for food aid in Ethiopia. CIRRELT-2013-30, online, https://www.cirrelt.ca/DocumentsTravail/CIRRELT-2013-30.pdf (accessed 20 December 2013).

Rashid, S. (2010) The cereal availability in Ethiopia, 2007/2008. A study in support of the Mars-food action of the European Union, IFPRI, Addis Ababa.

Rashid, S. and Lemma, S. (2011) Strategic grain reserves in Ethiopia, institutional design and operational performance. IFPRI Discussion paper 01054, Markets, trade and Institutions division, Addis Ababa, Ethiopia, online, http://www.ifpri.org/sites/default/files/publications/ifpridp01054.pdf (accessed 20 December 2013).

Rashid, S. and Negassa, A. (2011) Policies and performance of Ethiopian cereal markets. Ethiopia Strategy Support Program II (ESSP II) Working Paper 21, IFPRI, Addis Ababa, online, http://www.ifpri.org/sites/default/files/publications/esspwp21.pdf (accessed 20 December 2013).

Sabates, W.R. and Devereux, S. (2010) Cash transfers and high food prices: explaining outcomes on Ethiopia's productive safety net programme, *Food policy*, (35): 274–85.

Shoham, J. (2007) Mid-term evaluation of PRRO 10362.0: enabling livelihood protection and promotion in Ethiopia. WFP, online, http://www.alnap.org/resource/11266 (accessed 20 December 2013).

Tadege, A. (2007) Climate change national adaptation program of action of Ethiopia, Ministry of Water Resources and National Meteorological Services, Addis Ababa,

Ethiopia, online, http://unfccc.int/resource/docs/napa/eth01.pdf (accessed 20 November 2013).

Ulimwengu, J., Workneh, S. and Paulos, Z. (2009). Impact of soaring food price in Ethiopia: does location matter? IFPRI, Washington, DC.

United Nations Development Programme (UNDP) (2006a) Country evaluation: assessment of development results – Ethiopia, online, http://web.undp.org/evaluation/documents/ADR/ADR_Reports/ADR_Ethiopia.pdf (accessed 20 December 2013).

United Nations Development Programme (UNDP) (2006b) *Human Development Report.* Oxford University Press, New York.

United States Agency for International Development (USAID)-COMPETE (2010) Staple foods value chain analysis country report – Ethiopia. Chemonics International Inc., online, http://www.competeafrica.org/Files/ETHIOPIA_Staple_Foods_Value_Chain_Analysis_April_2010.pdf (10 December 2013).

United States Agency for International Development (USAID) (Africa Bureau and Population and Reproductive Health) and EFMH (2012) Three successful sub-Saharan Africa family planning programs: lessons for meeting the MDGs, Malawi Ministry of Health, Rwanda Ministry of Health. Africa Bureau, USAID, Washington, DC, online, http://www.fhi360.org/sites/default/files/media/documents/3-successful-family-planing-programs-africa.pdf (accessed 15 December 2013).

United States Agency for International Development (USAID)-USDA (2008) U.S. international food assistance report. USAID Development Experience Clearing House, Silver Spring, MD, online, http://pdf.usaid.gov/pdf_docs/PDACK880.pdf (22 December 2013).

van der Veen, A. and Gebrehiwot, T. (2011) Effect of policy interventions on food security in Tigray, Northern Ethiopia, *Ecology and Society*, 16 (1): 1–18.

Vhughen, D. and Gebru, A. (2012) Large-scale acquisitions of land in Ethiopia: placing land rights at the heart of development. Brief, Focus on Land in Africa, online, www.focusonland.com (accessed 10 November 2013).

von Braun, J. and Olofinbiyi, T. (2007) Famine and food insecurity in Ethiopia. Case study #7–4 of the program: food policy for developing countries: The role of government in the global food system, Cornell University, New York.

World Food Programme (WFP) (2012) Food aid flows. International Food Aid Information System, August, online, www.wfp.org (accessed 10 December 2013).

World Bank (1987) Agriculture: a strategy for growth, a sector review, Report No. 6512-ET, Washington, DC.

Zewdu, G.A. and Malek, M. (2010) Implications of land policies for rural-urban linkages and rural transformation in Ethiopia. In: Dorosh, P.A. and Rashid, S. (Eds) *Food and Agriculture in Ethiopia: Progress and Policy Challenges*. University of Pennsylvania Press, Philadelphia.

8 Tanzania's food security

Seeking sustainable agricultural intensification and dietary diversity

Sandy Fritz, Robyn Alders, Brigitte Bagnol, Halifa Msami and Karimu Mtambo

Introduction

Tanzania sits on the eastern coast of Africa with a population of almost 45 million (FAO, 2012a). On average, the Tanzanian economy has grown an attractive 7 per cent per annum over the last ten years (URT, 2012a), primarily as a result of mining. Mining, however, has few links forward or backward to the local economy, representing only 0.5 per cent of total employment in 2006 (Osberg and Bandara, 2012), and consequently has little impact on reducing high levels of poverty.

The sector most fundamental to Tanzania's economy is agriculture. Over 75 per cent of the population depend on agriculture for their livelihoods. Agriculture contributes about 95 per cent of the food consumed; it represents 25 per cent of GDP, 24 per cent of the national export revenue (URT, 2011a) and provides 65 per cent of raw material used in Tanzanian industries (Mbunda, 2011).

Although agriculture is the cornerstone of Tanzania's economy, the country does not enjoy food security and there are high levels of malnutrition. Throughout a relatively short history of independence, Tanzania has adopted many different strategies to increase food production and economic growth. The strategies have generally achieved this outcome, but without significantly improving nutrition or reducing poverty. In recent years, the importance of smallholder agriculture has been recognised, and this view is represented in the current development framework. However, the framework also incorporates policies encouraging increased foreign investment and larger farms with high-cost inputs. In this way Tanzania's food security policy is ambiguous. This chapter explores the contradictions, the potential challenges and the opportunities.

The following section presents an overview of Tanzania's current food production, distribution and constraints; the status of food security, poverty and nutrition; and a brief history of policy relevant to food security. The third section describes the government's current food security strategies; what drives them, how they sit within the African context, support from donors and response to the strategies. An analysis of the capacity of the current approach to provide food security in Tanzania is presented in the fourth section, along with examples of sustainable smallholder production. In the last section, the authors present recommendations and policy implications.

Tanzania's food security

Current food production, constraints and distribution

In Tanzania, different farming systems have evolved in line with local conditions. There are seven agroecological zones, generally falling into two main categories: the highland agroecological zone, and the arid and semi-arid zones. Traditionally, the small-scale farms of Tanzania were dispersed family units based on subsistence in less arid areas with pastoralism in the drier areas (Fratkin and Mearns, 2003). Most of the population is concentrated in the periphery of the country and this is where most of the food is produced. It must then be transported from these areas to dry central regions, particularly to the inner urban centres.

Farm size varies but most farmers operate between 0.5 and 2.5 ha. They, and livestock herders who keep an average of 50 head of cattle, utilise approximately 85 per cent of the arable land (Mnenwa and Maliti, 2010). Most are subsistence farmers growing maize and other crops such as cassava, beans, rice, bananas and sweet potatoes, sorghum (Coulson, 2011)[1] and millet. From 2000 to 2007 production in wheat and rice, along with export of cotton, tobacco and sugarcane, grew rapidly.[2] The growth had little impact on poverty or nutrition outcomes because it was concentrated in a few regions and primarily produced by larger-scale commercial farmers (Pauw and Thurlow, 2010).

The Maasai pastoralists historically occupy drier regions of the savannahs, arid lands and high plateaus and traded their cattle for grains. Some undertook limited cultivation to supplement their diet. Pastoralism remains an important livelihood today, providing meat, leather, wool and milk. The Maasai herd cattle, goats and sheep, primarily in the northern part of the country (Fratkin and Mearns, 2003). Pastoral systems are highly productive because herds are moved in response to seasonal and climatic variations, largely over lands not suitable for other forms of agriculture (Neely *et al.*, 2007). The mobility of pastoralists is currently declining, as pastureland is lost to private ranches, game parks and urban areas. The push to commercial production has created a divide between wealthier herd owners and poor Maasai. Many of the poor work for wealthier relatives and others have migrated to cities. Today the Maasai have the status of a minority indigenous people as their population is less than 200,000 (Fratkin and Mearns, 2003).

A number of factors constrain agricultural production. Low soil fertility (Verchot *et al.*, 2007) and degradation is a primary constraint. High input prices and a lack of credit means most smallholders continuously mine the soil by cultivating without fertilisers. Organic matter content of soils is declining. Deforestation rates are high as farmers are forced to abandon poor soils and encroach on forests, which are more fertile. Increased population is leading to reduced per capita land availability and a breakdown of traditional natural fallow systems that used to be the means of replenishing soil fertility (Ajayi *et al.*, 2007).

Agricultural production suffers a yield gap (actual yields compared to attainable yields) of 25–30 per cent as a result of irregular rainfall (Rockstrom *et al.*, 2009a). Famines resulting from floods or drought have become increasingly common since the mid-1990s (Orindi and Murray, 2005). Climate change is expected to make both weather conditions and agricultural production more volatile (Ahmed *et al.*, 2011) and result in:

- water scarcity due to increasing temperatures and decreasing rainfall;
- increased rainfall and temperatures in other areas, increasing the incidence of pests and diseases;
- salt-water intrusion affecting fresh water availability in coastal areas;
- increased vulnerability of Tanzania's mangroves (an important and productive ecosystem) to inundation;
- loss of biodiversity, expected to be a major blow to Tanzania's tourist industry;
- instability in the supply of staple grains and food prices. Maize yields may drop by 33 per cent.

(Orindi and Murray, 2005)

A spatial assessment to determine the impact of climate change on the production of six major crops in sub-Saharan Africa (SSA) identified Tanzania as one of several countries that are likely to face more serious undernutrition problems (Liu *et al.*, 2008). Local strategies to cope with food shortages (e.g. during drought and flood) include collecting wild fruits, selling assets and finding casual labour to tide families over until the next harvest (Orindi and Murray, 2005). While the availability of wild fruits is a significant aid and could play a stronger role in food security, the selling of assets erodes household resources and increases their vulnerability. Increasing food security requires adaptation to climate change by building resilient farming systems, communities and households. In the meantime, the response of the Government of Tanzania (GoT) to food shortages is to conduct rapid vulnerability assessment and provide free food for the most affected population, usually for a period of two to three months.

An additional constraint has been the lack of adequate extension services (Coulson, 2011). Although 75 per cent of the target of one agricultural extension officer in each of 12,000 villages was reached in 2012, assistance with production, processing and marketing opportunities is still limited (Uliwa and Fischer, 2004).

Finally, empowering women through gender balance is widely recognised as being critical to family health and nutrition and to increasing agricultural production (FAO, 2011). Women in Tanzania constitute the main part of the agricultural workforce. But they are disadvantaged by undernutrition (UNDP, 2011); lack of land ownership; reduced access to land and credit; and, compared to men, generally less access to formal employment and control over household assets and decision making (URT, 2010). This is a key constraint to improving agricultural production.

Tanzania has made good progress on gender issues with respect to educational enrolment at the primary and secondary levels. However, the literacy rate for women has shown only a slight improvement (URT, 2010). In rural areas 75 per cent of women report agriculture/livestock/forestry to be their main activity; 40 per cent of women in these areas are illiterate (NBS, 2007 cited in URT,

2010). Literacy in these roles is needed to access information posted on village and council notice boards, extension resources, modern technologies (URT, 2010) and contracts and business plans.

Tanzania's Women's Development and Gender Policy aims to create an environment conducive to empowering women. There has been active intervention to close the gender gap by increasing the number of female extension officers and increasing female participation in farmer field schools (FAO, 2011). In 2009, the government established the Tanzania Women's Bank to empower women through the provision of banking and credit facilities at very low interest rates. More generally, the percentage of women in leadership positions in public service has increased considerably, but less so in the districts (URT, 2010).

Beyond production constraints, there are a very limited number of markets and storage facilities; certainly, they do not exist in every village. This leads to a high level of post-harvest loss (30 per cent of cereal, 20 per cent of roots and tubers, 70 per cent of fruits and vegetables, 20 per cent of fishery products). There is inadequate budget allocation for such facilities and a breakdown of traditional best practices in preserving agricultural produce (UNDP, 2011).

Where markets do exist, small-scale farmers participate at relatively low levels.[3] They usually sell a great part of their produce at once instead of selling smaller quantities at a time, which might enable them to take advantage of considerable price variations over the season (Mkenda and van Campenhout, 2011). Marketing constraints include:

- poor quality roads – a major constraint to market efficiency (Mnenwa and Maliti, 2010);
- lack of electricity for food processing and storage facilities (Mnenwa and Maliti, 2010);
- lack of market information[4] or capacity to negotiate prices (Mnenwa and Maliti, 2010);
- poor credit availability, reducing flexibility (Mkenda and van Campenhout, 2011);
- taxes on produce sold out of the farmer's district and export restrictions (Mbunda, 2011).

Given marketing constraints, small-scale farmers are more concerned with reducing risk and managing income than maximising production (Green, 2012). Under existing agricultural development programmes, the GoT intends to further develop market infrastructure and increase investment in processing and packaging; and to encourage the private sector to play a major role in marketing of agricultural products.[5]

Cooperatives and producer organisations (POs) are able to support smallholders to a limited extent. These organisations have always played a key part in Tanzania's agriculture[6] and most agribusinesses rely on them to bulk up crops from smallholders. POs may provide bargaining power for smallholders; advocate for policy change; participate in decentralisation of government services;

facilitate adoption of new technologies; link members to new markets/out-grower schemes; and assist with access to financial services. But, generally, they are poorly resourced and do not have capacity to carry out these functions (Uliwa and Fischer, 2004).

Current food security, poverty and nutritional status

Tanzania is described as being more or less self-sufficient in food production since 2005 (URT, 2012a), gradually increasing to 113 per cent in 2012/13 and expected to reach 118 per cent in 2013/14 (Mtambo, 2013). Nevertheless, approximately 39 per cent of Tanzanians suffer from undernourishment (FAO, 2012b). More than a third of children under the age of 5 years are affected by chronic malnutrition. In the southern zone, the prevalence is greater than 50 per cent (URT, 2013). Childhood malnutrition is a result of poor nutrition of reproductive age women, inadequate dietary intake and disease (URT, 2013; UNDP, 2011). Indirectly it results from poverty, an unhealthy environment and poor access to health services (URT, 2011b). Stunting affects 42 per cent of children and 16 per cent are underweight (URT, 2013). The prevalence of wasting remained unchanged from 1999 to 2010 (URT, 2012a). The most notable micronutrient deficiencies in Tanzania are iron,[7] vitamin A and iodine deficiencies (UNDP, 2011). The geographic pattern of malnutrition in Tanzania suggests that areas of the country with cereal surpluses are also the areas with relatively high rates of malnutrition (UNDP, 2011) – demonstrating the significance of the World Food Summit definition of food security (FAO, 2012b) as requiring both sufficient production, and physical and economic access to food.

Despite a variety of strategies to reduce poverty and malnutrition, the number of poor increased by 1.3 million over a decade of economic growth to 2007, with vast geographic disparities in incidence and severity of poverty (UNDP, 2011). One-third of Tanzanians live on less than US$1/day, with poverty rates higher among rural households (37.6 per cent) than urban households (16.4 per cent) (NBS, 2009). The rural poor are thus the most vulnerable in Tanzania and a group that needs most attention in initiatives to improve food security.

Undernutrition creates an increased burden on the health care system and lost productivity. Deficiencies in iron, vitamin A and folic acid alone cost Tanzania over US$518 million/year, around 2.65 per cent of the country's GDP (World Bank, 2010a).

Public nutrition intervention in Tanzania dates back to the 1940s. Current interventions include vitamin A supplementation; an integrated package for anaemia; addressing related health problems; improving access to safe water; and salt fortified with iodine. A National Food Fortification Alliance has been formed to progress other fortification interventions. The National Nutrition Strategy targets include increased services (particularly at district levels); education and awareness; coordination with agriculture and industry; and supportive legislation (URT, 2011b). Programmes are supported through the World Food Programme, UNICEF (the United Nations Children's Fund) and others. These programmes are immensely important and critical to the health of Tanzanians. However, their scale and duration are testimony to a country/people without food security.

History of policies related to food security

Formerly known as Tanganyika, the country gained independence from Britain in 1961 and united with Zanzibar in 1964, becoming the United Republic of Tanzania. During the colonial period, the introduction of Western-style agriculture with strong commercial and export-oriented systems (Turshen, 1977) reduced dietary diversity by changing food preferences (Latham, 1997) and availability. In 1967, the GoT launched the Arusha Declaration on Socialism and Self-Reliance and established the concept of Ujamaa. This was an important step in the post-independence period, intended to pave the way for the future of food production and rural development. Ujamaa included collectivised agriculture and villagisation where five million smallholders and farm workers were displaced from traditional holdings to settlements of 250–600 households, establishing approximately 8,000 villages with a new system of village government (McCall, 1985). Most estates and plantations were nationalised into state farms. The objective was to eliminate external dependence, and achieve self-sufficiency in food production at all levels using Green Revolution technology. By the 1980s, production subsidies drained the government's budget and Ujamaa failed to deliver the expected results. The rate and scale of change and a lack of ownership and control of land by farmers was considered to have contributed to low productivity (Uliwa and Fischer, 2004).

As a result of these failures, the government turned to a neoliberal approach of privatisation, adopting the World Bank/International Monetary Fund Structural Adjustment Policies (SAP) from 1986 to the late 1990s. Reduced subsidies and open markets meant that small-scale producers had to face high input prices and increased competition. Lack of credit compelled farmers to use fewer inputs, switch to different crops and/or reduce areas under cultivation (Mwakalobo and Kashuliza, 1999 cited by Mkenda and van Campenhout, 2011). The economy suffered from a decline in demand due to the population's reduced purchasing power. The period of SAP has been described as one during which the focus changed frequently, the country and its people started losing direction and initiative, and donor-dependency filled the void (URT, undated a).

In 1998, the National Poverty Eradication Strategy (NPES) provided an overall framework targeting improved economic growth as a basis for poverty eradication by 2025. There have been a number of strategies under this framework. Growth in GDP did occur, but hunger and malnutrition continued, particularly in rural areas (UNDP, 2011).

A second generation of poverty reduction strategies known as MKUKUTA was initiated in 2001.[8] MKUKUTA I (2001–11) targeted annual GDP growth of 6 to 8 per cent by 2010, with the expressed goal of improving food availability and accessibility at household level (URT, 2012a). To target rural development, the government launched the Agricultural Sector Development Strategy (ASDS) to modernise, commercialise and increase production on subsistence farms, and integrate them into the market economy. The ASDS was implemented in 2006 under the Agricultural Sector Develop Programme (ASDP).[9] ASDP prioritises the provision of public goods that currently constrain agriculture (Cooksey, 2013). The degree to which current programmes focus on the target and priorities of ASDP is one of the ambiguities of current policy.

Current national strategies for food security

Tanzania is now implementing MKUKUTA II (2010–15). The ASDP continues but the *Kilimo Kwanza* (Agriculture First) programme emerged in 2009. *Kilimo Kwanza* was initiated by the private sector through the Tanzania National Business Council. It targets private sector investment, and aims to increase the agricultural growth rate from 4 to 10 per cent by adopting the methods of the Green Revolution; i.e. a high-technology input system focused on mechanisation, irrigation, improved seed and greater use of petroleum-based products such as chemical fertilisers and pesticides (Ngaiza, 2012; URT, 2012b). It involves amendments to the Land Act, moves to fast-track contract farming, infrastructure development and industrialisation of the agricultural sector (URT undated b).

Both ASDP and *Kilimo Kwanza* are implemented under the Tanzania Agriculture and Food Security Investment Plan (TAFSIP). The TAFSIP identifies priority areas for investments that will drive agricultural development in both the mainland and Zanzibar. TAFSIP is led by the agricultural sector ministries and is linked to the international community through the Ministry of Finance. TAFSIP recognises existing growth as skewed towards larger-scale production, and identifies the need to broaden the base of agricultural growth and embrace crops that are valuable to the poor in terms of income and nutrition. But since 2009, *Kilimo Kwanza* – which is centred on larger farms, input subsidies and mechanisation (Mbunda, 2011) – has become the government's central strategy for agricultural development (Ngaiza, 2012; Cooksey, 2013). In this section, we look at the drivers, the role of donors and response from the wider community. In the next section, we assess the risks associated with prioritising this initiative.

Factors driving the initiative and the role of donors

Factors driving the initiative are primarily economic opportunities. Domestically this includes the prospects of growth and support for infrastructure development from private investment and donors who will participate in the initiative. Also, because food is the largest single component of household expenditure representing, on average, 64 per cent of the household budget (NBS, 2009), targeting increased food production is aimed at reducing inflationary pressures (URT, 2012a).

International drivers include the increasing demand for food globally as a result of population growth; and rising incomes and changing diets in Asia creating more demand for horticultural products, meat and oils. Other drivers include the prospect that global food prices will continue to rise as: food production competes for resources (land, water, energy) with market demands for biofuels and timber; the impacts of climate change are felt; and as a result of rising land values (World Bank, 2008; Cotula *et al.*, 2009; Kaarhus *et al.*, 2010). Increased demand and rising prices represent good market opportunities. But in the context of food security, in Tanzania and globally, the crucial element is to ensure that increased production is environmentally and socially sustainable (Godfray *et al.*, 2010).

There is also a strong regional driver. Tanzania is a member of the African Union (AU).[10] The AU promotes increased investment in agriculture as the best option for economic development of African countries (Ngaiza, 2012). Under the framework of the AU's New Partnership for Africa's Development (NEPAD) Tanzania undertook a regional consultative process regarding agriculture and food security. The process culminated in the signing of a compact under the Comprehensive Africa Agriculture Development Programme (CAADP). It is operationalised in Tanzania through the country's investment plan, TAFSIP (URT, 2011a).

Another aspect of the regional processes is Tanzania's alignment with two African groups targeting private sector investments: the Alliance for a Green Revolution in Africa (AGRA);[11] and the New Alliance for Food Security and Nutrition ('New Alliance').[12] As part of these programmes and the CAADP Compact, support is provided to Tanzania from different funding sources (URT, 2011a).

One of the key roles that the government envisages for small-scale farmers is that of out-growers in a commercial agricultural corridor to be established, the Southern Agricultural Growth Corridor of Tanzania (SAGCOT). The corridor is a belt crossing the east-west centre of Tanzania (Kaarhus *et al.*, 2010). SAGCOT is expected to be largely funded by the private sector with support from the World Bank, IFAD and other donor partners (URT, 2011a). Private sector investments are aimed at scaling up specific commodity production (maize, soya, wheat, rice, sugarcane, red meat and high-value fruits) (Mbunda, 2011). SAGCOT is the first in a sequence of initiatives to develop agricultural corridors and provides a framework for public-private partnership to invest in value chain development (Ngaiza, 2012). The Norwegian fertiliser company, Yara International, has been instrumental in starting the initiative and will build a port warehouse to wholesale fertilisers. The government's fertiliser subsidy programme is expected to contribute towards increased demand for fertilisers (Kaarhus *et al.*, 2010).

Tanzania is one of the largest recipients of overseas development assistance (ODA), receiving US$26.85 billion between 1990 and 2010. There are 42 donors with four providing over 50 per cent of Tanzania's ODA: World Bank, the UK, Japan and the USA (Tripp, 2012). Nevertheless, Tanzania's commitment to providing incentives for private sector investments is considered to transform the CAADP/TAFSIP project from a traditional state-donor project approach to a more market-driven one. It is suggested that donor agencies are under pressure to align 'more closely with their national agribusiness corporations, and to carry some of the initial investment costs and risks' (Cooksey, 2013).

Wider response to the national initiatives

Kilimo Kwanza is supported by donors and through CAADP and other African programmes. But there are criticisms of both the strategy and the process by which it has been developed. One criticism is that generic agricultural growth has not previously altered the level of poverty, and that investment should address the specific requirements of farming systems in which poverty is highest (Mnenwa and Maliti, 2010). The perception that large, commercial farming is needed for agricultural development is criticised on the basis of the productivity of small-scale farmers globally (Kaarhus *et al.*, 2010; Coulson, 2011), and that the structure of growth (driven by large-scale farms in a few regions) is what constrains poverty reduction and fails to address nutritional needs (Pauw and Thurlow, 2010; URT, 2011a). The strategy is not sufficiently pro-poor (Osberg and Bandara, 2012).

Some authors report a lack of trust given the involvement of business elites with poor records and the risk of institutional failure and corruption (Kaarhus *et al.*, 2010; Cooksey, 2013). The process is said to have been collaborative but smallholders say they were not consulted and only heard about *Kilimo Kwanza* indirectly. It is difficult to establish whether smallholders are targeted by the strategy or how they can participate meaningfully. There is concern that donors and investors control the strategy (Mbunda, 2011).

A study commissioned by MVIWATA (*Mtandao wa Vikundi vya Wakulima Tanzania*, the National Network of Farmers Groups in Tanzania) and carried out by Sokoine University of Agriculture (SUA) indicates that:

- large-scale biofuel investment is likely to have negative impacts on the social and economic interests of small-scale farmers and ecological systems;
- the community has not been provided with legal support during negotiations for land acquisition and most smallholders did not participate in the negotiations;
- promises made during land acquisition negotiations to develop community infrastructure such as roads and schools have not been fulfilled.

(MVIWATA, 2013)

Twelve organisations representing African farmers; civil society organisations (CSOs), women's associations; journalists; and research, legal, business, traders and development groups have written to the AU regarding the implementation of NEPAD and CAADP. They argue that these initiatives started as something that generated hope and expectations for peasants and producers throughout Africa for the rebuilding of African economies by Africans. But they also stated that CAADP rapidly degenerated and lost the support of the African community as a result of insufficient dialogue with those most concerned, and a generic development plan heavily influenced by those outside of Africa. They view the process as an occasion 'for negotiating new aid' which lacks 'clarity concerning the destination of these investments' (Cissokho, 2012).

Analysis of current food security strategies

This section analyses how well aligned the current strategies are with providing food security[13] in Tanzania. It concentrates on the weaknesses of *Kilimo Kwanza*, especially in light of an increasing call globally for agricultural science and technology to move away from large-scale enterprises, to better address the needs of the small farmers and to lessen the environmental impacts of past agricultural practices (McIntyre *et al.*, 2009; De Schutter, 2010; Godfray *et al.*, 2010; GOS, 2011), particularly through sustainable agricultural intensification (SAI). SAI 'is defined as producing more output from the same area of land while reducing the negative environmental impacts and at the same time increasing contributions to natural capital and the flow of environmental services' (Pretty *et al.*, 2011).

Physical and economic access

Having physical and economic access means that sufficient food is either produced and marketed within Tanzania or imported; and that households – where they are not producing enough food for their own consumption – have the economic resources to purchase food.

Land and land use rights

Tanzania is one of the hot spots for international land acquisition related to biofuel production (Cotula *et al.*, 2009) and there is strong interest in leasing or purchasing land for food production for other countries, tourism and land speculation (Kaarhus *et al.*, 2010).

Under the Land Act (1999) all land in Tanzania is public land vested in the president as trustee on behalf of all citizens. Land is categorised as general land, reserved, and village land. Village land is the largest category representing about 70 per cent of the total land (Kaarhus *et al.*, 2010) and provides security for land owned or managed by villagers under customary right of occupancy (Hall, 2011).

The intention of *Kilimo Kwanza*'s Pillar 5 is to amend the Village Land Act to facilitate access to land for investors. Recent legislation provides for this, allowing the minister to identify any land as an irrigation area (Makoye, 2013a)[14] and permits villagers to be shareholders using their land as equity (URT, undated b).

A number of authors consider that these arrangements are not in the interest of villagers. The process undermines customary land use rights; and decision-making procedures for villagers to reject or shape the deals are weak. Given the incentives offered by government to attract investors (e.g. tax holidays and nominal rental fees), returns at the national or village level are minimal (Vermeulen and Cotula, 2010). Smallholders feel they are at risk of losing their land and therefore their livelihood and capacity to feed their families (Mbunda, 2011). A survey by Research on Poverty Alleviation (REPOA) in 2012 'found that only four percent of farmers had a land title, making them potentially vulnerable to dispossession' (Cooksey, 2013). Land surveying and titling are slow and expensive processes; but already land and asset ownership is changing. Large allocations of indigenous forest have been cleared for biofuel cultivation. The value of the forest resources has been grossly under-calculated (e.g. at Kilwa, a once-off compensation of US$9.50/ ha was distributed to the district and the village on a ratio of 60:40 in return for a 34,000 ha allocation) (Sulle, 2010 cited in Hall, 2011). In exchange for use of their land, villagers have been promised jobs, roads and services; but few of these promises have been realised (Kaarhus *et al.*, 2010).

Tanzania has aimed to emulate the rapid development of Asian countries (UNDP, 2011). Studwell's work (2013) reveals the outcomes of land reform in that region. A comparison of the agricultural development in various Asian countries highlights the importance of egalitarian land reform; focusing on increased productivity of small farms through the adoption of labour-intensive agriculture with low-cost inputs; and the importance of infrastructure, credit, extension services, storage facilities and marketing. Countries adopting such policies experienced rapid economic development, increased employment and equality, staved off food import dependency, and achieved higher food production – in particular, greater yields on small farms than on plantations, including for cash crops such as sugar and rubber. Countries that failed to adopt or implement strong egalitarian land reform policies, along with support for small farm development, continue to experience inefficient farming, lower yields and high levels of poverty – despite the abundance of natural resources.

Already in Tanzania, there are conflicts between farmers and pastoralists over the shortage of land. Current land acquisitions exacerbate these conflicts and raise concerns about sufficient public scrutiny; a lack of overall land management planning and coordination; and lack of principles to guide transactions so they are equitable to all Tanzanians (Arduino *et al.*, 2012; Makoye, 2013b).

Increased mechanisation and jobs and livelihoods

A survey of household farm implements in Tanzania showed that 92 per cent of farming households own a hand hoe, 8 per cent own other implements, and 10 per cent own or use tractors (UNDP, 2011). This is largely because the cost of purchasing and operating tractors is beyond most of the country's smallholders; and there is a shortage of services and spare parts (Mbunda, 2011). While the Tanzania government is aiming to establish such services, the use of tractors is considered by some to be inappropriate for conditions in Tanzania (Coulson, 2011; Mbunda, 2011). They are not well suited to the fragile soils, terrain, and the unseasonable floods.

The government has recognised that existing land degradation poses a major threat to agricultural productivity, and more appropriate technologies are needed. However references to trade-offs between productivity and resource management objectives (URT, 2011a) make the government's level of commitment to sustainability unclear and suggests that production and sustainability are mutually exclusive, when in fact they are mutually dependent and should be targeted by common strategies.

Mechanised farms are likely to require fewer farm workers and Tanzania's non-agricultural sectors of mining and industry are not generating enough jobs to provide employment for displaced farm workers (Osberg and Bandara, 2012).[15] The labour market is highly competitive, casual/piecemeal and poorly paid (Muller, 2012). A key contribution of agriculture to poverty reduction is through the labour market channel. But this contribution is unlikely to be realised where the agricultural strategy does not feature labour-intensive production (De Schutter, 2009). Where jobs have been promised, investors have disappeared without having paid employees for several months (Kaarhus *et al.*, 2010). In other cases, migrant workers have been brought into Tanzania from the country of the company acquiring the land (Leahy, 2009).

The approach is of particular concern given that for most crops there are no economies of scale in agricultural production (De Schutter, 2009). Small-scale farmers are highly efficient producers (Studwell, 2013),[16] particularly when supported by farmer organisations (World Bank, 2008; Pretty *et al.*, 2011).

In the investment corridor (SAGCOT), it will be important to safeguard small farmers from problems of the past such as not being paid and middlemen taking a big portion of the price (Coulson, 2011). The Southern Highlands, where SAGCOT will be located, are subject to extreme events of floods and droughts; and highly vulnerable to increased frequency of climate change impacts. Floods have often destroyed infrastructure and impaired food distribution and access by affected communities (Kangalawe, 2012). This vulnerability further exposes smallholders that participate in equity investment, specialisation and/or high-cost inputs. While out-grower schemes could be a win-win situation, it emphasises the need for climate-smart agriculture (FAO, 2010), low-cost inputs and diversity in cropping.

Safe and nutritious food

The multiple functions of agriculture are to provide livelihoods; commodity production; environmental services; and, most fundamentally, nutrition. Attention has recently been drawn to the need for closer ties between agriculture and nutrition (Masset *et al.*, 2011; Haddad, 2013; Wiggins and Keats, 2013).

Aggregate data indicates that agricultural growth has a greater impact on the income of the poor than non-agricultural growth (World Bank, 2008; Haddad, 2013). But research emphasises the lack of evidence between agricultural interventions and a positive impact on household or community nutritional status (Masset *et al.*, 2011). A significant majority of the interventions studied were located in SSA. Agricultural development in general is considered to have neglected nutrition as a direct outcome (Hawkes *et al.*, 2012). This is specifically the case in Tanzania (Pauw and Thurlow, 2010), although there are exceptions (e.g., Alders *et al.*, 2014).

Not all projects need to focus on specific nutritional outcomes, but the framework in which agricultural projects are developed and implemented should have

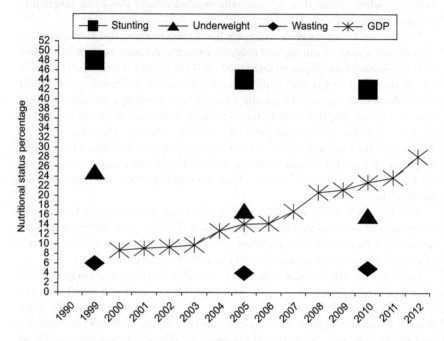

Figure 8.1 Growth and nutritional status of children.

Source: GDP 2000–03 adapted from URT, 2013;[1] Trading Economics, 2014; World Bank, 2014.

[1] Stunting, underweight and wasting from: http://www.who.int/nutgrowthd/database/countries/who_standards/tza.pdf cited by URT 2013:4.

nutrition at its centre. The framework must extend beyond production to include the availability of nutrient-rich foods at prices that poor people can afford; and/or increase their ability to pay (Hawkes *et al.*, 2012). Such a framework is more likely to provide direction about what type of agriculture and crops are promoted; their distribution; and how broadly the returns to investment are distributed (Wiggins and Keats, 2013). Appropriate indicators include measures that demonstrate: achievement against the Millennium Development Goals (MDGs), increased production, access to and consumption of high-nutrient foods; increased income of poor households; empowerment of women in decision making; improved access to information about nutrition (Haddad, 2013); labour-intensiveness as a measure of the intervention's capacity to increase employment; access to low-cost inputs; better storage; and improved processing, transport and markets that facilitate participation of poor households.

Nutritional security is a strategic objective of TAFSIP. However, TAFSIP states that there are 'potential tensions between policies that encourage agricultural commercialisation (often involving increased specialisation) and the need to maintain diversification of farming systems and diets' (URT, 2011a). It identifies improved diets as outcomes of the investment plan, but relies primarily on agricultural growth.

Two percent of the TAFSIP budget is allocated to food and nutrition security with the bulk of the remaining budget allocated to production and commercialisation (71 per cent) and irrigation (14 per cent). To achieve the targeted 6 per cent agricultural growth, the allocation of resources will be rationalised and 'there is the risk that smallholders will be marginalised, or at least fail to participate fully, against a background of rapid agricultural commercialisation' (URT, 2011a).

This apparent contradiction is fundamental to criticism of the TAFSIP as being ambiguous in its generality; attempting to be all things to all people; and without a consistent, coherent policy (Cissokho, 2012; Cooksey, 2013). The measure of nutritional indicators has not changed significantly over more than a decade while during that time the focus of government strategy was the same as what it is now – i.e. growth (Figure 8.1). Although growth is now targeted to agriculture, unless nutrition and smallholders are at the centre of the framework (rather than in a position at risk of being 'marginalised') is it unclear how achievements against a nutritional objective will be greater than they have been in the past.

The current approach has implications for what have been identified as key determinants of nutritional status. An institutional analysis of nutrition in Tanzania reported that undernutrition is not caused by food shortages, and that the key determinants are access and availability, which are strongly influenced by income and food prices (Leach and Kilama, 2009). Household income is largely determined by livelihood. Investment focused on large-scale specialised agriculture will support improved nutrition only if it helps smallholders to diversify and/or increases the income of the poor.

Agricultural diversity improves production and nutrition by:

- improving efficient use of water, sun and nutrients (Tilman *et al.*, 2001);
- improving diversity of foods at the level of household and local markets;
- reducing vulnerability to income loss because the household is not dependent on a single crop in the case of drought or low prices (De Weerdt, 2010);
- providing greater resilience to climate change through multiple crops and multi-storied production to buffer against storms (Holt-Gimenez, 2002);
- enhancing pollination and providing habitat for beneficial insects to increase control of agricultural pests (Tilman *et al.*, 2002);
- increasing livestock health, production levels, fertility and the birth weight of offspring by providing shelter from adverse conditions through agroforestry (Naylor and Ehrlich, 1997 cited by Robertson and Swinton, 2005);
- providing more opportunity to incorporate indigenous species.

There is a growing confidence on the part of institutions and their donors about the merits of agro-diversity and the use of indigenous species in progressing the MDGs of eradicating poverty and hunger and promoting social equity and environmental sustainability (Leaky *et al.*, 2005).

Projections suggest that malnutrition will worsen in SSA over the next decade, with the largest impact in East Africa, where the incidence of malnutrition is expected to increase by 25 per cent (Verchot *et al.*, 2007). This risk needs to be averted by putting nutrition at the centre of the framework guiding agricultural development.

Sustainability

To have food security 'at all times' (as the definition stipulates) means that sufficient quantity and quality of food is available on a consistent basis – in the present and into the future. This means that production must also be sustainable.

One of the primary undertakings of *Kilimo Kwanza* is to subsidise greater use of petroleum-based products (i.e. chemical fertilisers, pesticides and insecticides) and improved seed. In assessing the sustainability of this policy, it is worth reflecting on lessons learned from the Green Revolution (GR). Although the GR successfully increased agricultural output and reduced poverty in many parts of Asia, many small-scale farmers remained poor (FAO, 2011; Muller and Patel, 2004), and the GR did not work in SSA (UN, 2008). The GR created serious environmental damage (Huang *et al.*, 1995; Ali, 2004; McIntyre *et al.*, 2009) which in the coming decades will increase world food prices by 30–50 per cent in real terms (UNDP, 2011).

The GR has not reduced the absolute number of undernourished people, of which there are now 15 million more than in 1990/92 (FAO, 2009). The growth in crop yields resulting from GR technologies is now stagnating, and will not meet global food production requirements without expanding into natural ecosystems, additional loss of biodiversity and deterioration of water quality and soil condition (Cassman *et al.*, 2003; Godfray *et al.*, 2010).

The emphasis of *Kilimo Kwanza* on GR technologies must be considered in light of the widely recognised shortcomings of that approach and make policy and technology adjustments so as not to repeat the mistakes.

Improved seed

'Improved seeds' are part of the subsidised package being offered under *Kilimo Kwanza*. Tanzanian farmers currently use hybrid seed, which do not produce uniform offspring, and require farmers to purchase new seed every year, but they are not genetically modified organisms (GMOs). Under Tanzanian regulations, GMOs are not allowed to be imported, transported, stored or used in the country. Persons involved in these activities are liable for personal loss or injury including damage to the environment and to biological diversity (Mtui, 2012). These regulations are currently under review.[17] Research into GMOs is undertaken in Tanzania to, for example, develop maize that requires less nitrogen fertiliser, and drought tolerant maize. However, scientists cannot conduct field trials and are waiting for new regulations (Schmickle, 2013).

Tanzania's cooperation with the New Alliance, which involves groups such as plant breeder Monsanto, presents incentive to change their regulations relating to GMOs. Monsanto has said that seeds to African farmers will be royalty-free (Schmickle, 2013). This kind of concession on the part of Monsanto is significant but there is no guarantee that this offer does not provide an opening for regulation change in Tanzania allowing other GMOs to follow, not necessarily with the same concession.

Full discussion of these issues is beyond the scope of this chapter. However, it is not clear how changing the GMO regulation aligns with stated support for on-farm seed production (Ngaiza, 2012) or how risks (e.g. variable yields, increasing liability and cost to farmers, and the need to protect genetic diversity) would be managed. Farmers need to have good quality seed that is accessible, affordable and reliable. But careful consideration must be given to the impacts of using GMOs, along with the overall context in which they are used. For example, the value of drought tolerant plants in providing food security is limited unless actions to mitigate climate change are also taken, and broader climate-smart agricultural techniques are adopted.

Fertiliser subsidies and soil management

Kilimo Kwanza provides vouchers that represent subsidies for 50 per cent of the purchase price for 100kg of fertiliser and seed sufficient for one acre. Similar subsidy programmes introduced elsewhere in SSA have raised questions about their sustained affordability for either the state or farmers. In Malawi, fertiliser prices rose dramatically during the programme, leading to an estimated budget shortfall of US$80 million (Denning *et al.*, 2009). Fertiliser prices also rose in Zambia, with a 70 per cent decline in fertiliser use after the elimination of subsidies (Ajayi *et al.*, 2007).

Reliance on synthetic fertilisers contributes to nutrient leaching, erosion and eutrophication of water bodies, adding costs to the public. 'As much as a third of the [agricultural] productivity gains from technical progress in China and Pakistan have been negated by soil and water degradation and this does not include the offsite pollution costs' (World Bank, 2008).[18] This does not suggest that synthetic fertilisers should not be used. Particularly where soil has been degraded, some immediate source of fertility is required. What is important is that farmers understand the potential hazards of fertilising practices to soil and water, and to their own livelihoods; and that an integrated strategy for long-term soil fertility is initiated. As part of this strategy, the incorporation of organic matter is critical to increase the water-holding capacity of soil and thereby build resilience to drought, rising temperatures, and erosion. Failure to build long-term soil health reduces food security.[19]

In Tanzania, farmers have access to subsidised inputs but not access to information about using the inputs (Mbunda, 2011). Concurrent with the subsidy programme in Malawi, the Millennium Village Programme provided extension services that encouraged farmers to intercrop maize with groundnut seed and pigeon pea, which supplied up to 60kg nitrogen per hectare, reducing dependency on the expensive mineral fertilisers while at the same time providing soil surface protection, diversity in cropping and cash income (Denning *et al.*, 2009).

Elsewhere, the use of legumes and fertiliser trees in cropping systems has been found to produce as much as 150kg nitrogen per hectare (Verchot *et al.*, 2007).

The trees also reduce erosion, and provide a source of firewood and carbon storage (Tilman *et al.*, 2002). In Malawi, Tanzania and Zambia over 200,000 farmers are testing or using agroforestry fallows or agroforestry intercrops as part of soil fertility (Verchot *et al.*, 2007). Policy and institutional factors have been identified as one of the obstacles to more widespread adoption of agroforestry (Ajayi *et al.*, 2007).[20]

Phosphorus deficiencies are widespread in Tanzania and a constraint to agricultural productivity (Verchot *et al.*, 2007). There is an overall rising awareness of vulnerability to global supply and price of phosphorus. In 2008, there was an 800 per cent price spike in phosphate rock, driven by an increased demand. 'The price has not returned to pre-2008 levels and is trending back upwards' (White and Cordell, 2012).

Traditionally phosphate was supplied through the integration of livestock into the cropping system. By separating livestock from cropping, the livestock's phosphorus-rich excretions are no longer available to crops. Without livestock, farmers need to purchase expensive and increasingly scarce fertilisers (Tilman *et al.*, 2002; White and Cordell, 2012).

Recognition of these problems has drawn attention (globally and in SSA) to integrated soil fertility management. The greatest efficiency of synthetic nitrogen is achieved with the first increments of added fertiliser; efficiency declines at higher levels of application (Tilman *et al.*, 2002). Studies of 160,000 households in Zimbabwe showed that when natural fertilising techniques were combined with the use of 8–10kg/ha of synthetic fertiliser, production and food security increased by between 30 and 50 per cent depending on the amount of rainfall (Verchot *et al.*, 2007).

The fertiliser voucher scheme excludes the poorest and most vulnerable because they are unable to afford the 50 per cent cost-share (UNDP, 2011).[21] While the burden of environmental impacts has to be borne by the public, subsidies to private goods such as fertilisers favour larger farmers who can afford to purchase the larger amount of fertiliser. Such subsidies structure economic growth in a way that constrains rather than targets poverty reduction and rural development. Such subsidies are less productive than investments in core public goods such as agricultural research, extension and rural infrastructure (World Bank, 2008: 41). Another approach is supporting integration of livestock at the household level for improved soil nutrients, as well as nutrition and an alternative income source (Njuki, 2010).

Water and increasing irrigation

Although Tanzania's water resources are described as abundant, increasing water demand intensifies water scarcity during the dry season (Van Koppen *et al.*, 2004) and are causing a drift to groundwater use. The extent of resource stress is difficult to assess due to inadequate data/information on aquifers. It is clear that some aquifers are threatened by pollution and are already overexploited (Mato and Mujwahuzi, 2010).

There are concerns about the capacity to manage the rapid growth in water use given the lack of knowledge about small-scale irrigation technology and sound water management practices (UNDP, 2011); and the lack of incentives for conservation, particularly by large-scale users (Van Koppen *et al.*, 2004). Existing large-scale land deals have resulted in contamination of downstream water sources rendering water supply to local communities (in one case, to a population of 45,000) unfit for human consumption. Tanzania has laws[22] to protect water quality, but there are large gaps between the intent of legislation and its implementation (Arduino *et al.*, 2012).

A study of the potential scale of water deficiencies in the next 30 years and the implications for food security identified Tanzania's renewable freshwater resources as diminishing below the amount required per person per year. Once countries drop below this threshold, water resources become a limiting factor to food production. 'For countries that lack the financial capacity to import, starvation is likely to occur' (Yang *et al.*, 2003).

Up to 50 per cent of total rainfall can be lost in non-productive evaporation in semi-arid tropical croplands. Hence, water availability largely depends on water productivity and improving water use efficiency at the national, district and farm level. The Comprehensive Assessment of Water Management in Agriculture (2007) emphasises the need for rainfed agriculture to continue to play a crucial and dominant role in providing food and livelihoods, not only by capturing water at farm level but, importantly, by increasing plant water uptake and reducing soil evaporation. This can be done by using farming systems[23] to hold water in the landscape; maintaining high spatial configuration of different land use types (Rockstrom *et al.*, 2009a); and adopting the same soil building techniques as required for healthy fertility (Wiggins and Keats, 2013). The key concern is that *Kilimo Kwanza* appears more focused on providing irrigation than on conserving the resource on which irrigation relies.

Beyond the issues of protecting water quantity and quality there is the issue of equity. The infrastructure required for irrigation is expensive, presenting a problem for a single or even a group of smallholders. It is considered that this will most likely result in land suitable for irrigation going to foreign large-scale investors (Mbunda, 2011). Although increased water harvesting is needed to smooth out water availability to crops over the season, it is not clear whether the issues of equity and sustainability have been adequately addressed.

Examples of sustainable smallholder production in Tanzania

In summary, although TAFSIP documents broader objectives, the weight of discussion, promotion and budget appear heavily geared to the GR. Given the scope of potential problems, the current strategies would benefit by an increased focus on smallholders to provide the necessary links to poverty reduction (Pauw and Thurlow, 2010; Studwell, 2013), and include both smallholder support (e.g. infrastructure, extension, coordination) (Poulton *et al.*, 2010) and expertise in areas of health and sustainable agriculture that can inform the farming community of the issues and options they face.

UN agencies (e.g. UNEP, FAO and UNCTAD)[24] have promoted the potential of small-scale sustainable farming to meet food security needs. This is increasingly supported by scientific literature, international collaborations (De Schutter, 2009; McIntyre *et al.*, 2009; Wiggins, 2009; Godfray *et al.*, 2010; GOS, 2011; Pretty *et al.*, 2011; Rosset *et al.*, 2011) and by on-ground programmes throughout the world. Such initiatives are under way in Tanzania and are presented here in order to assert their feasibility, to illustrate the expertise currently involved and to lay the groundwork for considering how projects such as these can be scaled up.

The FAO is working with the GoT and farmers in a transboundary agroforestry programme in the Kagera River catchment to reverse land degradation while improving farmers' livelihoods and food security (FAO, 2006). Other agroforestry projects have been proposed to reduce conflict between farmers and pastoralists. The model integrates nitrogen-fixing trees with annual crops and pastoral activities, increasing resilience in dry farming systems and cereal yields by 100 per cent; providing fodder, fuel wood and charcoal; and controlling the parasitic weed, *striga*. Participants include the World Agroforestry Centre working with local universities and meteorological and research organisations (Kimaro *et al.*, 2012).

One Farm Africa (in Kenya and Tanzania) is working with 500 small farmers growing a range of high-nutrient indigenous[25] and exotic vegetables. The project targets an increase of farmer income to US$3,000–4,500 per year and includes training in crop and seed production, business and marketing (Pretty *et al.*, 2011:15). In a similar project, over 75 indigenous fruit trees (IFTs) have been identified in the Miombo woodlands, which bear edible, nutrient-rich fruits. Tanzania has a long history of using wild plants for nutritional and medicinal purposes and the use of these plants has been associated with improved human health outcomes (Cordeiro, 2012). They are important food sources during the rainy season when traditional crops are not yet ready for harvest. The International Centre for Research in Agroforestry (ICRAF) is working with smallholders to bring IFTs into wider cultivation to enhance nutrition and income. There are already successful cottage industries in Tanzania processing the fruits of IFTs into juice, jam, wine, yogurts and other products; and training other groups to do the same (Saka and Msonthi, 1994 cited in Akinnifesi *et al.*, 2004).

Export Promotion of Organic Products from Africa (EPOPA) works with FAIDA MaLi and MVIWATA[26] investing in out-grower schemes to develop niche markets for spices and fruits. The main need for these enterprises is strong extension for the technically difficult crops (Uliwa and Fischer, 2004).

Sustainable intensification of maize-legume cropping systems for food security in Eastern and Southern Africa (SIMLESA) and other organisations work with smallholders in Tanzania to improve productivity and reduce yield risks (ACIAR, 2013) in maize and upland rice (Riches *et al.*, 2005).

A multi-sectoral five-year project involving key GoT ministries and universities are working with the University of Sydney to reduce childhood undernutrition and enhance the role of women in farming. It aims to improve the efficiency of family poultry-crop systems, improve access to a nutritionally optimal combination of food from plant and animal[27] sources, and raise nutritional awareness and knowledge. Crops such as sunflower, amaranthus, millet and sorghum provide a broader range of nutrients than hybrid maize, and flexibility to manage farmers' risks in the face of variable climate (Alders *et al.*, 2014).

Recommendations and policy implications

The opportunities for agricultural growth through investment, and the need to improve nutrition and the livelihoods of smallholders, are not necessarily mutually exclusive. But linking the two requires broader consideration of the environmental and socioeconomic context in which agriculture is situated. Recommendations in this section are promoted with the intention of achieving these mutual goals, and of realising Tanzania's Vision 2025 of *'an agriculture sector that is modernised, commercial, highly productive and profitable and utilises natural resources in a sustainable manner'* (URT, 2011a). Implementing sustainable practices centred on smallholders can be more complex due to regional specificity. To be successful, more coordination is needed between disciplines, between ministries and between small-scale farmers. Much can be learned from past and ongoing projects – reducing constraints and improving livelihood and nutrition outcomes.

Recommendations

Private investment can contribute to agricultural development in ways which do not involve large-scale land acquisitions but instead focus on processing, packaging and marketing. This approach matches the assets of investors (capital, technology, markets) with those of local communities (land, labour and local knowledge); and it supports smallholders to diversify into high-value crops (Wegner and Zwart, 2011).

Vermeulen and Cotula (2010) examined alternative business models to large-scale land acquisitions. Central findings of their work include the importance of secure land rights; ensuring that smallholders have an understanding of different business models that work under different conditions; business structures with an appropriate level of risk for smallholders; and national governments and development agencies playing a key role in making these alternatives possible and successful. They report a growing trend among African governments to require that investors contribute to local development.

Ways in which investors can contribute to local development start with recognising the connection of their business to the positive effects that a living wage, health, and opportunities for employee training and advancement have on productivity. Sharing the value of business is critical to growing both local and global economies. Such positive effects are created by redefining productivity and enabling local cluster development (Porter and Kramer, 2011).

The government can encourage contracts that focus on high-nutrient foods involving intensive labour which smallholders make efficient use of (Poulton *et al.*,

2010). They can make investment opportunities conditional on a requirement for indigenous labour, fair wages and working conditions, regulations of agricultural chemicals and natural resource management, and sharing user rights (to water, timber, grazing) with local community. Government can support proposals that offer opportunities of equity share arrangements for labourers (Bienabe *et al.*, 2004 cited in Louw *et al.*, 2008), include smallholders as suppliers to supermarket chains, and encourage the development of alternative marketing options to promote competition. It is important to ensure that administration and taxation of investments offer a fair return to Tanzanians (Van Koppen *et al.*, 2004), and that the details of investors' commitments to infrastructure and jobs are secured in writing prior to finalising agreements.

Other actions that support the majority of farmers and natural resources include: (1) transferring subsidies from agro-chemicals to fund the adoption by smallholders of farming methods that improve soil structure and build long-term fertility (Tilman *et al.*, 2002); and (2) establishing indices within the TAFSIP to more precisely target the outcomes of natural resource management and the engendering of agriculture (such as the number of women owning land and accessing credit). Evaluation is critical, as is responding to the measure of established indicators.

Donor partners and international agencies can make their support conditional on the demonstration of nutrition, livelihood and/or natural resource management outcomes; and supporting the market participation of smallholders through, for example, funding of feeder roads, storage capacity, credit and cell phone based communications (Mkendu and van Campenhout, 2011).

Producer organisations should be supported in facilitating extension targeting the needs of specific agroecological zones; encouraging the development of SAI (Poulton *et al.*, 2010) and climate-smart (Pinto, 2009; FAO, 2010), multi-layered production systems (Holt-Gimenez, 2002); and promoting understanding about what agricultural methods and inputs can complement or contradict biological processes and ecosystem services on which farmers rely (Pretty *et al.*, 2011).

Research and development organisations should be supported to work with farming communities to address information needs; assess and archive traditional knowledge and practices; pilot approaches that protect both genetic resources and equitable intellectual property rights (IAASTD, 2009); and to develop business opportunities such as the supply of predators for integrated pest management, fertilisers made from waste products and development and manufacturing of farm equipment suitable for smallholders and local soils and terrains.

Globally, 73 per cent of rangelands are degraded. The substantial capacity to rehabilitate these lands through a process of sequestering carbon is a significant part of the climate change solutions (Neely *et al.*, 2007).[28] Participatory research should be undertaken in this area;[29] as well as related work to maintain biodiversity and the migration needs of pastoralists in search of pasture and water (Orindi and Murray, 2005).

Coordination (e.g. between research, extension and education; and between health, agriculture and environmental management) can be supported by establishing a process by which the relevant ministries come together to integrate overlapping policy areas, make joint decisions and identify outcomes, indicators, activities and budgets according to common goals. Nutritional outcomes and eco-logically sustainable development would also benefit by increased coordination between non-government organisations working in health, agricultural and environmental programmes.

Policy implications

Continued growth and development relies on sustainability and inclusiveness, which require an environment of shared value. Porter and Kramer define the concept of shared value as 'policies and operating practices that enhance the competitiveness of a company while simultaneously advancing the economic and social conditions in the communities in which it operates' (Porter and Kramer, 2011).

As Tanzania encourages private investment it is important to review how pol-icies (e.g. land reform, credit, tax/depreciation, lease arrangements) can cre-ate shared value; how investments can best support conservative use of natural resources and the multifunctional role of agriculture (in providing nutrition, eco-nomic growth, livelihoods, and ecosystem services). Laying the groundwork to ensure that the economy continues to grow means evaluating the transfer of tech-nologies on offer – avoiding path dependency and being '[locked in] to low value-added activities' (Humphrey, 2004), and developing policies that promote learning and innovation.

Active promotion of small-scale operations supports economic growth in the short term because more people have good nutrition and health for improved live-lihood capacity and more money to spend in the marketplace. In the long term, the population has the skills, knowledge and experience to expand businesses. There is little point in creating conditions that contribute to smallholders exiting agriculture until non-agricultural jobs are available. The process of making those jobs available is growing the economy through agriculture with policies based on inclusiveness (Studwell, 2013).[30] Given the prominence of small farms, pol-icies that incentivise agro-diverse smallholder production should be implemented before determining what is 'too small'. Where farms are not fully commercial due to size, the policy framework should recognise their contribution to nutrition and environmental services – values that can exist alongside off-farm income. Policies that support these values contribute to reducing the public cost of malnutrition. As the economy transitions to manufacturing, it is important that smallholders exiting agriculture are in a position of informed choice.

Notes

1 After famines farmers plant drought-resistant sorghums and cassavas but they eventually return to planting maize because it is more profitable (Coulson, 2011).
2 The fisheries subsector also grew during this period (Pauw and Thurlow, 2010).

3 While most farmers produce maize, only 38 per cent of those interviewed by Mkenda and van Campenhout (2011) reported selling maize once or more during the previous year.

4 Big traders operate through mobile phones while small local traders commonly send bicycle runners to check quality and price with growers. Local traders report that they can get maize at cheaper prices when famers have no information on the price of maize in other villages. Marketing research showed that only 20 per cent of farmers sampled were able to negotiate a price for their maize (Mnenwa and Maliti, 2010).

5 The GoT has introduced a warehouse receipt system where growers can receive a receipt for depositing and storing their crop until the price is favourable. The receipt serves as collateral for loans. However, it is difficult for warehouses to take small amounts and still give farmers a good price; and quality is mixed (Kaarhus *et al.*, 2010).

6 Tanzania has a complex history of agricultural organisations including farmer-initiated producer organisations (POs); government-initiated POs; cooperative societies at village, regional and national levels; crop authorities; national marketing boards (Uliwa and Fischer, 2004; Mkendu and van Campenhout, 2011); and a nationwide small-producers network (MVIWATA) with members in all regions of Tanzania (Pinto, 2009).

7 Sixty-nine percent of children <5 years old are anaemic (URT, 2013), and 41 per cent of women of reproductive age. This is primarily due to iron deficiency. Anaemia impairs growth and learning, lowers resistance to infectious diseases, reduces physical work capacity and increases the risk of maternal death and delivering a low birth weight infant (URT, 2011b).

8 MKUKUTA is an acronym for *Mkakatiwa Kukuza Uchumina Kupunguza Umaskini* and translates to National Strategy for Growth and Reduction of Poverty. A corresponding strategy for Zanzibar is called MKUZA. Reference in this paper to MKUKUTA is intended to cover both strategies.

9 ASDP is a joint initiative of the Ministry of Agriculture, various other natural resource ministries and donor agencies.

10 Tanzania is also part of the African Free Trade Zone (FTZ), improving access to markets within the zone and providing stronger bargaining power when negotiating international deals (BBC News, 2008).

11 AGRA is an alliance of the government, private sector, farmers and CSOs. AGRA promotes policies that support value chain development. AGRA identifies Tanzania as one of four breadbasket regions in Africa in which they concentrate their investment (AGRA, 2013).

12 The New Alliance is a collective of African and donor governments organising private sector investment to increase agricultural productivity and farmer incomes in Africa. It includes investments of US$3 billion from 45 of the largest multinational corporations (Cooksey, 2013) and from companies based in Tanzania (Agro EcoEnergy) for US$425 million (New Alliance, 2013).

13 'Food security exists when all people, at all times, have physical and economic access to sufficient, safe and nutritious food that meets their dietary needs and food preferences for an active and healthy life' (FAO, 2012a).

14 The implication here is that irrigation land should be irrigated. If villages cannot afford irrigation, the land will more likely go to investors (Mbunda, 2011).

15 'In terms of labour absorption, the agriculture sector employed 82.1 and 76.5 percent of total employment in 2001 and 2006 respectively. Although the percentage has fallen somewhat, the sector is still a large employer of labour compared to industry which accounted for 2.6% and 4.2% of employment in the same years' (Mkenda and van Campenhout, 2011). Wiggins (2009) also points out that over the last 20 years agricultural growth in Africa has been highest in countries where the bulk of output comes from small farms; and countries with large-farm sectors are well down the growth ranking.

16 The World Bank adheres to the proposal of an 'inverse size-productivity relationship' favouring small farms. In regions with low population densities and low mobility,

agricultural intensification will require larger farm sizes (World Bank, 2010b cited by Hall, 2011). But increasing population density is more commonly the problem in Tanzania.

17 *Tanzania Daily News*, Kiishweko (2013) 'Debate on safety of GMOs rages on', 25 August 2013, online, allafrica.com/stories/201308250158.html (accessed 30 August 2013).

18 The cost of soil erosion in Kenya 'is equivalent to 3.8 per cent of GDP and equal in magnitude to national electricity production or agricultural exports' (Cohen *et al.*, 2005 cited by Verchot *et al.*, 2007).

19 'Only 14 per cent of the [African] continent is relatively free of moisture stress' (Eswaran, 1997). 'Soil fertility degradation, including soil organic matter depletion, in smallholder farms affects 200 million hectares of cultivated land in 37 African countries and is becoming increasingly recognized as a primary constraint to agricultural development' (Sanchez *et al.*, 1997; Conway, 1998; Verchot *et al.* 2007: 9–10).

20 'Forests, trees and agroforestry systems contribute to food security and nutrition in many ways, but such contributions are usually poorly reflected in national development and food security strategies. Coupled with poor coordination between sectors, the net result is that forests are mostly left out of policy decisions related to food security and nutrition' (FAO, 2013).

21 On average, Tanzanian farmers use 9kg of fertiliser per hectare (Verchot *et al.*, 2007). The fertiliser subsidies are reportedly targeted at disadvantaged farmers with less than two acres (Kaarhus *et al.*, 2010). However, a key criterion is the ability to pay the remaining 50 per cent of the price for 100kg of fertiliser and improved seed (Yongolo, 2013, personal communication).

22 2006 Water Sector Development Strategy and 2009 Water Resources Management Act.

23 Examples from SSA show that converting from conventional ploughing to conservation agriculture resulted in maize yield improvements ranging between 20 and 120 per cent with water productivity improving from 10 to 40 per cent. Yield improvements in Tanzania were approximately 75 per cent (Rockstrom *et al.*, 2009a cited in Rockstrom *et al.*, 2009b).

24 United Nations Environment Programme, UN Food and Agriculture Organization, and UN Conference on Trade and Development.

25 In spite of the abundance of 280 indigenous African leafy vegetables, they remain unexploited and underutilised (Smith and Eyaguirre, 2007).

26 MVIWATA also works with smallholder farmers and livestock keepers to construct grain storage facilities and initiate new income-generating activities such as poultry farming, bee keeping, skin collection/processing, tree nurseries and vegetable growing.

27 Animal source foods (of both domestic and wild origin) are rich in energy, protein and micronutrients that have greater bioavailability than vegetable sources. This initiative is especially important in areas that are marginal for cropping (Alders *et al.*, 2014).

28 'Rangelands are estimated to store up to 30 percent of the world's soil carbon in addition to the substantial amount of above-ground carbon stored in trees, bushes, shrubs and grasses' (White *et al.*, 2000; Grace *et al.*, 2006; Neely *et al.*, 2007).

29 Possibly through the National Carbon Monitoring Centre with funding from donor partners, international agencies and/or climate change funding.

30 See Studwell (2013) for an excellent discussion on policies that incentivise production and inclusiveness, avoiding perverted outcomes such as concentration of ownership and rent-seeking.

References

ACIAR (2013) SIMLESA Program, Australian Centre for International Agricultural Research, online, http://aciar.gov.au/page/simlesa-program (accessed 30 October 2013).

AGRA (2013) Who we are: strategy – for an African green revolution, online, http://www.agra.org/AGRA/en/who-we-are/-strategy--for-an-African-green-revolution/#sthash.lXXhOs1D.dpuf (accessed 10 October 2013).

Ahmed, S.A., Diffenbaugh, N.S., Hertel, T.W., Lobell, D.B., Ramankutty, N., Rios, A. and Rowhani, P. (2011) Climate volatility and poverty vulnerability in Tanzania, *Global Environment*, 21 (1): 46–55.

Ajayi, O.C., Akinnifesi, R.K., Sileshi, G. and Chakeredza, S. (2007) Adoption of renewable soil fertility replenishment technology in southern African region: lessons learnt and the way forward, *Natural Resources Forum*, 31: 306–17.

Akinnifesi, F.K., Kwesiga, F.R., Mhango, J., Mkonda, A., Chilanga, T. and Swai, R. (2004) Domesticating priority for Miombo indigenous fruit trees as a promising livelihood option for smallholder farmers in Southern Africa. In: Albrigo, L.G. and Galan, S.V. (Eds). *Proc XXVI IHC – Citrus, Subtropical and Tropical Fruit Crops*, Acta Hort. 632, publication supported by CIDA.

Alders, R., Aongola, A. Bagnol, B., Kimboka, S., Kock, R., Li, M. Maulaga, W., McConchie, R. Mor, S., Msami, H., Muleng, F., Mwala, M., Mwale, S., Rushton, J., Victor, R., Yongolo, C. and Young, M. (2014) Using a one health approach to promote food and nutrition security in Tanzania and Zambia, *Planet@Risk* [in press].

Ali, A.M.S. (2004) Technological change in agriculture and land degradation in Bangladesh: a case study, *Land Degradation & Development*, 15: 283–98.

Arduino, S., Colombo, G., Ocamp, O.M. and Panzeri, L. (2012) Contamination of community potable water from land grabbing: a case study from rural Tanzania, *Water Alternatives*, 5 (2): 344–59.

BBC (British Broadcast) News (2008) African free trade zone is agreed, BBC News, online, http://news.bbc.co.uk/2/hi/business/7684903.stm (accessed 22 October 2008).

Bienabe, E., Coronel, C., Lecoq, J. and Liagre, L. (2004) Linking smallholder farmers to markets: lessons learnt from literature review and analytical review of selected projects, CIRAD TERA TA 60/15 73, World Bank, Breton.

Cassman, K.G., Dobermann, A.R., Walters, D.T. and Yang, H. (2003) Meeting cereal demand while protecting natural resources and improving environmental quality, Agronomy and Horticulture Department at Digital Commons, University of Nebraska, Lincoln.

Cissokho, M. (2012) Letter from African civil society critical of foreign investment in African agriculture at G8 Summit, International Food and Development Policy, online, http://www.foodfirst.org/en/Challenge+to+Green+Revolution+for+Africa (accessed 21 May 2012).

Cohen, M.J., Brown, M.T. and Shepherd, K.D. (2005) Estimating the environmental costs of soil erosion at multiple scales in Kenya using energy synthesis, *Agriculture, Ecosystems and Environment*, 114(2): 249–69.

Cooksey, B. (2013) The Comprehensive Africa Agriculture Development Program (CAADP) and agricultural policies in Tanzania: Going with or against the grain? Working paper produced as part of the FAC Political Economy of Agricultural Policy in Africa (PEAPA) work stream. March, online, www.future-agricultures.org (accessed 20 January 2014).

Cordeiro, L. (2012) Household dietary diversity, wild edible plants, and diarrhea among rural households in Tanzania, *Journal of Medicinally Active Plants*, 1 (3): 98–105.

Cotula, L., Vermeulen, S., Leonard, R. and Keeley, J. (2009) Land grab or development opportunity? Agricultural investment and international land deals in Africa, IIED/FAO/IFAD, London/Rome.

Coulson, A. (2011) Kilimo kwanza: a new start for agriculture in Tanzania? Institute of Local Government Studies, online, http://btsociety.org/app/images/events/kilimo_kwanza_paper.pdf (accessed 14 November 2013).

Denning, G., Kabambe, P., Sanchez, P., Malik, A., Flor, R. (2009) Input subsidies to improve smallholder maize productivity in Malawi: toward an African green revolution, *PLoS Biology*, 7 (1): e1000023. DOI:10.1371/journal.pbio.1000023.

De Schutter, O. (2009) Large-scale land acquisitions and leases: a set of core principles and measures to address the human rights challenge. Briefing note, UNHCR, Geneva, 11 June.

De Schutter, O. (2010) Report submitted by the Special Rapporteur on the right to food, UNHCR, 16th session, agenda item 3, UN General Assembly, New York, online, HRC website (accessed 9 June 2011).

De Weerdt, J. (2010) Moving out of poverty in Tanzania: evidence from Kagera, *The Journal of Development Studies*, 46 (2): 331–49.

Food and Agriculture Organization (FAO) (2006) Transboundary Agro-Ecosystem Management Programme (TAMP) for the Kagera River Basin, Project Brief, December, online, www.fao.org/fileadmin/templates/nr/images/.../kagera_brief_dec06.doc (accessed 21 August 2013).

Food and Agriculture Organization (FAO) (2009) The state of food insecurity in the world, economic crises: impacts and lessons learned, FAO, Rome.

Food and Agriculture Organization (FAO) (2010) Climate-smart agriculture; policies, practices and financing for food security, adaptation and mitigation, FAO, Rome.

Food and Agriculture Organization (FAO) (2011) State of Food and Agriculture 2010–11. Women in agriculture, closing the gender gap for development, FAO, Rome.

Food and Agriculture Organization (FAO) (2012a) CountryStat – Tanzania, online, http://www.countrystat.org/home.aspx?c=TZA&p=ke (accessed 15 August 2013).

Food and Agriculture Organization (FAO) (2012b) Hunger report. FAO website, online, http://www.fao.org/hunger/en/ (accessed 14 April 2013).

Food and Agriculture Organization (FAO) (2013) Forests for food security and nutrition, online, http://www.fao.org/forestry/food-security/en/ (accessed 30 October 2013).

Fratkin, E. and Mearns, R. (2003) Sustainability and pastoral livelihoods: lessons from East African Maasai and Mongolia, *Human Organization*, 2 (62): 112–22.

Godfray, H.C.J., Beddington, JR, Crute, I.R., Haddad, L., Lawrence, D., Muir, J.F., Pretty, J., Robinson, S., Thomas, S.M. and Toulmin, C. (2010) Food security: the challenge of feeding 9 billion people, *Science*, 327: (812), online, www.sciencemag.org (accessed 4 June 2012).

Government Office for Science (GOS) (2011) Foresight: the future of food and farming. Final Project Report, The Government Office for Science, London.

Grace, J., San Jose, J., Meir, P., Miranda, H. and Montes, R. (2006) Productivity and carbon fluxes of tropical savannah, *Journal of Biogeography*, 33: 387–400.

Green, M. (2012) Understanding rural transformation in Tanzania. REPOA Policy Research for Development No. 35, November 2012.

Haddad, L. (2013) From nutrition plus to nutrition driven: how to realize the elusive potential of agriculture for nutrition? *Food and Nutrition Bulletin*, 34 (1).

Hall, R. (2011) The many faces of the investor rush in Southern Africa: towards a typology of commercial land deals, *ICAS Review Paper Series*, 2 (1).

Hawkes, C., Turner, R., Waage, J. (2012) Current and planned research on agriculture for improved nutrition: a mapping and a gap analysis. Report for DFID, 21 August.

Holt-Gimenez, E. (2002) Measuring farmers' agro ecological resistance after Hurricane Mitch in Nicaragua: a case study in participatory, sustainable land management impact monitoring, *Agriculture, Ecosystems and Environment*, 93: 87–105.

Huang, J. and Scott, R. (1995) Environmental stress and grain yields in China, *American Journal of Agricultural Economics*, 77 (4): 853–64.

Humphrey, J. (2004) Upgrading in global value chains. Working paper No. 28, Policy Integration Department, World Commission on the Social Dimension of Globalization,

ILO, Geneva, online, http://www.ilo.int/wcmsp5/groups/public/---dgreports/---integration/documents/publication/wcms_079105.pdf (accessed 6 March 2014).

IAASTD (2009) International assessment of agricultural knowledge, science and technology for development. Executive summary of the Synthesis Report, Island Press.

Kaarhus, R., Haug, R., Hella, J.P. and Makindara, J.R. (2010) Agro-investment in Africa: impact on land and livelihoods in Mozambique and Tanzania. Noragric report No. 53, Department of International Environment and Development Studies, Norwegian University of Life Sciences.

Kangalawe, R.Y.M. (2012) Food security and health in the southern highlands of Tanzania: a multidisciplinary approach to evaluate the impact of climate change and other stress factors, *African Journal of Environmental Science and Technology*, 6 (1): 50–66.

Kimaro, A.A., Sileshi, G.W., Mpanda, M., Majule, E.A. and Swai, E. (2012) Africa RISING early wins project proposal: evidence-based scaling-up of evergreen agriculture for increasing crop productivity, fodder supply and resilience of the maize-mixed and agro pastoral farming systems in Tanzania and Malawi, World Agroforestry Centre, 16 April, online, http://cgspace.cgiar.org/bitstream/handle/10568/16883/earlywinproposal_esa_evergreen.pdf?sequence=1 (accessed 17 August 2013).

Latham, M.C. (1997) Human nutrition in the developing world. FAO, Rome, online, http://portals.wi.wur.nl/foodnut/latham/Lathamchap7.htm (accessed 26 January 2014).

Leach, V. and Kilama, B. (2009) Institutional analysis of nutrition in Tanzania, REPOA (Research on Poverty Alleviation) Special Paper 09.31.

Leahy, S. (2009) Agriculture: foreigners lead global land rush. *Inter Press Service News*, 5 May, online, http://www.ipsnews.net/news.asp?idnews=46724 (accessed 6 May 2014).

Leaky, R.R.B., Tchoundjeu, Z., Schreckenberg, K., Shackleton, S.E. and Shackleton, C.M. (2005) Agroforestry tree products: targeting poverty reduction and enhanced livelihoods, *International Journal of Agricultural Sustainability*, 3 (1):1–23.

Liu, J., Fritz, S., van Wesenbeek, C.F.A., Fuchs, M., You, L., Obersteiner, M. and Yang, H. (2008) A spatially explicit assessment of current and future hot spots of hunger in sub-Saharan Africa in the context of global change, *Global and Planetary Change*, 64: 222–35.

Louw, A., Jordaan, D., Ndanga, L. and Kirsten, J.F. (2008) Alternative marketing options for small-scale farmers in the wake of changing agri-food supply chains in South Africa, *Agrekon*, 47 (3): 287–308.

Makoye, K. (2013a) Tanzania adopts irrigation law to help farmers battle climate change, posted to Thomson Reuter Foundation website, 4 September, online, http://www.trust.org/item/20130904190945-6crok/ (accessed 9 October 2013).

Makoye, K. (2013b) Tanzania farmers accuse biofuel investors of land grab, posted to Thomson Reuter Foundation website 18 July, online, http://www.trust.org/item/20130718134927-q50zx (accessed 9 October 2013).

Masset, E., Haddad, L., Cornelius, A. and Isaza-Castro, J. (2011) A systematic review of agricultural interventions that aim to improve nutritional status of children, EPPI-Centre, Social Science Research Unit, Institute of Education, University of London.

Mato, R.R. and Mujwahuzi, M. (2010) Groundwater governance case study: Tanzania. groundwater use, characterization and vulnerability (URT), online, http://xa.yimg.com/kq/groups/22477246/889666431/name/Aquifer?characteristics (accessed 15 August 2013).

Mbunda, R. (2011) Kilimo kwanza and small-scale producers: an opportunity or a curse? Research report, Hakiardhi. Department of Political Science, University Dar es Salaam on behalf of Land Rights Research and Resources Institute.

McCall, M. (1985) Environmental and agricultural impacts of Tanzania's villagization programme. In: Clarke, J.I. *et al.* (Eds), *Population and Development Projects in Africa.* Cambridge University Press, Cambridge: 123–40.

McIntyre, B.D., Herren, H.R., Wakhungu, J. and Watson, R.T. (Eds) (2009) *International Assessment of Agricultural Science and Technology for Development.* Island Press, Washington, DC.

Mkenda, B.K. and van Campenhout, B. (2011) Estimating transaction costs in Tanzania supply chains. Working paper No. 11/0898, International Growth Centre, IFPRI, online, www.theigc.org (accessed 15 August 2013).

Mnenwa, R. and Maliti, E. (2010) A comparative analysis of poverty incidence in farming systems of Tanzania, REPOA (Research on Poverty Alleviation), Special Paper 10/4.

Mtambo, K. (2013) Food Security Division, Ministry of Agriculture, Food Security and Cooperative, Tanzania, personal communication, 16 December.

Mtui, G. (2012) Biosafety systems in Eastern and Central Africa, *African Journal of Environmental Science and Technology*, 6 (2): 80–93.

Muller, A.R. and Patel, R. (2004) Shining India? Economic liberalisation and rural poverty in 1990s. Food First Institute for Food and Development Policy, Policy Brief No.10, May, online, www.foodfirst.org (accessed 28 October 2008).

Muller, B.E.T. (2012) The poverty of the smallholder ideal: highlighting Tanzania's rural labour market. Development Viewpoint No. 71, March, Centre for Development Policy and Research website, online, http://www.soas.ac.uk/cdpr/publications/dv/the-poverty-of-the-smallholder-ideal-highlighting-tanzanias-rural-labour-market.html (accessed 15 August 2013).

MVIWATA (2013) New study: large-scale investment likely to disadvantage smallholder farmers, online, http://www.mviwata.org/news/new-study-large-scale-investment-likely-to-disadvantage-smallholder-farmers/ (accessed 1 October 2013).

Mwakalobo, A. and Kashuliza, A. (1999) Smallholder farming systems in a liberalized market environment in Tanzania: some empirical analysis in some areas of Mbeya region, Sokoine University, Morogoro, Tanzania.

National Bureau of Statistics (NBS) (2009) Household Budget Survey 2007. Dar es Salaam, online, http://www.nbs.go.tz (accessed 31 October 2013).

Naylor, R.L. and Ehrlich, P.R. (1997) Natural pest control services and agriculture. In: Daily, G.C. (Ed.) *Nature's Services: Societal Dependence on Natural Ecosystems.* Island Press, Washington, DC.

Neely, C., Bunning, S. and Wilkes, A. (2007) Review of evidence on dryland pastoral systems and climate change: implications and opportunities for mitigation and adaptation. Land and Water Discussion Paper No. 8, FAO, Rome.

New Alliance (2013) New alliance for food security and nutrition policy brief Part I, online, http://www.one.org/us/policy/policy-brief-on-the-new-alliance/ (accessed 10 October 2013).

Ngaiza, R.S. (2012) Presentation at FAO-University of Nairobi regional workshop on an integrated policy approach to commercializing smallholder maize production, Nairobi, Kenya, 6–7 June, Department of Policy and Planning, Tanzania and Ministry of Agriculture Food Security and Cooperatives.

Njuki, J. (2010) The role of gender in strengthening the causal linkages between livestock production and human nutrition. Presentation at the BECA-CSIRO workshop on human nutrition, ILRI, Nairobi, 26–29 April.

Orindi, V.A. and Murray, L.A. (2005) Adapting to climate change in East Africa: a strategic approach. Gatekeepers Series 117, International Institute for Environment and Development.

Osberg, L. and Bandara, A. (2012) 'Running with two legs'. Why poverty remains high in Tanzania and what to do about it. Working paper No. 2012/01, April, Department of Economics, Dalhousie University, Canada.

Pauw, K. and Thurlow, J. (2010) Agricultural growth, poverty, and nutrition in Tanzania, IFPRI Discussion Paper 00947, Development Strategy and Governance Division, January 2010.

Pinto, A.C. (2009) Agricultural cooperatives and farmers' organizations: role in rural development and poverty reduction, Agricord, Swedish Cooperative Centre, UN-Department of Economic and Social Affairs (DESA), online, http://www. un. org/esa/ socdev/egms/docs/2009/cooperatives/Pinto.pdf (accessed 2 October 2013).

Porter, M.E. and Kramer, M.R. (2011) Creating shared value. *Harvard Business Review*, 30 November, online, http://hbr.org/2011/01/the-big-idea-creating-shared-value/ar/ pr (accessed 4 March 2014).

Poulton, C., Dorward, A. and Kydd, J. (2010) The future of small farms: new directions for services, institutions, and intermediation, *World Development*, 38 (10): 1413–28.

Pretty, J., Toulmin, C. and Williams, S. (2011) Sustainable intensification in African agriculture, *International Journal of Agricultural Sustainability*, 9 (1): 5–24.

Riches, C.R., Mbwaga, A.M., Mbapila, J. and Ahmed, G.J.U. (2005) Improved weed management delivers increased productivity and farm incomes for rice in Bangladesh and Tanzania, *Aspects of Applied Biology*, 75: 127–38.

Robertson, G.P.I. and Swinton, S.M. (2005) Reconciling agricultural productivity and environmental integrity: a grand challenge for agriculture, *Frontiers in Ecology and the Environment*, 3 (1): 38–46.

Rockstrom, J., Falkenmark, M., Karlberg, L., Hoff, H., Rost, S. and Gerten, D. (2009a) Future water availability for global food production: the potential of green water to build resilience to global change, *Water Resources Research*, 44, DOI:10.1029/2007WR006767.

Rockstrom, J., Karlbery, L., Wani, S.P., Barron, J., Hatibu, N., Oweis, T., Bruggeman, A. Farahani, J. and Qiang, Z. (2009b) Managing water in rain-fed agriculture: the need for a paradigm shift, *Agricultural Water Management*, 97: 543–50.

Rosset, P.M., Sosa, B.M., Jaime, A.M.R. and Lozano, D.R.A. (2011) The Campesino-to-Campensino agroecology movement of ANAP in Cuba: social process methodology in the construction of sustainable peasant agriculture and food sovereignty, *The Journal of Peasant Studies*, 38 (1): 161–91.

Saka, J.D.K. and Msonthi, J.D. (1994) Nutritional value of edible fruits of indigenous wild trees in Malawi, *Forest Ecology and Management* 64: 245–8.

Sanchez, P.A., Shephard, K.D., Soule, M.J., Place, F.M., Buresh, R.J., Izac, A.N., Mokunye, A.U., Kwesiga, F.R., Ndiritu, C.G. and Woomer, P.L. (1997) Soil fertility replenishment in Africa: an investment in natural resource capital. In: Buresh, R.J. and Sanchez, P.A. (Eds) *Replenishing Soil Fertility in Africa*, ICRAF/Social Science Society of America: Special Publication, Madison, WI, 51: 1–46.

Schmickle, S. (2013) Tanzania becomes a battleground in fight over genetically modified crops, *Washington Post*, online, http://www.washingtonpost.com/world/africa/tanzania-becomes-a-battleground-in-fight-over-genetically-modified-crops/2013/10/06/94ee9c2c-27ac-11e3-ad0d-b7c8d2a594b9_story.html (accessed 10 October 2013).

Smith, F.I. and Eyaguirre, P. (2007) African leafy vegetables: their role in the World Health Organization's global fruit and vegetables initiative, *African Journal of Food, Agriculture, Nutrition and Development*, 7 (3), online, http://www.bioline.org.br/request?nd07019 (accessed 14 August 2013).

Studwell, J. (2013) *How Asia Works: Success and Failure in the World's Most Dynamic Region*. Profile Books, London.

Sulle, E. (2010) Scramble for land in Tanzania. Presentation at the regional workshop on commercialisation of land and 'land grabbing' in Southern Africa hosted by the Institute for Poverty, Land and Agrarian Studies (PLAAS), University of the Western Cape, Cape Town, 24–25 March.

Tilman, D., Cassman, K.G., Matson, P.A. and Naylor, R.L. (2002) Agricultural sustainability and intensive production practices, *Nature*, 418: 671–7.

Tilman, D., Reich, P.B., Knops, J. Wedin, D. and Mielke, T. (2001) Diversity and productivity in a long-term grassland experiment, *Science*, 294 (5543): 843–5.

Trading Economics (2014) online, www.tradingeconomics.com/tanzania/gdp (accessed 10 July 2014).

Tripp, A.M. (2012) Donor assistance and political reform in Tanzania. ReCom/UN University/World Institute for Development Economics Research (UNU-WIDER), Working Paper No. 2012/37, April.

Turshen, M. (1977) The impact of colonialism on health and health services in Tanzania, *International Journal of Health Services*, 1:7–35.

Uliwa, P. and Fischer, D. (2004) Assessment of Tanzania's producer organizations experience and environment. USAID Tanzania Economic Growth Office.

United Nations (UN) (2008) The Millennium Development Goals Report 2008, United Nations, New York.

United Nations Development Programme (UNDP) (2011) Tanzania, accelerating progress toward the MDGs (addressing poverty and hunger), UNDP.

United Republic of Tanzania (URT) (undated a) The Tanzania Development Vision 2025, online, http://www.tanzania.go.tz/vision.htm (accessed 23 September 2013).

United Republic of Tanzania (URT) (undated b) Ten Pillars of Kilimo Kwanza. Implementation Framework, online, www.tzonline.org_pdf_tenpillarsofkilimokwanza. pdf (accessed 22 September 2013).

United Republic of Tanzania (URT) (2010) Tanzania Gender Indicators Booklet 2010. Poverty Eradication and Economic Empowerment Division, Dar es Salaam, Tanzania.

United Republic of Tanzania (URT) (2011a) Tanzania Agriculture and Food Security Investment Plan (TAFSIP) 2011/12 to 2020/21. Main document, 18 October.

United Republic of Tanzania (URT) (2011b) National Nutrition Strategy July 2011/12 – June 2015/16. Ministry of Health and Social Welfare.

United Republic of Tanzania (URT) (2012a) Poverty and Human Development Report 2011 (National Strategy for Growth and Reduction of Poverty). Research and Analysis Working Group, MKUKUTA Monitoring System, Ministry of Finance, May.

United Republic of Tanzania (URT) (2012b) Global Agriculture and Food Security Programme Request for Funding: Public Sector Window. Tanzania Agriculture and Food Security Investment Plan, GAFSP Gap Financing Proposal, March.

United Republic of Tanzania (URT) (2013) Nutrition Country Paper: The United Republic of Tanzania (Draft) CAADP Agriculture Nutrition Capacity Development February Workshops, p. 4.

Van Koppen, B., Sokile, C., Hatibu, N., Lankford, B. Mahoo, H. and Yanda, P.Z. (2004) *Formal Water Rights in Tanzania: Deepening the Dichotomy?* International Water Management Institute, Colombo, Sri Lanka.

Verchot, L.V., Place, F., Shepherd, K.D. and Jama, B. (2007) Science and technological innovations for improving soil fertility and management in Africa. A report for the

NEPAD Science and Technology Forum, World Agroforestry Centre website, online, http://www.worldagroforestrycentre.org/ (accessed 12 September 2013).

Vermeulen, S. and Cotula, L. (2010) *Making the Most of Agricultural Investment: A Survey of Business Models that Provide Opportunities for Smallholders*. IIED/FAO/IFAD/SDC, London/Rome/Bern, pp. 23, 18.

Wegner, L. and Zwart, G. (2011) Who will feed the world? The production challenge, Oxfam, online, www.oxfam.org (accessed 29 April 2013).

White, R., Murray, S. and Rohweder, M. (2000) *Pilot Analysis of Global Ecosystems: Grassland Ecosystems*. World Resources Institute, Washington, DC, 112 pp.

White, S. and Cordell, D. (2012) Time for policy action on global phosphorus security, The conversation, online, https://theconversation.com/time-for-policy-action-on-global-phosphorus-security-5594 (accessed 1 March 2012).

Wiggins, S. (2009) Can the smallholder model deliver poverty reduction and food security for a rapidly growing population in Africa? Expert meeting on 'How to feed the World in 2050', Rome, 24–26 June, FAO, Economic and Social Development Department.

Wiggins, S. and Keats, S. (2013) Smallholder agriculture's contribution to better nutrition, Overseas Development Institute. Report commissioned by the Hunger Alliance.

World Bank (2008) Agriculture for Development. World Development Report 2008, pp. 60–3, online, http://web.worldbank.org/WBSITE/EXTERNAL/EXTDEC/EXTRESEARCH/EXTWDRS/0,,contentMDK:23062293~pagePK:478093~piPK:477627~theSitePK:477624,00.html (accessed 12 August 2009).

World Bank (2010a) Nutrition at a Glance: Tanzania, online, http://siteresources.worldbank.org/NUTRITION/Resources/281846-1271963823772/Tanzania.pdf (accessed 10 May 2013).

World Bank (2010b) The global land rush: can it yield sustainable and equitable benefits? World Bank, Washington, DC, 8 September.

World Bank (2014) 2004–12 data from http://databank.worldbank.org/data/views/reports/tableview.aspx (accessed 10 July 2014).

Yang, H., Reichert, P., Abbaspour, K.C. and Zehnder, A.J.B. (2003) A water resources threshold and its implications for food security, *Science and Technology*, p. 5, online, http://www.aseanfood.info/Articles/11014497.pdf (accessed 12 August 2013).

Yongolo, C.S.A. (2013) Personal communication, Division of Research and Development (Crops) Ministry of Agriculture, Food and Cooperatives, Government of United Republic of Tanzania, Dar es Salaam.

9 Food security in Malawi

Disputed diagnoses, different prescriptions

Rachel Bezner Kerr and Raj Patel

Introduction

Overview

Malawi has experienced high levels of food insecurity over the past 30 years, prompting the government to actively explore new policy approaches to address hunger in a predominantly rural economy. A small landlocked country in southern Africa, Malawi has a current estimated population of 16 million people, approximately 85 per cent of whom rely on agriculture for their livelihood (World Bank, 2013a). Most people live in rural areas in smallholder farming households, planting on average one hectare (ha) of crops – a mixture of maize, legumes, tubers and cash crops such as tobacco, sugar and cotton (Jayne *et al.*, 2006; Fisher and Lewin, 2013). Landholdings are higher on average in the north, where 59 per cent of people cultivate more than 1 ha, and lowest in the southern region of the country, where only 32 per cent of households have more than 1 ha of land to cultivate (Fisher and Lewin, 2013). The level of population density is 164 for the country as a whole, with a higher number in the south (185 people per km²), followed by the central (154) and northern (56) regions (Fisher and Lewin, 2013; World Bank, 2013a).

Food production

Approximately half of all calories consumed by the smallholders in Malawi come from their own food production (Dorward and Chirwa, 2011). Maize is the dominant staple crop in the country, estimated to make up over 60 per cent of area planted and 70 per cent of calories consumed (Ellis and Manda, 2012). The predominance of maize in Malawi began with the demands of slave caravans, and accelerated during the colonial period, as the British promoted maize production for colonial institutions such as prisons, mines and estates (Vaughan, 1987). The post-colonial dictatorship of Kamuzu Banda also promoted maize as a primary staple crop for smallholders, through agricultural extension and the Agricultural Development and Marketing Corporation (ADMARC). Tobacco was, and remains, responsible for the large majority of Malawi's foreign exchange.

Banda's authoritarian regime had an uneasy social contract with rural Malawians, which focused on increasing national food security by promoting primarily maize through the provision of fertilizer subsidies and a guaranteed supply of maize seeds and markets in rural ADMARC depots (Harrigan, 2001). A debt crisis and subsequent structural adjustment policies implemented in the 1980s broke this contract, by removing fertilizer subsidies, agricultural credit and other public expenditures on agriculture (Sahn and Arulpragasam, 1991; Harrigan, 2008). Input prices rose sharply while maize prices fell, rural depots were closed and credit removed, all of which led to increased rural poverty and food insecurity (Peters, 2006). The last decade has been called by Ellis and Manda (2012) as 'a decade of two halves' with the first half characterized by very low and declining maize production, reaching a nadir in 2004/05, followed by a steep reversal from 2005 onwards (Ellis and Manda, 2012). Although the Government of Malawi and others attribute this success to the implementation of a nationwide agricultural input subsidy programme (Denning *et al.*, 2009), a number of scholars have been sceptical of the accuracy of government production figures (Jayne *et al.*, 2008; Ellis and Manda, 2012; Chirwa and Dorward, 2013).

Food access

Current estimates suggest that approximately one-third of Malawians are food insecure, lacking access to sufficient, safe and nutritious food to meet their daily needs (Ellis and Manda, 2012), but this number varies annually depending upon rainfall, food prices and many other factors. A recent national survey indicated southern Malawi had the highest levels of food insecurity. Households that are headed by a widow, divorced or separated woman, and poor households are more likely to be food insecure (NSO, 2012). Food production is dependent on a unimodal rainfall pattern, and food insecurity is highly seasonal, peaking just before the harvest period at the same time that farming households have peak agricultural labour requirements. On average Malawian households experience food shortages for three months of the year, and compensate for this shortage by eating less preferred foods, reducing the number and size of meals, and prioritizing children's meals over adults' (NSO, 2012). Households also turn to other coping strategies such as borrowing from family and friends, or working as casual labourers (called *ganyu*) on other people's farms (NSO, 2012).

Since the majority of Malawians purchase at least some of their food, their income level plays a major role in sustaining household food security. Although economic growth in Malawi has averaged 7 per cent for 2006–10, more than half the population lives below the poverty line. Extremely low wages contribute to this high level of poverty (De Schutter, 2013). Some studies suggest that poverty levels have only marginally declined in the last decade, from 52.5 per cent in 2004 to 50.7 per cent in 2010 (NSO, 2012; De Schutter, 2013), but a recent survey suggests that poverty increased in rural areas; 57 per cent of people in rural areas live below the poverty line (NSO, 2012). Malawi remains one of the poorest countries in the world (UNDP, 2013), and inequality in the country has worsened over

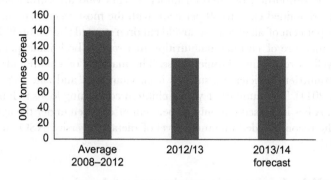

Figure 9.1 Malawi total cereal imports 2008–13.
Source: Adapted from FAO, 2013.

the last decade (NSO, 2012). Wealthier households consume on average more than nine times as much food as poor households (NSO, 2012). One-quarter of Malawians are considered 'ultra-poor', with an income below the level needed to purchase a minimum daily recommended calorie intake (NSO, 2012).

Maize price fluctuations have major impacts on food security levels in Malawi. Prices are affected by several factors, including rainfall, farming practices and government policies. In addition to farming households producing an adequate maize supply, the Strategic Grain Reserve stockpiles a national grain supply, and ADMARC purchases and sells maize, and, in the last decade, provided subsidized fertilizer and maize seed to farming households. Some maize is also imported annually, primarily from South Africa, Zambia, Tanzania and Mozambique (see Figure 9.1) (Jayne *et al.*, 2010; FAO, 2013).

Since there is only one maize harvest a year, and most maize consumed by households comes from local supplies, there is considerable seasonal fluctuation of maize prices: on average a 60 per cent difference between the lowest and highest price (Ellis and Manda, 2012). In addition to seasonal variation, in the last decade, due to a combination of differences in rainfall, changing government policies about storing and importing maize, and variations in supply of fertilizer and other inputs, the overall price of maize has varied considerably, ranging from 5 to 25 Malawi kwacha per kg (MK/kg) (Ellis and Manda, 2012). Maize price fluctuations and increases have negative implications for households that purchase maize. Many households run out of their own maize supplies after six months, therefore, at the height of agricultural labour requirements, are often squeezed by high prices and short supply.

Consumption patterns

While national levels of food production have increased in the last decade, chronic malnutrition has not significantly reduced since 1990 (NSO and ICF

Macro, 2011). The proportion of children under 5 years who are chronically malnourished has remained close to 50 per cent, with the most recent national survey finding 47 per cent of all under 5-year-old children stunted (NSO and ICF Macro, 2011), a measure of chronic malnutrition that reflects both inadequate food intake as well as recurrent, chronic illness. The majority of children also suffer from micronutrient deficiencies such as iron, vitamin A and zinc (NSO and ICF Macro, 2011). The number of young children consuming foods rich in iron and vitamin A has increased but only 29 per cent of children under the age of 5 years met the recommended minimum level of dietary diversity (NSO and ICF Macro, 2011).

Historical, political, economic, environmental and social drivers

There are conflicting views about the key drivers of food insecurity in Malawi, but many agree that it is a combination of historical, political, economic, environmental and social factors, which interact at multiple levels. Some scholars emphasize the role of history in shaping national and international policies, which tended to benefit elites and international companies, while promoting a monocropped maize system that discourages diversified diets or incomes (Vaughan, 1987; Bryceson, 2006; Bezner Kerr, 2010; Chinsinga, 2011a). A second set of scholars focuses on economic factors as the key driver alongside political management of agricultural inputs, maize prices and food shortages (Jayne et al., 2006; Harrigan, 2008; Devereux, 2009; Ellis and Manda, 2012). Some authors point to problems with a state-run system of input distribution, which is viewed as ineffective and prone to corruption (Crawford et al., 2003). Environmental factors are often presented as the main driver, with a focus on *production*, namely the low productivity of smallholder farmers, which is blamed on declining soil fertility, variable rainfall, labour-intensive methods, small landholdings and low use of agricultural inputs (Denning et al., 2009). The fact that Malawi is a landlocked country is also considered crucial, since both agricultural inputs and imported maize prices are higher than countries with access to shipping (Fisher and Lewin, 2013). At the household level, most scholars agree that some key drivers of food insecurity are unequal gender relations, and HIV/AIDS (Bezner Kerr, 2005; Wodon and Beegle, 2006; Bignami-Van Assche et al., 2011). This section will discuss each set of factors in turn.

Historical factors: establishment of an unequal agrarian system

As a British protectorate (then Nyasaland) from the late 1800s until 1964, Malawi's economy was shaped by colonial forces, with economic development of a few key export crops, and agricultural research and transportation systems developed to support British interests (Vail, 1983). In southern Malawi, European settlers, though few in number, took over an estimated 3.7 million ha of land during the colonial period, on which they established missions and tobacco, tea and cotton estates

(Ng'ong'olo, 1990). Smallholder African farmers in this region were displaced and worked for the estates. A 'hut tax' was imposed in 1892, requiring each household to pay tax to the British government; this tax led to high levels of male migration, since there were few mines or estates established throughout Malawi (Bryceson, 2006). This pattern of male migration established a persistent pattern of women doing the majority of farming labour (Bryceson, 2006). In addition, the British government looked to Malawian smallholder African farmers to provide food crops for their prisons, hospitals, mines and estates. The colonial government invested in a few key crops for export, namely tea, cotton and tobacco, with the agricultural research programme largely focused on these crops (Mandala, 1995).

The British colonial government provided extension advice, seeds, credit and subsidized fertilizer to a few African large landholders but taxed the majority of smallholder farmers through price controls, initially with the Marketing of Native Produce Ordinance in 1935, then the establishment of the Farmers Marketing Board in the 1950s (Kalinga, 1993).

Until now, all of the post-colonial governments could be termed neo-patrimonial: states centred around one person (the president) who dispenses patronage through the power and resources of the state to sustain political power (Booth *et al.*, 2006). Banda's post-colonial dictatorship of 30 years built on the colonial dual agrarian policy for estates and smallholders. Banda's regime redistributed thousands of hectares for tobacco estate production, to the benefit of his political allies and supporters, and ensured that the majority of agricultural research and extension was focused on estate crops (Kydd and Christiansen, 1982; Ellis *et al.*, 2003). In 1965, the Land Act was passed which allowed for customary land to be taken for state leasehold, and a growing class of large landholders specializing in tobacco began to lease this land (Ellis *et al.*, 2003). At the same time, Banda promoted maize production for smallholders, through the establishment of ADMARC, the National Seed Company of Malawi, fertilizer and hybrid maize seed subsidies and an agricultural extension programme. Crop prices paid to smallholders were kept low, however, the surplus profits from the international sale of smallholder crops were mainly invested into estate production and the banking sector (Kydd and Christiansen, 1982). Maize research and support for smallholder production in general was limited, with all ADMARC investments in smallholder agriculture in the first two decades of Banda's rule making up 4.3 per cent of the total, compared to 51 per cent of ADMARC's investments into estate tobacco production (Kydd and Christiansen, 1982).

Under Banda's regime, inequality between urban and rural areas was exacerbated, with limited investment in rural infrastructure such as schools, health clinics or roads (Bryceson, 2006). The 1971 Wage Restraint Policy suppressed wage rates and trade unions, and migration was restricted. This highly unequal regime eventually ran up high debts. Falling commodity prices, rising fuel prices and a conflict in Mozambique (which cut off transport routes) in the 1970s precipitated a debt crisis in the early 1980s. This debt crisis occurred just as a shift towards neoliberal economic policies, led by the World Bank and the International Monetary Fund (IMF) and known as the 'Washington Consensus', began to occur around the globe. Banda had to agree to structural adjustment terms determined by the IMF and the World Bank, which included currency devaluation, market liberalization, reduction of agricultural extension, health and other public expenditures, dismantling the agricultural credit programme, and removal of fertilizer subsidies. Fertilizer prices rose dramatically, giving Malawi one of the highest price ratios of nitrogen to maize in the world (Edriss *et al.*, 2004). Maize production stagnated, fluctuating between 70 to 90 per cent of national requirements annually, and poverty rates increased, with estimates that smallholder income levels declined by 25 per cent while estate producers' income rose by 44 per cent in the structural adjustment period of the 1980s and 1990s (Sahn and Arulpragasam, 1991; Ellis *et al.*, 2003; Bryceson, 2006). Poor rural households, who relied on ADMARC for maize purchases during the lean season, experienced erratic supplies and rising maize prices (Peters, 2006). Women farmers experienced greater impacts from structural adjustment, due to reduced health services – which increased their domestic responsibilities – and reduced access to fertilizer and seed (Bryceson, 2006). Smallholder tobacco production increased post-structural adjustment, as part of efforts to increase exports, but largely benefited better-off smallholder farmers, due to the need for capital, labour and variable prices (Ellis *et al.*, 2003; Peters, 2006).

All of these historical factors – colonial and post-colonial land and agricultural policies, and structural adjustment programmes – led to a highly unequal agrarian system in which smallholder farmers had lost access to land, had few state supports, high prices for agricultural inputs and had been historically disadvantaged by state policies in comparison to estate farmers.

Gender relations, population and HIV/AIDS

Unequal gender relations worsen food security and nutrition for many smallholder households. Women have lower levels of education and fewer employment opportunities (NSO and ICF Macro, 2011). Higher educational attainment affects women's knowledge of food choices, nutrition and childcare, as well as their employment options, and has a positive association with child nutritional status (Ruel *et al.*, 1999). While food production and access is important, sufficient knowledge of healthy childcare and feeding practices, the ability to implement those practices, and adequate time to care for children are crucial factors to ensure well-nourished children (Sassi, 2012). Rural Malawian women contribute more than half the agricultural labour, income generation and carry out almost all childcare and domestic activities (e.g. water collection, food preparation), but have limited decision-making power over household resources (Bezner Kerr, 2008; NSO and ICF Macro, 2011). One study found that female-headed households in Malawi are more likely to invest in food and other resources that improve child nutrition compared to male-headed households, despite higher levels of poverty (Kennedy and Peters, 1993).

Young women marry at an early age in Malawi, with one report that nearly 50 per cent of girls aged 20–24 were married before the age of 18 (PRB, 2011).

Once married, women often experience limited decision-making power over crucial issues such as health care, household purchases and farming practices (Bezner Kerr, 2005; PRB, 2011). Low levels of education may be a factor in limiting women's decision making, with 21 per cent of rural women having no formal education (NSO and ICF, 2011). In rural areas, pregnancy soon follows; one in every four teenage girls has her first child between 15 and 19 years of age (NSO and ICF Macro, 2011). Teenagers in the lowest wealth bracket are more than twice as likely to have had a child than teenagers in the highest wealth bracket, while 45 per cent of teenagers with no education have had their first child by the age of 19 (NSO and ICF Macro, 2011). Teenage motherhood has implications for educational attainment, food security and their children's subsequent nutrition.

Population growth rates remain high in Malawi, with total fertility rates estimated at 5.7 children over a woman's lifetime (NSO and ICF Macro, 2011). The high birth rates are in part related to improved survival rates, high poverty rates, as well as gender inequality, such as women's low decision-making power over fertility, low educational attainment and few employment opportunities. Families in rural areas and in poorer households are likely to have more children, which increases the number of household members to support. High population growth, combined with high population density, small landholdings and increased pressure for land acquisition for mining, biofuels and other large-scale land investments also mean that farming families increasingly have limited land to grow food (De Schutter, 2013).

Current adult HIV prevalence is estimated at 11 per cent, which increases household costs and food requirements for those living with HIV (Shah *et al.*, 2002; Bignami-Van Assche, 2011; UNAIDS, 2013). Unequal gender relations are a factor in the persistently high HIV prevalence rates (Bryceson, 2006). Infection rates for young women are estimated to be four times higher than for male youth (NSO and ICF Macro, 2011). The most recent national survey found that more than a third of Malawian women aged 15–49 years have experienced physical violence and 15 per cent of women report that their first sexual intercourse experience was forced (NSO and ICF Macro, 2011). Dominant ideas about masculinity and gender inequality reinforce sexual violence, multiple partners and limited use of condoms by men with their partners (Ghosh and Kalipeni, 2005; NSO and ICF Macro, 2011), which helps HIV prevalence rates to persist.

Families with an HIV positive member are more likely to be food insecure, owing to greater labour and income requirements to care for the HIV positive member and have higher nutritional requirements, while having fewer adults to farm and earn a livelihood (Bernell *et al.*, 2006). One study found that women in HIV-affected families were more likely to reallocate their time to cash-generating activities, which took them away from both food production and childcare (Bignami-Van Assche *et al.*, 2011). One longitudinal study concluded that extended kin members played a significant role in supporting AIDS-affected families, but given high levels of poverty and food insecurity, their resources were limited (Peters *et al.*, 2008).

Environmental and geographical factors

Malawi has 3.6 million ha of arable land available for cultivation (World Bank, 2013b). The vast majority of agricultural production is rainfed, with the rainy season occurring between November and April. Maize, the staple crop for 90 per cent of Malawian households (FAOSTAT, 2013), requires a relatively high amount of nitrogen to gain adequate yields. The farming system, which revolves around monocropped maize production, places smallholder farmers at greater risk of food insecurity. Smallholder farmers add few organic materials to soils, relying primarily on inorganic fertilizer for crop production, which fosters greater degradation through soil acidification.

National surveys of soil quality indicate that most soils in Malawi are nitrogen deficient, but have adequate organic matter and phosphorus to support small-holder cultivation, although there is considerable variability (Snapp, 1998). There is also evidence of extensive land degradation, through land clearing, soil erosion and limited application of organic matter (Nakhumwa and Hassan, 2012). Degraded soils have reduced water capacity, ability to retain nutrients and therefore reduce smallholder farmer households' ability to withstand droughts or other environmental shocks.

A related environmental problem that Malawi faces is deforestation. Forests play a crucial role in providing income, energy sources and ecosystem services (GoM, 2010). The annual rate of decline of primary forests in Malawi accelerated from 2.6 per cent (1990–2000) to 3.8 per cent in the last decade (FAO, 2010), now making up 27 per cent of total land area in 2005 (Jumbe and Angelsson, 2007). Studies indicate that some land clearing is for charcoal production (used for households and tobacco production), timber and other forest products, or household fuelwood collection, while the majority of clearing is for agricultural production (Bandyopadhyay et al., 2012; Chibwana et al., 2012). There is a small but significant relationship between poverty and forest clearing (Bandyopadhyay et al., 2012). Poor government policies also play a major role in deforestation (Zulu, 2010). Those most affected by forest loss are often women and children, who are responsible for forest-related household tasks, such as fuelwood or wild food collection (Bandyopadhyay et al., 2012).

Malawi faces challenges in terms of climate variability, which influences food security. As part of the semi-arid region of southern Africa, Malawi has highly variable rainfall patterns, and climate change predictions suggest an increase in variability, intensity of both droughts and floods and less precipitation overall (Funk et al., 2008; IPCC, 2007). The country experienced three severe droughts in the 1990s and one in 2001/2 (Ellis et al., 2003). Climatic and land use changes in this region of southern Africa are anticipated to reduce the overall agricultural production, quality and availability of water (IPCC, 2007; Palamuleni et al., 2011).

All of these environmental factors (poor and degraded soils, variable climate and deforestation) interact with political-economic conditions to exacerbate food insecurity for smallholder farming households.

Political-economic conditions

The political management of agriculture, food and related policies in the two decades following democratic rule also bear considerable responsibility for persistent food insecurity (Devereux, 2009). There were food shortages in 1987 and 1992–1994, which exacerbated political tension and helped to lead to Banda ceding power in 1994 (Harrigan, 2001; Englund, 2002; Harrigan, 2003). The first government under democratic rule, led by President Bakili Muluzi, became known for high levels of patronage, financial mismanagement and a shift in political alliances to the southern region business community (Englund, 2002; Chirwa and Dorward, 2013). There were ongoing structural reforms, including trade liberalization and privatization, which further reduced the small domestic manufacturing sector to about 12 per cent of the economy in 1999 (Chinsinga, 2002). The period of Muluzi's rule was also characterized by severe macroeconomic mismanagement, including rampant inflation, declining value of the Malawian Kwacha, and the issue of bonds to finance budget deficits (Chirwa and Dorward, 2013). The Muthalika and Joyce Banda governments have also been wracked with major corruption scandals that have led to donor withdrawal of support, high debt loads and inflation.

Muluzi's political support was from the southern commercial business elite, and this shift in political alliances, combined with increased fertilizer use, declining soil fertility and growing land pressure, increased the state's focus on maize self-sufficiency as a source of political patronage (Chirwa and Dorward, 2013). The Starter Pack Programme, overseeing universal distribution of free fertilizer and hybrid seed, began in 1998. This programme was downsized to the Targeted Input Programme, which had an official objective of social protection for the most vulnerable households, but also served as a source of mass patronage for Muluzi and political allies (Chirwa and Dorward, 2013).

Malawi experienced a major food crisis in 2001/02, caused by a combination of IMF stipulations to reduce national grain stores as part of structural adjustment, government miscalculation of the availability of tubers, disputes with donors relating to the severity of the crisis, and a series of information errors, transportation and communication mishaps (Devereux, 2002). Shifting donor perspectives about how to address food security is an important aspect of politics (Harrigan, 2003). Starting in the 1990s, Malawi became increasingly dependent on foreign donors for national programmes, with foreign donors playing an increasingly prominent role in decision making on food policy (Smale and Jayne, 2003). Malawi is currently a 'highly indebted poor country' and as such is very dependent on donor assistance to carry out any agricultural and food security programmes. Over the last decade, there has been an increased focus by donors on the impacts of policies on the more vulnerable households (Chirwa and Dorward, 2013). Individual donor differences driven by political ideology, domestic and humanitarian concerns, and shifting theories about development have also affected international donor approaches. The inconsistency of donor policies, combined with high reliance on donor funding, has made this aspect an important influence on food security (Chirwa and Dorward, 2013). Increasingly, agriculture and food policy-making has become a political issue, including regional patronage in distribution of various benefits, and heated debates with donors about policy approaches to address food insecurity (Chinsinga, 2011b). The special case of agricultural input subsidies in Malawi will be discussed in the next section.

Fertilizer subsidies and alternative solutions

Malawi's 'miracle': the Agricultural Input Subsidy Programme

Malawi has garnered international attention for its approach to combatting food insecurity since its implementation of the Agricultural Input Subsidy Programme (AISP) in 2006. We concentrate on this policy in the discussion below because it has been the single most important – and expensive – focus of food and agriculture policy in Malawi. Declarations of Malawi 'solving hunger' and a 'hunger-free nation' have been heralded within and beyond Malawi (Denning *et al.*, 2009; Sachs, 2012). President Bingu wa Mutharika, who had won the election as a member of the United Democratic Front (UDF) party and subsequently left that party to form his own, initiated the AISP in large part to gain popular political support at a time of high political tension and calls for his impeachment (Chirwa and Dorward, 2013). The fertilizer subsidy programme was highly popular, and despite increased repression and corruption, Mutharika was able to win a second term in office, mainly because of this programme's popularity (Chinsinga, 2012). Following his second election, Mutharika became increasingly repressive, corrupt and combative with critics within and outside Malawi, leading to fuel shortages, rising prices, political unrest and a political and economic crisis until his death in 2012.

The logic of the AISP was that both poor and non-poor rural farmers have limited access to affordable fertilizer and seeds in Malawi, in part due to poor roads, low levels of foreign exchange and an undeveloped input market, which leads to price volatility. Reduced fertilizer prices would allow Malawian farmers to increase productivity, and incomes through the increased sale of maize, and in turn maize prices would fall, which would increase the affordability of maize for net purchasers and, therefore, national food security would increase overall (Chirwa and Dorward, 2013). The Mutharika government also saw the subsidy programme as an opportunity to gain the political support of both the rural masses and the middle classes, who viewed national food security as an important priority (Sahley *et al.*, 2005; Chirwa and Dorward, 2013).

The programme's main features over a five-year period has been to provide a coupon to farmers to purchase fertilizer, maize seed and sometimes other agricultural inputs (e.g. legume and cotton seed) at considerably reduced rates – between 64 and 94 per cent reduced rate compared to commercial prices. Over half of farming households in Malawi were estimated to receive one or more coupons each year.

The Ministry of Agriculture and Food Security guidelines stated that beneficiaries of the programme were supposed to be 'full time smallholder farmers who cannot afford to purchase one or two bags of fertilizer at prevailing commercial prices, as determined by local leaders in their areas' and that coupons should be given 'just before they go to a market point to purchase inputs, to minimize chances of abusing them' (Chirwa and Dorward, 2013). In the programme's later years, there was greater emphasis on targeting vulnerable, at-risk households, including widows, AIDS-affected and the elderly.

Impacts of the AISP

The most commonly cited impact of the subsidy programme was an increase in national maize production from 1.4 million megatons (MT) in 2004/5 before the subsidy, to between 2.6 to 3.8 million MT in subsequent subsidy years (Dugger, 2007; Denning *et al.*, 2009). Although widely trumpeted as evidence of programme effectiveness, there are a number of questions about these figures. First, as discussed earlier, low production in earlier years was due to several factors, including low rainfall and late availability of fertilizer. Second, the estimates of hybrid maize yields, increasing from 2,500kg/ha to 3,000kg/ha, are inconsistent with on-farm studies, almost all of which are below 2,000kg/ha (Government of Malawi and World Bank, 2006; Holden and Lunduka, 2010a; NSO, 2010; Ricker-Gilbert, 2011). There is considerable evidence that the government overestimated maize yields, partly because of the political nature of the programme and partly because of discrepancies in yield estimate methods (Chinsinga, 2012; Chirwa and Dorward, 2013). Other studies on the impact of the AISP maize yields suggest that maize production did increase nationally and at the household level, but the exact amount varies (Chirwa and Dorward, 2013).

Food security was positively associated with the subsidy (Dorward and Chirwa, 2010; Fisher and Lewin, 2013,) but more recent studies have found that about one-third of the population remains highly food insecure, and 42 per cent of rural households experienced food insecurity in 2010/11 (NSO and ICF Macro, 2011). Qualitative studies also suggest that the subsidy increased maize production that season for the majority of coupon recipients, although the majority remain net buyers of maize (SOAS *et al.*, 2008; Dorward and Chirwa, 2010; Holden and Lunduka, 2010a; Chirwa and Dorward, 2013). Most households who reported strong impacts on their food security were already better off prior to receiving the coupons, while those who were still net buyers of maize reported lower maize prices and higher *ganyu* wages as two positive impacts from the AISP (Chirwa and Dorward, 2013).

In addition to a direct impact on food production and food security during that season, the subsidy may increase incomes. One study found increases in the number of households reporting improved well-being and reduced poverty for that season, but the estimated impact was small; while another found no impact (Ricker-Gilbert, 2011; Chirwa and Dorward, 2013). There has been inconsistent evidence on the impacts of the subsidy on real incomes, due in part to difficulties in getting accurate measures of income. There is evidence of an overall increase in real wages for most years, which is at least partly attributed to the AISP (SOAS

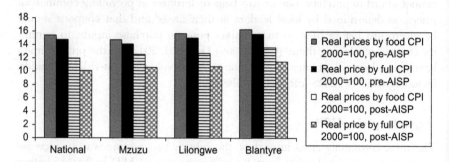

Figure 9.2 Average real maize prices in 2001 and 2011, at national level and in three major cities in Malawi.

Source: Calculated from nominal maize prices in Chirwa and Dorward (2013: 152), and NSO (2014).

et al., 2008; Ricker-Gilbert, 2011; Chirwa and Dorward, 2013). Rural poverty rates have in fact increased slightly in the last five years, but being able to tease out the specific links to the AISP is difficult on account of multiple confounding factors (De Schutter, 2013).

Overall nominal maize prices have almost doubled from pre-AISP prices (Chirwa and Dorward, 2013), but while inflation drove up nominal prices in Malawi by around 300 per cent, maize prices increased less than that. Non-food inflation was higher over this period than food inflation and, in real terms, deflating by the consumer price index (CPI), the price of maize decreased over the AISP period (Figure 9.2). These figures are, however, based on annual inflation rates.

Problems with the AISP

There are numerous problems in implementing such a large-scale programme. First, fertilizer had to be purchased in a timely fashion, since it had to be shipped to the nearest port, transported and then moved to the various depots across the country. Various political disputes, rising fertilizer and fuel prices, transportation problems, limited storage space at depots, poor roads, delayed printing and distribution of coupons all made late availability of fertilizer a problem most years. Fertilizer was distributed on time (by mid-December) to all depots in only two years of the programme (Chirwa and Dorward, 2013).

There were also difficulties with a transparent and fair coupon allocation and in the distribution programme, with evidence of local leaders sometimes favouring kin and other supporters. In numerous years, there was political allocation of coupons based on support for a given political party (Chinsinga, 2012) or the presence of an MP in a village (SOAS *et al.*, 2008). There was also evidence of corruption in beneficiary identification, for example, 'ghost' families created so that field staff could obtain coupons, splitting of households to obtain more coupons, as well as evidence of beneficiaries paying for coupons. One study found an average of 14 per cent price increase from the subsidized rate (Holden and Lunduka, 2010b), and other studies found a range of 3–5 per cent price increase (Chirwa and Dorward, 2013). In addition, there was widespread reporting of retailers asking for bribes to redeem the coupons, ranging from 9–27 per cent of the coupon price (Chinsinga, 2009; Farmers Union of Malawi, 2011). While only an estimated 20 per cent of people paid the bribe, women were found to be more vulnerable to paying it (Farmers Union of Malawi, 2011). There were also other types of fraud reported, including theft and counterfeit coupons (Chinsinga, 2009; Chirwa and Dorward, 2013). Chirwa and Dorward (2013) estimate that approximately 30 per cent of coupons were 'captured' or diverted from smallholder farmers in 2006/7 and this number was reduced to a little over 10 per cent in 2011/12.

One outcome of the coupon distribution problems (related to rising political, social and economic inequalities) was a reduced impact on the poor compared to the better off, and therefore lower impact on food insecurity. Numerous studies have found that better-off households in terms of livestock and assets received more coupons and applied more fertilizer than poor households (Ricker-Gilbert, 2011; Chibwana *et al.*, 2012; Holden and Lunduka, 2012). The poor were also more likely to share their fertilizer than the non-poor, with significantly lower fertilizer applications overall.

Impacts on crop diversification are less positive, with evidence that receipt of a subsidy coupon increased the likelihood of maize and tobacco production at the expense of legumes (Chibwana *et al.*, 2012). While legumes have been officially included in the AISP for several years, legume coupons are not always distributed, and are often unavailable for sale by seed companies (Chinsinga, 2011a). Fewer crops grown means increased risk of crop failure, fewer income-generating strategies, less diverse diets (since much of the food crop is consumed by the household), and in the case of legumes, less organic material and nitrogen added to the soils. Holden and Lunduka (2012) found that subsidy use was associated with a small but significant use of livestock manure, but this correlation may be related to wealth – since livestock ownership is one measure of wealth in Malawi – and was positively associated with subsidy use. There is also evidence that the AISP has increased hybrid maize seed use, and may have reduced local maize use, thereby reducing varietal diversity (Chinsinga, 2011a; Bezner Kerr, 2013). While hybrid maize varieties may have higher yields under high soil fertility conditions, they are not reproducible at farm level, while local maize varieties have other beneficial qualities, including high flour production, yield stability under low rainfall and soil fertility (Snapp *et al.*, 2010; Chinsinga, 2011a; Bezner Kerr, 2013).

The programme is also very costly, due to the rising cost of fertilizer, rising fuel prices, limited foreign exchange and distribution to remote rural areas on poor roads. The majority of the AISP cost was borne by the Government of Malawi, which spent between 7 and 16 per cent of the overall national budget on the programme, upwards of US$214 million at the highest point (Table 9.1).

Table 9.1 Main features and costs of the Agricultural Input Subsidy Programme 2005/6–2011/12.

Characteristic	2005/6	2006/7	2007/8	2008/9	2009/10	2010/11	2011/12
Total subsidized fertilizer sales (MT)	131,388	174,688	216,553	197,498	159,584	160,531	139,901
% farm family households receiving a coupon	n.a.	54	n.a.	67	n.a.	79	n.a.
Fertilizer coupon value (MK/bag)	7,750	2,480	3,299	7,951	3,841	5,237	6,536
Redemption price (MK/bag)	950	950	900	800	500	500	500
Subsidy %	64	72	79	91	88	91	93
Subsidized maize seed (MT)	n.a.	4,524	5,541	5,365	8,652	10,650	8,245
Legume seed	0	0	24	1	1,551	2,726	2,562
Net recorded and estimated cost (US$ million)	32.00	73.90	107.26	274.91	108.49	143.57	133.91
Direct donor support (US$ million)	0	9.51	7.13	37.75	17.48	22.05	44.85
Malawi government support (US$ million)	n.a.	64.39	100.13	214.04	100.92	129.12	95.84
Cost % MoAFS budget	n.a.	46.8	57.2	67.6	52.7	60.1	48.9
Cost, % national budget	n.a.	6.8	8.2	16.2	6.5	8.0	7.1
Cost, % GDP	n.a.	2.5	3.1	6.6	2.5	3.0	n.a.

Source: Adapted from Chirwa and Dorward, 2013.

Note: n.a. – not available.

In later years, the rising cost of fuel and persistent fuel shortages were partly blamed on the AISP by critics, and led to an increase in political unrest as well as donor unease with the programme (Bezner Kerr, 2012; Chinsinga, 2012). National debt loads increased considerably, in part as a result of the AISP programme, from 8.2 per cent in 2005 to 15.7 per cent in 2010, almost doubling the debt load in less than a decade (Chirwa and Dorward, 2013). The high debt load, rising prices, fuel shortages and foreign exchange deficit led President Joyce Banda to devalue the Malawian Kwacha in 2013, and inflation has gone from below 10 per cent to over 30 per cent (NSO, 2013). The lingering impacts of the high cost of the AISP thus remain to be seen.

It is worth noting, however, that the increased infrastructure provided so that the AISP programme could succeed – notably a large and growing network of private agro-dealerships – has provided tangible benefits to one key set of stakeholders: large multinational corporations. Monsanto Malawi's sales increased 85 per cent between 2007 and 2010. Concerns have been raised among a range of commentators and non-governmental organizations about the benefits to such corporations as a result of Malawi's recent agricultural strategies (Curtis and Hilary, 2012). What cannot easily be measured, however, is the cost of *not* funding alternative approaches to the problem of food security. We now turn to a discussion of alternatives.

Policy recommendations for achieving food and nutritional security in Malawi

Several major alternative approaches to addressing food insecurity will be discussed here, echoing the calls and analysis of the Malawian context by the United Nations Special Rapporteur on the Right to Food (De Schutter, 2013): promotion and research on agroecological methods, farmer education, legal frameworks to support the right to food (wage laws, protection of land rights), cash transfers to those households vulnerable to food insecurity, gender equality policies and the strengthening of democracy.

Agroecological approaches to improving food security for smallholders

Some scholars, including the authors of this chapter, contend that the AISP strategy, which promotes reliance on commercial fertilizer and hybrid maize to increase food security, is a short-term solution that may worsen conditions for farmers and Malawi's economy long term (Mhango and Dick, 2011; Bezner Kerr, 2012). Advocates of an agroecological approach argue that crop diversification is both more sustainable and has multiple positive impacts on livelihoods, nutrition, food security and ecosystem health (Bezner Kerr *et al.*, 2010; De Schutter, 2010; Snapp *et al.*, 2010; Chinsinga *et al.*, 2011a; Mhango and Dick, 2012; Patel, 2013). One nationwide study found that a more biodiverse cropping system, particularly integration of shrubby semi-perennial legumes, builds up soil quality, reduces the need for fertilizer application, increases soil cover, reduces the likelihood of soil erosion, while most important from a farmer perspective, reduces yield variability while maintaining maize yields (Snapp *et al.*, 2010).

Other studies have noted the importance that a diverse cropping system plays in buffering farming households, making them less vulnerable to drought, price changes and other livelihood shocks. Cassava, for example, is a useful drought tolerant crop that can be 'stored' in the soil until harvested (Brooks, 2014). Sorghum and finger millet are drought tolerant indigenous grains that were used as the 'back-up' crop for maize during periods of drought in northern Malawi. However, these grains have increasingly been dropped from the farming system on account of government policies that promoted tobacco and maize (Bezner Kerr, 2014). Another major feature of agroecological approaches is improved soil quality through the integration of organic materials, soil conservation and other methods (Snapp *et al.*, 2002; Bezner Kerr *et al.*, 2007b). Improved soil quality increases soil nutrient holding and water carrying capacity during drought, which increases yield stability during low precipitation years (Snapp *et al.*, 2014).

Investing in farmer education

Agroecological approaches include strengthening farmer education to foster observation, experimentation and adaptation to a given ecological, social and economic context. The recent UN Mission to Malawi called for the government to revise and strengthen agricultural extension so that it is more responsive to poor farmers with limited resources (De Schutter, 2013). Farmer-led research and experimentation increases the range of solutions and draws on local knowledge (Snapp *et al.*, 2002; Bezner Kerr *et al.*, 2007b). Transformational educational approaches that foster idea sharing, experimentation, reflection and farmer-to-farmer teaching encourage innovation, problem solving and exchange between people who understand the local context (Satzinger *et al.*, 2009). There are considerable opportunity costs from spending over half of the agriculture budget on a narrow set of technologies, and the funds might have had longer-lasting impacts for more people if invested in an agricultural extension programme that fostered this type of farmer learning rather than a limited set of purchased technologies.

Attention to gender inequality

Scholars argue that there is a need to pay attention to gender and other social inequalities, if increased yields are to translate into improved child nutrition (Berti *et al.*, 2004; Hawkes and Ruel, 2006; Bezner Kerr *et al.*, 2008). Increased food production does not directly translate into improved child nutrition; attention to child feeding practices, appropriate care during illness, and access to other resources (e.g. health care, clean water, sanitation, education) are crucial to ensure improved child nutrition. One study found that grandmothers were advocating early introduction of watery porridge to infants, which had negative impacts on child growth (Bezner Kerr *et al.*, 2007a). Women also had difficulty carrying out exclusive breastfeeding due to considerable labour constraints reinforced by gender inequality at the household level (Bezner Kerr *et al.*, 2008). A dialogue-based approach to addressing this problem led local people to discuss the various causes of child malnutrition, which were rooted in power inequalities at the household level as well as broader trends such as poverty and HIV/AIDS (Bezner Kerr *et al.*, 2008; Satzinger *et al.*, 2009). Inter-generational discussion groups combined with farmer-led research on agriculture and nutrition strategies led to improvements in child nutrition for participating households (Bezner Kerr *et al.*, 2008; Satzinger *et al.*, 2009). The authors argued that attention to power inequalities at the household, community and national level is crucial for addressing nutrition (Bezner Kerr, 2008; Bezner Kerr *et al.*, 2008; Patel *et al.*, forthcoming).

Legal protections and legislation for land, wages and food

Land shortages are a major problem for smallholder farmers, with the majority of households farming less than one hectare of land, in part due to historical conditions discussed above that created land inequalities. The GoM has promoted large-scale corporate agricultural production with links to global markets as one means to address food security, as signalled through their signing of the New Alliance for Food Security and Nutrition in 2013. This agreement paves the way for increased foreign investment, including releasing 200,000 ha of land to foreign investors and facilitating foreign land acquisition, a trend observed in other countries in Africa. The GoM is developing a new Land Bill, but there is concern that this bill will not protect rural communities from increased land acquisition by foreign corporations (De Schutter, 2013). In his mission to Malawi, the UN Special Rapporteur for the Right to Food recommended strengthening the Land Bill to ensure ceilings on land acquisition as well as adequate safeguards to prevent land being transferred without community assent (De Schutter, 2013). Further, he recommended that protection of communal land tenure, adequate compensation for land loss, and women's rights to land be strengthened (De Schutter, 2013). Legislation which facilitated redistribution of some of the estimated 2.4 million ha of underutilized land (most of which is estate land) to those households with no or little land who are interested in farming would address a major structural constraint to food security for poor Malawians.

A second structural constraint to food security is that of extremely low wages, with the minimum wage fixed at US$1.12 per day, one of the lowest in the world (De Schutter, 2013). Current labour laws do not adequately protect workers from exploitation, and the minimum wage is not adequate to ensure a right to food. Enforced living-wage legislation would be a major policy shift to improve food security in Malawi. Adequate labour inspection, awarding public contracts to those companies who provide a living wage, and ensuring the right to collective bargaining in all sectors are other means by which food security could be strengthened (De Schutter, 2013). Further, tabling the Tobacco Tenancy Labour Bill to Parliament, which addresses some of the poor working conditions for tobacco sharecroppers in Malawi, would enhance working conditions and increase access to food for workers in this sector.

Cash transfers to the 'ultra-poor'

Another approach to addressing food security, successfully applied in other contexts, is direct cash transfers to poor, highly food insecure households. Note that agroecological approaches or, indeed, a fertilizer subsidy can only reach those with land. For the landless, land poor, labourers or the unemployed in rural areas, such projects are unlikely to matter a great deal – even if lower maize prices result, the ultra-poor will reap only a quantum of benefit. A cash transfer not only allows households to survive, but can over time translate into gains in productivity, poverty reduction and improvements in nutrition, health and other measures of social welfare (Lagarde et al., 2007; Gertler et al., 2012). This kind of targeted programme addresses the credit constraints faced by extremely poor households that prevent them from investing in activities to get out of poverty.

Malawi initiated a Social Cash Transfer (SCT) programme in 2006, to address the needs of the highly poor (Schubert and Kambewa, 2006). Initially a pilot programme, the SCT targeted labour-constrained rural households who had few assets and were defined as 'ultra-poor' (Boone et al., 2013). The overall goal of the programme was to improve the health, nutrition and education of the poorest 10 per cent of Malawian households (Schubert and Kambewa, 2006; Miller et al., 2011). Studies of the programme indicate that less than 5 per cent of these poor households receive a fertilizer subsidy, often because they were landless, so there was little overlap with the AISP (Boone et al., 2013). The average household participating in the SCT received the equivalent of US$14 per month, which was enough to raise their living standard to above the national average (Boone et al., 2013). There were no conditions attached to participation in the programme, unlike similar programmes initiated in Latin America (Molyneux, 2006), though families were urged through social marketing efforts to invest in their households' health, nutrition and education (Boone et al., 2013).

Evidence from several studies found that there was a significant improvement of food security, increased dietary diversity (Miller et al., 2011), increased time spent on their farms and household care, while time spent on ganyu (casual farm labour) decreased (Boone et al., 2013). Households also increased both production and consumption of their own food, and had more productive agricultural assets such as hoes and chickens, following participation in the SCT programme (Boone et al., 2013). Overall, this programme was effective at reaching the extremely destitute in Malawi.

Deepening of democratic rule

All of these recommendations require a government that is accountable, committed to social justice, responsive and transparent in the management of funds and programmes. The relatively new democratic system in Malawi has considerable problems with corruption, mismanagement and rule by those who are focused on political patronage and acquiring wealth. The government is also highly dependent on foreign support, making it vulnerable to influence from international donors, corporations and non-governmental organizations. As Sen suggests (1981), efforts are needed to strengthen democratic rule in Malawi, through processes such as participatory budgeting, regular consultation at the community level, and insisting on greater accountability of politicians to their constituents through legislation and popular pressure, if food security is to be effectively addressed.

Conclusions

In this chapter, we reviewed the major political, economic, environmental and social factors that drive food insecurity in Malawi, one of the poorest countries in sub-Saharan Africa. For largely political and economic reasons, the diagnosis of hunger as an insufficiency of maize production has led to a technological focus on agricultural inputs and the well-publicized Agricultural Input Subsidy Programme (AISP), which reduced the price of fertilizer and hybrid maize seed for the majority of smallholder farmers in the last decade. While there is sound evidence that this programme increased maize production, thereby increasing farmer incomes, the programme has been expensive. It crowded out other solutions and provided only short-term gains to the challenges associated with food insecurity and malnutrition. It is of some concern that current initiatives, such as the New Alliance for Food Security and Nutrition, tend to repeat these errors, especially when there is evidence that the AISP also decreased crop diversity and had little impact on child malnutrition. The literature on food security and nutrition points to the importance of gender relations, crop diversity and basic ability to command access to food. With these diagnoses for food insecurity in mind, an agroecological alternative to the AISP was discussed, which increased farmer knowledge of a range of possibilities for improving land quality, crop diversity and livelihood strategies, while paying greater attention to gender and other social inequalities that influence child nutrition. Finally, the Malawi SCT was also discussed, which provides cash to the most destitute households, and has been shown to improve food security and nutrition for the poorest households.

Solutions to food security in a case such as Malawi vary partly because of debates about the ultimate causes of food insecurity. Proponents of the AISP tend to argue that farming households are food insecure because they lack access to the right technologies. Those who favour the agroecological approach suggest that the problem lies in the social and economic relations that reinforce inequalities in food access, as well as constrain the knowledge of sustainable alternative solutions.

References

Bandyopadhyay, S., Shyamsundar, P. and Baccini, A. (2012) Forests, biomass use and poverty in Malawi, *Ecological Economics*, 70: 2461–71.

Bernell, S., Edwards, M. and Weber, B. (2006) Restricted opportunities, unfortunate personal choices, ineffective policies? What explains food insecurity in Oregon, *Journal of Agricultural and Resource Economics*, 31 (2): 193–211.

Berti, P.R., Krasavec, J. and Fitzgerald, S. (2004) A review of the effectiveness of agriculture interventions in improving nutrition outcomes, *Public Health Nutrition*, 7 (5): 799–809.

Bezner Kerr, R. (2005) Food security in northern Malawi: historical context and the significance of gender, kinship relations and entitlements, *Journal of Southern Africa Studies*, 31: 53–74.

Bezner Kerr, R. (2008) Gender and agrarian inequality at the local scale. In: Snapp, S.S. and Pound, B. (Eds) *Agricultural Systems: Agroecology and Rural Innovation*, Elsevier Press, San Diego: 279–306.

Bezner Kerr, R. (2010) The land is changing: contested agricultural narratives in northern Malawi. In: McMichael, P. (Eds) *Contesting Development: Critical Struggles for Social Change*. Routledge Press, Florence.

Bezner Kerr, R. (2012) Lessons from the old Green Revolution for the new: social, environmental and nutritional issues for agricultural change in Africa, *Progress in Development Studies*, 12 (2 & 3): 213–29.

Bezner Kerr, R. (2013) Seed struggles and food sovereignty in northern Malawi, *Journal of Peasant Studies*, DOI: 10.1080/03066150.2013.848428.

Bezner Kerr, R. (2014) Lost and found crops: agrobiodiversity, indigenous knowledge, and a feminist political ecology of sorghum and finger millet in northern Malawi, *Annals of the Association of American Geographers*, 104 (3): 577–93, DOI: 10.1080/00045608.2014.892346.

Bezner Kerr, R., Berti, P. and Chirwa, M. (2007a) Breastfeeding and mixed feeding practices in Malawi: timing, reasons, decision makers, and child health consequences, *Food and Nutrition Bulletin*, 28 (1): 90–9.

Bezner Kerr, R., Dakishoni, L. and Shumba, L. (2008) We grandmothers know plenty: breastfeeding, complementary feeding and the multifaceted role of grandmothers in Malawi, *Social Science and Medicine*, 66 (5): 1095–105.

Bezner Kerr, R., Snapp, S., Chirwa, M., Shumba, L. and Msachi, R. (2007b) Participatory research on legume diversification with Malawian smallholder farmers for improved human nutrition and soil fertility, *Experimental Agriculture*, 43: 437–53.

Bignami-van Assche, S., Anglewicz, P., van Assche, A., Fleming, P. and van de Ruit, C. (2011) HIV/AIDS and time allocation in rural Malawi, online, http://www.demographic-research.org/Volumes/Vol24/27/ DOI: 10.4054/DemRes.2011.24.27 (accessed 2 May 2014).

Boone, R., Covarrubias, K., Davis, B. and Winters, P. (2013) Cash transfer programs and agricultural production: the case of Malawi, *Agricultural Economics*, 44: 365–78.

Booth, D., Cammack, D., Harrigan, J., Kanyongolo, E., Mataure, M. and Ngwira, N. (2006) Drivers of change and development in Malawi, Working paper No. 261: Overseas Development Institute, London; Institute for Policy Research, Analysis and Dialogue, Blantyre.

Brooks, S. (2014) Enabling adaptation? Lessons from the new Green Revolution in Malawi and Kenya, *Climatic Change*, 122: 15–26.

Bryceson, D.F. (2006) Ganyu casual labour, famine and HIV/AIDS in rural Malawi: causality and casualty, *Journal of Modern African Studies*, 44 (2): 173–202.

Chibwana, C., Fisher, M. and Shively, G. (2012) Cropland allocation effects of agricultural input subsidies in Malawi, *World Development*, 40: 124–33.

Chinsinga, B. (2002) The politics of poverty alleviation in Malawi: a critical review. In: Englund, H. (Ed.) *A Democracy of Chameleons*, Nordiska Afrikainstitutet, Uppsala, Sweden: 25–42.

Chinsinga, B. (2009) Participation of civil society in the monitoring of the Agricultural Input Subsidy Programme (AISP). A monitoring exercise carried out for the Consortium of FUM, CISANET and MEJN, Zomba: Chancellor College, University of Malawi.

Chinsinga, B. (2011a) Seeds and subsidies. The political economy of input subsidies in Malawi, *IDS Bulletin*, 42 (4): 59–69.

Chinsinga, B. (2011b) Agro-dealers, subsidies and rural market development in Malawi: a political economy enquiry, FAC Working paper No. 31, Future Agricultures Consortium, Brighton.

Chinsinga, B. (2012) The political economy of agricultural policy processes in Malawi: a case study of the fertilizer subsidy programme, Working paper No. 39, Future Agricultures Consortium, Brighton.

Chirwa, E. and Dorward, A. (2013) *Agricultural Input Subsidies: The Recent Malawi Experience.* Oxford University Press, Oxford.

Crawford, E., Kelly, V., Jayne, T. and Howard, J. (2003) Input use and market development in sub-Saharan Africa: an overview, *Food Policy*, 28: 277–92.

Curtis, M. and Hilary, J. (2012) The hunger games: How DFID support for agribusiness is fuelling poverty in Africa. War on Want, London, online, http://www.waronwant. org/attachments/The%20Hunger%20Games%202012.pdf (accessed 2 July 2014).

De Schutter, O. (2010) Report submitted by the United Nations Special Rapporteur on the Right to Food. United Nations, Geneva.

De Schutter, O. (2013) United Nations Special Rapporteur for the Right to Food: Mission to Malawi from 12–22 July 2013 – End of mission statement. United Nations, Geneva, online, http://www.ohchr.org/EN/Issues/Food/Pages/Visits.aspx (accessed 6 May 2014).

Denning, G., Kabambe, P., Sanchez, P., Malik, A., Flor, R., Harawa, R., Nkhoma, P., Zamba, C., Banda, C., Magombo, C., Keating, M., Wangila, J. and Sachs, J. (2009) Input subsidies to improve smallholder maize productivity in Malawi: toward an African green revolution, *PLoS Biology*, 7 (1): e1000023.

Devereux, S. (2002) The Malawi famine of 2002: causes, consequences and policy lessons, *IDS Bulletin*, 33: 70–8.

Devereux, S. (2009) Why does famine persist in Africa?, *Food Security*, 1: 25–35.

Dorward, A.R. and Chirwa, E.W. (2010) Evaluation of the 2008/9 Agricultural Input Subsidy Programme, Malawi: maize production and market impacts. University of London, SOAS.

Dorward, A.R. and Chirwa, E.W. (2011) The Malawi agricultural input subsidy programme: 2005/6 to 2008/9, *International Journal of Agricultural Sustainability*, 9: 232–47.

Dugger, C.W. (2007) Ending famine, simply by ignoring the experts, *New York Times*, 2 December.

Edriss, A., Tchale, H. and Wobst, P. (2004) The impact of labour market liberalization on maize productivity and rural poverty in Malawi. Robert Bosch Foundation, Policy Analysis for Sustainable Agricultural Development (PASAD) Project, University of Bonn, Germany.

Ellis, F., Kutengule, M. and Nyasulu, A. (2003) Livelihoods and rural poverty reduction in Malawi, *World Development*, 31 (9): 1495–510.

Ellis, F. and Manda, E. (2012) Seasonal food crises and policy responses: a narrative account of three food security crises in Malawi, *World Development*, 40 (7): 1407–17.

Englund, H. (2002) *A Democracy of Chameleons: Politics and Culture in the New Malawi.* Nordic Africa Institute, Uppsala, Sweden.

Farmers Union of Malawi (2011) Promoting the participation of civil society in the management of the farm input subsidy programme (FISP). Farmers Union of Malawi, Lilongwe.

FAOSTAT (2013) Food and Agriculture Organization Statistics (FAOSTAT), online, http://faostat-gateway/ (accessed 30 April 2013).

Fisher, M. and Lewin, P. (2013) Household, community, and policy determinants of food insecurity in rural Malawi, *Development Southern Africa*, 30 (4–5): 451–67.

Food and Agriculture Organization (FAO) (2010) Global Forest Resources Assessment 2010: Country report Malawi, FAO, Rome.

Food and Agriculture Organization (FAO) (2013) Global information and early warning system on Food and Agriculture Country Brief, Malawi, FAO, Rome.

Funk, C., Dettinger, M.D., Michaelsen, J.C., Verdin, J.P., Brown, M.E., Barlow, M. and Hoell, A. (2008) Warming of the Indian Ocean threatens eastern and southern African food security but could be mitigated by agricultural development, *PNAS*, 105:11081–6.

Gertler, P., Martinez, S., and Rubio-Codina, M. (2012) Investing cash transfers to raise long-term living standards, *American Economics Journals: Applied Economics*, 4 (1): 164–92.

Ghosh, J. and Kalipeni, E. (2005) Women in Chinsapo, Malawi: vulnerability and risk to HIV/AIDS, *Journal of Social Aspects of HIV/AIDS*, 2 (3): 320–32.

Government of Malawi (GoM) (2010) Malawi State of the Environment and Outlook Report. Ministry of Natural Resources, Energy and Environment, Government of Malawi, Lilongwe.

Government of Malawi and World Bank (2006) Malawi Poverty and Vulnerability Assessment: Investing in Our Future, Ministry of Economic Planning and Development, Lilongwe.

Harrigan, J. (2001) *From Dictatorship to Democracy: Economic Policy in Malawi, 1964–2000.* Ashgate, UK: Aldershot.

Harrigan, J. (2003) U-Turns and full circles: two decades of agricultural reform in Malawi 1981–2000, *World Development*, 31: 847–63.

Harrigan, J. (2008) Food insecurity, poverty and the Malawian starter pack: fresh start or false start? *Food Policy*, 33 (3): 237–49.

Hawkes, C. and Ruel, M.T. (2006) Policy and practice – the linkages between agriculture and health: an inter-sectoral opportunity to improve the health and livelihoods of the poor, *Bulletin of the World Health Organization*, 84 (12): 984.

Holden, S. and Lunduka, R. (2010a) Impacts of the fertilizer subsidy programme in Malawi: targeting, household perceptions and preferences. Noragric Report, Ås, Norway.

Holden, S. and Lunduka, R. (2010b) The political economy of input subsidies in Malawi: targeting efficiency and household perceptions. Draft for comment, School of Economics and Business, Norwegian University of Life Sciences, Ås, Norway.

Holden, S. and Lunduka, H. (2012) Who benefits from Malawi's targeted farm input subsidy program? *Forum for Development Studies*, DOI:10.1080/08039410.2012.6 88858, 1–25.

Intergovernmental Panel on Climate Change (IPCC) (2007) Climate Change 2007: impacts, adaptation and vulnerability. Contribution of Working Group II to the 4th Assessment Report of the IPCC. Cambridge University Press, Cambridge, UK.

Jayne, T.S., Zulu, B. and Nijhoff, J.J. (2006) Stabilizing food markets in Eastern and Southern Africa, *Food Policy*, 31 (4): 328–41.

Jayne, T.S., Chapoto, A., Minde, I. and Donovan, C. (2008) The 2008/09 food price and food security situation in Eastern and Southern Africa: implications for immediate and longer run responses. International Development Working Paper, Michigan State

University, East Lansing, online, http://www.aec.msu.edu/fs2/papers/idwp97.pdf (accessed 3 May 2014).

Jayne, T.S., Mather, D. and Mghenyi, E. (2010) Principal challenges confronting smallholder agriculture in sub-Saharan Africa, *World Development*, 38: 1384–98.

Jumbe, C.B.L. and Angelsen, A. (2007) Forest dependence and participation in CPR management: empirical evidence from forest co-management in Malawi, *Ecological Economics*, 62: 661–72.

Kalinga, O.E. (1993) The master farmers' scheme in Nyasaland 1950–62: a study of a failed attempt to create a 'yeoman' class, *African Affairs*, 92: 367–87.

Kennedy, E. and Peters, P. (1993) Household food security and child nutrition: the interaction of income and gender of household head, *World Development*, 20: 1077–85.

Kydd, J. and Christiansen, R. (1982) Structural change in Malawi since independence: consequences of a development strategy based on large-scale agriculture, *World Development*, 10 (5): 355–75.

Lagarde, M., Haines, A. and Palmer, N. (2007) Conditional cash transfer for improving uptake of health interventions in low- and middle-income countries: a systematic review, *JAMA*, 298 (16): 1900–9.

Mandala, E. (1995) We toiled for the white man in our own gardens: the conflict between cotton and food in colonial Malawi. In: Isaacman, A. and Roberts, R. (Eds) *Cotton, Colonialism and Social History in Sub-Saharan Africa*. Heinemann and James Currey, Portsmouth, NH and London: 285–306.

Mhango, J. and Dick, J. (2011) Analysis of fertilizer subsidy programs and ecosystem services in Malawi, *Renewable Agriculture and Food Systems*, 26 (3): 200–7, DOI:10.1017/S1742170510000517.

Miller, C., Tsoka, M. and Reichert, K. (2011) The impact of the social cash transfer scheme on food security in Malawi, *Food Policy*, 36: 230–8.

Molyneux, M. (2006) Mothers at the service of the new poverty agenda: progresa/oportunidades, Mexico's conditional transfer programme, *Social Policy and Administration*, 40 (4): 425–49.

Nakhumwa, T.O. and Hassan, R.M. (2012) Optimal management of soil quality stocks and long-term consequences of land degradation for smallholder farmers in Malawi, *Environment Resource Economics*, 52: 415–33.

N'gong'ola, C. (1990) The state, settlers and indigenes in the evolution of land law and policy in colonial Malawi, *International Journal of African Historical Studies*, 23: 27–58.

NSO (2012) Integrated Household Survey 2010–11. Household socioeconomic characteristics report, National Statistical Office, Zomba, Malawi.

NSO (2013) Headline Inflation Rates, online, http://www.nsomalawi.mw/index.php/latest-publications/consumer-price-indices/65-headline-inflation-rates.html and http://www.nsomalawi.mw/index.php/component/content/article/3-reports/156--the-consumer-price-index-time-series.html (accessed 20 January 2014).

NSO (2014) Malawi Consumer Price Indices, online, http://www.nsomalawi.mw/latest-publications/consumer-price-indices/index.php (accessed 20 January 2014).

NSO and ICF Macro (2011) Malawi: Demographic and Health Survey 2010, National Statistical Office and ICF Macro, Zomba, Malawi and Calverton, MA.

Palamuleni, L.G., Ndomba, P.M. and Annegarn, H.J. (2011) Evaluating land cover change and its impact on hydrological regime in Upper Shire river catchment, Malawi, *Regional Environmental Change*, 11: 845–55.

Patel, R. (2013) The long green revolution, *Journal of Peasant Studies*, 40(1): 1–63.

Patel, R., Bezner Kerr, R. and Shumba, L. (forthcoming) Cook eat man woman: understanding the new alliance for food security and nutrition in Malawi, and its alternatives, *Journal of Peasant Studies*.

Peters, P. (2006) Rural income and poverty in a time of radical change in Malawi, *Journal of Development Studies*, 42: 322–45.

Peters, P., Walker, P. and Kambewa, D. (2008) Striving for normality in a time of AIDS in Malawi, *Journal of Modern African Studies* 46 (4): 659–87.

Population Reference Bureau (PRB) (2011) The world's women and girls: 2011 data sheet, www.prb.org. Washington, DC.

Ricker-Gilbert, J. (2011) Household-level impacts of fertilizer subsidies in Malawi. Unpublished PhD Thesis, Michigan State University.

Ruel, M.T., Levin, C.E., Armar-Klemesu, M., Maxwell, D. and Morris, S.S. (1999) Good care practices can mitigate the negative effects of poverty and low maternal schooling on children's nutritional status: evidence from Accra. FCND Discussion paper No. 62, IFPRI, Washington, DC.

Sachs, J. (2012) How Malawi fed its own people, *New York Times*, 19 April, online, http://www.nytimes.com/2012/04/20/opinion/how-malawi-fed-its-own-people.html?ref=global-home&_r=0 (accessed 6 May 2014).

Sahley, C., Groelsma, R., Marchione, T. and Nelson, D. (2005) *The Governance Dimension of Food Security in Malawi*. USAID, Lilongwe.

Sahn, D.E. and Arulpragasam, J. (1991) The stagnation of smallholder agriculture in Malawi: a decade of structural adjustment, *Food Policy*, 16 (3): 219–34.

Sassi, M. (2012) Short-term determinants of malnutrition among children in Malawi, *Food Security*, 4: 593–696.

Satzinger, F., Bezner Kerr, R. and Shumba, L. (2009) Farmers integrate nutrition, social issues and agriculture through knowledge exchange in northern Malawi, *Ecology of Food and Nutrition*, 48 (5): 369–82.

School of Oriental and African Studies (SOAS), Wadonda Consult, Overseas Development Institute & Michigan State University (2008) Evaluation of the 2006/7 agricultural input supply programme, Malawi. Final report, March, SOAS, London.

Schubert, B. and Kambewa, P. (2006) Designing a pilot social cash transfer scheme for Malawi. First report, UNICEF, Lilongwe.

Sen, A.K. (1981) *Poverty and Famines: An Essay on Entitlement and Deprivation*. Oxford University Press, New York.

Shah, M.K., Osborne, N., Mbilize, T. and Vilili, G. (2002) Impact of HIV/AIDS on agricultural productivity and rural livelihoods in the central region of Malawi. CARE International in Malawi, Lilongwe.

Smale, M. and Jayne, T.S. (2003) Maize in eastern and southern Africa: seeds of success in retrospect, EPTD Discussion paper No. 97.

Snapp, S.S. (1998) Soil nutrient status of smallholder farms in Malawi, *Communications in Soil Science and Plant Analysis*, 29 (17–18): 2571–88.

Snapp, S.S., Kanyama-Phiri, G.Y., Kamanga, B., Gilbert, R. and Wellard, K. (2002) Farmer and researcher partnerships in Malawi: developing soil fertility technologies for the near term and far term, *Experimental Agriculture*, 38: 411–31.

Snapp, S.S., Blackie, M.J., Gilbert, R.A., Bezner Kerr, R. and Kanyama-Phiri, G.Y. (2010) Biodiversity can support a greener revolution in Africa 2010, *Proceedings of the National Academy of Sciences*, 107 (48): 20840–5.

Snapp, S.S., Bezner Kerr, R., Smith, A., Ollenburger, M., Mhango, W., Shumba, L, Gondwe, T. and Kanyama-Phiri, G.Y. (2014) Modeling and participatory, farmer-led approaches to food security in a changing world: a case study from Malawi, *Scheresse*, 24: 350–8, DOI: 10.1684/sec.2014.0409.

United Nations Development Programme (UNDP) (2013) Human Development Report 2013, United Nations Development Programme, New York.

United Nations Programme (Joint) on HIV/AIDS (UNAIDS) (2013) Malawi Country Report, online, http://www.unaids.org/en/regionscountries/countries/malawi/ (accessed 3 May 2014).

Vail, L. (1983) The making of the 'dead north': a study of Ngoni rule in northern Malawi, c1855–1907. In: Peires, J.B. (Ed.) *Before and After Shaka: Papers in Nguni History*. Rhodes University, Grahamstown, South Africa, pp. 230–67.

Vaughan, M. (1987) *The Story of an African Famine: Gender and Famine in 20th Century Malawi*. Cambridge University Press, London.

Wodon, Q. and Beegle, K. (2006) Labour shortages despite underemployment? Seasonality in time use in Malawi. In: Blackden, C.M. and Wodon, Q. (Eds) *Gender, Time Use, and Poverty in Sub-Saharan Africa*. World Bank, Washington, DC, 97–116.

World Bank (2013a) Economic Indicators. Washington, DC, online, http://wdi.worldbank.org/table/1.1 (accessed 6 January 2014).

World Bank (2013b) Data Indicators. Washington, DC, online, http://data.worldbank.org/indicator/AG.LND.ARBL.HA (accessed 5 January 2014).

Zulu, L.C. (2010). The forbidden fuel: charcoal, urban woodfuel demand and supply dynamics, community forest management and woodfuel policy in Malawi, *Energy Policy*, 38 (7): 3717–30.

10 Making the agri-food system work for the poor

The construction of food and nutrition security in Brazil

Thaís Leonardi Bassinello and Crispim Moreira

Introduction

In Brazil, the use of the terms food security and human right to food were first registered in official documents in the mid-1980s. In 1985, the Ministry of Agriculture elaborated the document 'Food Security: Proposal for a Policy to Fight Hunger', with the focus on the socioeconomic aspects of food security. In the following year, the first National Food and Nutrition Conference[1] brought about the inclusion of a nutritional dimension to food security as well as establishing food as a right (CONSEA, 2009).

Although these first initiatives differ with the more recent use of the term 'food security', they already signalled two key aspects in the understanding of food security action (i.e. related to *how* that goal should be pursued) in Brazil. The first is the intersectoral nature of food security, indicating the need for a government body capable of coordinating the formulation and the implementation of public interventions in multiple areas; and the second is that civil society should participate in the formulation and monitoring of such public policies through a high-level council that would advise the president in food security matters.

These early proposals had little repercussion for almost a decade in Brazil. Driven by social claims, the food security agenda officially re-emerged in 1993, in the aftermath of the impeachment of the first democratically elected president in 30 years. By the end of that decade, the Brazilian civil society had shaped the concept of food and nutrition security (*segurança alimentar e nutricional* – SAN) through a process in which several social mobilizations played a role.

In 2003, already in the context of a consolidated democracy, the newly elected government declared SAN the priority of its social policy. The participatory policy process that ensued led to the institutionalization of the SAN agenda with the establishment of the National Food and Nutrition Security System (*Sistema Nacional de Segurança Alimentar e Nutricional* – SISAN) in 2006.

In this sense, SAN in Brazil should be understood as a social construction, jointly developed by the Brazilian government and civil society over the past three decades. The two main constructs that emerged from that interaction were: the definition of SAN as a human right – which emphasizes the responsibilities of the Brazilian State towards this right; and SISAN, which is the participatory and intersectoral governance structure for SAN in Brazil. Both constructs emphasize SAN as a strategic and permanent objective of policies concerning all domains of the agri-food system.

This chapter aims at presenting a historical account of the Brazilian construction of SAN, highlighting the most important developments during the two periods mentioned above: the first, between 1993 and 2002, when food security and related agendas were mainly embraced by civil society; and the second, after 2003, when the agenda was institutionalized as a system of public policies. In addition, this chapter also presents the main understandings about the causes of food insecurity in Brazil that the policies – reinforced or instituted within SISAN – were intended to address: food production, distribution and consumption dimensions. In general, these policies aimed at supporting family-based agriculture for domestic market supply, reinstating the role of the State in food provisioning, and increasing access to food through poverty reduction policies. Possible future developments, as well as results of nationwide studies, are also included in the chapter wherever relevant.

Social mobilization and democracy as the basis of food security in Brazil (1993–2002)

With the fight for re-democratization, the Brazilian civil society became a protagonist in several public arenas (Pinto, 2005). Between 1993 and 2002, the country witnessed three mobilizations in particular that would have deep implications for its food security history.

First, the Citizenship Action against Hunger, Poverty and for Life, firmly placed the issue of hunger on the national agenda, leading to the organization of a food security council, plan and conference. Second, on the other side of the agri-food spectrum, deep transformations were operating within the Brazilian rural syndicalism already since the 1970s, paving the way for the emergence of family farming as a distinctive category within the rural domain[2] and its de facto legitimization with the creation of a credit support policy in 1996. Third, in 2001, the participative construction of the Zero Hunger Project connected both the family farming and the fight against hunger and poverty agendas by putting forward the understanding of SAN that currently prevails in Brazil.

The citizenship action, the food security council, plan and conference

In 1993, the Movement for Ethics in Politics – the leading social movement responsible for the presidential impeachment of 1992 – started the Citizenship Action against Hunger, Poverty and for Life, as its new ethical campaign. The proposal put forward by the Citizenship Action had its basis in the National Food Security Policy introduced in 1991 by the Parallel Government[3] (Pessanha, 2002). The ties of the movement with the opposition forces at the time should not, however, disqualify the legitimate social engagement that supported its accomplishments.

The constitution of the Citizenship Action had the objective to 'mobilize, and above all, sensitize the society to the necessity of fundamental and urgent changes that could transform the country's economic, political and social reality that is leading to social exclusion, hunger and poverty' (CONSEA, 1995, quoted in Vasconcelos, 2004). The movement operated through over 5,000 local committees that were quickly established to advocate for and implement actions to ameliorate the living conditions of deprived people.

The Citizenship Action managed to make the highest policymaking body in Brazil aware of these actions. In April 1993 – only a month after President Itamar Franco had committed to the implementation of the food security proposal – a National Plan of Fight against Hunger and Misery was launched, followed by a presidential decree that created *Conselho Nacional de Segurança Alimentar* – CONSEA (the National Food Security Council), comprising 9 ministers and 21 representatives of the civil society (Vasconcelos, 2004).

In the following year, under the leadership of CONSEA, the first National Food Security Conference took place, in which 2,000 government officials and representatives of civil society organizations and social movements participated. The conference put forward the vision of food security as a 'set of principles, policies, measures and instruments that permanently guarantee access to food at adequate prices, in enough quantity and quality to meet nutritional requirements for a dignified and healthy life as well as other citizenship rights' (Burlandy, 2009).

In 1995, with the change in government, CONSEA was deactivated; President Fernando Henrique Cardoso instituted instead the Solidarity Community Programme[4] and its Council. The Citizenship Action lost strength with the debate changing to focus on the launch of the Solidarity Community and of the *Plano Real*[5] (Vasconcelos, 2004). The short-lived experience at the federal level, however, did not impede several municipal and state governments referring to this broad understanding of food security within their actions (CONSEA, 2009). In addition, the country progressively adopted the vocabulary of human rights in its policies and legislation, and the right to food was included in the 1996 National Human Rights Plan (Burlandy, 2009).

The legitimization of family farming as a social and productive category

In the 1990s, farmers in Brazil faced market liberalization already experiencing reduced credit availability and income levels. In 1991, the South Common Market, Mercosul, was created between five South American countries. (Mercosul is an economic and political agreement whose purpose is to promote free trade and the fluid movement of goods, people and currency.) In response, autonomous farmers, mainly from the southern region of Brazil, started mobilizing themselves and publicly demonstrating their dissatisfaction. Their main concern was for future competition coming from the Mercosul integration (Schneider *et al.*, 2004).

In response to the social pressure, in 1996, the government created *Programa Nacional de Fortalecimento da Agricultura Familiar* – PRONAF (the National Programme for the Strengthening of Family Farming), linked to the Solidarity Community Programme. Access to credit through PRONAF was the first, and still is the most important, public policy aimed at family farmers. Its creation signalled the recognition and legitimization, by the State, of the specificities of a new social category – family farmers – as 'protagonist[s] of a viable economic project' (Picolotto, 2008). The Declaration of Aptitude to PRONAF was the instrument created to identify family farmers and/or their associations.

In 2006, the Law of Family Farming established the guidelines for the formulation of a national family farming policy. It also officially defined family farmers as persons carrying out activities in rural areas, who simultaneously comply with criteria relating to the size of the area owned (i.e. smallholders), utilization of labour (i.e. mainly from family members), income (i.e. mostly originated from the rural establishment) and administration (i.e. self-management) (Lei No. 11.326., 2006).

The Zero Hunger Project and the concept of food and nutrition security

The Zero Hunger Project – a proposal of food security policy for Brazil, commissioned by the *Instituto Cidadania*[6] – was launched in 2001 as a means of bringing back food security into the political agenda of the country. The preliminary text received contributions from more than 100 specialists, including many participants of the Brazilian Forum of Food and Nutrition Security,[7] preceded by meetings in three different cities that gathered over 1,000 participants at each meeting. The preliminary text was sent to civil society organizations, members of Congress, churches, unions, businessmen and national and international specialists, whose contributions were incorporated in the final text (Takagi, 2006).

The concept of SAN adopted in the document was that:

> food and nutrition security is the guarantee of everyone's right to access quality food, in sufficient quantity and in a permanent way, based on healthy food practices and without compromising access to other essential needs nor the future food system, therefore it must be realized with sustainable bases. Every country should be sovereign to secure its food security, respecting the cultural characteristics of each people that are manifested in the act of feeding. It is the responsibility of the National States to guarantee this right and they shall obligatorily do it in articulation with civil society, each part fulfilling its specific attributions.
>
> (Instituto Cidadania, 2001a, quoted in Takagi, 2006)

For the purposes of this discussion, four important aspects in the concept deserve attention. The first one is that SAN is defined as a right, therefore emphasizing the responsibility of the Brazilian State in respecting, protecting, providing and promoting this right. In fact, the National Food and Nutrition Security Law, adopted in 2006, adds to the set of State responsibilities those of informing, monitoring, controlling and evaluating the right to food, as well as guaranteeing mechanisms for its enforceability. The aspect of indivisibility of rights is also contemplated in the definition. The second aspect is that it brings back the centrality of social participation in SAN policymaking.

The third and fourth aspects are related to more concrete issues. Farmers' unions, academia and some governmental institutions have been striving to attach values such as modernity, efficiency, solidarity and sustainability of family farming (Picolotto, 2011). In this context, the reference to sustainability is, in practical terms, an indirect reference to the category. More directly, the Zero Hunger Project considered 'an agricultural policy that favours family farming in Brazil, aiming at increasing food production and protecting the low income farmer' as essential (Instituto Cidadania, 2001b). Last, the construction that SAN should be based on 'healthy food practices' qualifies the access to food, in that it should serve the prevention of nutritional diseases, including obesity, which is on the rise in Brazil.

The analysis developed in the Zero Hunger Project identified the roots of food insecurity in (1) insufficient agricultural supply; (2) problems regarding the intermediate level of the food chain (i.e. distribution and commercialization); and (3) lack of purchasing power caused by high unemployment and under-employment rates and low salaries (Instituto Cidadania, 2002, quoted in Yasbek, 2004). The solution to the problem would be the implementation and coordination of a number of policies, some already existing in Brazil and some brought in during the construction of the proposal.

Post 2003: Workers' Party and the institutionalization of food and nutrition security

After the establishment of CONSEA and the events of 1993–94, the idea of a food security policy continued to be advanced by the Workers' Party in the three subsequent presidential campaigns (1994, 1998 and 2002) (Frei Betto, 2003). With President Luiz Inácio Lula da Silva winning the elections in 2002, CONSEA, now called the National Food and Nutrition Security Council,[8] was reinstated. Zero Hunger was conceptualized as a programme (*Programa Fome Zero*), with defined priorities. These included five structural programmes[9] (agrarian reform, strengthening of family farming, 'co-existence with the semi-arid',[10] overcoming illiteracy, and employment generation) and five specific programmes (popular restaurants, food banks, strengthening of school feeding, food-specific cash transfer and food education) (Takagi, 2006).

However, the main programme of the first national government – to declare food and nutrition security the priority of social policy – 'mobilized Brazilian society without having a proper plan of what to do with it [Zero Hunger]' (Rocha, 2009), which generated disappointment and criticism. As a consequence, the government reorganized the project's structure. Zero Hunger was then described as a strategy and its interventions (i.e. public programmes) were grouped under four axes: food access; income generation; strengthening of family farming; and articulation, mobilization and social control – reinforcing the need for coordination among executive actors as well as with the civil society.

The establishment of the food and nutrition security system

With CONSEA once again becoming functional and, with the reformulation of the governmental strategy, the establishment of SAN within the Brazilian policy and legal frameworks was progressively advanced by a series of events in the following years. In 2004, the second National Food and Nutrition Security Conference took place and deliberated for the creation of the national SAN system to guarantee the human right to adequate food as a permanent public policy objective in Brazil (CONSEA, 2004).

In 2006, SISAN was instituted with the passing of the National Food and Nutrition Security Law, which also formalized the Brazilian definition of SAN:

> Food and nutrition security is the realization of everyone's right to regular and permanent access to quality food, in sufficient quantity, without endangering access to other essential needs, based on food practices that promote health, that respect cultural diversity and that are socially, economically and environmentally sustainable.
>
> (Lei No. 11.346, 2006)

SISAN has a dual coordination mechanism. The first one is CONSEA, responsible for proposing the directives and priorities of the National Food and Nutrition Security Policy and National Food and Nutrition Security Plan to the Federal Government, as well as monitoring their implementation. The second is the Interministerial Food and Nutrition Security Chamber.[11] The Chamber is responsible for drawing up and coordinating the implementation of both the SAN Policy and Plan, by pointing out directives, goals, funding sources and follow-up instruments of monitoring and evaluation.

The work of the Chamber must take into consideration the directives of CONSEA, which, in turn, have as reference the deliberations emanating from the National SAN Conferences. The National Conference is also responsible for the overall evaluation of SISAN. The last two groups of actors that integrate SISAN are (1) the SAN entities at State, district and municipal levels,[12] and (2) private institutions that manifest interest in joining and respecting the principles of the system. The governance of SAN in Brazil, therefore, lies with SISAN (see Figure 10.1).

In 2009, a strong social mobilization emerged once again to request the inclusion of the right to food in the Federal Constitution (CONSEA, 2009), and in 2010 the constitutional amendment came into effect. The priority given to SAN actions in Brazil can also be verified in the country's budget allocation. The budget for food security programmes and actions totalled R$13.4 billion in 2004, and was progressively expanded in the following years, reaching R$25.8 billion in 2010 (CONSEA, 2010).

Food and nutrition security programmes along the agri-food system

In 2010, a Presidential Decree instituted the National SAN Policy, indicating that its objectives were, on general lines,

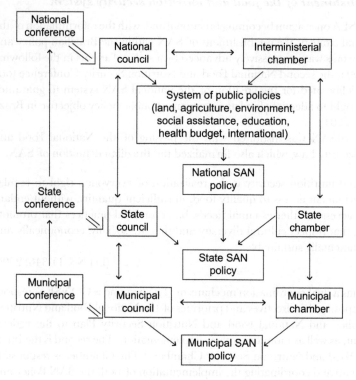

Figure 10.1 The National Food and Nutrition Security System in Brazil.
Source: Adapted from CONSEA, 2009.

to promote sustainable food production and distribution systems, of agro-ecological basis, that respect biodiversity and strengthen family farming, the indigenous populations and traditional communities, and that guarantee consumption and access to an adequate and healthy diet, respecting the diversity of the national food culture.

(Decreto No. 7.272, 2010)

With these guiding objectives, the Inter-ministerial Chamber structures the National Plan, which consolidates the programmes and actions to be implemented in the area of SAN over a given period. The systemic emphasis conferred by the Policy indicates that SAN programmes should be pursued in food production, distribution and consumption, but the goal of inter-sectorality also means that a single programme might influence more than one dimension of the agri-food system.

Food production: supporting family farming for domestic market supply

The agricultural sector in Brazil is marked by the juxtaposition of two models of agricultural production, each one evoking a different model of 'national

Table 10.1 Comparison between family and non-family farming according to the 2006 Agricultural Census (selected dimensions).

	Family farming %	*Non-family farming* %
Agricultural establishments	84.4	15.6
Total area of agricultural establishments in the country	25	75
Total population employed in agricultural establishments in the country	75	25
Agricultural credit	20	80
Total rural income	33	67
Agricultural production value	38	62

Source: Adapted from CONSEA, 2010.

development': the export-oriented model, based on large-scale monocultures, and the family farming model, based on small properties with a diversified production directed at supplying the domestic market (CONSEA, 2007). Through the lenses of SAN, this dual model also represents a contradiction: whereas 70 per cent[13] of the food that reaches the Brazilian table is produced by family farmers, rural development in Brazil has historically been dictated by commercial agribusinesses. The agricultural census of 2006 generated data on this duality as it incorporated the definition of family farming approved by law in that year in its data collection. Its results highlighted the extreme rural inequality present in Brazil (see Table 10.1).

The origin of this dual system lies in the partial and excluding process of agricultural modernization that took place in Brazil in the 1960s and 70s.[14] It was during the military dictatorship that the discussion on how to advance agricultural productivity took place. Two different views polarized the debate: one proposed agrarian reform; and the other was pro adoption of technological packages and maintenance of the agrarian structure (Zamberlan and Froncheti, 2001, quoted in De Andrades and Ganimi, 2007). With rural credit as the core, around which technical assistance, agricultural research, insurance and warehousing were organized (Belik and Paulillo, 2001, quoted in Miralha, 2006), the Brazilian State supported and expanded the agribusiness, to the economic advantage of mainly commercial farmers – who did enjoy the benefits of increased productivity and production – and suppliers of technological packages. As a result, the production growth of traditional exports was (and still is) much higher than the growth of agricultural production destined for domestic consumption.[15]

The consequence of the agricultural modernization was a rapid expansion of productive areas in what were before untouched, or barely touched, fragile ecosystems, such as the Cerrado (the Brazilian interior savannah) and the Amazon.[16] Even so, although available agricultural production was enough to feed the population, agricultural prices remained high (Belik *et al.*, 2001). At the beginning of the 2000s, oscillating prices and increased dependency on food imports were perceived as threats to food security (Takagi, 2006).

As explained above, it was only at end of the 1990s, with the institution of PRONAF, that the strengthening of family farming became an object of public policies, having a strong articulation with the SAN paradigm from 2003 onwards.[17] With a view to promoting SAN, Zero Hunger sustained – and the National Policy maintains – the position of promoting increased production of food, at reduced costs by family farmers, through the implementation of programmes of technical assistance, access to credit and support to commercialization, among others. Zero Hunger's rationale was that other programmes that targeted improving the incomes of the poor and food insecure would create extra demand for the increased food production.

Among the consequences of the renewed commitment to family farmers was the expansion of PRONAF. In 2003, PRONAF was incorporated in a broader set of public interventions aimed at supporting the programme, the Harvest from Family Farming Plan (see Box 10.1). In the ten years that followed the Plan's establishment, the income of family farming grew by 52 per cent, allowing 3.7 million people to move from the lower- to middle-income class (Agência Brasil, 2013).

Box 10.1   Harvest from Family Farming: interventions aimed at supporting family farmers

The Harvest from Family Farming Plan articulates the set of public policies endeavouring to strengthen family farming with the objective of raising and protecting incomes, promoting adoption of technological innovations and stimulating food production.

The Plan's main interventions, launched annually since 2003, are:

- PRONAF (credit).
- *Programa de Aquisição de Alimentos* – PAA (Programme for Acquisition of Food from Family Farming).
- *Programa Nacional de Alimentação Escolar* – PNAE (National School Feeding Programme).
- Technical assistance and rural extension.
- Guaranteed Harvest Programme (in case of losses in semi-arid region due to climate risks).
- Family farming insurance (to farmers that establish contract with funding lines of PRONAF).
- *Política de Garantia de Preços Mínimos para a Agricultura Familiar* – PGPM-AF (Policy of Minimum Price Guarantee for Family Farming). This purchases food from family farming at fair prices for public stock formation.
- Programme of Price Guarantee for Family Farming (secure discounts in the repayment to PRONAF in case of decrease in market prices).

The 2013/2014 Plan allocated R$39 billion to the programmes: 54 per cent to PRONAF; 3 per cent to PAA; 3 per cent to PNAE; and the remaining 40 per cent to other programmes and actions.

Food distribution: reinstating the role of the state in food provisioning

Rather than focusing on the aspect of food distribution, the conceptual formulation of SAN in Brazil privileged an emphasis on the issue of food provisioning (*abastecimento alimentar*), which is understood as a broad and diverse set of activities mediating food production and consumption. According to Maluf (1999), food provisioning covers aspects related to the access to food and its connection to food availability, that is, its production and commercialization.

Governmental interventions in the field of food provisioning started in the 1960s for two reasons. First, increased production in areas increasingly distant from urban centres required improved structures for food distribution. Second, food prices were hiked, due to speculation (Belik *et al.*, 2001). In response, the Federal government (but also state and municipalities) decided to directly regulate the area by establishing spaces where supply and demand could meet, thus facilitating organization of flows and transparency in price formation. Therefore, an extensive network of wholesale and retailing facilities was created under the coordination of *Compania Brasileira de Abastecimento* – COBAL (the Brazilian Provisioning Company).

Centrais de Abastecimento – CEASAs (Provisioning Centres) are government-owned or mixed-capital corporations created mostly during the 1970s to organize and promote the wholesale commercialization of vegetables and fruits in metropolitan regions. Until the creation of the *Sistema Nacional de Centrais de Abastecimento* – SINAC (National System of Provisioning Centres) in 1972, under the coordination of COBAL, commercialization of these products took place 'literally on the streets' of most cities. There was a huge loss of products, resulting in producers not having any incentive to supply them (Mourão, 2008).

In the 1980s, 34 CEASAs were started in urban areas as wholesale market centres not only of horticulture produce but of other products as well, with plans to implement a whole new set of activities to support the processing of agricultural products. In 1985, however, the debate on the privatization of state companies started taking place in Brazil, and the government decided to privatize the CEASAs. With 'no wholesaler willing to take over the functions of government' (Mourão, 2008), an alternative solution was needed. After 16 years, during which 32 producers' markets and 158 retail facilities were also established, SINAC was brought to an end in 1988, and CEASAs started being administered by states and municipalities.

In 1990, the *Compania Nacional de Abastecimento* – CONAB (National Provisioning Company) was established as a result of the merging of three State-owned corporations linked to complementary food provisioning policies: administration of regulating stocks, warehousing, and distribution (COBAL). CONAB was therefore created to implement the agricultural policy and the policy of minimum price guarantee (*Política de Garantia de Preços Mínimos* – PGPM) in the food provisioning sector, as well as to fix the minimum quantity of regulating and strategic food stocks.

Under PGPM, in existence since 1966, there are several instruments in place to sustain agricultural prices and regulate domestic market supply. The classic instrument is Direct Federal Government Acquisition, through which CONAB purchases agricultural products when prices are low, stores them, and releases the produce when market prices surpass the benchmarked 'price of public stocks release', with a view of satisfying the domestic demand. In the course of the 1990s, however, with the Federal government pursuing market deregulation and a 'minimum State' goal, the CONAB system was dismantled. In 2003, the levels of stocks were at their lowest. While there had once been over 400 public warehouses operating in Brazil, CONAB was operating 33 by the end of 2002 (Takagi, 2006).

Also during the 1990s, the absence of a systemic coordination had many negative impacts in the CEASAs, including a poorer operational efficiency. Some critics, however, question the impact of the CEASAs in food provisioning even before the end of SINAC. Belik *et al.* (2001) conclude that CEASAs 'never functioned as a space of approximation of producers and consumers', given that they were taken over by private agents (wholesaler traders) (Belik *et al.*, 2001). This extra layer of intermediation also meant that increased commercialization had little effect on supply. According to Maluf, a significant factor affecting the CEASAs was the concentration of retail in large supermarket chains, because supermarkets acquire products from wholesalers or larger producers, not from CEASAs (Maluf, 1999). In this arrangement, producers that meet quality and quantity requirements benefit from selling to supermarkets, whereas small-scale farmers are generally excluded from the process.

With Zero Hunger, there was a revision of the role of the State in food provisioning as well as the articulation of this policy area with the broader objectives of SAN and support to family farming:

> The provisioning structures are part of the elements that determine the conditions for the population to access food; however, it is the private economic agents that have control over these structures. In the food market, the oligopoly in the supermarket sector (the five largest chains have 46 per cent of the market) have effects in determining prices for smallholders' production and in sustaining high profit margins in the sales to consumers. It is up to governments to promote actions regarding food distribution and price regulation, committing themselves with institutional provisioning.
>
> (CONSEA, 2011)

The renewed focus on food provisioning led to the revival of the CONAB and CEASA systems. CONAB now operates 93 warehouses. Apart from PGPM, the corporation also operates part of the *Programa de Aquisição de Alimentos* (PAA) and PGPM-AF (both part of the Harvest from Family Farming Plan) and assembles food baskets that are sent to communities vulnerable to food insecurity due to climatic shocks or other reasons.[18] As for the CEASAs, the Federal government launched the National Programme of Modernization of the Horticultural Market, under the coordination of CONAB, in 2005. The objectives of this programme are many, such as reducing costs to allow small-scale retailers to supply cheaper products to their final consumers, helping producers add value, and supplying directly to the retail trade. It also aims at 'expanding the functions of CEASAs, turning them into privileged areas for the implementation of public policies, especially in health, education and food security' (CONAB, 2013).

A National Food Provisioning Policy, produced within SISAN, is under discussion now in Brazil. Reflecting both the conceptual construction of SAN as well as the praxis of institutional feeding programmes such as PAA and PNAE (see Box 10.2), the objectives of the future policy include the promotion of access to food, the improvement of the mechanism of governmental food purchases and of the commercialization of family farming products, the minimization of abusive forms of intermediation and food waste reduction (CAISAN, 2012).

Box 10.2   Provisioning circuits for public food shortages: the cases of PAA and PNAE

PAA and PNAE are two programmes that intend to explore the potential of institutional markets to support the commercialization of products, as well as increase incomes, of family farmers, while improving access to quality food. By connecting producers and consumers in a given locality, they can be seen as food provisioning actions with a focus on stimulating the formation of public short food circuits.

The proposal for *Programa de Aquisição de Alimentos* – PAA (Programme for the Acquisition of Food from Family Farming) emerged in CONSEA in 2003. Through the PAA, municipalities, states and *Compania Nacional de Abastecimento* – CONAB (National Provisioning Company) buy food from family farmers and direct it to organizations that are part of the network of social protection and promotion, as well as to public food and nutrition facilities (popular restaurants, food banks and community kitchens), specific groups of people and vulnerable families. All these actions have the objective of improving the access of food insecure people (who are using these public services exactly for this reason) to quality products. In addition, part of the food purchased by CONAB is used for the formation of strategic stocks. Some 3,100,257 tons of food were purchased between 2003 and 2010, leading not only to increased farmers' incomes and improved consumption of high quality, diverse products, but also to stronger local economies.

The *Programa Nacional de Alimentação Escolar* – PNAE (National School Feeding Programme) has been implemented in Brazil since the 1950s. In 2009, a new school feeding legislation established that at least 30 per cent of the programme's resources have to be used in the purchase of food from family farming. In practice, this meant that another market the size of PAA was opened up to farmers in that year. PNAE is hoping to meet the nutritional requirements of 43 million students during their stay in class, contributing to their growth, development, learning and educational performance, as well as promoting the formation of healthy food habits.

Food consumption: increasing access to food through reduction of poverty and inequality

One of the main lines of argument at its onset for Zero Hunger critics was that widespread hunger no longer existed in Brazil. Based on the results of a series of surveys that had collected data on anthropometrical indicators (at that time the last one being in 2003), critics pointed to the population's nutritional transition, characterized by the decrease in undernourishment and an increase in overnourishment (see Table 10.2).[19]

Table 10.2 Prevalence of weight deficit and excess in over 20-year-olds: Brazil, 1974–2009.

	Deficit of weight		*Excess of weight*	
	Female adult population	*Male adult population*	*Female adult population*	*Male adult population*
1974–5	11.8	8	28.7	18.5
1989	6.4	4.4	41.4	29.9
2002–3	5.6	3.1	40.9	41.4
2008–9	3.6	1.8	48	50.1

Source: Adapted from ENDEF 1974/1975, PNSN 1989, POF 2002/2003 and POF 2008/2009, presented in CONSEA, 2010.

Figure 10.2 The determinants of food insecurity (access dimension) in Brazil.
Source: Authors' own elaboration.

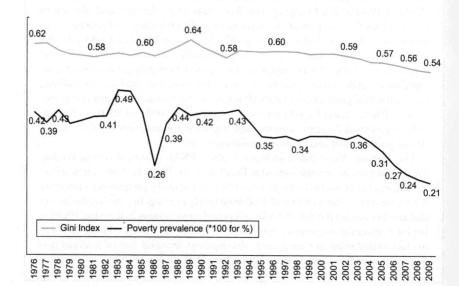

Figure 10.3 Evolution of income inequality and poverty prevalence in Brazil.
Source: Adapted from IPEA, 2013.

In contrast, the Zero Hunger Project had presented the figure of 44 million people (27.8 per cent of the total population at the time) as its target number of beneficiaries. However, the methodology that the authors of the project used was constructed to reflect the number of people 'vulnerable to hunger', measured by an estimate of the population below the chosen poverty line, rather than one reflecting the number of people actually 'going hungry' in Brazil[20] (Takagi, 2006).

At the core of Zero Hunger's efforts to improve food consumption was, there-fore, the establishment of permanent policies that would reduce poverty, building upon the tenet that hunger in Brazil is caused by lack of income and purchasing power rather than by lack of availability of food. In fact, more than reducing poverty, the goal was to attack the roots of poverty. De Barros and colleagues postulated that 'Brazil is not a poor country, it is a country with many poor deter-mined by a perverse inequality in income distribution and in opportunities for socioeconomic inclusion' (De Barros *et al.*, 2000). In this sense, if food insecurity (access dimension) is largely determined by poverty, poverty is largely determined by inequality in Brazil (see Figure 10.2).

In the two decades prior to the launch of *Plano Real* in 1994, the poverty rate in Brazil was generally above 40 per cent (IPEA, 2013). In the two years after the introduction of the Plan, the percentage of people living in poverty fell signifi-cantly. However, after this period, the poverty rate remained more or less stable until 2003, when it started falling again, accompanied, this time, by a reduction in income inequality (see Figure 10.3).

In this context, the merit of poverty reduction policies established in Brazil from 2003 onwards is that not only did they improve food access in the short term, but that they also reduced inequality, providing a basis for a more sustainable SAN in the long term. This was expressed in the motto 'share to grow' advanced during President Lula's governments. Two of the main poverty reduction policies were the conditional cash transfer *Bolsa Família* (see Box 10.3) and the increase in the minimum wage.

Box 10.3 *Bolsa Família*: income transfer to poor, food insecure households

Bolsa Família is a conditional cash transfer programme. Families considered to be poor receive the benefit as long as they comply with the programme's conditionalities in the areas of education, health and social assistance. The transferred value depends on the size of the family, age of its members and household income. Families with-draw the monthly benefit with a magnetic card, preferably issued to the woman of the household.

The programme was designed to generate multiple benefits: income transfer alle-viates poverty in the short term; conditionalities reinforce access to the basic social rights of education, health and social assistance; and complementary programmes and actions, such as professional qualification and microcredit, aim at supporting families in overcoming their situation of vulnerability.

In 2013, the budget of the programme was R$24 billion, representing around 0.4 per cent of the Brazilian GDP. Furthermore, rather than an expenditure, it repre-sents an investment. For each R$1.00 spent in the programme, the GDP increases R$1.78 (SAE, 2013).

Table 10.3 Classification of households according to Brazilian food insecurity scale, 2004 and 2009.

	2004 %	2009 %
Food secure	65.0	69.8
Mildly food insecure	18.0	18.7
Moderately food insecure	9.9	6.5
Severely food insecure	7.0	5.0

Source: Adapted from CONSEA, 2010.

The minimum wage policy was already established in Brazil in the 1940s, and it was the responsibility of the Federal Government and National Congress to ensure that it was implemented across the country. Between the end of the 1980s and the beginning of the 1990s, with inflation, the real value of the minimum wage decreased, but started increasing again in 1995, with a more accentuated growth from 2002 on. Between April 2002 and January 2010, it had increased in real terms by 53.67 per cent. The purchasing power of the minimum wage more than doubled between 1995 and 2010, presenting a strong correlation with the reduction of poverty levels in Brazil in the same period (CONSEA, 2010).

According to the *Instituto de Pesquisa Econômica Aplicada, Bolsa Família* was responsible for 7.26 per cent of the poverty reduction verified in 2003. In 2012, however, it was responsible for 28 per cent of the decrease in poverty. In the absence of the programme, poverty in Brazil would have been 36 per cent higher by 2012. *Bolsa Família* was also responsible for 12 per cent of the reduction in inequality verified between 2002 and 2012 (SAE, 2013). In more direct food access terms, a 2008 inquiry revealed that beneficiary families spent 87 per cent of the transferred value in food purchases (CONSEA, 2010).

In 2004, a different food access indicator – *Escala Brasileira de Insegurança Alimentar* – EBIA (the Brazilian Food Insecurity Scale) was applied for the first time, and reapplied in 2009 (see Table 10.3). EBIA measures the perception, of household members, of their access to food. EBIA is understood as a direct and specific indicator of SAN, complementary to indirect indicators such as poverty rates (CONSEA, 2010). In 2004, 35.5 million Brazilians were in a situation of severe or moderate food insecurity, that is, lacking access to sufficient quantity of food, whereas in 2009 the number had dropped to 25.4 million.

The future of food and nutrition security in Brazil

The Brazilian experience with income-based policies shows that they were very effective in increasing access to food. However, income indicators only partially reflect the concept of SAN – a shortcoming also present in the EBIA – as they cannot capture the quality of the ingested food or information related to its mode of production, dimensions that are clearly spelled out in the Brazilian definition of SAN and relate to worrying food-associated challenges and trends in the country.

In terms of food quality, households have reduced the purchase of wholesome foods that are part of the traditional diet (such as rice, beans and tubers), while the consumption of biscuits, soft drinks and frozen meals has increased by 400, 400 and 82 per cent respectively between 1974/5 and 2002/3 (CONSEA, 2010). Although presenting a positive relation with income, being overweight is strongly present in all income groups, and obesity has been recognized as an epidemic in Brazil.

In terms of mode of production, the productive paradigm brought about with the Green Revolution, based on the adoption of technological packages, has formed deep roots in the country. It is not by chance that Brazil is the largest pesticide buyer in the world. More recently, however, agroecological techniques have been recognized as effective in improving production, reducing costs and raising product added value (CONSEA, 2010), while also protecting the environment and the health of both producers and consumers. Given that low borrowing capacity and fear of contracting debt are generally seen as reasons why family farmers do not adopt improved production technologies (CONSEA, 2010), a useful debate is related to what kind of technologies farmers adopt to improve production once they access credit.[21]

In this context, two factors can be expected to play an important role in further advancing SAN in Brazil. The first is the acknowledgment of the limits of poverty reduction policies in improving diets. As challenges related to food consumption, such as obesity, are not specifically present among the poor, the nutrition security dimension of SAN is likely to become more salient in the future. The second is the promotion of agroecological conversion through dissemination of and access to social technologies. In fact, the Brazilian government has already taken steps towards this with the launch of the National Agroecology and Organic Production Plan in 2013. While the majority of the resources will be made available as rural credit, the Plan presents a strong articulation with PRONAF, although it also aims at connecting the produce to institutional markets such as PAA and PNAE.

In this sense, reinforced intersectoral policies involving the domains of food production, health care, including preventive health, and food education and awareness, among others such as the ones being currently debated under the proposal for a National Food Provisioning Policy, are still key for achieving SAN in Brazil. Nonetheless, it cannot be forgotten that the biggest challenge Brazilian policies still face is that of reducing inequality. For example, despite all the efforts, chronic child malnutrition is twice as high in families benefiting from *Bolsa Família* as in the general population, and five times higher in beneficiary families from the Northeast Region (Nilson and da Silva, 2009).

Conclusions and policy implications

This chapter aimed at presenting a historical account of the construction of SAN in Brazil, as well as an overview of the main policies aimed at improving the functioning of the agri-food system within the SAN framework. The understanding of SAN as a human right and the establishment of a system of governance in the area confer a character of permanency to the implementation of these policies. Civil society mobilization was a fundamental driver for the process of developing SAN in Brazil and policy inputs originating from its organizations and movements are continuously incorporated into the SAN policymaking through the structure of SISAN. Collaboration with the national academia was also important throughout the process.

Up to now, the main SAN policies focused on supporting family farming production, reaffirming the role of the state in food provisioning, and increasing access to food through poverty reduction. In each dimension, important lessons for other countries can be drawn, although the Brazilian experience particularly warns against the adoption of 'winner solutions' to promote food security. For instance, many developing countries are interested in learning from the Brazilian experience, by purchasing from smallholders to supply the school feeding market; however, there are difficulties in replicating the programme in the absence of specific actions aimed at supporting smallholder production; in Brazil, these actions were brought about primarily through social mobilization.

In terms of food production, therefore, the most important event for SAN was the State's recognition in 1996 of family farmers as actors of a viable economic project. The economic potential of the segment was confirmed ten years later, with hard data collected in the agricultural census. Family farming generates a much higher production value and income value per hectare than non-family farming establishments. Besides generating more jobs and producing more food, the model of production adopted by family farmers utilizes available productive resources – smaller areas and little funding – in an efficient way. In terms of food consumption, not only were income-based policies successful in increasing access to food, they were also very innovative because they aimed at attacking the roots of hunger, instead of its symptoms, which used to be the rationale of previous interventions such as the food supplementation programmes of the 1970s.[22] Nonetheless, it is necessary that Brazil keeps SAN as the articulating axis of social policies, rather than poverty reduction alone, given the limits of income policies in fulfilling the broader aspirations of SAN.

In short, improving food security in Brazil will depend on addressing the problems of 'developed countries', and on continuing the fight against inequality and persistent 'underdevelopment' problems in the country. The fundamental driver for sustained SAN will continue to be transformative public policies that protect and promote socioeconomic rights, operating in this nation. And this depends, at least in part, on the presence of systems (like SISAN) being embraced by the Brazilian State, so that these policies can be long-lasting, consistent, intersectorally articulated and based on a perspective of universal access.

Notes

1 Conferences are periodical events that serve as instruments of social participation in policymaking in Brazil. Conferences are held for many different areas and some have decision-making power over their respective policy domain.

2 Under the representation of the National Confederation of Workers in Agriculture (CONTAG), the 'rural workers' group was unified in their quest for agrarian reform and labour rights since 1963. Changes started taking place in the context of agricultural modernization, economic crisis and questioning of the authoritarian government at the end of the 1970s. The incapacity of CONTAG to propose and take solutions forward led to a process that imploded the homogenizing rural workers' category, leading to the surfacing of new rural identities, agendas and representation actors (Picolotto, 2008). In this process, 'autonomous, family-based, smallholders' rose in prominence within farmers' unions, with a decline in the political importance of landless, wage-earning rural workers.

3 The Workers' Party, having lost the elections of 1989, constituted a 'Parallel Government' as a means to exercise a qualified opposition to the government of President Fernando Collor de Mello. Frei Betto, a Dominican friar, militant of pastoral and social movements, gave a personal account of the creation of the Citizenship Action: 'I participated in a meeting in São Paulo in which the Parallel Government launched the National Food Security Programme. On the occasion, Lula tasked Betinho (Herbet José de Souza) with taking the cause to the streets, giving birth to the Citizenship Action' (Frei Betto, 2003).

4 The Solidarity Community aimed at fighting poverty by changing the management of (mostly) pre-existing programmes through civil society participation and coordination among the three levels of government. The programme had five priority areas: health, food and nutrition; urban services; rural development; jobs and income; and protection of rights.

5 *Plano Real* was a comprehensive programme aimed at economic stabilization and reform initiated in 1994.

6 With the impeachment, Parallel Government had no reasons for existing anymore. The NGO *Instituto Cidadania* was therefore constituted as a place for discussion and production of public policy proposals.

7 The Brazilian Forum of Food and Nutrition Security, now the Brazilian Forum of Food and Nutrition Security and Sovereignty, created in 1998, comprises a wide range of organizations, networks, social movements, research institutions and individuals linked to the fields of health, nutrition, human rights, agroecology, family farming, solidarity economy and popular education in the fight for the Right to Adequate Food and Food Sovereignty.

8 CONSEA currently comprises 38 counsellors from different civil society organizations and movements and 19 from different ministries.

9 'Structural policies' were deemed to reduce vulnerability to food insecurity through the increase in family income, the universalization of social rights and the reduction in income inequality, and 'specific policies' would reduce food insecurity in specific population groups (Instituto Cidadania, 2001b). The Zero Hunger Project, later Zero Hunger Programme, also contemplated 'local policies', which were to be implemented according to the targeted area (rural or urban).

10 The Brazilian semi-arid region is the most populous semi-arid region in the world. Civil society organizations and public bodies have put forward the concept of 'co-existence with the semi-arid' in Brazil. It expresses the idea that human life is possible in the region if families adapt to the environment, taking advantage of its nature instead of fighting against it. One of the main actions to promote co-existence with the semi-arid is the construction of cisterns that collect rainwater during the brief period of rains. Funded by the government and implemented by a large network of specialized NGOs, 273,000 cisterns providing water for household consumption and 2,892 for agricultural production were constructed between 2003 and 2009 (CONSEA, 2010). Before these actions, 'to fight the drought' was the main aim of interventions in the region.

11 The 19 ministries that are part of CONSEA currently comprise CAISAN. Coordination of CAISAN lies with the Ministry of Social Development and Fight Against Hunger.

12 The adhesion of states and municipalities to SISAN is voluntary and conditioned to the establishment of council formed by government and civil society and of an intersectoral executive body for the management of food and nutrition security programmes.

13 According to the Agricultural Census of 2006, family farmers were responsible for 87 per cent of the national production of cassava, 70 per cent of beans, 46 per cent of maize, 38 per cent of coffee, 34 per cent of rice, 21 per cent of wheat, 58 per cent of milk, held 59 per cent of swine, 50 per cent of poultry and 30 per cent of cattle, and were responsible for 63 per cent of horticultural produced value.

14 In 1985, for instance, 20 years after the introduction of the Green Revolution in Brazil, 87 per cent of rural establishments did not have access to the agricultural modernization credit (De Andrades and Ganimi, 2007).

15 For instance, sugarcane production grew by 146 per cent, soy production by 200 per cent, beans by 55 per cent, rice by 63 per cent, and wheat by 95 per cent between 1990 and 2008 (CONSEA, 2010).

16 Deforestation was only one of the negative consequences of agricultural modernization, which also include loss of biodiversity, pest proliferation, increased use of pesticide, water contamination and loss of soil fertility, among others. In socioeconomic terms, the undemocratic selection of establishments that benefited from modernization led to an intense process of rural expropriation and land and income concentration, land conflicts, rural exodus and disorganized urbanization (De Andrades and Ganimi, 2007).

17 It is important to notice that this was only one of the ways in which family farmers were linked to the SAN discussion; the other was that many family farmers were poor and food insecure themselves, and were part, therefore, of the target group for policies aimed at increasing food access, such as cash transfers.

18 Part of the products of the baskets come from PAA, and this integration reduces the baskets' costs and increases coverage in terms of number of beneficiaries.

19 Child malnutrition indicators were not included in the table because they are more related to the phenomenon of poverty rather than exclusively hunger, but underweight affected 4.6 per cent of under 5s in Brazil in 2003, and 1.8 per cent in 2009. Stunting affected 8.7 per cent of under 5s in 2003, and 6.7 per cent in 2009.

20 The distinction made by Monteiro (2003) between hunger, malnutrition and poverty supports the approach of Zero Hunger that the eradication of poverty would encompass the eradication of hunger. The author defines poverty as a condition in which elementary human necessities, including food, are not met; nutritional deficiencies, or malnutrition, are diseases that are either caused by food ingestion that is inadequate in energy or nutrients, or by inadequate biological utilization of ingested food; chronic hunger, or chronic energy deficiency (one specific type of malnutrition) occurs when regular food does not offer adequate energy intake for the maintenance of the body. In sum, eradication of poverty would lead to eradication of hunger, although not of malnutrition (especially in the case of children).

21 There is, however, diversity among these farmers. While the majority lack investment resources, some do operate with input intensive methods. In fact, one of the main criticisms of PRONAF is that it is driven by a banking logic that privileges low risk clients, i.e. the already more capitalized family farmers, actually excluding those who would benefit most from it.

22 For a detailed account of the programmes to fight hunger in Brazil from 1930 to 2003, see Vasconcelos (2005).

References

Agência Brasil (2013) *Agricultores familiares terão crédito de R$21 bilhões para a safra 2013/2014*, online, http://agenciabrasil.ebc.com.br/noticia/2013-06-06/agricultores-familiares-terao-credito-de-r-21-bilhoes-para-safra-20132014 (accessed 20 November 2013).

Belik, W. and Paulillo, L.F. (2001) O financiamento da produção agrícola brasileira na década de 90: ajustamento e seletividade. In: Leite, S.P. (Ed.) *Políticas Públicas e Agricultura no Brasil*, Ed. da UFRGS, Porto Alegre.

Belik, W., da Silva, J.G. and Takagi, M. (2001) Políticas de combate à fome no Brasil, *São Paulo em Perspectiva*, 15 (4).

Burlandy, L. (2009) A construção da política de segurança alimentar e nutricional no Brasil: estratégias e desafios para a promoçãoda intersetorialidade no âmbito federal de governo, *Ciência & Saúde Coletiva*, 14 (3): 851–60.

CAISAN (2012) Proposta de Projeto de Lei para a criação da Política Nacional de Abastecimento Alimentar. Aprovado pelo Pleno Executivo da CAISAN em 6 October 2011. Plenária do CONSEA. Brasília, 29 November, online, http://www2.planalto. gov.br/consea/plenarias/apresentacoes/apresentacao-01-novembro-2012 (accessed 27 November 2013).

CONAB (2013) Modernização dos mercados atacadistas de hortigranjeiros – prohort, online, http://www.conab.gov.br/detalhe.php?a=561&t=2 (accessed 20 November 2013).

CONSEA (1995) I Conferência Nacional de Segurança Alimentar (Relatório Final). Brasília, 1994.

CONSEA (2004) II Conferência Nacional de Segurança Alimentar e Nutricional: A construção da Política Nacional de Segurança Alimentar e Nutricional (Relatório Final). Olinda, 2004.

CONSEA (2007) III Conferência Nacional de Segurança Alimentar e Nutricional: Por um Desenvolvimento Sustentável com Soberania e Segurança Alimentar e Nutricional (Documento Final). Fortaleza, 2007.

CONSEA (2009) Construção do Sistema e da Política Nacional de Segurança Alimentar e Nutricional: a experiência brasileira, online, https://www.fao.org.br/download/ Seguranca_Alimentar_Portugues.pdf (accessed 10 October 2013).

CONSEA (2010) A Segurança Alimentar e Nutricional e o Direito Humano à Alimentação Adequada no Brasil: Indicadores e Monitoramento da Constituição de 1988 aos dias atuais, online, http://www2.planalto.gov.br/consea/biblioteca/publicacoes/a-seguranca-alimentar-e-nutricional-e-o-direito-humano-a-alimentacao-adequada-no-brasil (accessed 10 November 2013).

CONSEA (2011) 4ª Conferência Nacional de Segurança Alimentar e Nutricional: Caderno de Discussões, online, http://www2.planalto.gov.br/consea/biblioteca/publicacoes/caderno-de-discussao-4a-conferencia-nacional-de-seguranca-alimentar-e-nutricional (accessed 16 November 2013).

De Andrades, T.O. and Ganimi, R.N. (2007) Revolução verde e a apropriação capitalista, *CES, Revista*, 21: 43–56.

De Barros, R.P., Henriques, R. and Mendonça, R. (2000) Desigualdade e Pobreza no Brasil: retrato de uma estabilidade inaceitável, *Revista Brasileira de Ciências Sociais*, 15 (42):123–42.

Decreto No 7.272 (2010) Decreto Nº. 7.272, de 25 de Agosto de (2010) Regulamenta a Lei nº 11.346, de 15 de setembro de 2006, que cria o Sistema Nacional de Segurança Alimentar e Nutricional – SISAN com vistas a assegurar o direito humano à alimentação adequada, institui a Política Nacional de Segurança Alimentar e Nutricional – PNSAN, estabelece os parâmetros para a elaboração do Plano Nacional de Segurança Alimentar e Nutricional, e dá outras providências, online, http://www.planalto.gov.br/ccivil_03/_ato2007-2010/2010/decreto/d7272.htm (accessed 27 November 2013).

Frei Betto (2003) A fome como questão política, *Estudos Avançados*, 17 (38).

Instituto Cidadania (2001a) Fome Zero: Uma proposta de política de segurança alimentar para o Brasil, São Paulo.

Instituto Cidadania (2001b) Fome Zero: Uma proposta de política de segurança alimentar para o Brasil. Documento Síntese, versão 3.

Instituto Cidadania (2002) Projeto Fome Zero, versão 3.

IPEA (2013) Taxa de pobreza, online, http://www.brasil.gov.br/sobre/economia/indicadores/disoc_rdcg/indicadorview (accessed 9 September 2013).

Lei No. 11.326 (2006) Lei No. 11.326, de 24 de Julho de, 2006. Estabelece as diretrizes para a formulação da Política Nacional da Agricultura Familiar e Empreendimentos Familiares Rurais, online, http://www.planalto.gov.br/ccivil_03/_ato2004–2006/2006/lei/l11326.htm (accessed 21 November 2013).

Lei No. 11.346 (2006) Lei No. 11.346, de 15 de Setembro de 2006. 'Cria o Sistema Nacional de Segurança Alimentar e Nutricional – SISAN com vistas em assegurar o direito humano à alimentação adequada e dá outras providências, online, http://www.planalto.gov.br/ccivil_03/_ato2004-2006/2006/lei/l11346.htm (accessed 21 November 2013).

Maluf, R.S. (1999) Ações públicas locais de abastecimento alimentar, Pólis Papers No. 5.

Miralha, W. (2006) Questão agrária brasileira: origem, necessidade e perspectivas de reforma hoje, *Revista NERA*, 9 (8): 151–72.

Monteiro, C.A. (2003) Fome, desnutrição e pobreza: além da semântica, *Saúde e Sociedade*, 12 (1).

Mourão, I.R.A. (2008) Manual I. Breve história do sistema de ceasas no Brasil (1960 a 2007). Brasília.

Nilson, E.A.F. and da Silva, A.C.F. (2009) Evolução da desnutrição infantil no Brasil e o alcance da meta dos objetivos de desenvolvimento do milênio. Em: Saúde Brasil 2009: Uma análise da situação da saúde e da agenda nacional e internacional de prioridades em saúde. Secretaria de Vigilância em Saúde/MS.

Pessanha, L.D.R. (2002) A experiência Brasileira em políticas públicas para a garantia do direito ao alimento. Textos para discussão. Escola Nacional de Ciências Estatísticas. Número 5.

Picolotto, E.L. (2008) A emergência da categoria 'agricultor familiar' como sujeito de direitos na trajetória do sindicalismo rural Brasileiro. Artigo apresentado no XLVI Congresso da Sociedade Brasileira de Economia, Administração e Sociologia Rural, Rio de Janeiro.

Picolotto, E.L. (2011) As mãos que alimentam a nação: agricultura familiar, sindicalismo e política. Tese de Doutorado. UFRRJ. Instituto de Ciências Humanas e Sociais, Rio de Janeiro.

Pinto, C.R.J. (2005) A sociedade civil e a luta contra a fome no Brasil (1993–2003), *Sociedade e Estado*, 20 (1): 195–228.

Rocha, C. (2009) Developments in national policies for food and nutrition security in Brazil, *Development Policy Review*, 27 (1): 51–66.

SAE (2013) IPEA: cada R$1 gasto com bolsa família adiciona R$1,78 ao PIB (valor econômico, em 15 October 2013), Brasília, TER, online, http://www.sae.gov.br/site/?p=18659 (accessed 20 November 2013).

Schneider, S., Mattei, L. and Cazella, A.A. (2004) Histórico, caracterização e dinâmica recente do PRONAF – Programa Nacional de Fortalecimento da Agricultura Familiar. In: Schneider, S., Silva, M.K., and Marques, P.E.M. (Eds) *Políticas Públicas e Participação Social no Brasil Rural*. Porto Alegre: 21–50.

Takagi, M. (2006) A implantação da política de segurança alimentar e nutricional no Brasil: seus limites e desafios. Tese de Doutorado. Unicamp. Instituto de Economia. Campinas.

Vasconcelos, F.A.G. (2004) Fome, solidariedade e ética: uma análise do discurso da ação da cidadania contra a fome, a miséria e pela vida, *História, Ciências, Saúde-Manguinhos*, 11 (2).

Vasconcelos, F.A.G. (2005) Combate à fome no Brasil: uma análise histórica de Vargas a Lula, *Revista de Nutrição*, 18 (4).

Yasbek, M.C. (2004) O programa fome zero no contexto das políticas sociais brasileiras, *São Paulo em Perspectiva*, 18 (2).

Zamberlan, J. and Froncheti, A. (2001) Agricultura ecológica: preservação do pequeno agricultor e o meio ambiente. Vozes, Petrópolis.

11 The future of food security

Summary and recommendations

Udaya Sekhar Nagothu

Introduction

Food security is a global concern affecting millions of people worldwide, particularly in Asia and Africa. The global food price crisis in 2008 has shown that the issue of food security is interlinked and incredibly complicated with much wider implications than expected. Viewing food security as a 'wicked problem' is thus a positive step in acknowledging and accepting the serious challenges that the world is facing (Perrett, 2013). Approaching food security with such a view may encourage the emergence of new and innovative ways to tackle these problems.

There is definitely a growing interest in the food security topic, and governments all over the world are increasingly prioritizing the issue. Given the likely fluctuations in food availability and food access due to a number of factors including increase in food prices, food shortages resulting from climate change, poor entitlements and weak policy frameworks, issues of food security will continue to be prominent globally (FAO, 2011a). The cases studies presented in this book reveal both similarities and differences between food provision in a range of vulnerable countries and the various ways food security is being addressed.

The book opened with an introductory chapter providing a brief analysis of diverse views of the food security discourse supported by an extensive literature survey. Chapter 1 reminds us that in many parts of the world hunger remains a perennial problem due to poverty, economic inequality and unjust and unsustainable food production and distribution systems. Sen (1981) argued that hunger is most often a result of people not having *access* to enough food rather than there *not being enough food produced*. This argument is true for millions of households in Africa and Asia, where lack of entitlements and poverty have been the main determining factors for not having access to the food, resulting in food insecurity.

The first chapter also discussed the impacts of climate, population and economic factors on food security. It pointed out that at the same time the global food system is also characterized by large amounts of food waste and overconsumption, both in the developed countries and economies in transition. Economic growth brings changes in lifestyles and diets – increasing the prevalence of obesity and related health risks worldwide. These changes coincide with a rapidly changing global food system. Globalization and international trade is now a permanent feature of the food security landscape, affecting food transactions worldwide, including countries such as Myanmar, Bangladesh and Malawi, among others. All this is happening in a context of tenuous global economic security, urbanization, changing demographic patterns and global warming.

Chapter 1 recommends that the current strong focus on increasing food production as a response to global food insecurity must be matched simultaneously with support for the development of food systems that are ecologically, economically and socially sustainable; and can effectively address problems of food access and nutrition for all people. Essentially, if we expect to create or sustain something close to an optimal balance of the social, environmental and economic aspects of food security, the current course will simply not suffice. One of the strong views advocated is that the debate on food security should shift its focus from the traditional productionist discourse towards searching for approaches that create sustainable food systems (Patel, 2007).

The book's summary (final) Chapter 11 has revisited and assessed the variety of ways that different countries were dealing with food security issues – in the hope of finding ways to establish the contours of a future sustainable food system. This chapter synthesizes findings from the disparate chapters and summarizes the main challenges and drivers of food security from the nine country cases. Towards the end, some conclusions are provided about the most suitable options of addressing food (in)security.

A brief summary of the country case studies

Chapter 2 on China examined food security practice in the country since the 1950s including their main challenges and drivers, and how China managed to improve its food availability from a level of severe scarcity (1950s to 1970s) to one of abundance by the 1980s. One of the main arguments is that the removal of control over farmers and giving them more autonomy provided strong incentives to produce more food. Thus shifting from a collective to individual household-based farming was the first major step that boosted food production in China. With the introduction of economic reforms, although grain output increased, the output of other foods also doubled between 1978 and 2012.

Other major drivers that contributed to food production in China were the removal of controls over agricultural markets, increased investments in agricultural research and development, subsidies to farmers and the implementation of protective floor prices for major cereal crops. China's deregulation of agricultural markets helped to create more efficient allocation of resources, which in turn helped to raise food production. Experiences elsewhere also show that deregulating agricultural markets helped to improve resource allocation and increase output (Zhou, 2013).

Investments in agricultural research and extension paid off as evident from the high yields and boost in overall production levels in China during the 1970s and 1980s. The increase in agricultural production resulted in high environmental costs, which is still a serious issue to be addressed in China. Chapter 2 used the normative framework according to which attention should be given not only to the features of the food itself, but also to the range of factors determining the security of food supply and access when addressing food security. According to the analysis, the food availability and nutrition intake by Chinese people has notably improved; nevertheless there are other concerns that need to be addressed.

Major concerns for the future of food security in China are the large population, growing economic inequality, rapid urbanization, non-transparency in grain reserve management, corruption, land and water resources continuously diverted away from agriculture for the purpose of industrialization and urbanization, food adulteration, quality and safety, food wastage and issues related to environmental sustainability. These problems exist largely due to lack of accountability, poor monitoring system, low penalties and lack of freedom of media in the country. The growing income inequality is alarming, and could lead to social instability and food insecurity especially on the nutritional front. Food security concerns in China will have a global impact. China has to deal with these challenges diligently in order to achieve a balanced food security policy and practice for now and the future. There is an immediate need in China to make political, social and economic reforms to move towards a more sustainable and integrated food systems approach, linking agricultural production, food access, nutrition, human health and environment. There should be more transparency in the government programmes and food security policy, and the media should be given freedom to promote awareness about nutrition, health and environmental sustainability. China has the capacity to make necessary investments, but needs a major shift in the way it approaches the food security development paradigm in the future.

Chapter 3 highlighted the main constraints and drivers of food security in the island country of the Philippines. The current modest improvements in food security in the country can largely be attributed to science and technology development, government support programmes, education and awareness of health and nutrition. However, climate change and climate variability are viewed as major constraints to food security. The Philippines is in a vulnerable location with a long coastline subject to sea level rise and salinity. It is frequented by annual typhoons and floods leading to serious destruction of life and property. These extreme events, combined with man-made deforestation, have resulted in serious land and coastal erosion. Land will be a major limiting factor in the Philippines, as the population is increasing. Migration from rural areas and increasing urbanization is likely to put further pressure on land suitable for agricultural production. In response, the authors proposed a need for a new national land use plan and supporting policy measures to prevent conversion of agricultural lands for other uses; taxation measures that will persuade agricultural landowners to adopt sustainable practices; and improvement in land reclassification process and suitable agro-ecological farming systems. Diversification of crops and increased consumption of diversified foods should be strengthened in the Philippines to meet the recommended energy and nutrient intake to include food items rich in iron, folate, vitamin A and iodine together with other foods that promote the absorption of these nutrients.

The authors emphasized the need for strengthening the present agricultural extension system in the Philippines by introducing innovative approaches (such as mobile phone systems) to deliver extension, credit, insurance and other services. With literacy level higher than other developing countries, the contribution of such a modernized system could be wider, reaching people living in remote and vulnerable areas where road networks are not good (Baconguis, 2010). The current agricultural extension system should be broadened to offer services that promote and link various elements of food security such as nutrition and health. In planning for future food security, the nutritional requirements should be prioritized, as is presently not the case. Regular monitoring of food security and nutritional programmes at the household level is important. An integrated policy framework to support overall convergence of measures to promote food production, access, utilization, nutrition and health could largely address the food insecurity in the country.

In Chapter 4, the authors provided a very comprehensive analysis of the current status of food security, the various factors responsible for the current status and the future scenarios in Myanmar. The country will be exposed to far-ranging changes in the global and regional geopolitical and socioeconomic environment as part of its political and economic transition to democracy (ADB, 2012) after more than two decades of military regime. Land reforms were introduced in 2012 that still lack clarity, and the major question is: *will the government prioritize food security?* This is in contrast with Vietnam where more clearly defined land rights in the 1980s were critical to boosting farm productivity. Improving food security outcomes will depend on the political will, with a mix of policies that promote higher household incomes (particularly among the rural poor), improve education, and raise awareness of how food can best be used to meet nutrition needs.

The first step in unleashing the potential for growth in the smallholder agricultural sector and improving household food and nutrition security should be to privatize land tenure and allow farmers to select the crops they want to grow (e.g. relaxing 'rice first' policies). We have seen how such measures have contributed to food production in China and Vietnam. Currently rice is the dominant crop in Myanmar. Smallholder agriculture should be based on diverse crops to increase farmers' resilience to climate change and help address household-level food and nutrition security. There is a need to invest in agriculture water management and irrigation both in rainfed and irrigated systems that will be critical for Myanmar. Simultaneously, reforms in agricultural support institutions and infrastructure with increased access to markets and extension will help smallholders. Investment in research, extension and education, which is currently low, needs to be substantially bolstered to build and retain adequate human capital. Investment is also needed to improve emergency food and seed reserves – with a clear mandate to include the participation and oversight of small-scale farmers and civil society (ActionAid, 2011). A similar approach has yielded positive results in Brazil, where smallholders are involved in planning.

Other required actions include improvement of rural finance and the need for convergence of programmes and policies that promote basic health and nutrition with agricultural sector growth. The measures could include support for the national nutrition surveillance system extending into rural areas targeting pregnant women and children, promoting nutrition education and healthy cooking and establishment of home gardens for growing nutrient-rich crops (vegetables, fruits and legumes). Fisheries are a major source of protein for the poor, and opportunities for improving small-scale fisheries need to be investigated and promoted in the future. The government in Myanmar does not prioritize nutrition and health outcomes. At this stage when the country is in the process of reorganizing itself and introducing reforms it is important to coordinate across government sectors, as well as between government, NGOs, civil society and the private sector to ensure successful food and nutrition security outcomes. The country should see the transition process as a well-timed opportunity to provide food security to its people.

In Chapter 5, the main constraints and drivers responsible for the current food security situation in Bangladesh were analysed. Despite claims that it has reached self-sufficiency in food production at the macro-level, millions of people still suffer from food insecurity, particularly malnutrition. High population density and urbanization, climate change leading to droughts and floods, limited agricultural land and water resources and increasing food prices are some of the main challenges for food insecurity in the country. Bangladesh is highly exposed to threats from climate change as evident from the latest IPCC report (2013) and also other country-specific studies. The country is subject to heavy cyclones and floods inundating thousands of hectares, increasing salinity and damaging property and infrastructure each year. The rural poor possess high sensitivity to extreme events and low coping capacity. Thus, measures to increase the resilience of the rural people should be one of the foremost priorities of the country. Rice production dominates the agricultural landscape, but there is a need to encourage crop diversity in order to improve the diversity of food basket in the country. Cropping systems suitable to future climate change (e.g. vertical or pyramid culture for vegetable production) are slowly gaining popularity in the southern saline and flood prone belt.

The chapter recommends that credit and technology support should be given to farmers to improve crop diversity and adopt suitable climate resilient systems. Improving household nutritional security in Bangladesh should start by diversifying food production to attain self-sufficiency in the non-cereal foods that also contribute to dietary diversity, as recommended by Akanda (2010). Bangladesh has recently enacted a number of interesting programmes and policies to provide employment, food and social welfare to the rural poor. Some of these programmes target women, children and the landless who fall into the poorest categories of society. Fatima (2012) suggests that the implementation of midday meals in schools, development of food banks and food distribution systems for the poor (safety nets) will significantly improve the country's food and nutritional security. The Government of Bangladesh has constituted the Ministry of Food and Disaster Management to integrate all activities linked to food security in the country. The results are yet to be seen, but it is a positive step towards integration of all relevant sectors including agriculture, nutrition and health to address food insecurity.

Chapter 6 on India explored the major drivers and challenges to address the three elements of food and nutrition security (food production and availability, access, utilization and nutrition) in the country. The internal factors (demography, economic growth and poverty, policies) and the external impact factors (climate change, globalization and trade) and their implications on food security were discussed where relevant. Until now, India has focused on agriculture and food production. Despite the claims of success during the Green Revolution, food accessibility and nutritional security remain unresolved problems especially for the country's poor, women and children. There were limitations and negative impacts of the Green Revolution and the need for alternative solutions recognized (Pingali, 2012). The efforts made by the government since the 1980s through popular programmes such as the Targeted Public Distribution System did not yield the desired results. Currently, the percentage of population suffering from malnutrition is high in the country. These are mostly women, children and the poor, suggesting that economic and social factors play a key role in determining food access and utilization in India.

With the new Right to Food Act (2013), the government has the obligation to provide food to all its citizens. The intentions of the Act are good and if properly implemented will help the country to address the food security issues to a large extent. The new Act is considered by many as a major step in India's fight against hunger (Swaminathan, 2013). But much debate has been generated regarding the sustainability of the programme in the long run (Kishore *et al.*, 2013). The chapter questions whether the country will be able to implement this Act in its true sense; and how the resources needed for its implementation can be generated? Key factors influencing success will depend on equal and efficient devolution of decision-making powers and implementation of a system to redress grievances between central government and the states. The Right to Food Act should be systematically implemented with its strengths and weaknesses well documented in order to continuously improve its functioning. The Government of India understands the importance of a rural-oriented economic growth process. The numerous programmes and policies are a reflection of that vision. However, due to corruption and lack of transparency in the implementation of the programmes, the benefits often do not reach the right beneficiaries. This cannot continue any longer and governments should be held accountable for inefficiency and misuse of resources. It is critical that the processes are equitable, target the poorest and are effective in implementation. There is a need to strengthen the link between agriculture, crop diversity and nutrition in the country suited to different agro-climatic zones. The future welfare programmes in the country should have a nutrition-focused outreach targeting high-risk households, especially children below two years of age and pregnant women (Bajpai and Dholakia, 2011). The chapter acknowledges that it is a big challenge to make changes in the current system, but at the same time, it is a window of opportunity to combine the goals of better food, healthy environment and reduced poverty.

Chapter 7 discussed the main drivers of food insecurity in Ethiopia and analysed the data on key indicators of food availability, accessibility, utilization and stability. Severe land degradation, poverty, population growth and climate change have exacerbated the problem of food insecurity. Some of the domestic policies/ programmes such as land tenure do not motivate long-term conservation investments. Ongoing large-scale land leasing to private investors will make only a small contribution to food security, and current food aid programmes do not solve long-term food insecurity problems. The 'business as usual' agricultural practices will no longer improve national and/or household food security under the country's future climate change scenario. Future food security will depend to a great extent on Ethiopia's ability to tackle the following three challenges: the move towards sustainable, ecological and climate-smart agriculture underpinned by science-based knowledge; the need to promote the production of staple and other foods to reduce Ethiopia's reliance on foreign food aid; and, in the long term, a structural transformation towards a greener and more diversified economy.

Some of the measures proposed for improving food security in Ethiopia include: support for the new land tenure policy; conservation measures to rehabilitate degraded agricultural lands; increasing the amount of land cultivated under water and energy saving irrigation systems; improving access to markets by expanding the communication and road transport systems; and reducing post-harvest losses by promoting effective agricultural product value chains. The country needs to strengthen linkages among agricultural research, extension services and farmers. It needs to empower women in decision-making processes, establish farmer training centres, and build national food reserves to improve food and nutrition security.

Chapter 8 provided a comprehensive analysis of the state of food security in Tanzania where the contradictions, the challenges and the opportunities were explored. The authors gave credit to various initiatives in the past to address food security. At the same time, they were highly critical of the failures and gaps in the policies that result in a continued high level of poverty and malnutrition in the country. On the one hand, the current development framework in Tanzania puts emphasis on smallholder agriculture; but on the other, the framework also incorporates policies encouraging increased foreign investment and larger farms with high-cost inputs, thus making food security policy ambiguous.

Opportunities for agricultural growth through investment, and the need to improve nutrition and the livelihoods of smallholders, are not necessarily mutually exclusive. But linking the two requires broader consideration of the environmental and socioeconomic context in which agriculture operates. Private investment can contribute to agricultural development by focusing on processing, packaging and marketing rather than large-scale land acquisitions (Wegner and Zwart, 2011). But investments must be consistent with the country's nutritional needs and a wide distribution of incomes.

The chapter presents evidence of the need for more sustainable, diversified and climate-smart agriculture; and argues for policies such as supporting the role of women in agriculture and shifting subsidies away from agro-chemicals to support farmer adoption of practices that improve soil structure and build long-term fertility. It emphasizes the multifunctional role of agriculture in providing nutrition, economic growth, livelihoods and environmental management. Active promotion of small-scale operations (the majority of farms in Tanzania) supports economic growth in that more people have money to spend in the marketplace and improved access to good nutrition, increasing livelihood capacity. In the long term, more people gain the skills, knowledge and experience to expand businesses. Where farms are not fully commercial due to size, the policy framework should recognize their contribution to nutrition and environmental services – values that can exist alongside off-farm income. Policies that support these values contribute to reducing the public cost of malnutrition. Coordination (e.g. between research, extension and education; and between health, agriculture and environmental management) can be supported by establishing a process by which the relevant ministries come together to integrate overlapping policy areas, make joint decisions and identify outcomes, indicators, activities and budgets according to common goals.

In Chapter 9 on Malawi, the authors reviewed the major political, economic, environmental and social factors that drive food insecurity in Malawi, one of the poorest countries in sub-Saharan Africa. Largely due to political and economic reasons, the diagnosis of hunger as an insufficiency of maize production has led to a technological focus on agricultural inputs in the country. Consequently, in the last decade, the well-publicized Agricultural Input Subsidy Programme (AISP) was introduced to provide fertilizer and hybrid maize seed at cheaper prices for the majority of smallholder farmers. While there is good evidence that this programme increased maize production and increased farmer incomes, the programme crowded out other solutions and failed to address the overall food insecurity and malnutrition. The chapter expressed some concern that current initiatives, such as the New Alliance for Food Security and Nutrition, would repeat the mistakes of AISP that in fact decreased crop diversity and had little impact on child malnutrition.

Solutions to food security in a case such as Malawi vary in part due to debates about the ultimate causes of food insecurity. Proponents of the AISP tend to argue that farming households are food insecure because they lack access to the right technologies. Those who favour the agroecological approach suggest that the problem lies in the social and economic relations that reinforce inequalities in food access, as well as limited knowledge of sustainable solutions. Two major alternative approaches to addressing food security were discussed in the chapter, namely agroecological systems and cash transfers. The authors argue that the agroecological approach helps not only in diversifying cropping systems but also in increasing farmer knowledge about soil conservation strategies, crop rotation and other methods, which ultimately helps to build long-term community resilience in a region against environmental stresses. Crucial to the approach, from the authors' perspective, is attention to power inequalities at the household, community and scientist-farmer level, combined with farmer research (Bezner Kerr, 2010). Cash transfers is also viewed positively as it not only allows households to survive ultra-poverty but, if it is sufficiently generous, allows investment in food, health, education and other needs, which can over time translate into gains in productivity, reductions in poverty and improvements in nutrition, health and other measures of general social welfare (Handa and Davis, 2006; Lagarde *et al.*, 2007; Gertler *et al.*, 2012).

Chapter 10 presented the Brazilian experience in addressing food security. The historical account of the construction of Brazil's food and nutritional security framework (SAN) was analysed, as well as an overview of the main policies aimed at improving the functioning of the agri-food system within the framework. The human right to adequate food has been a milestone in the national food policy debate for several years, supported by a constitutional amendment that made the right to food legal. It reflects concern about two major issues originally involved in the discussions – rural development and health – that are also evident in the term 'food and nutritional security', which is widely used in Brazil rather than purely 'food security'. These concerns have been fundamental to the development of recent food schemes, through support for the production and consumption of diversified and nutritionally balanced food items.

To date, the main food and nutrition policies in Brazil have focused on supporting family farming, thereby reducing the role of the state in food provisioning, and increasing access to food through poverty reduction. Important lessons for other developing countries can be drawn from the Brazilian experience. A decade of experience (1996–2006) confirms that family farming generates a much higher production value and income value per hectare than non-family farming establishments. Besides generating more jobs and producing more food, the model of production adopted by family farmers utilizes available productive resources – smaller areas and little funding – in an efficient way.

The Brazilian policies in general aimed at attacking the roots of hunger, instead of its symptoms, and hence the reasons for the positive results. However, the biggest challenge is the one of reducing economic inequality. Its popular 'cash transfers' (*Bolsa Família*) programmes were very effective in increasing access to food. However, it is also clear that poverty reduction alone will not lead to improved diets; obesity is also a significant problem in Brazil, and not specifically present among the poor. This emphasizes the need for intersectoral policies involving the domains of food production, health care (including preventive health) and food education and awareness, among others.

Key factors that determine food security

The various country cases have briefly analysed the major challenges and drivers that were responsible for the failures and successes until now in addressing food security. The chapters were drafted by authors from different disciplinary backgrounds and ideological positions that also influenced the discussions in their respective chapters. The authors' diverse views and experiences have in a way provided some originality to the book, supported by an extensive literature survey on food security. As discussed earlier in the book, it is not easy to point to one single factor and say this is the reason for failure or success of food security. The different factors are linked with non-linear interdependency. Overall, six major issues can be identified that have played a key role in determining the food security outcomes in the different countries. These are not discussed in any order of priority,

The role of science and technology

The first key issue to be discussed here is the role of science and technology and its contribution to food security as experienced in different country cases (China, India, Philippines, Bangladesh and Brazil among others). It is no doubt that countries that have invested in research and development and extension services have benefited and reached self-sufficiency in food production at the macro-level. Unfortunately, the majority of research in the 1970s and 1980s focused on three major cereal crops (rice, wheat, maize) and contributed to monocultures – to the extent that in countries such as Bangladesh (rice) and Malawi (maize), almost 90 per cent of the agricultural landscape is dominated by one single crop, and still applies today. This has been the mainstream food production paradigm advocated throughout the Green Revolution, supported by heavily subsidized agrochemicals, seeds, water and power.

Although yields of major cereal crops have increased during the decades in which monocultures have proliferated, they were unsustainable and responsible for deforestation and loss of biodiversity. The three crops of rice, wheat and maize have replaced previously diverse crop patterns dominated by millets, beans and other local crops. As argued in Chapters 8 and 9, government policies to support maize production through subsidies has literally replaced millets and other traditional crops that have the potential to provide a diverse food basket to the rural poor in Africa. Several governments are now coming forward with crop diversification strategies (e.g. India, Bangladesh) and agroecological approaches. Unless smallholders, who constitute almost 85 per cent of the farm owners, are provided with the necessary technological, institutional and market support, they cannot take part in the ongoing crop diversification process. In fact, various chapters (Philippines, Myanmar, Bangladesh, Tanzania and Malawi) proposed a shift towards an agroecological systems approach as a sustainable option to address the food and nutritional security in the future. Agroecological systems are seen as a viable option for smallholders where integration of soil conservation strategies using low cost local inputs, crop rotation and other cropping systems is possible, which ultimately helps to build long-term community resilience and also provides the agriculture-nutrition connect (Bezner Kerr *et al.*, 2007; Giovannucci *et al.*, 2012). Agroecological systems have also been recognized as effective in reducing production costs and raising product added value (CONSEA, 2010), while also protecting soil, water, biodiversity and the health of both producers and consumers. The Brazilian government has already taken steps towards this with the launch of the National Agroecology and Organic Production Plan in 2013. Reallocation of resources, capacity building and knowledge development within each country may be needed to boost agroecology at the farm level (De Schutter, 2011).

Science and technology will continue to play a key role in addressing problems of food insecurity. Future research programmes should target crops and systems that can address risks from climate change, reduce pressure on land and water resources, crops that address the nutritional needs of the poor and smallholders. The link between researchers, extension agencies and farmers should be strengthened to develop and implement demand-driven research agendas (Garvey, 2012). Government and private sector should invest in long-term research programmes not affected by national policies and foster international cooperation. Necessary policy support should follow to support the long-term nature of specific scientific developments involving breeding of crop varieties to adapt to different climate, food and nutrition conditions.

Population growth and changing demographic patterns

The second key issue is population growth and changing demographic patterns that will impact the future of food security. It is estimated the global population will reach 9.1 billion by 2050 (FAO, 2009), increasing especially in sub-Saharan Africa where the majority of the next one billion people will be added. This was discussed in most of the chapters including India, China, Bangladesh, Tanzania, Ethiopia and the Philippines. It is believed that an increase in population will mean demand for more food, but at the same time, more people mean more land for settlements and urbanization, in competition with agriculture. Area of land dedicated to agriculture and technology these days plays a central role in determining a country's food production (Maisonet-Guzman, 2011). In addition to the increase in population numbers, the concern in some countries is more about urbanization, the changing demographic patterns as observed in China that will have a more aged population in the coming decades, and a relatively younger population in India and Bangladesh.

In all countries, one common trend that we have started to see is the outmigration from rural areas; that is, a shift towards urbanization and fewer people left to farm in the rural areas. By 2035, it is estimated that nearly two-thirds of the world's population will be living in cities. This will imply more pressure on resources and change in consumption patterns. Often outmigration is linked to economic reasons and the search for better livelihood options. In order to prevent outmigration, farming should be attractive for youth in the future and governments should encourage rural youth to remain in the agriculture sector. The agriculture sector will need to be a key area of focus, for both public and private funds in the future, especially in countries where agriculture is the main source of occupation. Farmers are key stakeholders and managers of ecosystems, and should be rewarded for the public goods they provide such as clean water, protected soils, landscapes and biodiversity.

It is mostly men who migrate and women stay back in the villages to provide food and nutritional security to the households. As it is, food security is highly gender biased in the developing world. Women are often marginalized in terms of land ownership, benefits of credit programmes, food distribution or nutrition schemes. While gender inequality is gradually reducing in the urban middle class due to economic growth and women taking part in the mainstream development, the situation has not changed much among Africa's rural poor (Tanzania, Malawi, Ethiopia) and to some extent in South Asia (India, Bangladesh, Myanmar). From a food security perspective the trend of migrating out of rural areas is not positive; it creates a greater burden on smallholders and rural women to produce food for the expanding urban middle class in the developing economies. Thus, the engendering of agriculture as recommended in Chapter 8 applies not only to Tanzania, but also to other countries following a similar growth model, and that includes Malawi, Ethiopia and also many Asian countries given the significant role of women in agriculture and also their contribution to household food security. The plethora of gender-specific hindrances women face in regard to the basic resources of production are often interrelated and demand comprehensive strategy approaches. In future, the role of gender in food security should be recognized by policy.

Land tenure, entitlements and reforms

The third major issue is land tenure, entitlements and reforms that played a key role in shaping the food security at the household level in many countries. A study by Young *et al.* (2001) showed that entitlements to land, alternative income sources and community support played a key role in determining food access in emergency situations. The majority of country cases discussed in this book pointed out that land tenure is a key factor that determines a household's food production and food access capabilities. Experience has shown that lack of tenure and property rights to cultivate land has been a disincentive for farmers to invest in land in many countries. Ethiopia is a good example where short-sighted land tenure policies of the state have increased food insecurity and led to severe deforestation and land degradation in the country (Amsalu, 2012). The consequences are still visible and other countries should learn from past mistakes and not repeat them in the future. In most countries in Asia and Africa, farmers did not own land until the 1970s; they either leased land from large private landowners as in India or obtained cultivating rights from the state as in China, Ethiopia, Myanmar and Tanzania.

Chapter 4 reported that in Myanmar 50 per cent of all rural households have no land use rights to cultivable land according to the 2013 census (Wilson and Wai, 2013). This problem is exacerbated by the lack of land tenure guarantees for small farmers, and, in recent years, the expansion of agribusiness and associated 'land grabbing' by both domestic and foreign enterprises (FSWG, 2011). Land grabbing is happening on a large scale in Tanzania, Ethiopia and Malawi and other countries across Africa. This has to be stopped as it will neither provide livelihoods to the local communities nor contribute positively to food security of any country. On the contrary, it alienates local communities from lands on which they enjoyed traditional rights for grazing, water and other resources. China has shown that where farming households have control over their land and the associated services (credit, extension and water rights) major production increases can be realized. Giving clear title deeds over land improves the possibility for smallholders' access to credit, extension services and rights to use water resources and thereby food security. One of the strong recommendations to governments is that current and future policies should aim at providing clear rights and entitlements to land and other resources to the rural poor, women and smallholders where needed.

Climate change

The fourth, and an equally key factor, is climate change and its impacts on food production, which is already being felt in many countries. In recent years, a lot of literature is available showing the importance of this factor and its likely impacts on food security. The recent IPCC report (2013) predicted that production of major cereals would be affected at a global level due to global warming; leading to increase in daily average temperatures, change in rainfall patterns and more extreme events. Most country cases presented in this book including the Philippines, Myanmar, Bangladesh, India, Ethiopia and Malawi have reported that they are highly exposed to risks from climate change. These countries will experience frequent extreme events in the form of floods and droughts that will directly affect crops, livestock, property and infrastructure. Lands along the coast will be affected by salinity and thereby reduce the productive agricultural land. Today, farmers in some of the coastal areas can only grow brackish water shrimps. It was also reported that in Bangladesh people in the areas affected by frequent floods suffer from severe malnutrition and lack of access to food in some cases. Smallholders, women and children in rural areas will be the groups most vulnerable to climate change impacts and, as noted in these countries, the impacts on society and the environment will be long lasting.

Governments and communities need to prepare for the worst and develop adaptation strategies that are low cost and not too risky for small-scale farmers. Promoting climate-smart agriculture systems that can deal with resource scarcities and help mitigate and adapt to climate change must remain the overarching goal in the regions vulnerable to climate risks. Several low cost and easily adaptable measures such as farm ponds for rainwater harvesting, retention of crop residues, soil mulching, integration of livestock into farm units, need-based water application and alternative production systems are examples of building blocks to climate resilient farming systems (FAO, 2013). Countries need to set up early warning systems, capacity building programmes and funds to continuously support the various programmes. Public-private partnership models can play an important role to support climate adaptation.

Good governance

The fifth key factor is good governance and policies with a goal to eradicate poverty, reduce economic inequality and move towards sustainable food security systems. Lele and colleagues (2013) emphasize that governance issues affect the choice of policies, institutions and outcomes for addressing these daunting challenges. Their study based on experiences from India, China and other countries concluded that current governance issues are inadequate, lack strategic clarity in some cases where they exist, and provide unequal distribution of power, access to resources and capability to exercise a sound influence, which will produce equitable and sustainable outcomes. Often the dominant, short-sighted policies of some governments do not consider the rights of the poorest. We have seen that in Ethiopia, Tanzania, India and Malawi.

The recent initiatives in India and Brazil are governed by the human rights dimension of food, which places responsibility on governments to ensure that all citizens have access to enough nutritious food and that it is produced in a sustainable manner. This becomes critical in countries where hunger and malnutrition are the result of poverty, social injustice and inequality, rather than simply a failure to produce enough food. Good governance for food security should be seen as a means to achieve the desired goal (FAO, 2011b). The commitment to a right to food, as already initiated in Brazil and India, is an important step in that direction. Brazil offers an interesting lesson for other countries to learn. The Brazilian debate also rests on the perception that food and nutritional security requires both short-term actions (such as immediate access to food and emergency interventions) and long-term structural changes (such as social movements and policies against inequality and social exclusion) to address the causes. These actions are aimed at increasing family income and redistributing resources. This approach is consistent with a comprehensive vision of food and nutritional security that reaffirms its diverse dimensions and the consequent need for a multi-sectoral intervention.

Although short-term interventions (e.g. agricultural subsidies, cash transfers, food distribution and food vouchers) are important, long-term policy and programme support is needed to make agriculture an engine of growth and poverty reduction. Subsidy programmes have put a tremendous burden on each country's national expenditure and diverted the funds that otherwise could have been used for improving rural infrastructure. Environmental consequences of the subsidies have been far-reaching, as farmers resorted to indiscriminate use of agrochemicals leading to serious pollution of the land and fresh water sources. This is particularly evident in China, India, Bangladesh, Tanzania and Malawi, where farmers have relied heavily on subsidized fertilizer programmes since the Green Revolution. It is likely that the governments will slowly phase out subsidy programmes due to financial reasons (as we are already witnessing in India), thus transferring the burden over to smallholders who will not be able to bear the expenditure. Where subsidies continue, they should preferably be used to improve soil structure and build long-term fertility rather than to fund agrochemicals (Tilman *et al.*, 2002).

Investments from the private sector may become important in the future, but there should also be strong policy support to develop initiatives that engage smallholders in the process. It is critical to integrate smallholders more fully into national and global food systems – including health systems, value chains and markets. In order to facilitate this engagement, institutions and policies must be designed for the benefit of smallholders, which will assist flows of necessary knowledge, training and capacity building and other resources. Brazil has shown that a targeted approach to support family farms can give better results, as reported in Chapter 10. The programme reinforces the benefits of access not only to cash transfers and micro-credit, but also to the basic social rights of education, health and social assistance.

International trade

The sixth and final factor is the impact of international trade on food and nutritional security. Global trade of agricultural commodities has significantly increased since the 1980s and influences producers and consumers worldwide. Large multinational companies and supermarkets influence what crops are grown by small-scale farmers and eaten by consumers in remote corners of the world. Market prices have more influence on the type of food to be produced and sold than does the nutritional value of crops. This trend neither supports smallholders to diversify crop production nor enables consumers to choose nutritious food from the market. Global trade barriers and tariffs will influence the national agricultural development plans and policies. Clearly, there is a greater need to integrate and support the development of local, national and global initiatives that can effectively address problems of food production, access and nutrition.

The way forward

With the serious challenges the world is facing today, we clearly need new paradigms to design future food security systems. This implies that strong voices calling for a New Green Revolution, with a focus on 'sustainable intensification' and technologically driven research and development, should be seriously considered. A wiser call would be for food security systems that are integrated, diverse and resource efficient. Perhaps the solutions to hunger and abatement of negative environmental impacts will not lie in one single system, but a combination of systems, sometimes termed an Evergreen Revolution (Swaminathan, 2013) or a mosaic approach (UNCTAD, 2013). Future systems and efforts to address food security must target the poorest and most needy communities across the economic and social spectrum and, at the same time, reduce the ecological footprint of food systems (Popkin, 2003).

As information is likely to be the key to transforming food systems, governments should further the integration of basic science and policy choices and innovation (Dubé *et al.*, 2012). Investments in innovative research will benefit in the long term. Scaling up innovative research results will be more effective through multi-sector networks connected at different levels with well-designed information and communication systems that will enable all stakeholders to access information and respond appropriately. Instead of using traditional silo thinking (agriculture policies vs trade policies vs economic development policies vs health policies), a goal for policymakers should be to develop integrated policy frameworks where agriculture, economy (including equity), nutrition and health converge. Policies framed with a systemic design will promote healthy lifestyles and environments, and build and support healthy communities, in both cities and rural areas.

Finally, governments, civil society and international agencies should work together to improve transparency and efficiency in the formulation and implementation of food security-related policy and programmes. This implies that they have to seriously deal with corruption, fix accountability and improve bureaucratic efficiency. It is most fundamental to recognize and ensure that national resources are effectively used to reduce poverty and economic inequality and thereby improve food and nutritional security. High priority should be given to protect the environment, as we address food security challenges in the future, and thereby promote sustainable food and nutrition security systems.

References

ActionAid (2011) No more food crises: the indispensable role of food reserves, online, http://www.actionaid.org/sites/files/actionaid/polcy_briefing_-_the_role_of_food_reserves.pdf (accessed 12 December 2013).

Akanda, A.I. (2010) Rethinking crop diversification under changing climate, hydrology and food habit in Bangladesh, *Journal of Agriculture and Environment for International Development*, 104 (1–2): 3–23.

Amsalu, A. (2012) Eradicating extreme poverty and hunger in Ethiopia: a review of development strategies, achievements, and challenges in relation with MDG1. NCCR North–South Dialogue 45. Working paper, special research project 4: Beyond the MDGs. NCCR North–South, Berne, Switzerland.

Asian Development Bank (ADB) (2012) Myanmar in transition: opportunities and challenges. ADB, Mandaluyong City, Manila.

Baconguis, R.T. (2010) Issues and challenges in the governance of the Philippine agricultural extension system, UPLB Professorial Lecture, University of the Philippines, Los Baños, Laguna, 6 December.

Bajpai, N. and Dholakia, R.H. (2011) Improving the integration of health and nutrition sectors in India, online, http://globalcenters.columbia.edu/content/improving-integration-health-and-nutrition-sectors-india (accessed 30 April 2014).

Bezner Kerr, R. (2010) The land is changing: contested agricultural narratives in northern Malawi. In: McMichael, P. (Ed.) *Contesting Development: Critical Struggles for Social Change*. Routledge Press, Florence, pp. 98–115.

Bezner Kerr, R., Snapp, S., Chirwa, M., Shumba, L. and Msachi, R. (2007) Participatory research on legume diversification with Malawian smallholder farmers for improved human nutrition and soil fertility, *Experimental Agriculture*, 43: 437–53.

CONSEA (2010) A segurança alimentar e nutricional e o direito humano à alimentação adequada no Brasil: indicadores e monitoramento da constituição de 1988 aos dias atuais, online, http://www2.planalto.gov.br/consea/biblioteca/publicacoes/a-seguranca-alimentar-e-nutricional-e-o-direito-humano-a-alimentacao-adequada-no-brasil (accessed 10 November 2013).

De Schutter, O. (2011) Agro ecology and the Right to Food. Report submitted by the Special Rapporteur on the right to food to UN Human Rights Council, 20 December 2010, online, http://www.srfood.org/images/stories/pdf/officialreports/20110308_a-hrc-16-49_agroecology_en.pdf (accessed 3 September 2013).

Dubé, L., Pingali, P. and Webb, P. (2012) Paths of convergence for agriculture, health and wealth, *Proceedings of the National Academy of Sciences*, 109 (31): 12294–301.

Fatima, S. (2012) Bangladesh: striving for food security, online, http://www.saglobal affairs.com/back-issues/1319-bangladesh-striving-for-food-security.html (accessed 21 September 2013).

Food and Agriculture Organization (FAO) (2009) How to feed the world in 2050. Report from the high-level expert forum in Rome, 12–13 October, online, http://www.fao.org/fileadmin/templates/wsfs/docs/expert_paper/How_to_Feed_the_World_in_2050.pdf (accessed 20 June 2013).

Food and Agriculture Organization (FAO) (2011a) Right to food – making it happen, online, http://www.fao.org/docrep/014/i2250e/i2250e.pdf (accessed 30 June2013).

Food and Agriculture Organization (FAO) (2011b) Good food security governance: the crucial premise to the twin-track approach, online, http://www.fao.org/fileadmin/templates/righttofood/documents/project_f/fsgovernance/workshop_report.pdf (accessed 5 May 2014).

Food and Agriculture Organization (FAO) (2013) Climate-smart agriculture. Sourcebook, online, http://www.fao.org/docrep/018/i3325e/i3325e.pdf (accessed 15 August 2013).

Food Security Working Group (FSWG) (2011) Upland land tenure security in Myanmar: an overview, online, http://www.myanmarfswg.net/land%20tenure%20briefing%20paper-eng.swf (accessed 24/09/13).

Garvey, K. (2012) Global food security: the role of science and technology, 17–19 October, Wilton Park Conference report, WP1189, UK, online, https://www.wiltonpark.org.uk/wp-content/uploads/WP1189-Report.pdf (accessed 5 May 2014).

Gertler, P.J., Sebastian, W.M. and Rubio-Codina, M. (2012) Investing cash transfers to raise long-term living standards, *American Economic Journal: Applied Economics*, 4(1): 1–32.

Giovannucci, D., Scherr, S.J., Nierenberg, D., Hebebrand, C., Shapiro, J., Milder, J. and Wheeler, K. (2012) Food and agriculture: the future of sustainability (1 March). The sustainable development in the 21st century (SD21) report for Rio+20, United Nations, New York, online, http://ssrn.com/abstract=2054838 or http://dx.doi.org/10.2139/ssrn.2054838 (accessed 30 April 2014).

Handa, S. and Davis, B. (2006) The experience of conditional cash transfers in Latin America and the Caribbean, *Development Policy Review*, 24(5): 513–36.

Intergovernmental Panel on Climate Change (IPCC) (2013) The physical science basis. Summary for policymakers. Contribution of the Working Group I to the 5th Assessment Report of the IPCC, Cambridge University Press, Cambridge.

Kishore, A., Joshi, P.K. and Hoddinott, J. (2013) A novel approach to food security, online, http://www.ifpri.org/gfpr/2013/indias-right-to-food-act (accessed 29 April 2014).

Lagarde, M., Haines, A. and Palmer, N. (2007) Conditional cash transfers for improving uptake of health interventions in low- and middle-income countries: a systematic review. *Journal of the American Medical Association*, 298 (16):1900–10.

Lele, U., Klousia-Marquis, M. and Goshwami, S. (2013) Good governance for food, water and energy security, *Aquatic Procedia*, 1: 44–63.

Maisonet-Guzman, O.E. (2011) Food security and population growth in the 21st century, online, http://www.e-ir.info/2011/07/18/food-security-and-population-growth-in-the-21st-century/ (accessed 5 May 2014).

Patel, R. (2007) *Stuffed and Starved: The Hidden Battle for the World's Food System*. Portobello Books, London.

Perrett, E. (2013) Tackling the 'wicked problem' of food security: challenges and opportunities for Australian agriculture, online, http://inform.regionalaustralia.org.au/industry/agriculture-forestry-and-fisheries/item/tackling-the-wicked-problem-of-food-security-challenges-and-opportunities-for-australian-agriculture (accessed 5 May 2014).

Pingali, P.L. (2012) Green Revolution: impacts, limits, and the path ahead, online, http://www.ncbi.nlm.nih.gov/pmc/articles/PMC3411969/ (accessed 27 April 2014).

Popkin, B.M. (2003) The nutrition transition in the developing world, *Development Policy Review*, 21 (5–6): 581–97.

Sen, A. (1981) *Poverty and Famines: An Essay on Entitlements and Deprivations*. Oxford University Press, Oxford.

Swaminathan, M.S. (2013) From Bengal famine to right to food, *The Hindu*, 13 February, 2013, online, http://www.thehindu.com/todays-paper/tp-opinion/from-bengal-famine-to-right-to-food/article4409557.ece (accessed 13 September 2013).

Tilman, D., Cassman, K.G., Matson, P.A. and Naylor, R.L. (2002) Agricultural sustainability and intensive production practices, *Nature*, 418: 671–7.

UNCTAD (2013) Wake up before it is too late. Make agriculture truly sustainable now for food security in a changing climate. Trade and Environment Review 2013. United Nations Conference on Trade and Development, online, http://unctad.org/en/PublicationsLibrary/ditcted2012d3_en.pdf (accessed 30 September 2013).

Wegner, L. and Zwart, G. (2011) Who will feed the world? The production challenge. Oxfam, online, www.oxfam.org.

Wilson, S. and Wai, A. (2013) Food and nutrition security in Myanmar. Working paper prepared for USAID, online, http://fsg.afre.msu.edu/Myanmar/myanmar_background_paper_4_food_security.pdf (accessed 13 December 2013).

Young, H., Jaspers, S., Brown, R., Frize, J. and Khogali, H. (2001) Food security assessments in emergencies: a livelihood approach, online, http://www.odihpn.org/documents/networkpaper036.pdf (accessed 5 May 2014).

Zhou, Z.Y. (2013) *Developing Successful Agriculture: An Australian Case Study*. CABI, Wallingford, UK.

Index

A reference in **bold** indicates a table and figures are shown in *italics*.

For Product Safety Concerns and Information please contact our
EU representative GPSR@taylorandfrancis.com Taylor & Francis
Verlag GmbH, Kaufingerstraße 24, 80331 München, Germany